JIMMIE ROBINSON

FIVE WEAPONS

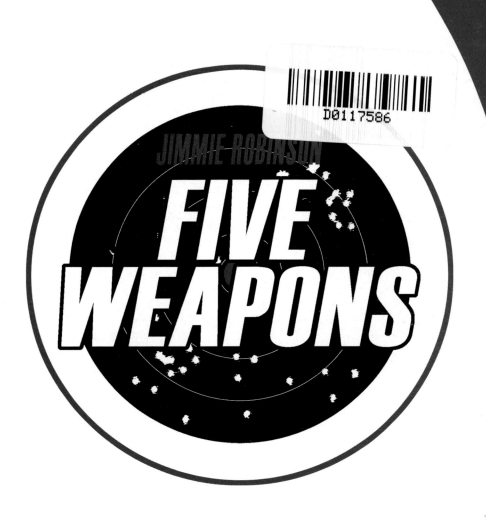

FIVE WEAPONS:
MAKING THE GRADE

FIRST PRINTING:
September, 2013

ISBN: 978-1-60706-779-5

Published by Image Comics, Inc. Office of publication: 2001 Center St. Sixth Floor, Berkeley, CA 94704. Copyright © 2013 JIMMIE ROBINSON. Originally published in single magazine form as FIVE WEAPONS #1-5. All rights reserved. FIVE WEAPONS™ (including all prominent characters featured herein), its logo and all character likenesses are trademarks of JIMMIE ROBINSON, unless otherwise noted. Image Comics® and its logos are registered trademarks of Image Comics, Inc. Shadowline and its logos are ™ and © 2013 Jim Valentino. No part of this publication may be reproduced or transmitted, in any form or by any means (except for short excerpts for review purposes) without the express written permission of Mr. Robinson. All names, characters, events and locales in this publication are entirely fictional. Any resemblance to actual persons (living or dead), events or places, without satiric intent, is coincidental. PRINTED IN USA. For information regarding the CPSIA on this printed material call: 203-595-3636 and provide reference # RICH –510061

International Rights / Foreign Licensing: -- foreignlicensing@imagecomics.com

CREATED, WRITTEN, ILLUSTRATED and LETTERED BY
JIMMIE ROBINSON

COLORED BY
PAUL LITTLE

EDITED BY
LAURA TAVISHATI

MARC LOMBARDI
COMMUNICATIONS
JIM VALENTINO
PUBLISHER/BOOK DESIGN

SPECIAL THANKS TO
GAIL FOLLANSBEE

IMAGE COMICS, INC.
Robert Kirkman - chief operating officer
Erik Larsen - chief financial officer
Todd McFarlane - president
Marc Silvestri - chief executive officer
Jim Valentino - vice-president

Eric Stephenson - publisher
Ron Richards - director of business development
Jennifer de Guzman - pr & marketing director
Branwyn Bigglestone - accounts manager
Emily Miller - accounting assistant
Jamie Parreno - marketing assistant
Emilio Bautista - sales assistant
Susie Giroux - administrative assistant
Kevin Yuen - digital rights coordinator
Tyler Shainline - events coordinator
David Brothers - content manager
Jonathan Chan - production manager
Drew Gill - art director
Jana Cook - print manager
Monica Garcia - senior production artist
Vincent Kukua - production artist
Jenna Savage - production artist
www.imagecomics.com

dedication...

"Thanks to my wife Gail,
        my daughters Ari and Jessica.

        And thanks to the real Tyler Shainline
                for being a good sport."

                Jimmie Robinson

"To Dave, Ian and the rest of the guys.
        Thanks for making comics fun again."
                Paul Little

BOOK ONE
JADE THE BLADE

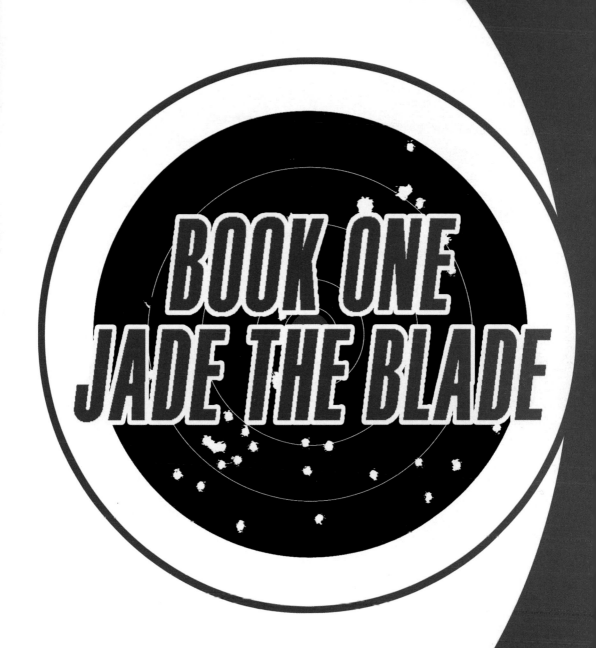

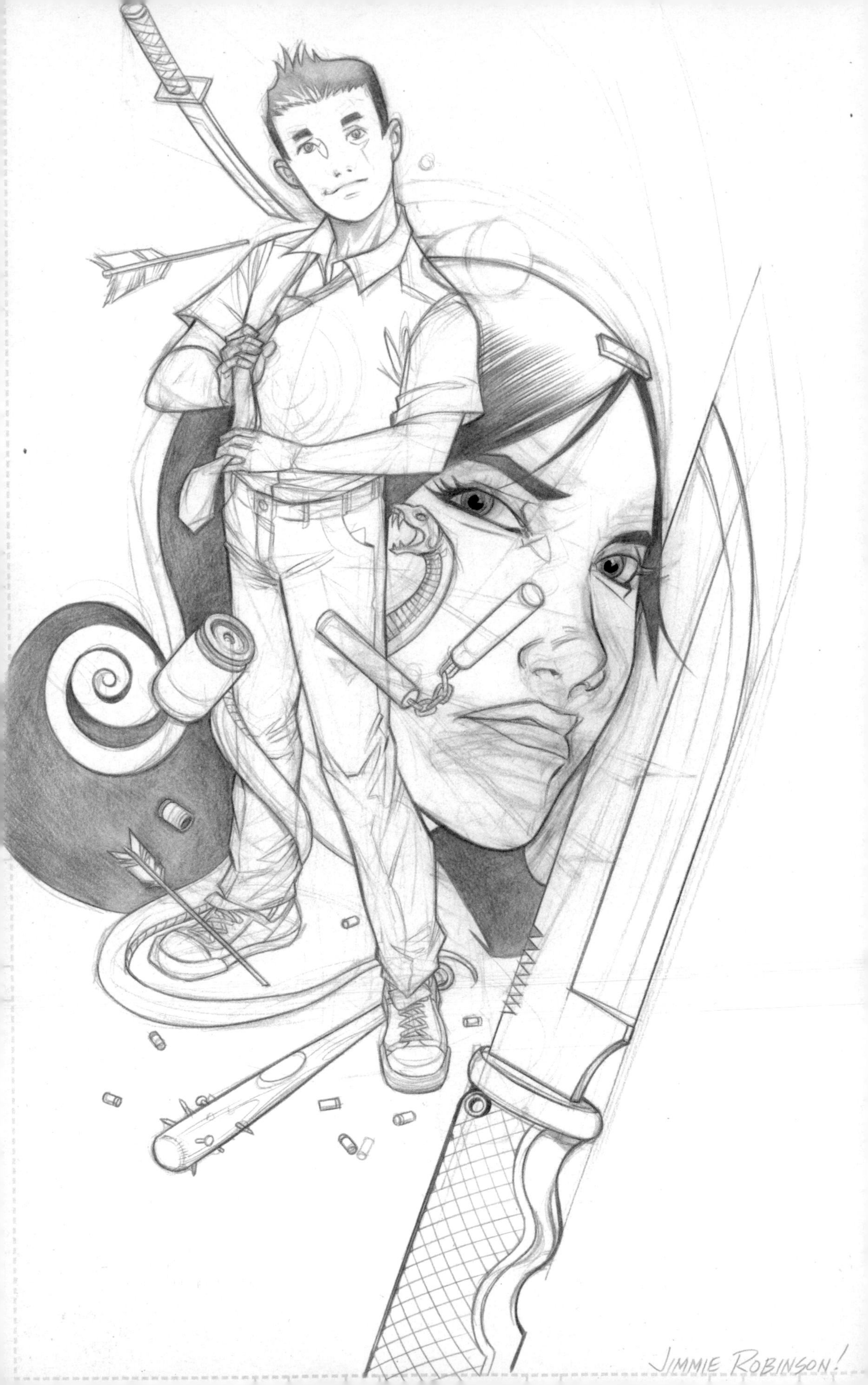
JIMMIE ROBINSON!

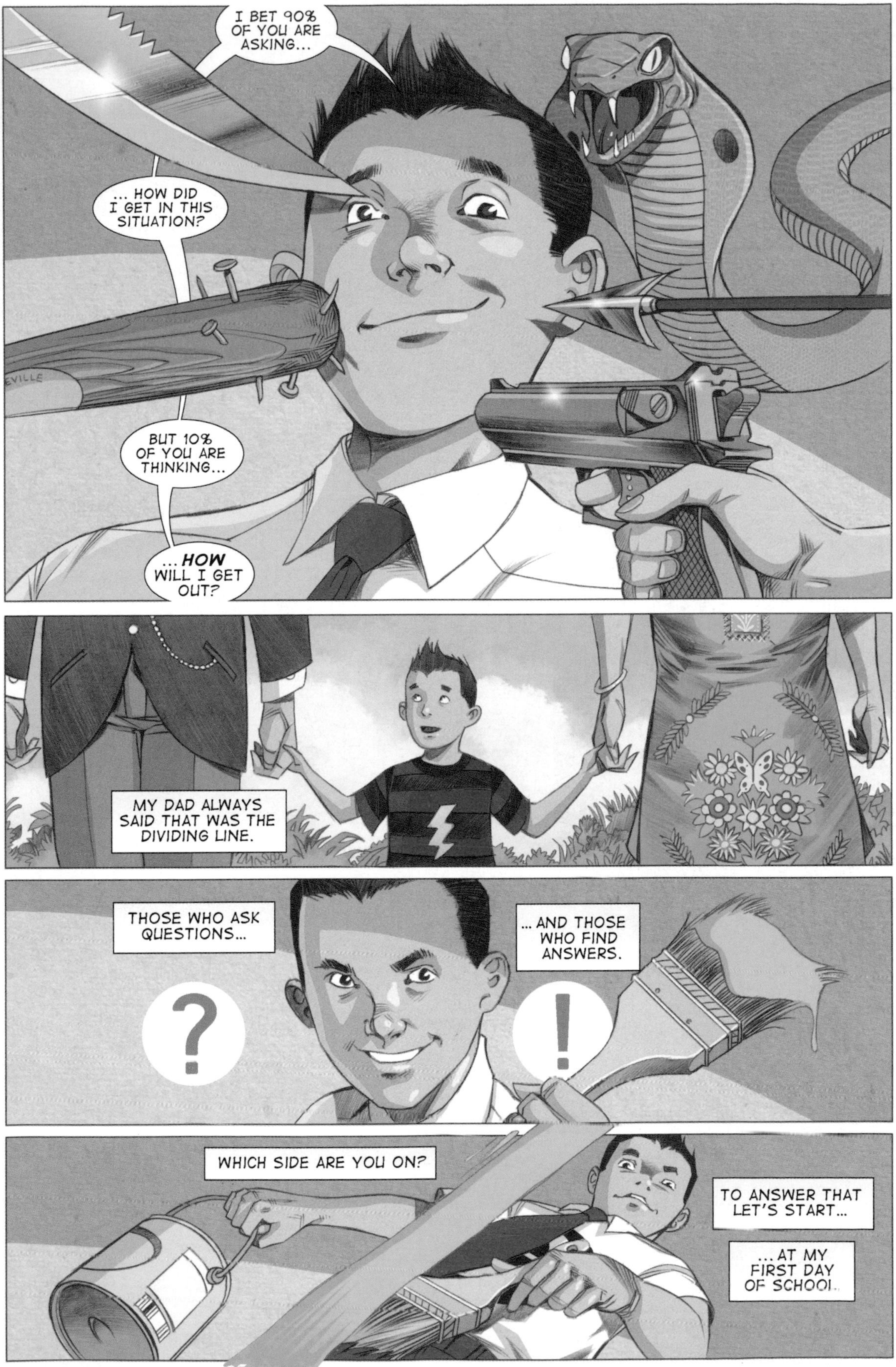
I BET 90% OF YOU ARE ASKING...
... HOW DID I GET IN THIS SITUATION?
BUT 10% OF YOU ARE THINKING...
... HOW WILL I GET OUT?
MY DAD ALWAYS SAID THAT WAS THE DIVIDING LINE.
THOSE WHO ASK QUESTIONS...
... AND THOSE WHO FIND ANSWERS.
?
!
WHICH SIDE ARE YOU ON?
TO ANSWER THAT LET'S START...
... AT MY FIRST DAY OF SCHOOL.

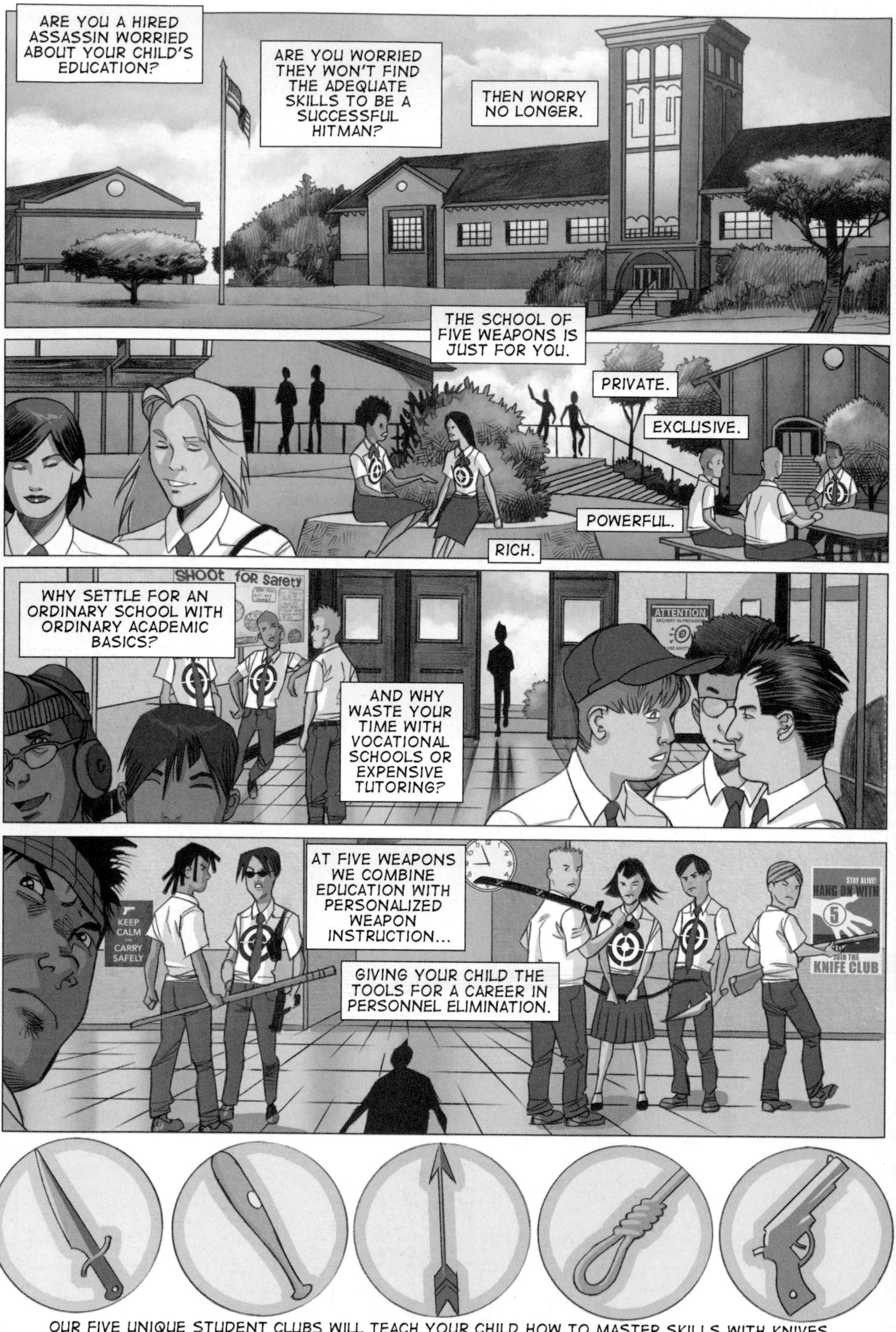
ARE YOU A HIRED ASSASSIN WORRIED ABOUT YOUR CHILD'S EDUCATION?
ARE YOU WORRIED THEY WON'T FIND THE ADEQUATE SKILLS TO BE A SUCCESSFUL HITMAN?
THEN WORRY NO LONGER.
THE SCHOOL OF FIVE WEAPONS IS JUST FOR YOU.
PRIVATE.
EXCLUSIVE.
POWERFUL.
RICH.
SHOOT FOR Safety
WHY SETTLE FOR AN ORDINARY SCHOOL WITH ORDINARY ACADEMIC BASICS?
ATTENTION
AND WHY WASTE YOUR TIME WITH VOCATIONAL SCHOOLS OR EXPENSIVE TUTORING?
KEEP CALM AND CARRY SAFELY
AT FIVE WEAPONS WE COMBINE EDUCATION WITH PERSONALIZED WEAPON INSTRUCTION...
STAY ALIVE! HANG ON WITH
5
JOIN THE KNIFE CLUB
GIVING YOUR CHILD THE TOOLS FOR A CAREER IN PERSONNEL ELIMINATION.

OUR FIVE UNIQUE STUDENT CLUBS WILL TEACH YOUR CHILD HOW TO MASTER SKILLS WITH KNIVES, STAVES, ARCHERY, EXOTIC WEAPONS, AND EVEN GUNS. DON'T DELAY, ENROLL YOUR CHILD TODAY.

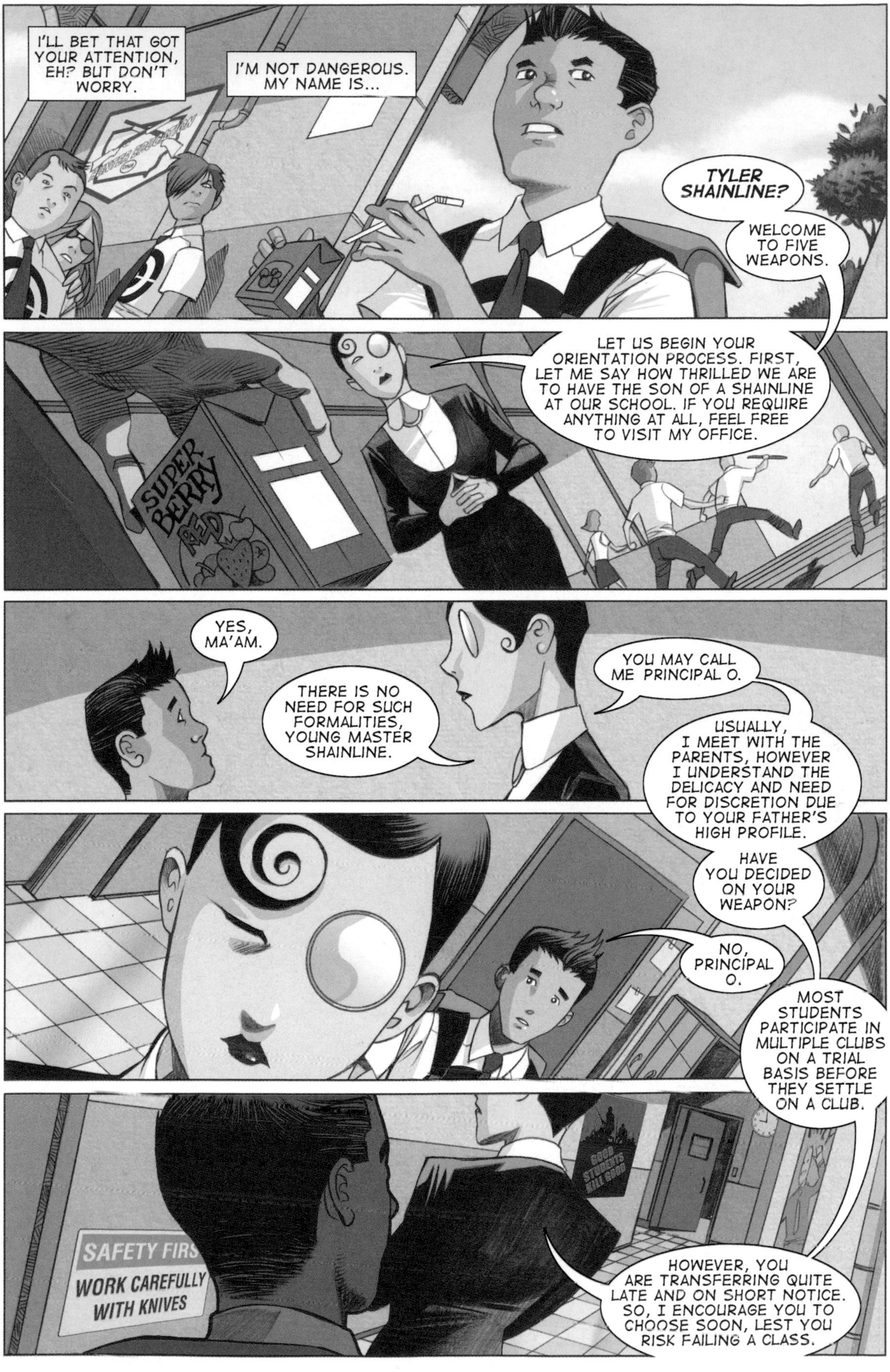
I'LL BET THAT GOT YOUR ATTENTION, EH? BUT DON'T WORRY.
I'M NOT DANGEROUS. MY NAME IS...
TYLER SHAINLINE?
WELCOME TO FIVE WEAPONS.
LET US BEGIN YOUR ORIENTATION PROCESS. FIRST, LET ME SAY HOW THRILLED WE ARE TO HAVE THE SON OF A SHAINLINE AT OUR SCHOOL. IF YOU REQUIRE ANYTHING AT ALL, FEEL FREE TO VISIT MY OFFICE.
SUPER BERRY RED
YES, MA'AM.
THERE IS NO NEED FOR SUCH FORMALITIES, YOUNG MASTER SHAINLINE.
YOU MAY CALL ME PRINCIPAL O.
USUALLY, I MEET WITH THE PARENTS, HOWEVER I UNDERSTAND THE DELICACY AND NEED FOR DISCRETION DUE TO YOUR FATHER'S HIGH PROFILE.
HAVE YOU DECIDED ON YOUR WEAPON?
NO, PRINCIPAL O.
MOST STUDENTS PARTICIPATE IN MULTIPLE CLUBS ON A TRIAL BASIS BEFORE THEY SETTLE ON A CLUB.
SAFETY FIRS
WORK CAREFULLY WITH KNIVES
HOWEVER, YOU ARE TRANSFERRING QUITE LATE AND ON SHORT NOTICE. SO, I ENCOURAGE YOU TO CHOOSE SOON, LEST YOU RISK FAILING A CLASS.

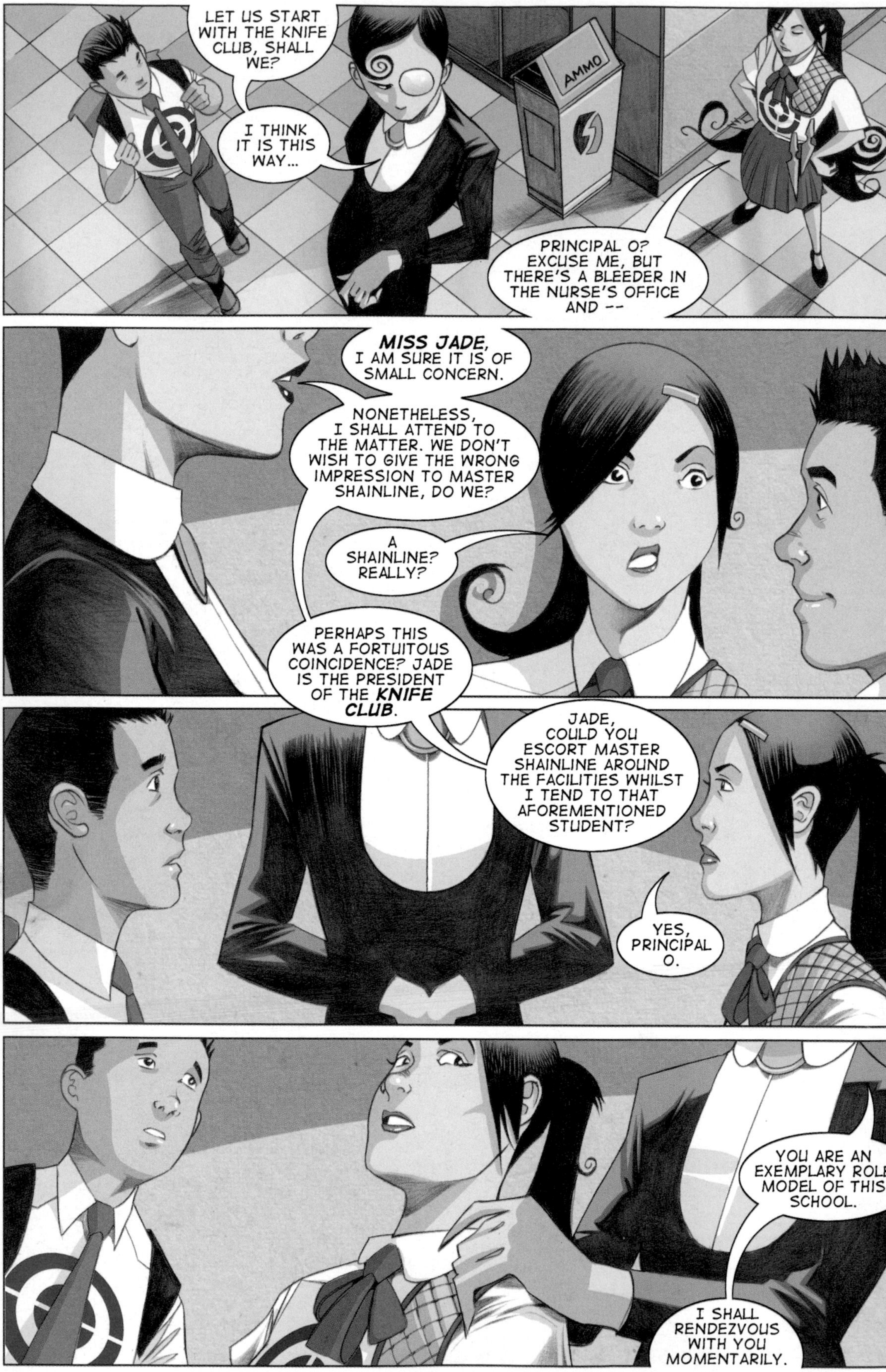
LET US START WITH THE KNIFE CLUB, SHALL WE?
I THINK IT IS THIS WAY...
AMMO
PRINCIPAL O? EXCUSE ME, BUT THERE'S A BLEEDER IN THE NURSE'S OFFICE AND --
MISS JADE, I AM SURE IT IS OF SMALL CONCERN.
NONETHELESS, I SHALL ATTEND TO THE MATTER. WE DON'T WISH TO GIVE THE WRONG IMPRESSION TO MASTER SHAINLINE, DO WE?
A SHAINLINE? REALLY?
PERHAPS THIS WAS A FORTUITOUS COINCIDENCE? JADE IS THE PRESIDENT OF THE KNIFE CLUB.
JADE, COULD YOU ESCORT MASTER SHAINLINE AROUND THE FACILITIES WHILST I TEND TO THAT AFOREMENTIONED STUDENT?
YES, PRINCIPAL O.
YOU ARE AN EXEMPLARY ROLE MODEL OF THIS SCHOOL.
I SHALL RENDEZVOUS WITH YOU MOMENTARILY.

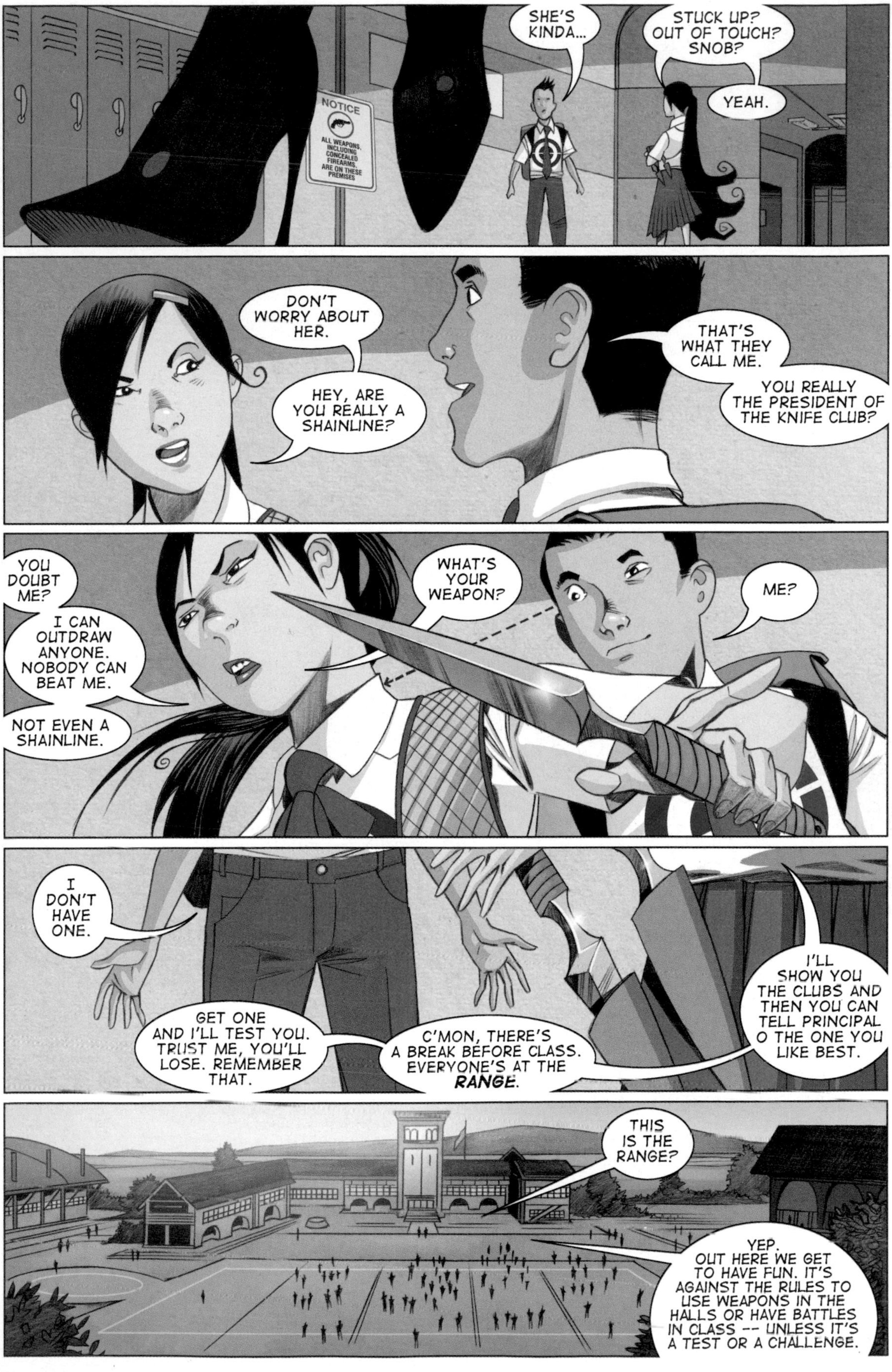
NOTICE
ALL WEAPONS, INCLUDING CONCEALED FIREARMS, ARE ON THESE PREMISES
SHE'S KINDA...
STUCK UP? OUT OF TOUCH? SNOB?
YEAH.
DON'T WORRY ABOUT HER.
HEY, ARE YOU REALLY A SHAINLINE?
THAT'S WHAT THEY CALL ME.
YOU REALLY THE PRESIDENT OF THE KNIFE CLUB?
YOU DOUBT ME?
I CAN OUTDRAW ANYONE. NOBODY CAN BEAT ME.
NOT EVEN A SHAINLINE.
WHAT'S YOUR WEAPON?
ME?
I DON'T HAVE ONE.
GET ONE AND I'LL TEST YOU. TRUST ME, YOU'LL LOSE. REMEMBER THAT.
C'MON, THERE'S A BREAK BEFORE CLASS. EVERYONE'S AT THE **RANGE**.
I'LL SHOW YOU THE CLUBS AND THEN YOU CAN TELL PRINCIPAL O THE ONE YOU LIKE BEST.
THIS IS THE RANGE?
YEP. OUT HERE WE GET TO HAVE FUN. IT'S AGAINST THE RULES TO USE WEAPONS IN THE HALLS OR HAVE BATTLES IN CLASS -- UNLESS IT'S A TEST OR A CHALLENGE.

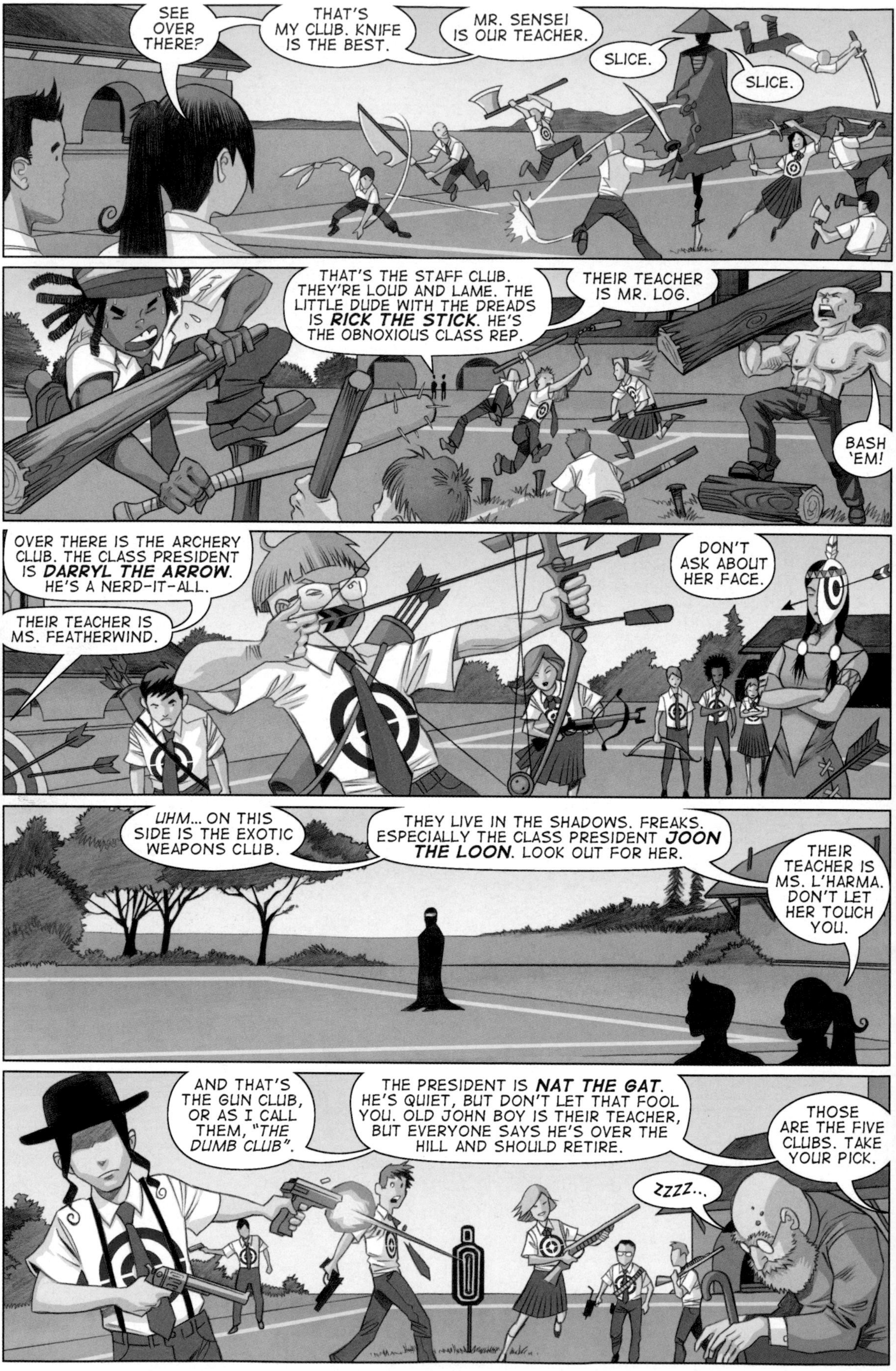
SEE OVER THERE?
THAT'S MY CLUB. KNIFE IS THE BEST.
MR. SENSEI IS OUR TEACHER.
SLICE.
SLICE.
THAT'S THE STAFF CLUB. THEY'RE LOUD AND LAME. THE LITTLE DUDE WITH THE DREADS IS RICK THE STICK. HE'S THE OBNOXIOUS CLASS REP.
THEIR TEACHER IS MR. LOG.
BASH 'EM!
OVER THERE IS THE ARCHERY CLUB. THE CLASS PRESIDENT IS DARRYL THE ARROW. HE'S A NERD-IT-ALL.
THEIR TEACHER IS MS. FEATHERWIND.
DON'T ASK ABOUT HER FACE.
UHM... ON THIS SIDE IS THE EXOTIC WEAPONS CLUB.
THEY LIVE IN THE SHADOWS. FREAKS. ESPECIALLY THE CLASS PRESIDENT JOON THE LOON. LOOK OUT FOR HER.
THEIR TEACHER IS MS. L'HARMA. DON'T LET HER TOUCH YOU.
AND THAT'S THE GUN CLUB, OR AS I CALL THEM, "THE DUMB CLUB".
THE PRESIDENT IS NAT THE GAT. HE'S QUIET, BUT DON'T LET THAT FOOL YOU. OLD JOHN BOY IS THEIR TEACHER, BUT EVERYONE SAYS HE'S OVER THE HILL AND SHOULD RETIRE.
ZZZZ...
THOSE ARE THE FIVE CLUBS. TAKE YOUR PICK.

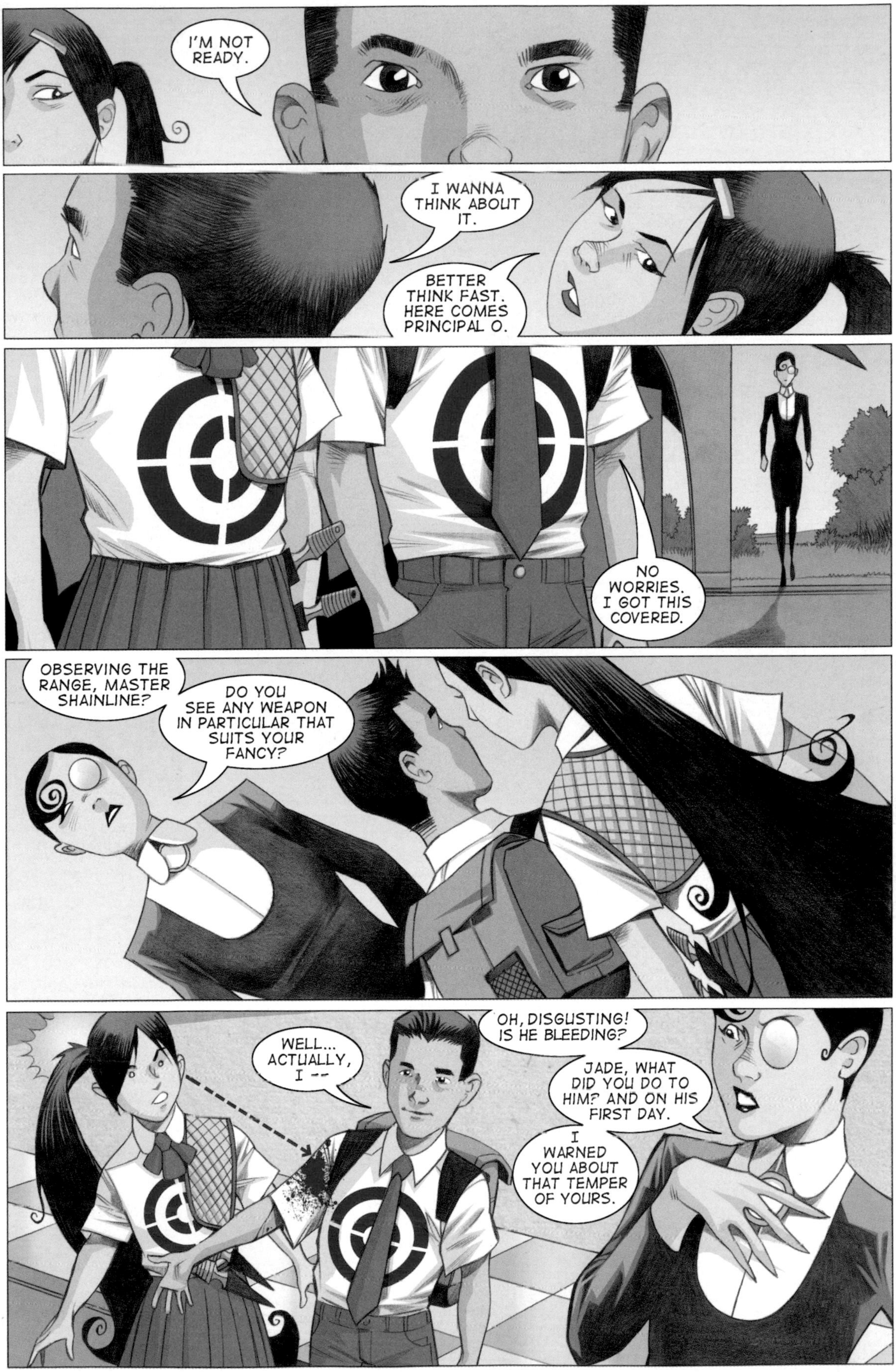
I'M NOT READY.
I WANNA THINK ABOUT IT.
BETTER THINK FAST. HERE COMES PRINCIPAL O.
NO WORRIES. I GOT THIS COVERED.
OBSERVING THE RANGE, MASTER SHAINLINE?
DO YOU SEE ANY WEAPON IN PARTICULAR THAT SUITS YOUR FANCY?
WELL... ACTUALLY, I --
OH, DISGUSTING! IS HE BLEEDING?
JADE, WHAT DID YOU DO TO HIM? AND ON HIS FIRST DAY.
I WARNED YOU ABOUT THAT TEMPER OF YOURS.

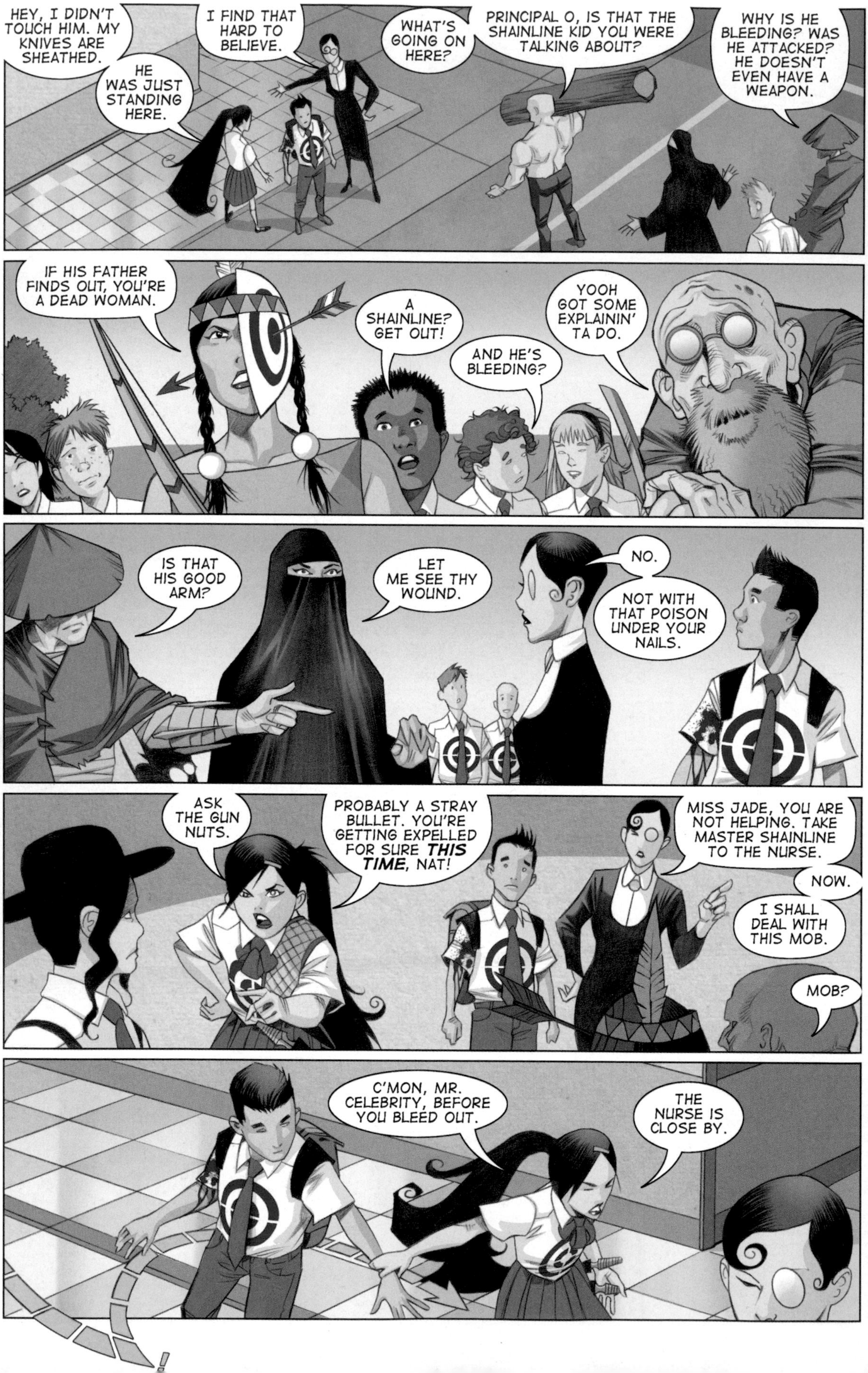

HEY, I DIDN'T TOUCH HIM. MY KNIVES ARE SHEATHED.
HE WAS JUST STANDING HERE.
I FIND THAT HARD TO BELIEVE.
WHAT'S GOING ON HERE?
PRINCIPAL O, IS THAT THE SHAINLINE KID YOU WERE TALKING ABOUT?
WHY IS HE BLEEDING? WAS HE ATTACKED? HE DOESN'T EVEN HAVE A WEAPON.
IF HIS FATHER FINDS OUT, YOU'RE A DEAD WOMAN.
A SHAINLINE? GET OUT!
AND HE'S BLEEDING?
YOOH GOT SOME EXPLAININ' TA DO.
IS THAT HIS GOOD ARM?
LET ME SEE THY WOUND.
NO.
NOT WITH THAT POISON UNDER YOUR NAILS.
ASK THE GUN NUTS.
PROBABLY A STRAY BULLET. YOU'RE GETTING EXPELLED FOR SURE THIS TIME, NAT!
MISS JADE, YOU ARE NOT HELPING. TAKE MASTER SHAINLINE TO THE NURSE.
NOW.
I SHALL DEAL WITH THIS MOB.
MOB?
C'MON, MR. CELEBRITY, BEFORE YOU BLEED OUT.
THE NURSE IS CLOSE BY.
!

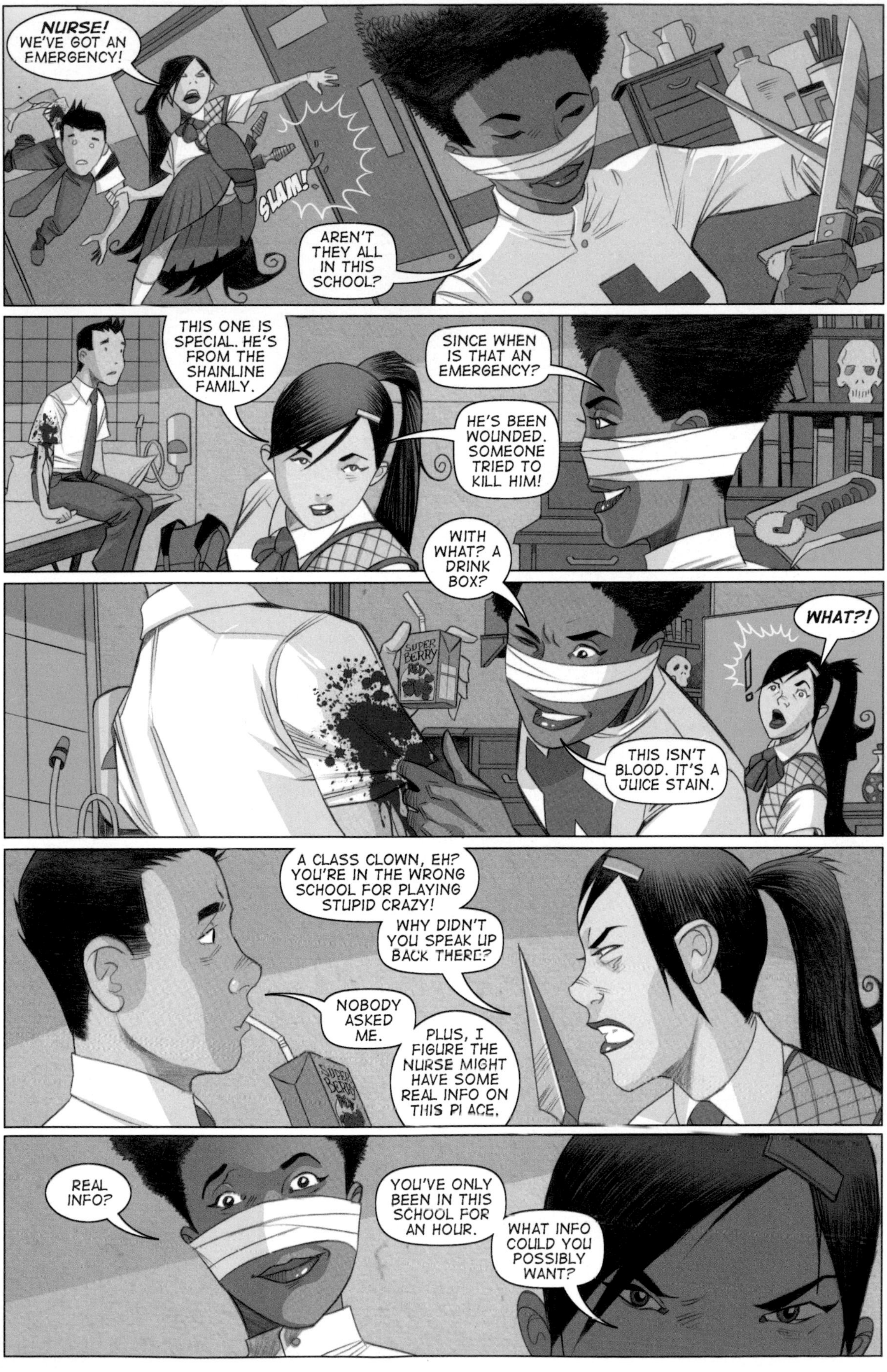
NURSE! WE'VE GOT AN EMERGENCY!
SLAM!
AREN'T THEY ALL IN THIS SCHOOL?
THIS ONE IS SPECIAL. HE'S FROM THE SHAINLINE FAMILY.
SINCE WHEN IS THAT AN EMERGENCY?
HE'S BEEN WOUNDED. SOMEONE TRIED TO KILL HIM!
WITH WHAT? A DRINK BOX?
SUPER BERRY
WHAT?!
THIS ISN'T BLOOD. IT'S A JUICE STAIN.
A CLASS CLOWN, EH? YOU'RE IN THE WRONG SCHOOL FOR PLAYING STUPID CRAZY!
WHY DIDN'T YOU SPEAK UP BACK THERE?
NOBODY ASKED ME.
PLUS, I FIGURE THE NURSE MIGHT HAVE SOME REAL INFO ON THIS PLACE.
REAL INFO?
YOU'VE ONLY BEEN IN THIS SCHOOL FOR AN HOUR.
WHAT INFO COULD YOU POSSIBLY WANT?

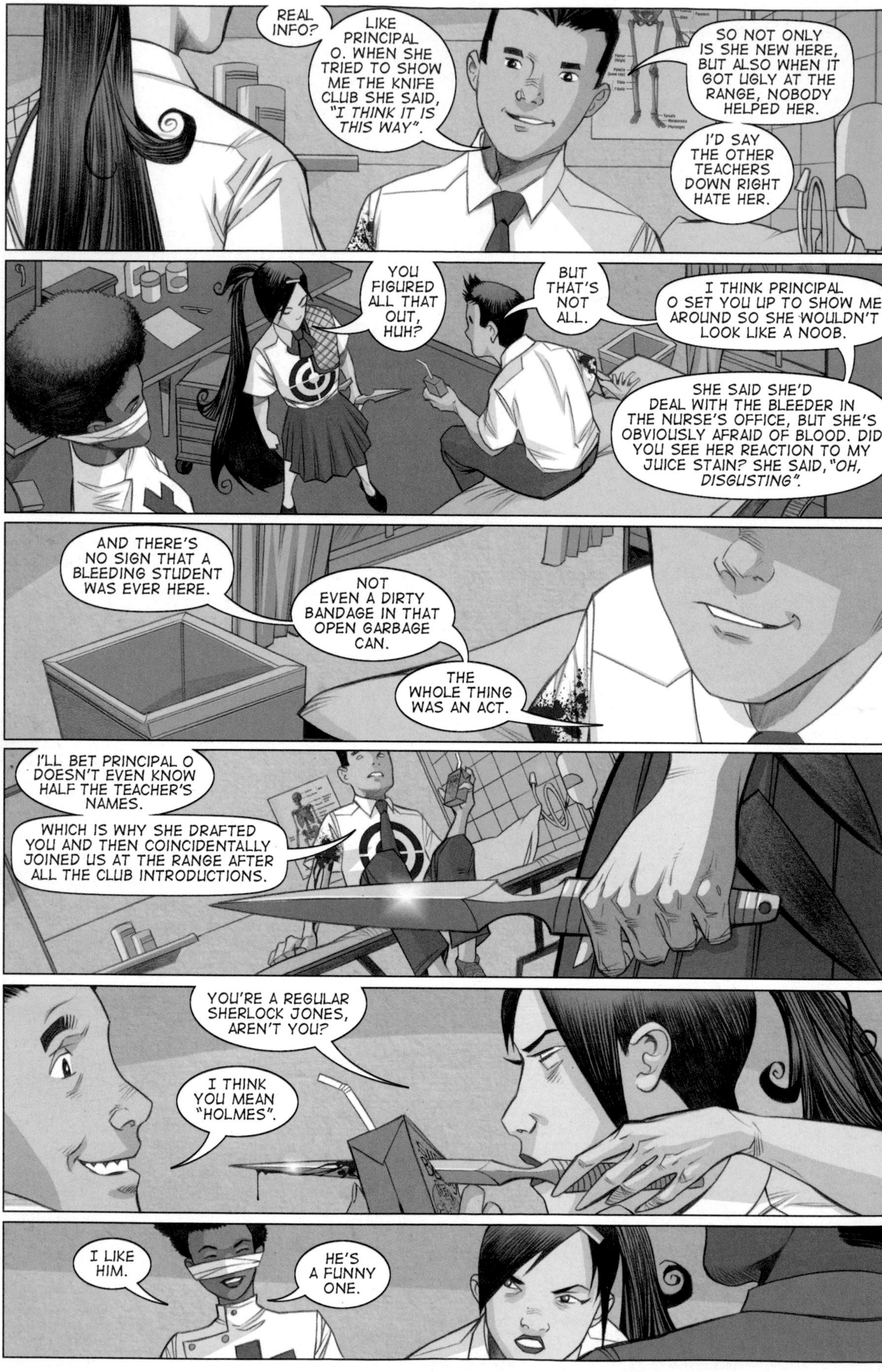
REAL INFO?
LIKE PRINCIPAL O. WHEN SHE TRIED TO SHOW ME THE KNIFE CLUB SHE SAID, "I THINK IT IS THIS WAY".
SO NOT ONLY IS SHE NEW HERE, BUT ALSO WHEN IT GOT UGLY AT THE RANGE, NOBODY HELPED HER.
I'D SAY THE OTHER TEACHERS DOWN RIGHT HATE HER.
YOU FIGURED ALL THAT OUT, HUH?
BUT THAT'S NOT ALL.
I THINK PRINCIPAL O SET YOU UP TO SHOW ME AROUND SO SHE WOULDN'T LOOK LIKE A NOOB.
SHE SAID SHE'D DEAL WITH THE BLEEDER IN THE NURSE'S OFFICE, BUT SHE'S OBVIOUSLY AFRAID OF BLOOD. DID YOU SEE HER REACTION TO MY JUICE STAIN? SHE SAID, "OH, DISGUSTING".
AND THERE'S NO SIGN THAT A BLEEDING STUDENT WAS EVER HERE.
NOT EVEN A DIRTY BANDAGE IN THAT OPEN GARBAGE CAN.
THE WHOLE THING WAS AN ACT.
I'LL BET PRINCIPAL O DOESN'T EVEN KNOW HALF THE TEACHER'S NAMES.
WHICH IS WHY SHE DRAFTED YOU AND THEN COINCIDENTALLY JOINED US AT THE RANGE AFTER ALL THE CLUB INTRODUCTIONS.
YOU'RE A REGULAR SHERLOCK JONES, AREN'T YOU?
I THINK YOU MEAN "HOLMES".
I LIKE HIM.
HE'S A FUNNY ONE.

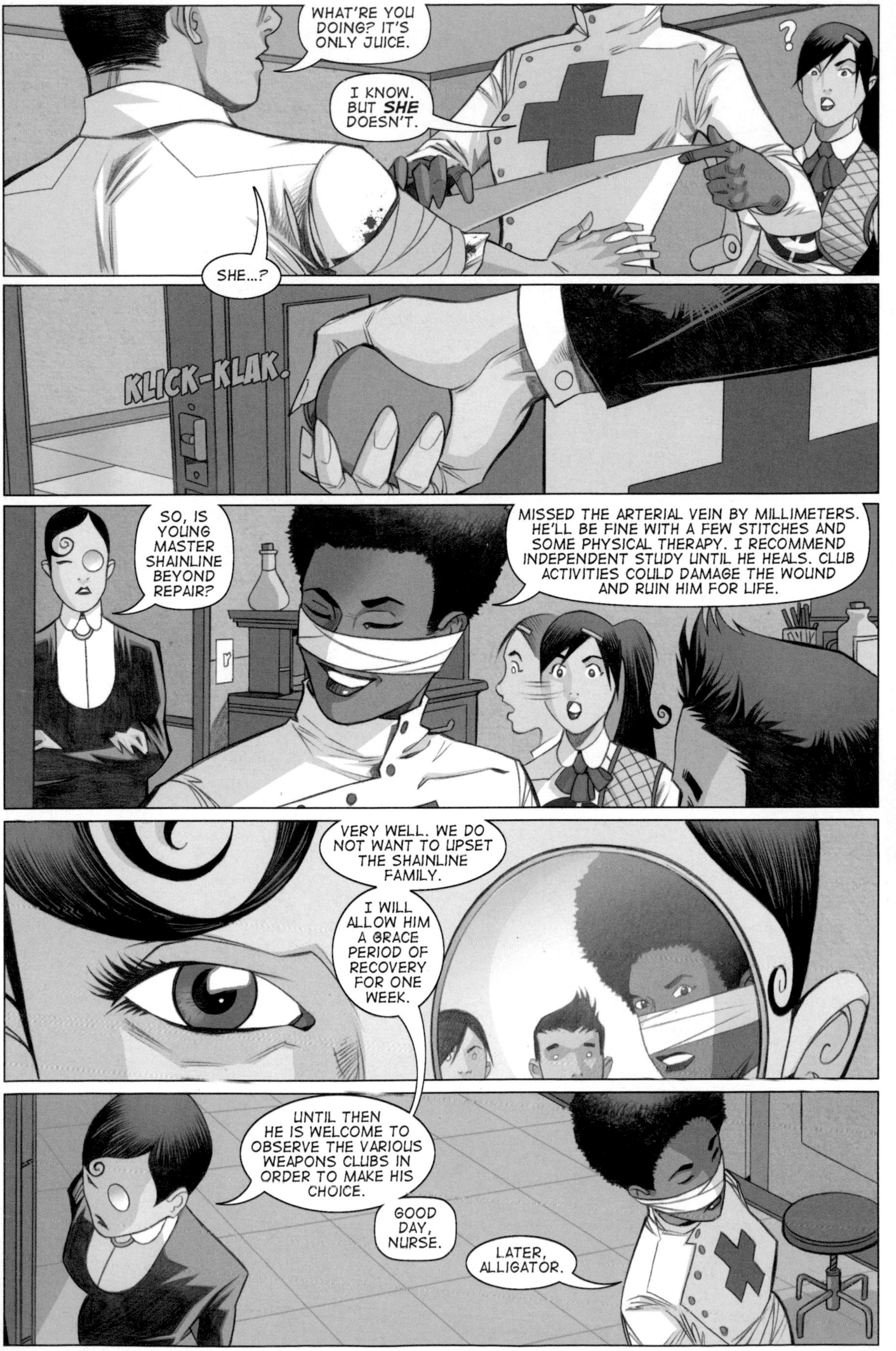
WHAT'RE YOU DOING? IT'S ONLY JUICE.
?
I KNOW. BUT SHE DOESN'T.
SHE...?
KLICK-KLAK.
SO, IS YOUNG MASTER SHAINLINE BEYOND REPAIR?
MISSED THE ARTERIAL VEIN BY MILLIMETERS. HE'LL BE FINE WITH A FEW STITCHES AND SOME PHYSICAL THERAPY. I RECOMMEND INDEPENDENT STUDY UNTIL HE HEALS. CLUB ACTIVITIES COULD DAMAGE THE WOUND AND RUIN HIM FOR LIFE.
VERY WELL. WE DO NOT WANT TO UPSET THE SHAINLINE FAMILY.
I WILL ALLOW HIM A GRACE PERIOD OF RECOVERY FOR ONE WEEK.
UNTIL THEN HE IS WELCOME TO OBSERVE THE VARIOUS WEAPONS CLUBS IN ORDER TO MAKE HIS CHOICE.
GOOD DAY, NURSE.
LATER, ALLIGATOR.

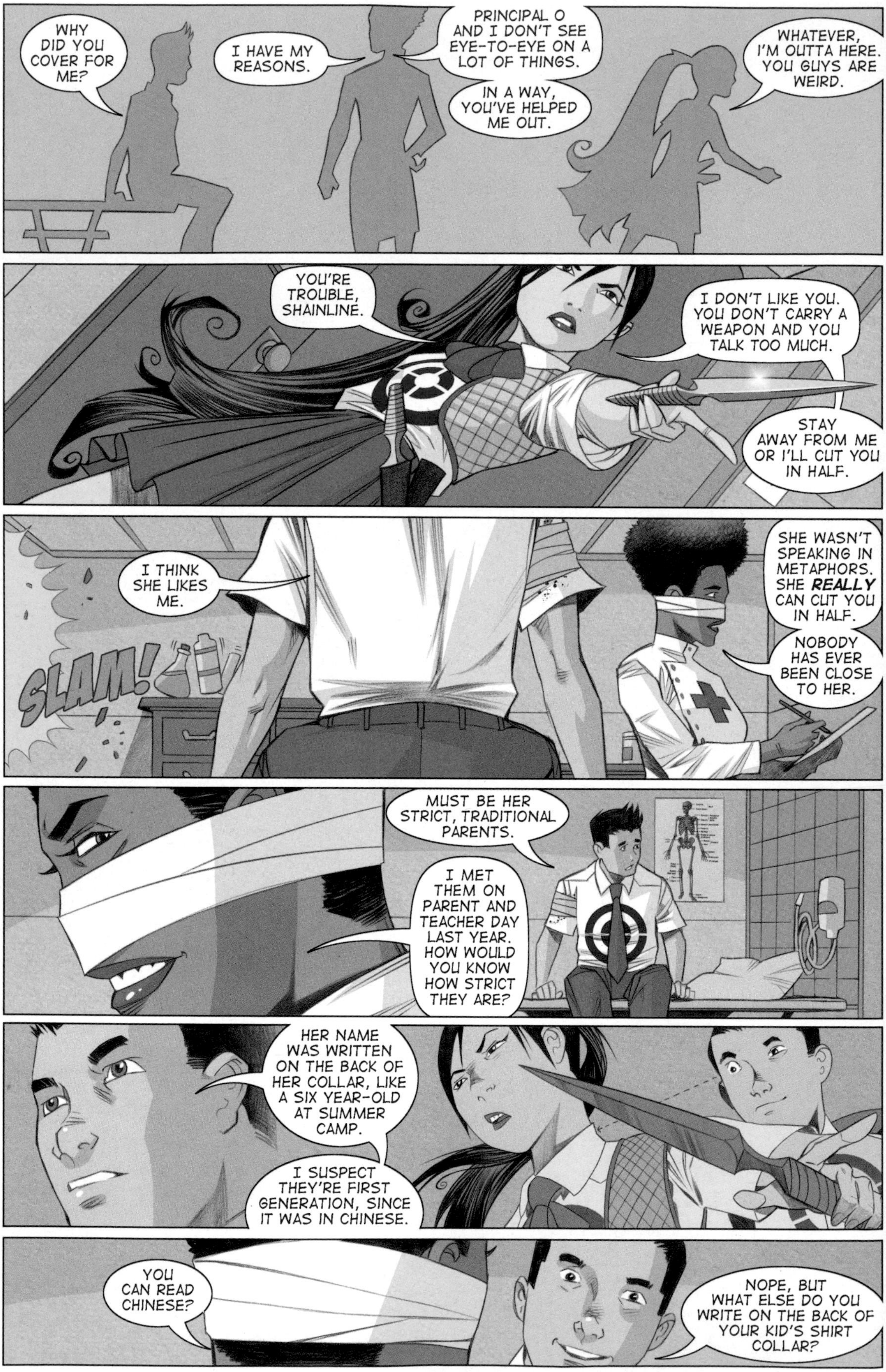
WHY DID YOU COVER FOR ME?
I HAVE MY REASONS.
PRINCIPAL O AND I DON'T SEE EYE-TO-EYE ON A LOT OF THINGS.
IN A WAY, YOU'VE HELPED ME OUT.
WHATEVER, I'M OUTTA HERE. YOU GUYS ARE WEIRD.
YOU'RE TROUBLE, SHAINLINE.
I DON'T LIKE YOU. YOU DON'T CARRY A WEAPON AND YOU TALK TOO MUCH.
STAY AWAY FROM ME OR I'LL CUT YOU IN HALF.
SLAM!
I THINK SHE LIKES ME.
SHE WASN'T SPEAKING IN METAPHORS. SHE *REALLY* CAN CUT YOU IN HALF.
NOBODY HAS EVER BEEN CLOSE TO HER.
MUST BE HER STRICT, TRADITIONAL PARENTS.
I MET THEM ON PARENT AND TEACHER DAY LAST YEAR. HOW WOULD YOU KNOW HOW STRICT THEY ARE?
HER NAME WAS WRITTEN ON THE BACK OF HER COLLAR, LIKE A SIX YEAR-OLD AT SUMMER CAMP.
I SUSPECT THEY'RE FIRST GENERATION, SINCE IT WAS IN CHINESE.
YOU CAN READ CHINESE?
NOPE, BUT WHAT ELSE DO YOU WRITE ON THE BACK OF YOUR KID'S SHIRT COLLAR?

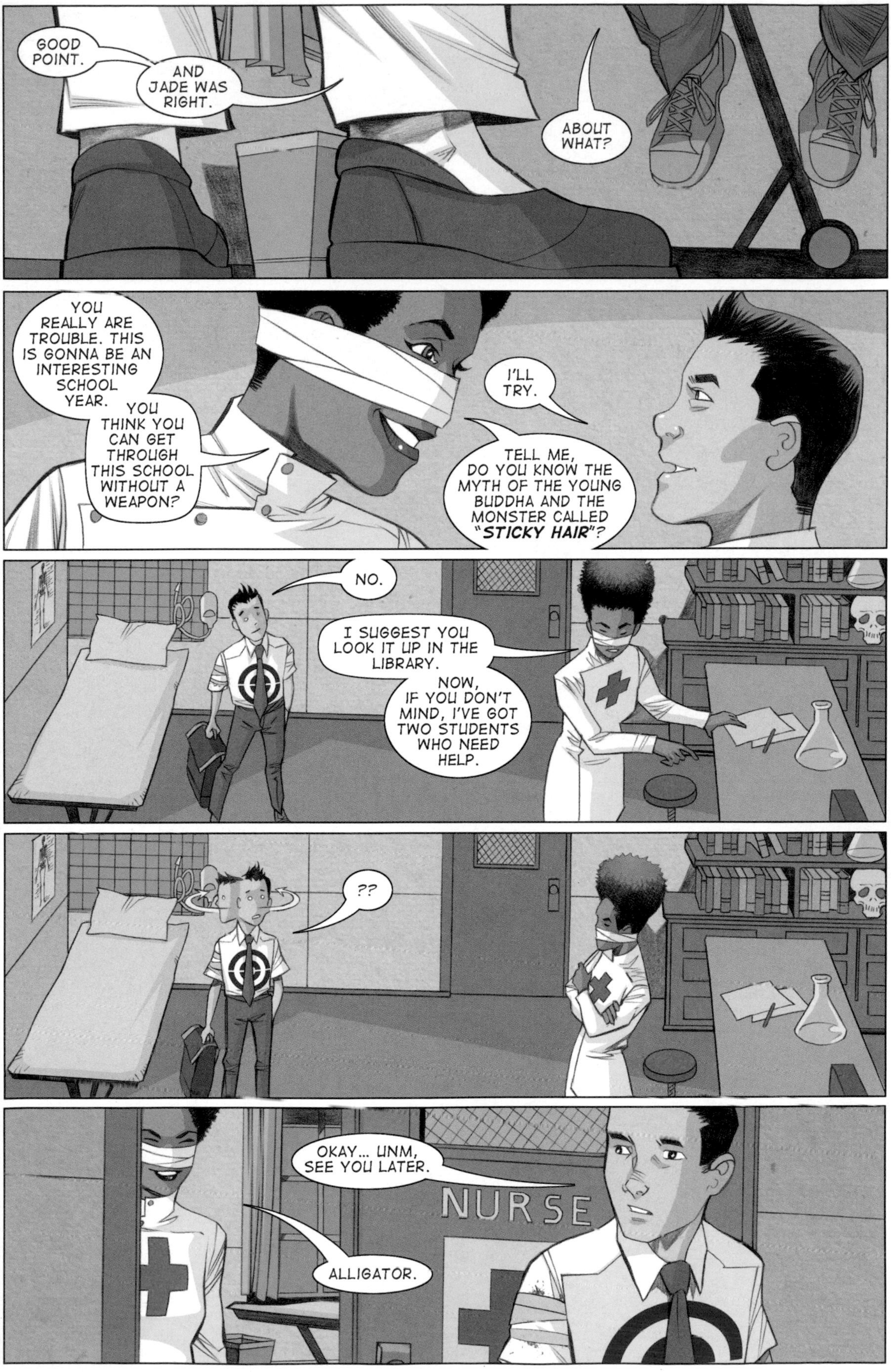
GOOD POINT.
AND JADE WAS RIGHT.
ABOUT WHAT?
YOU REALLY ARE TROUBLE. THIS IS GONNA BE AN INTERESTING SCHOOL YEAR.
YOU THINK YOU CAN GET THROUGH THIS SCHOOL WITHOUT A WEAPON?
I'LL TRY.
TELL ME, DO YOU KNOW THE MYTH OF THE YOUNG BUDDHA AND THE MONSTER CALLED "STICKY HAIR"?
NO.
I SUGGEST YOU LOOK IT UP IN THE LIBRARY.
NOW, IF YOU DON'T MIND, I'VE GOT TWO STUDENTS WHO NEED HELP.
??
OKAY... UNM, SEE YOU LATER.
NURSE
ALLIGATOR.

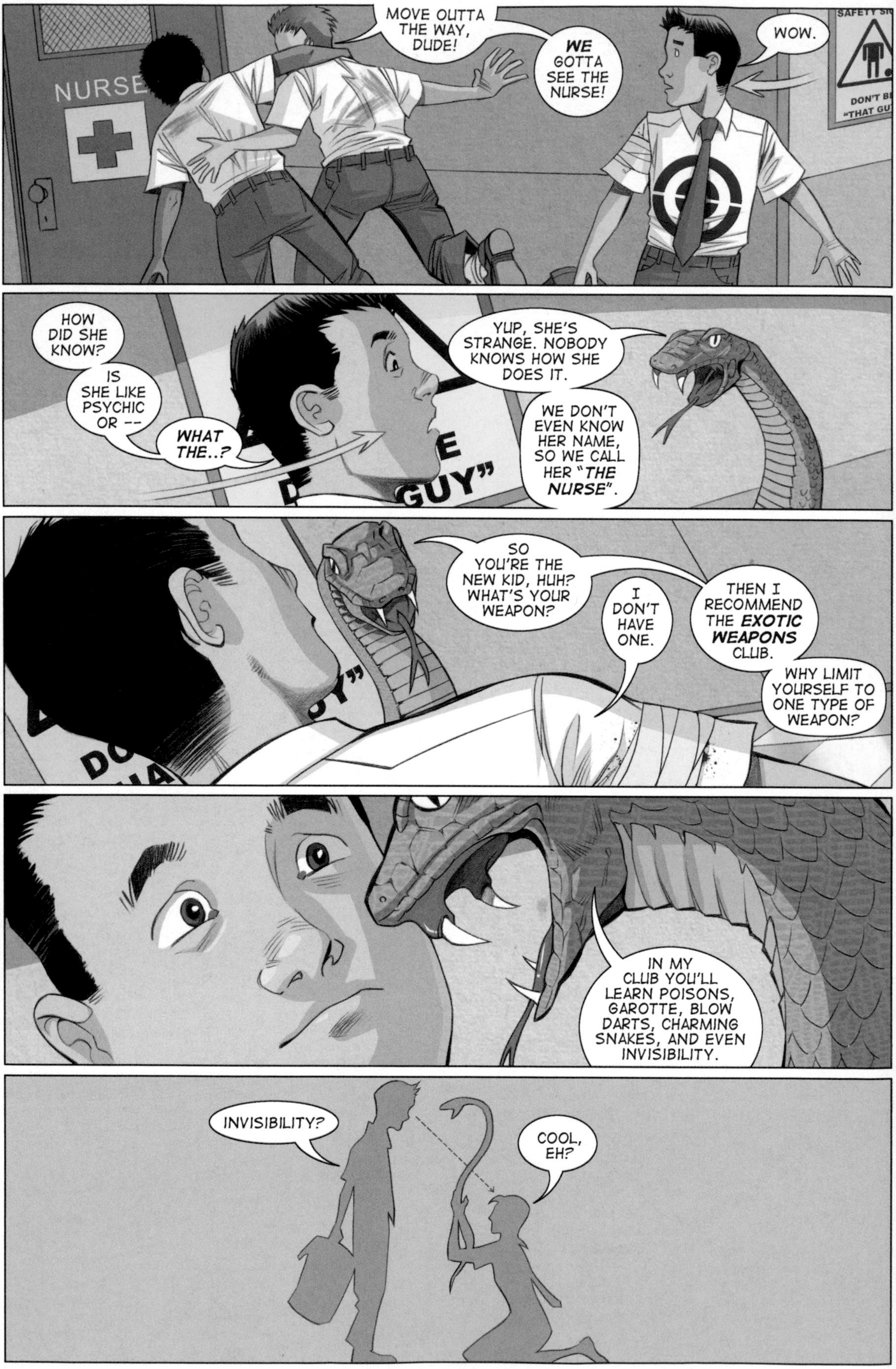
NURSE
MOVE OUTTA THE WAY, DUDE!
WE GOTTA SEE THE NURSE!
WOW.
SAFETY SI
DON'T B
"THAT GU
HOW DID SHE KNOW?
IS SHE LIKE PSYCHIC OR --
WHAT THE..?
YUP, SHE'S STRANGE. NOBODY KNOWS HOW SHE DOES IT.
WE DON'T EVEN KNOW HER NAME, SO WE CALL HER "*THE NURSE*".
SO YOU'RE THE NEW KID, HUH? WHAT'S YOUR WEAPON?
I DON'T HAVE ONE.
THEN I RECOMMEND THE ***EXOTIC WEAPONS*** CLUB.
WHY LIMIT YOURSELF TO ONE TYPE OF WEAPON?
IN MY CLUB YOU'LL LEARN POISONS, GAROTTE, BLOW DARTS, CHARMING SNAKES, AND EVEN INVISIBILITY.
INVISIBILITY?
COOL, EH?

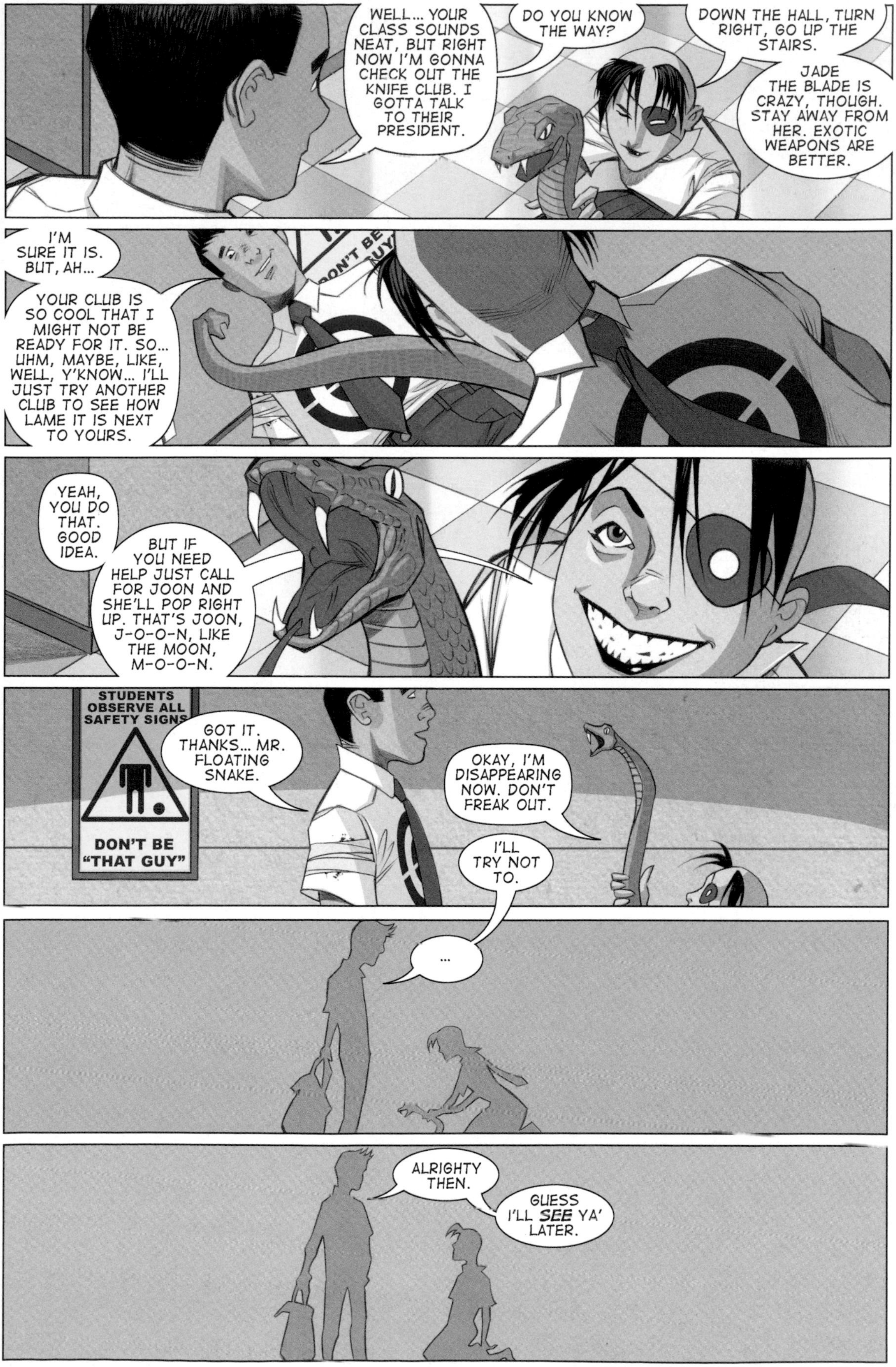
WELL... YOUR CLASS SOUNDS NEAT, BUT RIGHT NOW I'M GONNA CHECK OUT THE KNIFE CLUB. I GOTTA TALK TO THEIR PRESIDENT.
DO YOU KNOW THE WAY?
DOWN THE HALL, TURN RIGHT, GO UP THE STAIRS.
JADE THE BLADE IS CRAZY, THOUGH. STAY AWAY FROM HER. EXOTIC WEAPONS ARE BETTER.
I'M SURE IT IS. BUT, AH...
YOUR CLUB IS SO COOL THAT I MIGHT NOT BE READY FOR IT. SO... UHM, MAYBE, LIKE, WELL, Y'KNOW... I'LL JUST TRY ANOTHER CLUB TO SEE HOW LAME IT IS NEXT TO YOURS.
YEAH, YOU DO THAT. GOOD IDEA.
BUT IF YOU NEED HELP JUST CALL FOR JOON AND SHE'LL POP RIGHT UP. THAT'S JOON, J-O-O-N, LIKE THE MOON, M-O-O-N.
STUDENTS OBSERVE ALL SAFETY SIGNS
DON'T BE "THAT GUY"
GOT IT. THANKS... MR. FLOATING SNAKE.
OKAY, I'M DISAPPEARING NOW. DON'T FREAK OUT.
I'LL TRY NOT TO.
...
ALRIGHTY THEN.
GUESS I'LL SEE YA' LATER.

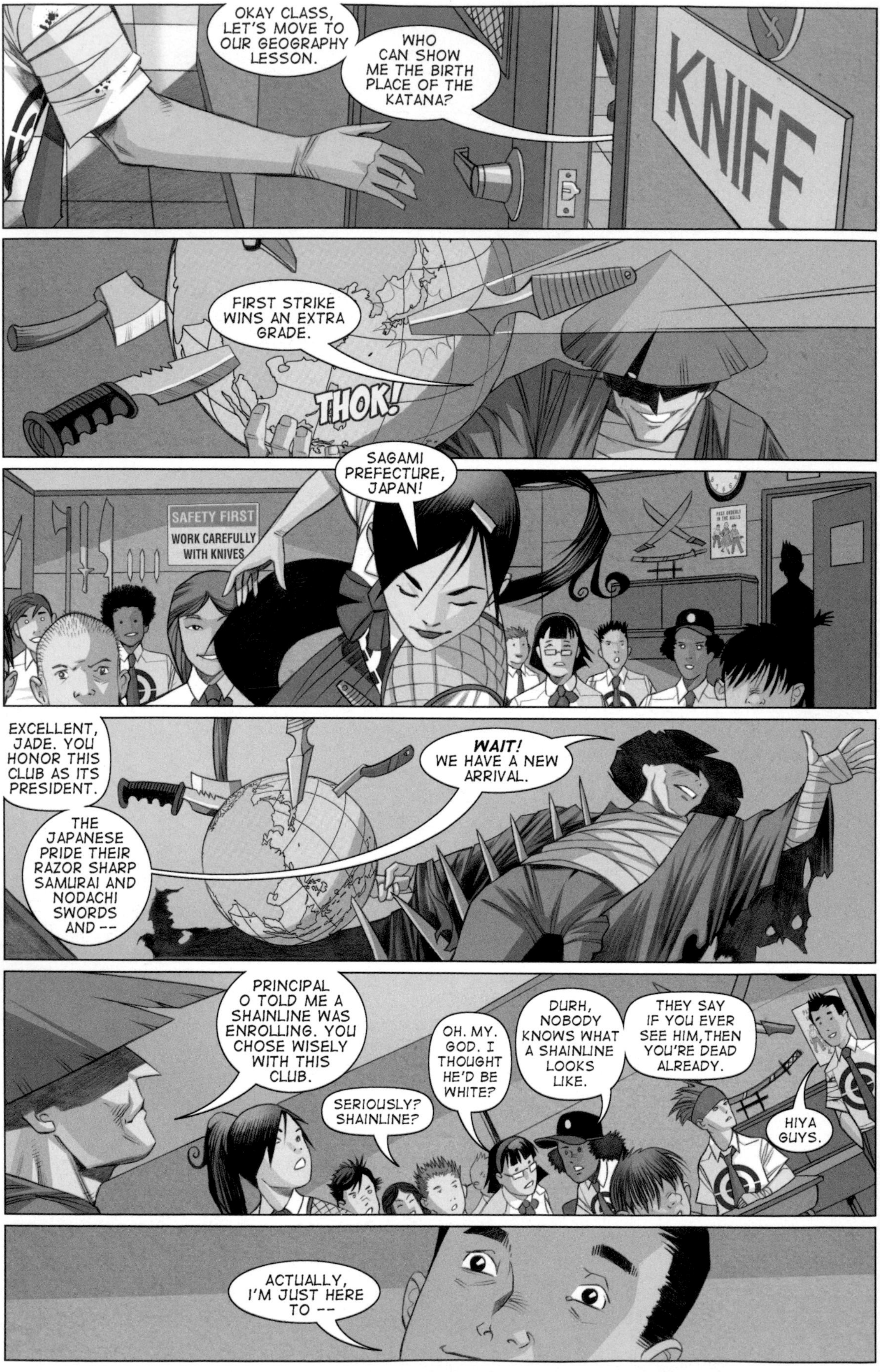

OKAY CLASS, LET'S MOVE TO OUR GEOGRAPHY LESSON.
WHO CAN SHOW ME THE BIRTH PLACE OF THE KATANA?
KNIFE
FIRST STRIKE WINS AN EXTRA GRADE.
THOK!
SAGAMI PREFECTURE, JAPAN!
SAFETY FIRST
WORK CAREFULLY WITH KNIVES
EXCELLENT, JADE. YOU HONOR THIS CLUB AS ITS PRESIDENT.
THE JAPANESE PRIDE THEIR RAZOR SHARP SAMURAI AND NODACHI SWORDS AND --
WAIT! WE HAVE A NEW ARRIVAL.
PRINCIPAL O TOLD ME A SHAINLINE WAS ENROLLING. YOU CHOSE WISELY WITH THIS CLUB.
SERIOUSLY? SHAINLINE?
OH. MY. GOD. I THOUGHT HE'D BE WHITE?
DURH, NOBODY KNOWS WHAT A SHAINLINE LOOKS LIKE.
THEY SAY IF YOU EVER SEE HIM, THEN YOU'RE DEAD ALREADY.
HIYA GUYS.
ACTUALLY, I'M JUST HERE TO --

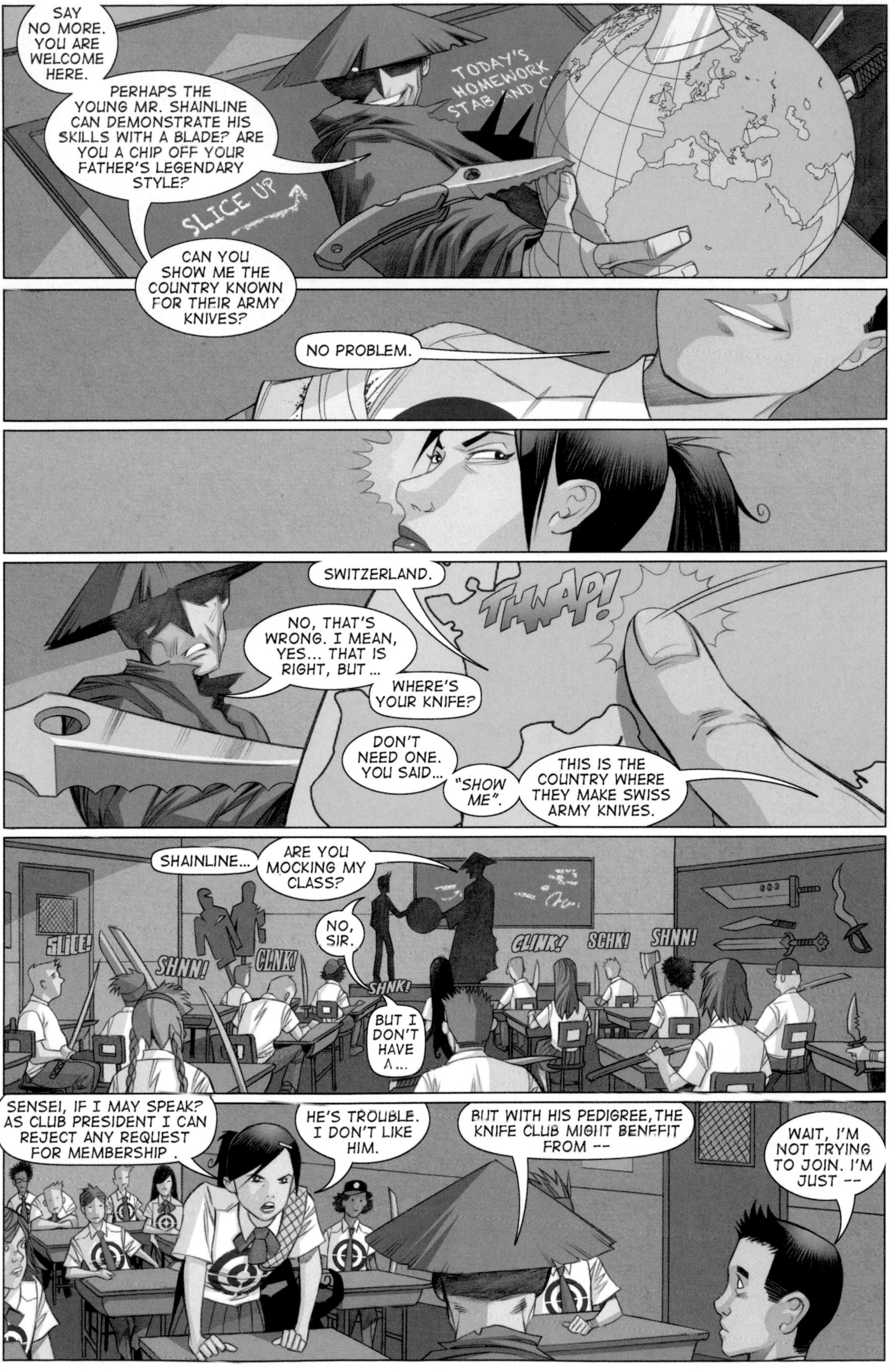
SAY NO MORE. YOU ARE WELCOME HERE.
PERHAPS THE YOUNG MR. SHAINLINE CAN DEMONSTRATE HIS SKILLS WITH A BLADE? ARE YOU A CHIP OFF YOUR FATHER'S LEGENDARY STYLE?
TODAY'S HOMEWORK STAB AND C
SLICE UP
CAN YOU SHOW ME THE COUNTRY KNOWN FOR THEIR ARMY KNIVES?
NO PROBLEM.
SWITZERLAND.
THWAP!
NO, THAT'S WRONG. I MEAN, YES... THAT IS RIGHT, BUT ...
WHERE'S YOUR KNIFE?
DON'T NEED ONE. YOU SAID...
"SHOW ME".
THIS IS THE COUNTRY WHERE THEY MAKE SWISS ARMY KNIVES.
SHAINLINE...
ARE YOU MOCKING MY CLASS?
NO, SIR.
SLICE!
SHNN!
CLINK!
CLINK!
SCHK!
SHNN!
SHNK!
BUT I DON'T HAVE A...
SENSEI, IF I MAY SPEAK? AS CLUB PRESIDENT I CAN REJECT ANY REQUEST FOR MEMBERSHIP .
HE'S TROUBLE. I DON'T LIKE HIM.
BUT WITH HIS PEDIGREE, THE KNIFE CLUB MIGHT BENEFIT FROM --
WAIT, I'M NOT TRYING TO JOIN. I'M JUST --

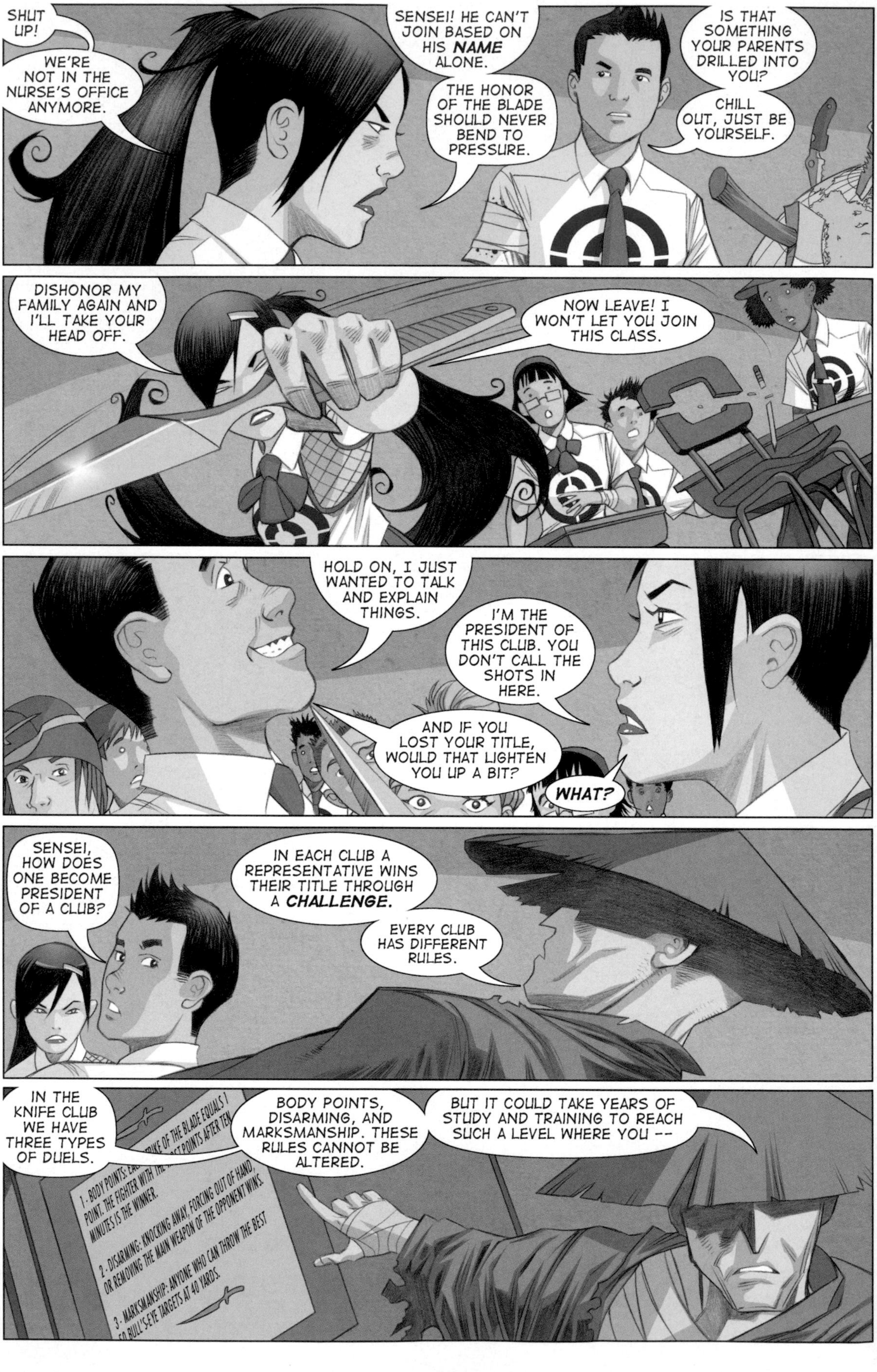
SHUT UP!
WE'RE NOT IN THE NURSE'S OFFICE ANYMORE.
SENSEI! HE CAN'T JOIN BASED ON HIS **NAME** ALONE.
THE HONOR OF THE BLADE SHOULD NEVER BEND TO PRESSURE.
IS THAT SOMETHING YOUR PARENTS DRILLED INTO YOU?
CHILL OUT, JUST BE YOURSELF.
DISHONOR MY FAMILY AGAIN AND I'LL TAKE YOUR HEAD OFF.
NOW LEAVE! I WON'T LET YOU JOIN THIS CLASS.
HOLD ON, I JUST WANTED TO TALK AND EXPLAIN THINGS.
I'M THE PRESIDENT OF THIS CLUB. YOU DON'T CALL THE SHOTS IN HERE.
AND IF YOU LOST YOUR TITLE, WOULD THAT LIGHTEN YOU UP A BIT?
WHAT?
SENSEI, HOW DOES ONE BECOME PRESIDENT OF A CLUB?
IN EACH CLUB A REPRESENTATIVE WINS THEIR TITLE THROUGH A **CHALLENGE.**
EVERY CLUB HAS DIFFERENT RULES.
IN THE KNIFE CLUB WE HAVE THREE TYPES OF DUELS.
BODY POINTS, DISARMING, AND MARKSMANSHIP. THESE RULES CANNOT BE ALTERED.
BUT IT COULD TAKE YEARS OF STUDY AND TRAINING TO REACH SUCH A LEVEL WHERE YOU --
1 - BODY POINTS: EA
POINT. THE FIGHTER WITH THE
MINUTES IS THE WINNER.
2 - DISARMING: KNOCKING AWAY, FORCING OUT OF HAND, OR REMOVING THE MAIN WEAPON OF THE OPPONENT WINS.
3 - MARKSMANSHIP: ANYONE WHO CAN THROW THE BEST
BULL'S-EYE TARGETS AT 40 YARDS.

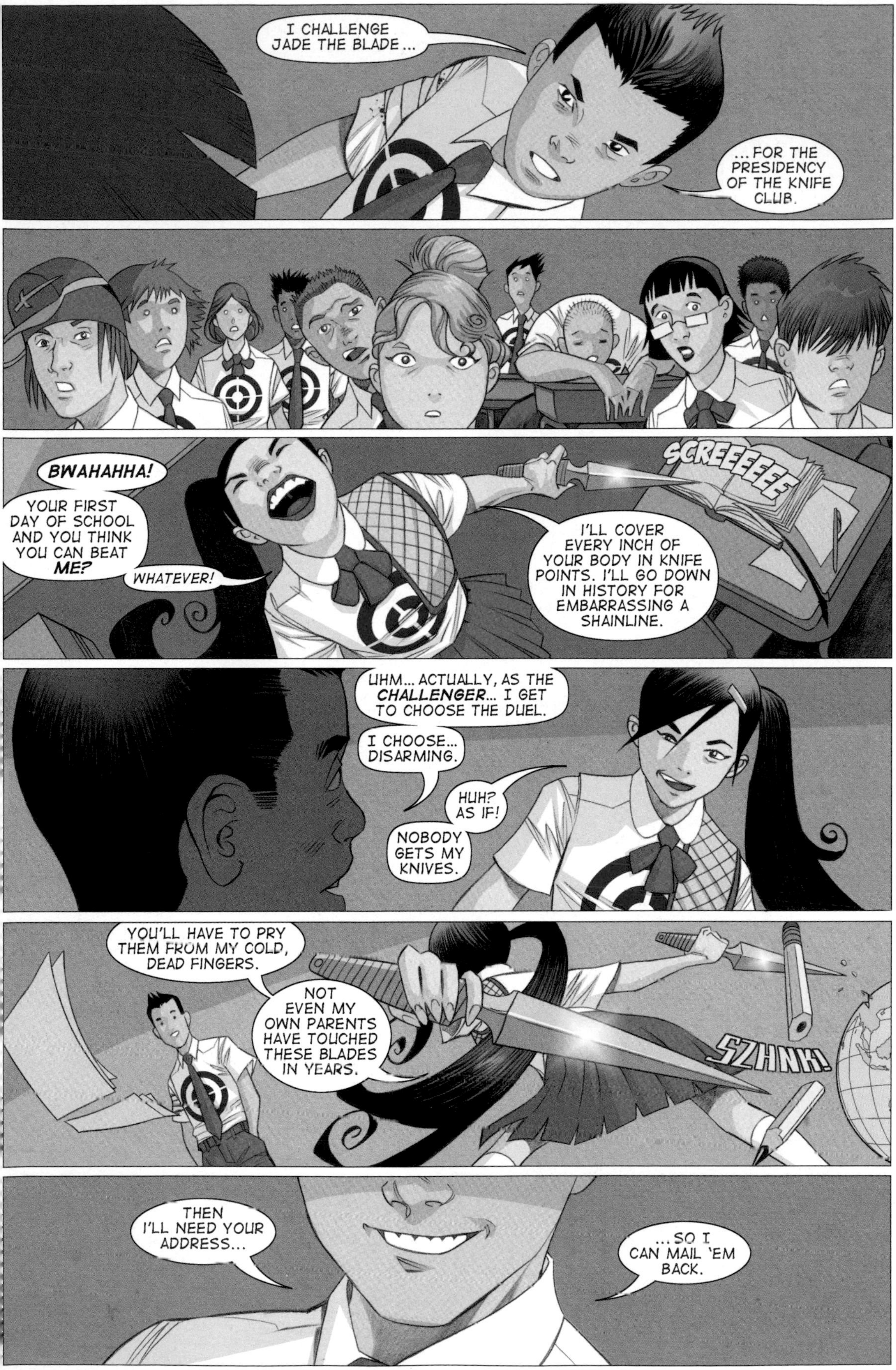

I CHALLENGE JADE THE BLADE...
...FOR THE PRESIDENCY OF THE KNIFE CLUB.
BWAHAHHA!
YOUR FIRST DAY OF SCHOOL AND YOU THINK YOU CAN BEAT ME?
WHATEVER!
SCREEEEEE
I'LL COVER EVERY INCH OF YOUR BODY IN KNIFE POINTS. I'LL GO DOWN IN HISTORY FOR EMBARRASSING A SHAINLINE.
UHM... ACTUALLY, AS THE CHALLENGER... I GET TO CHOOSE THE DUEL.
I CHOOSE... DISARMING.
HUH? AS IF!
NOBODY GETS MY KNIVES.
YOU'LL HAVE TO PRY THEM FROM MY COLD, DEAD FINGERS.
NOT EVEN MY OWN PARENTS HAVE TOUCHED THESE BLADES IN YEARS.
SZHNK!
THEN I'LL NEED YOUR ADDRESS...
...SO I CAN MAIL 'EM BACK.

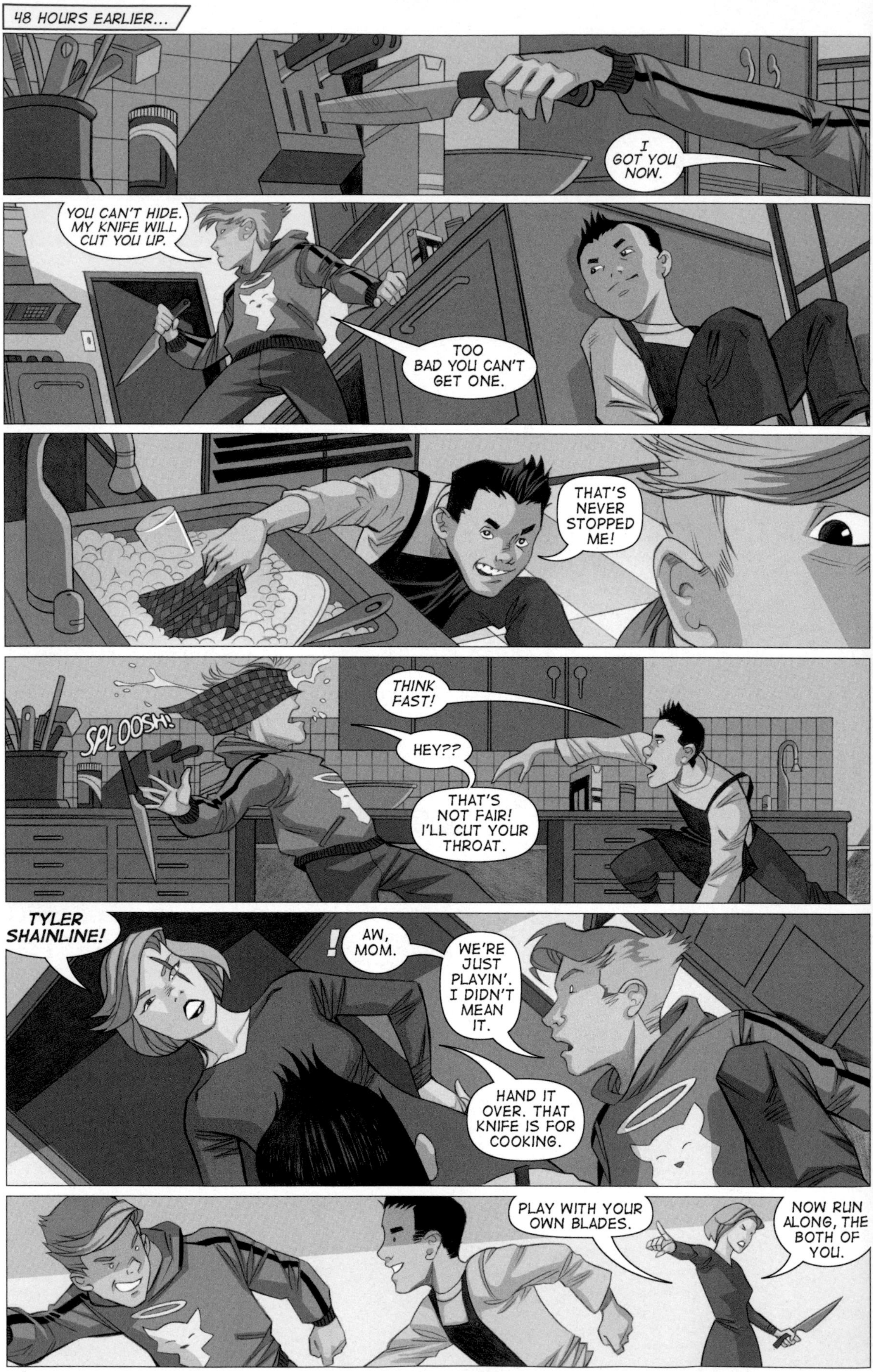
48 HOURS EARLIER...
I GOT YOU NOW.
YOU CAN'T HIDE. MY KNIFE WILL CUT YOU UP.
TOO BAD YOU CAN'T GET ONE.
THAT'S NEVER STOPPED ME!
THINK FAST!
SPLOOSH!
HEY??
THAT'S NOT FAIR! I'LL CUT YOUR THROAT.
TYLER SHAINLINE!
!
AW, MOM.
WE'RE JUST PLAYIN'. I DIDN'T MEAN IT.
HAND IT OVER. THAT KNIFE IS FOR COOKING.
PLAY WITH YOUR OWN BLADES.
NOW RUN ALONG, THE BOTH OF YOU.

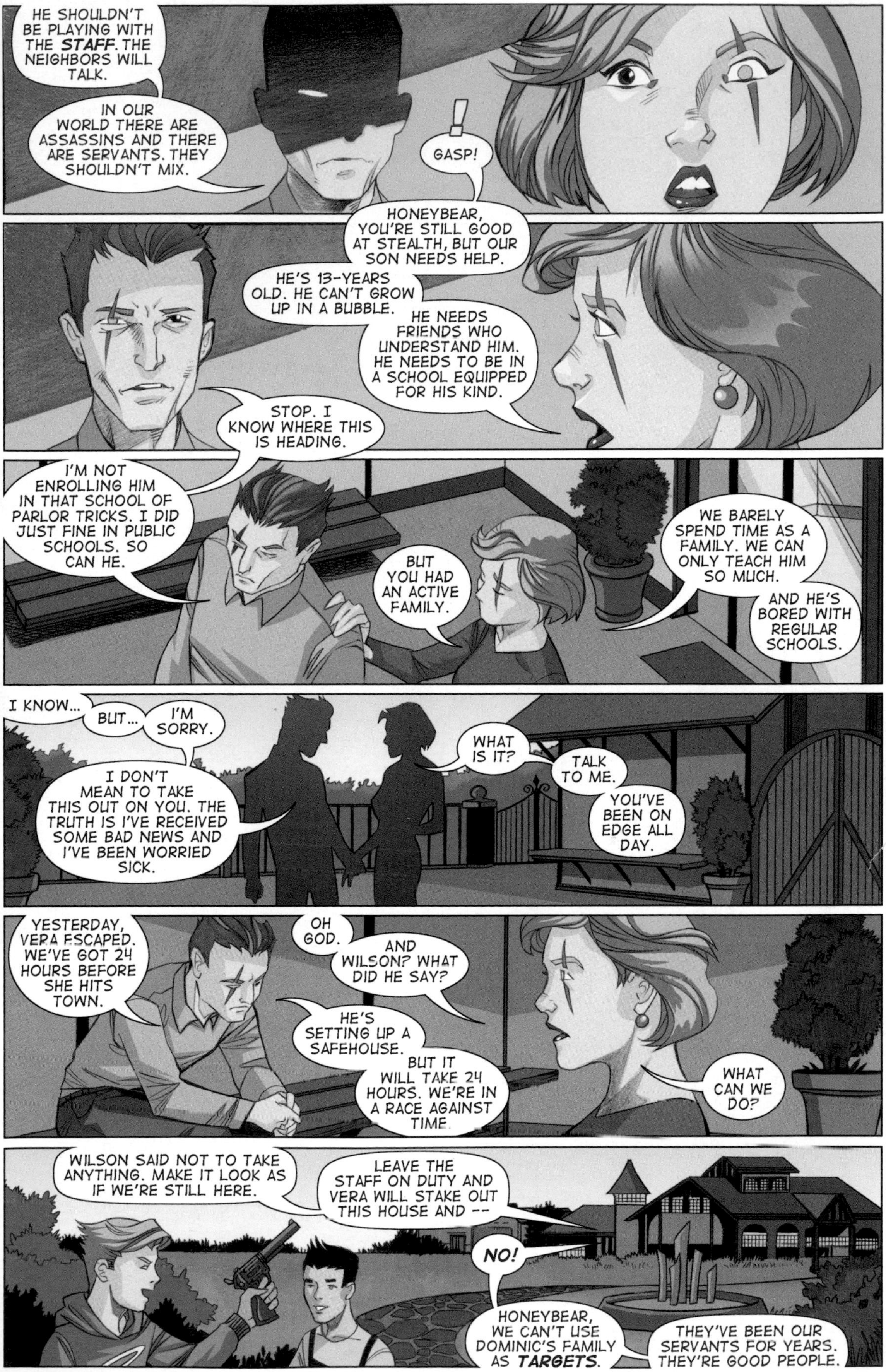
HE SHOULDN'T BE PLAYING WITH THE **STAFF**. THE NEIGHBORS WILL TALK.
IN OUR WORLD THERE ARE ASSASSINS AND THERE ARE SERVANTS. THEY SHOULDN'T MIX.
!
GASP!
HONEYBEAR, YOU'RE STILL GOOD AT STEALTH, BUT OUR SON NEEDS HELP.
HE'S 13-YEARS OLD. HE CAN'T GROW UP IN A BUBBLE.
HE NEEDS FRIENDS WHO UNDERSTAND HIM. HE NEEDS TO BE IN A SCHOOL EQUIPPED FOR HIS KIND.
STOP. I KNOW WHERE THIS IS HEADING.
I'M NOT ENROLLING HIM IN THAT SCHOOL OF PARLOR TRICKS. I DID JUST FINE IN PUBLIC SCHOOLS. SO CAN HE.
BUT YOU HAD AN ACTIVE FAMILY.
WE BARELY SPEND TIME AS A FAMILY. WE CAN ONLY TEACH HIM SO MUCH.
AND HE'S BORED WITH REGULAR SCHOOLS.
I KNOW...
BUT...
I'M SORRY.
I DON'T MEAN TO TAKE THIS OUT ON YOU. THE TRUTH IS I'VE RECEIVED SOME BAD NEWS AND I'VE BEEN WORRIED SICK.
WHAT IS IT?
TALK TO ME.
YOU'VE BEEN ON EDGE ALL DAY.
YESTERDAY, VERA ESCAPED. WE'VE GOT 24 HOURS BEFORE SHE HITS TOWN.
OH GOD.
AND WILSON? WHAT DID HE SAY?
HE'S SETTING UP A SAFEHOUSE.
BUT IT WILL TAKE 24 HOURS. WE'RE IN A RACE AGAINST TIME.
WHAT CAN WE DO?
WILSON SAID NOT TO TAKE ANYTHING. MAKE IT LOOK AS IF WE'RE STILL HERE.
LEAVE THE STAFF ON DUTY AND VERA WILL STAKE OUT THIS HOUSE AND --
NO!
HONEYBEAR, WE CAN'T USE DOMINIC'S FAMILY AS **TARGETS**.
THEY'VE BEEN OUR SERVANTS FOR YEARS. THEY'RE GOOD PEOPLE.

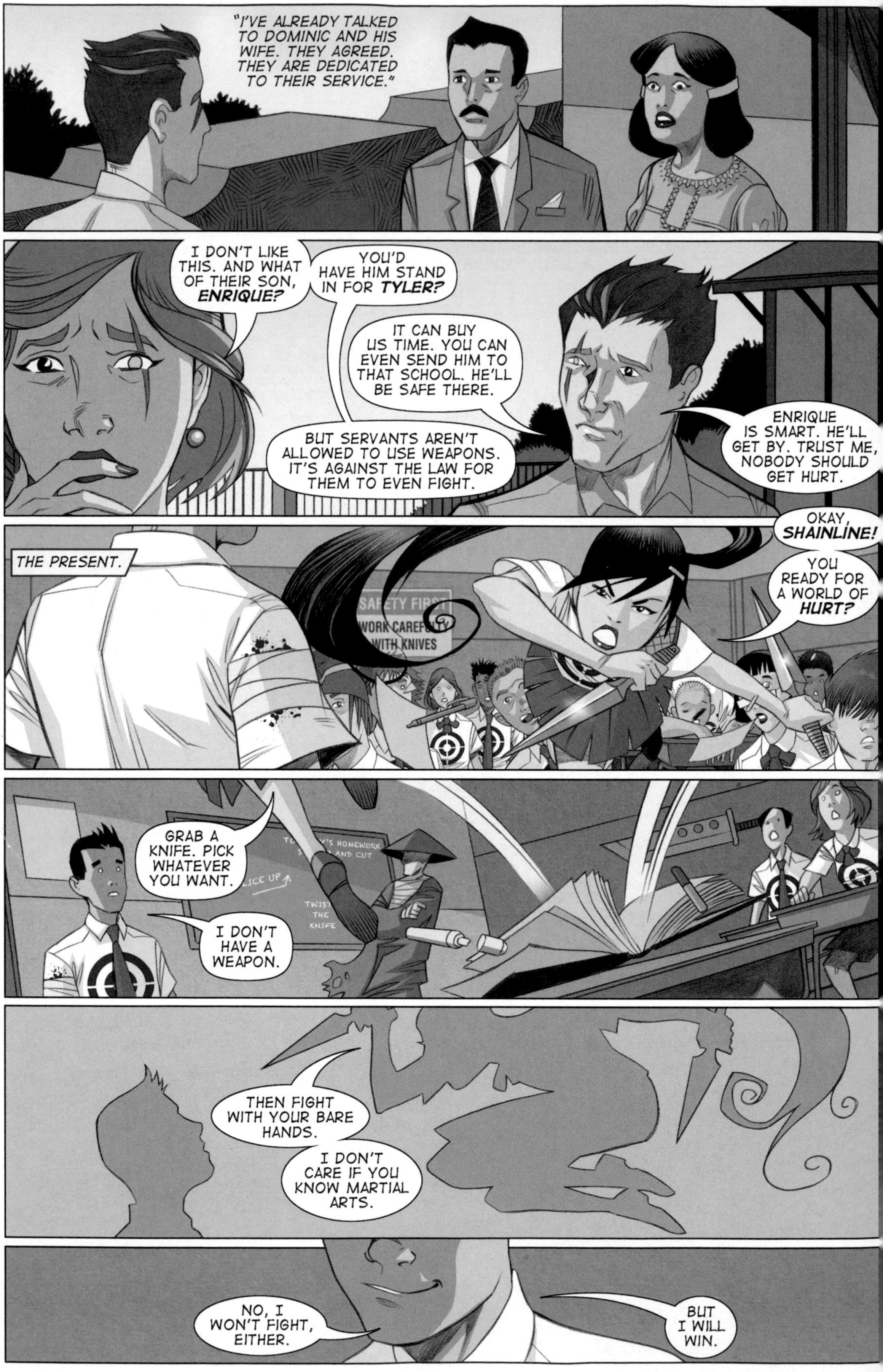
"I'VE ALREADY TALKED TO DOMINIC AND HIS WIFE. THEY AGREED. THEY ARE DEDICATED TO THEIR SERVICE."
I DON'T LIKE THIS. AND WHAT OF THEIR SON, ENRIQUE?
YOU'D HAVE HIM STAND IN FOR TYLER?
IT CAN BUY US TIME. YOU CAN EVEN SEND HIM TO THAT SCHOOL. HE'LL BE SAFE THERE.
BUT SERVANTS AREN'T ALLOWED TO USE WEAPONS. IT'S AGAINST THE LAW FOR THEM TO EVEN FIGHT.
ENRIQUE IS SMART. HE'LL GET BY. TRUST ME, NOBODY SHOULD GET HURT.
THE PRESENT.
SAFETY FIRST
WORK CAREFULLY WITH KNIVES
OKAY, SHAINLINE!
YOU READY FOR A WORLD OF HURT?
GRAB A KNIFE. PICK WHATEVER YOU WANT.
I DON'T HAVE A WEAPON.
THEN FIGHT WITH YOUR BARE HANDS.
I DON'T CARE IF YOU KNOW MARTIAL ARTS.
NO, I WON'T FIGHT, EITHER.
BUT I WILL WIN.

BOOK TWO
RICK THE STICK

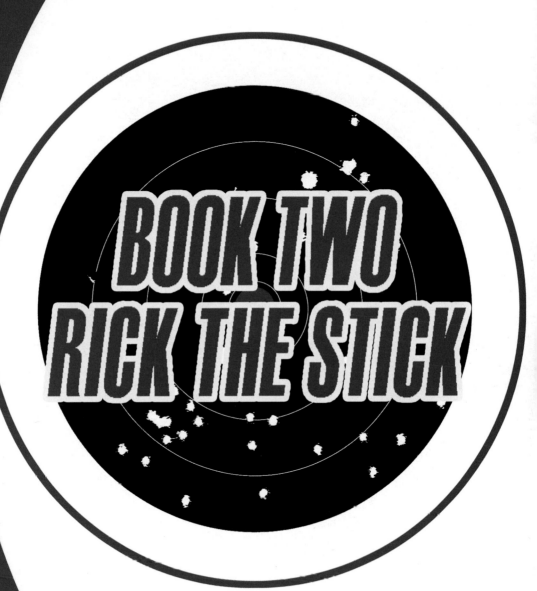

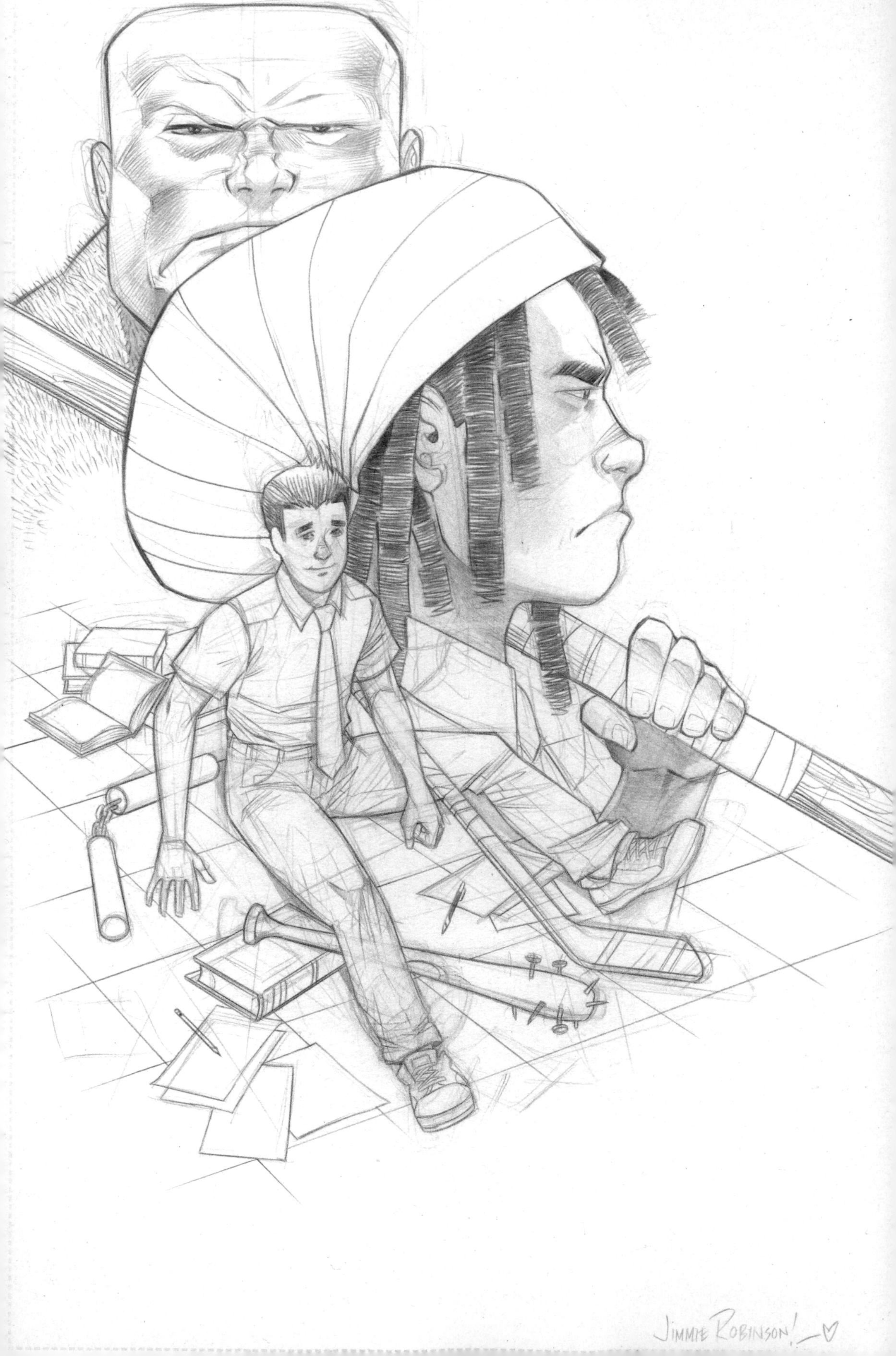
JIMMIE ROBINSON!

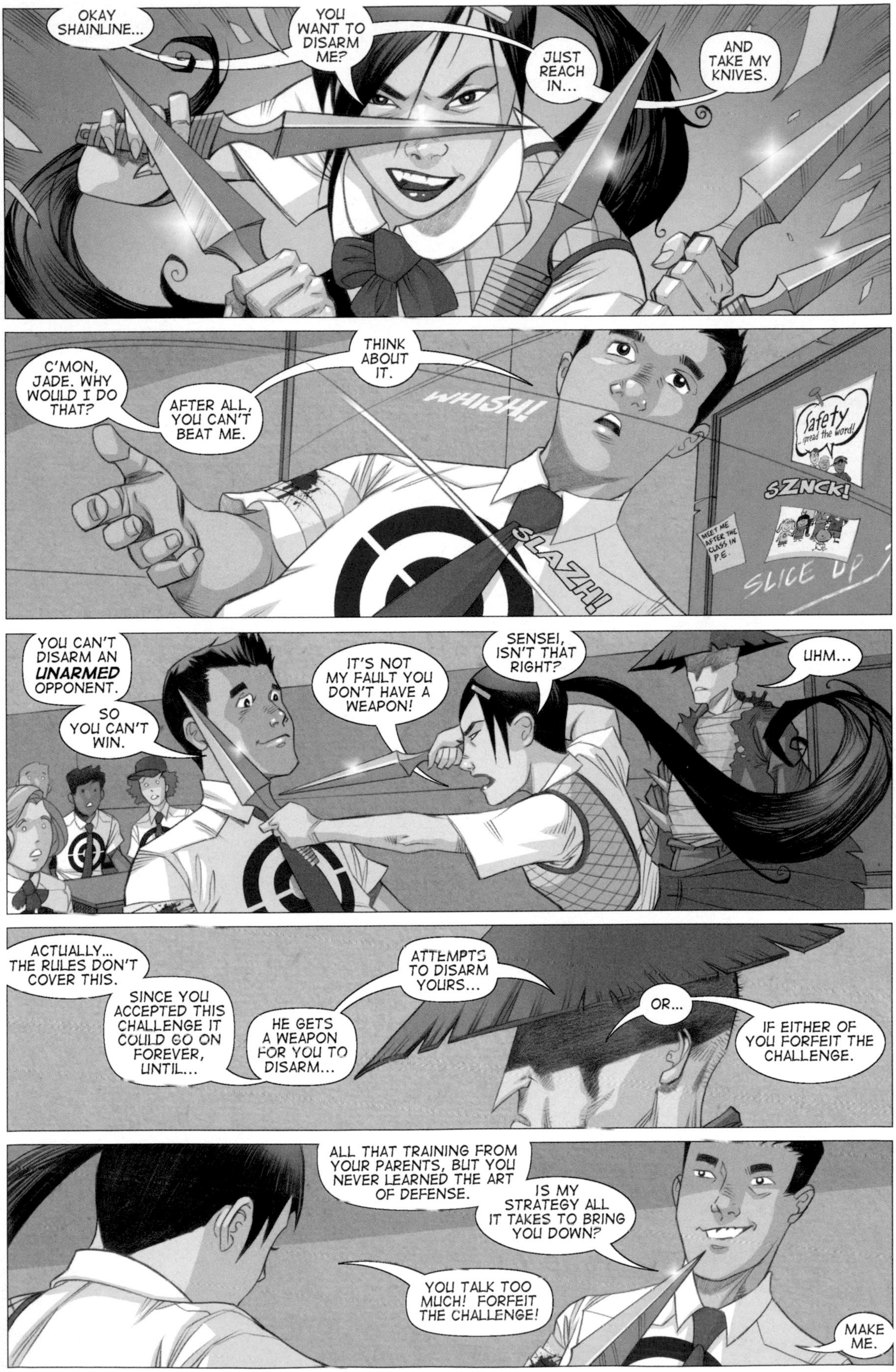
OKAY SHAINLINE...
YOU WANT TO DISARM ME?
JUST REACH IN...
AND TAKE MY KNIVES.
C'MON, JADE. WHY WOULD I DO THAT?
AFTER ALL, YOU CAN'T BEAT ME.
THINK ABOUT IT.
WHISH!
Safety ...spread the word!
SZNCK!
MEET ME AFTER THE CLASS IN P.E.
SLAZH!
SLICE UP
YOU CAN'T DISARM AN UNARMED OPPONENT.
SO YOU CAN'T WIN.
IT'S NOT MY FAULT YOU DON'T HAVE A WEAPON!
SENSEI, ISN'T THAT RIGHT?
UHM...
ACTUALLY... THE RULES DON'T COVER THIS.
SINCE YOU ACCEPTED THIS CHALLENGE IT COULD GO ON FOREVER, UNTIL...
HE GETS A WEAPON FOR YOU TO DISARM...
ATTEMPTS TO DISARM YOURS...
OR...
IF EITHER OF YOU FORFEIT THE CHALLENGE.
ALL THAT TRAINING FROM YOUR PARENTS, BUT YOU NEVER LEARNED THE ART OF DEFENSE.
IS MY STRATEGY ALL IT TAKES TO BRING YOU DOWN?
YOU TALK TOO MUCH! FORFEIT THE CHALLENGE!
MAKE ME.

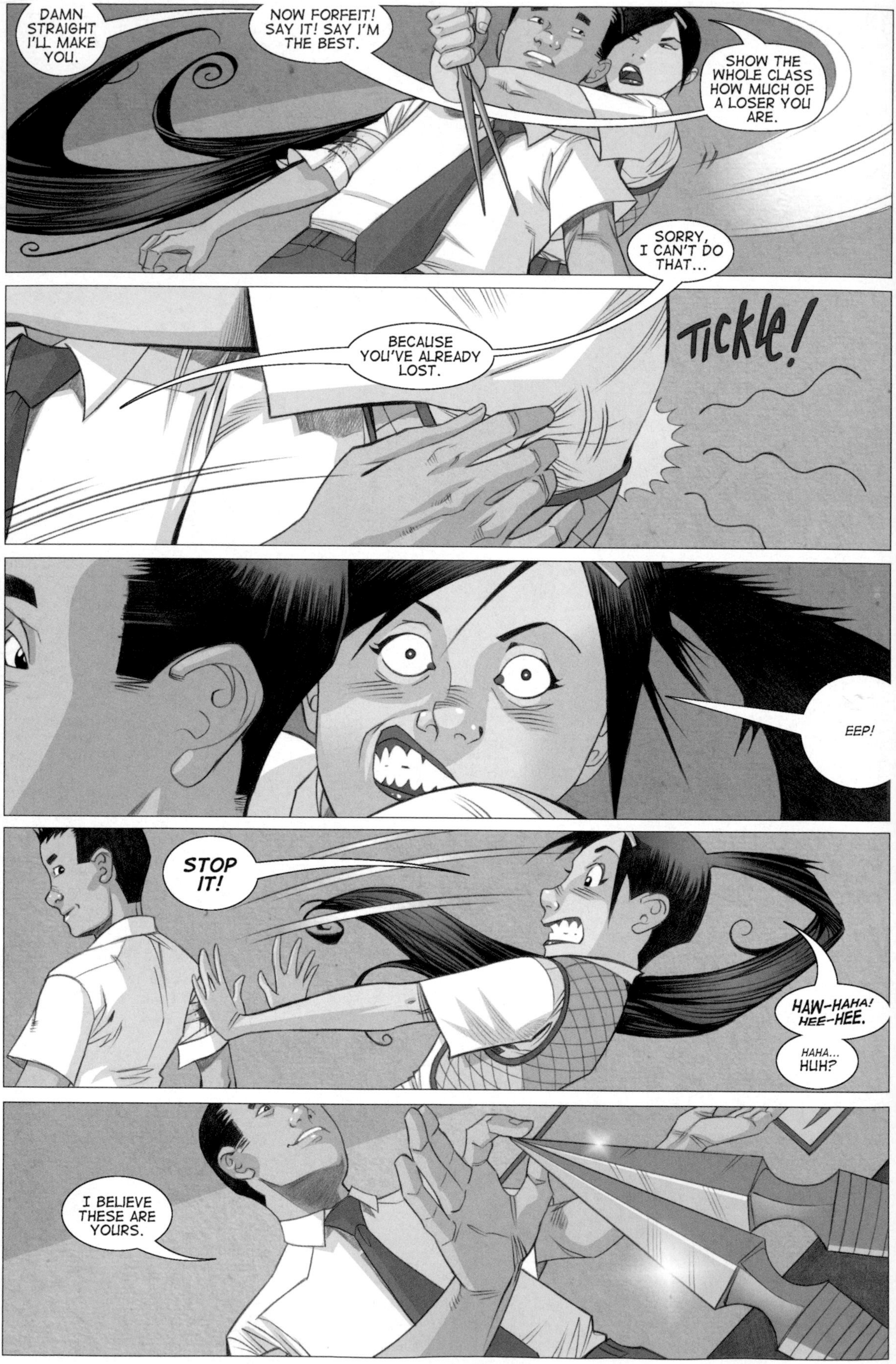
DAMN STRAIGHT I'LL MAKE YOU.
NOW FORFEIT! SAY IT! SAY I'M THE BEST.
SHOW THE WHOLE CLASS HOW MUCH OF A LOSER YOU ARE.
SORRY, I CAN'T DO THAT...
BECAUSE YOU'VE ALREADY LOST.
TICKLE!
EEP!
STOP IT!
HAW-HAHA! HEE-HEE.
HAHA... HUH?
I BELIEVE THESE ARE YOURS.

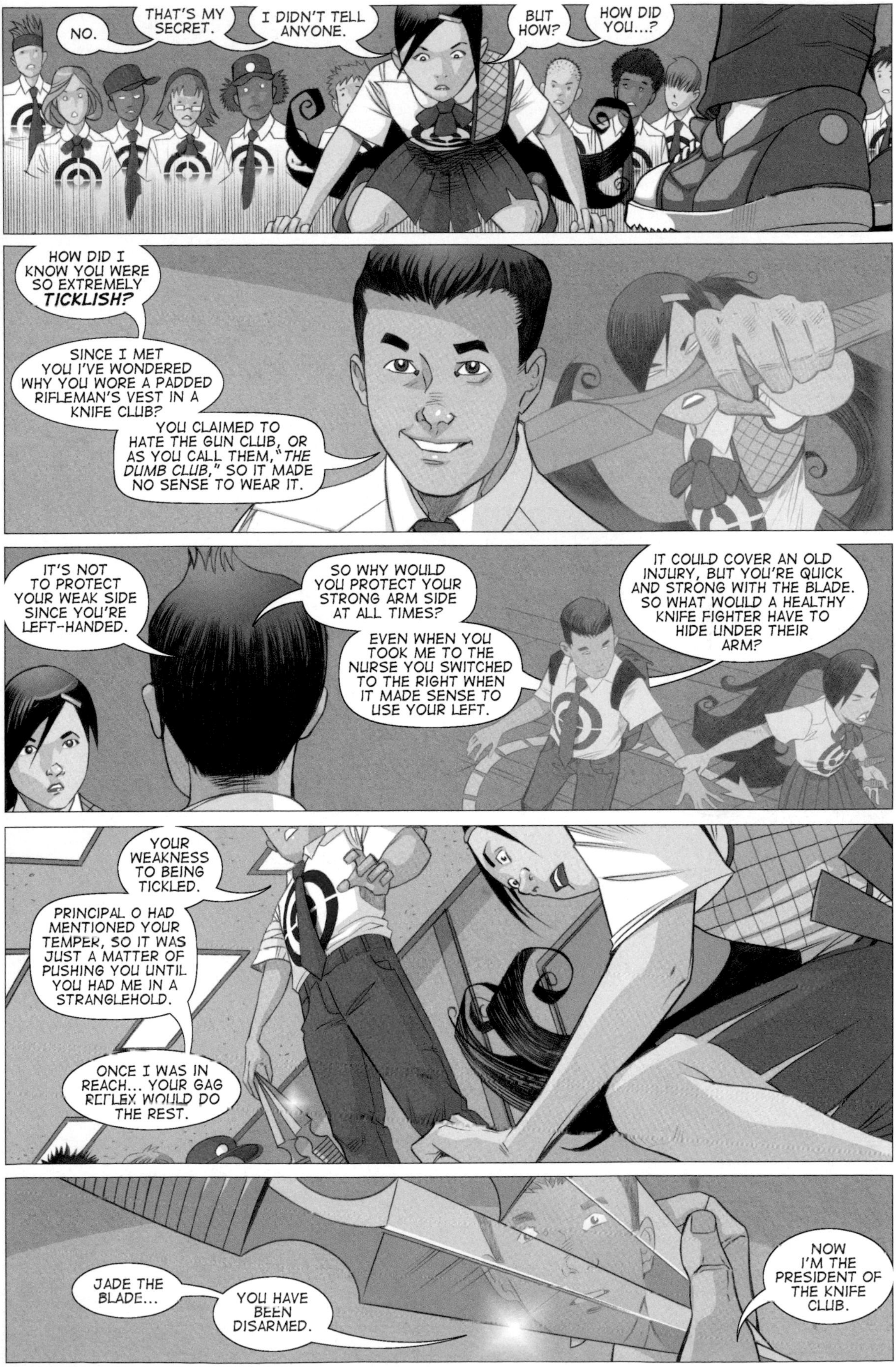
NO.
THAT'S MY SECRET.
I DIDN'T TELL ANYONE.
BUT HOW?
HOW DID YOU...?
HOW DID I KNOW YOU WERE SO EXTREMELY *TICKLISH?*
SINCE I MET YOU I'VE WONDERED WHY YOU WORE A PADDED RIFLEMAN'S VEST IN A KNIFE CLUB?
YOU CLAIMED TO HATE THE GUN CLUB, OR AS YOU CALL THEM, "*THE DUMB CLUB*," SO IT MADE NO SENSE TO WEAR IT.
IT'S NOT TO PROTECT YOUR WEAK SIDE SINCE YOU'RE LEFT-HANDED.
SO WHY WOULD YOU PROTECT YOUR STRONG ARM SIDE AT ALL TIMES?
EVEN WHEN YOU TOOK ME TO THE NURSE YOU SWITCHED TO THE RIGHT WHEN IT MADE SENSE TO USE YOUR LEFT.
IT COULD COVER AN OLD INJURY, BUT YOU'RE QUICK AND STRONG WITH THE BLADE. SO WHAT WOULD A HEALTHY KNIFE FIGHTER HAVE TO HIDE UNDER THEIR ARM?
YOUR WEAKNESS TO BEING TICKLED.
PRINCIPAL O HAD MENTIONED YOUR TEMPER, SO IT WAS JUST A MATTER OF PUSHING YOU UNTIL YOU HAD ME IN A STRANGLEHOLD.
ONCE I WAS IN REACH... YOUR GAG REFLEX WOULD DO THE REST.
JADE THE BLADE...
YOU HAVE BEEN DISARMED.
NOW I'M THE PRESIDENT OF THE KNIFE CLUB.

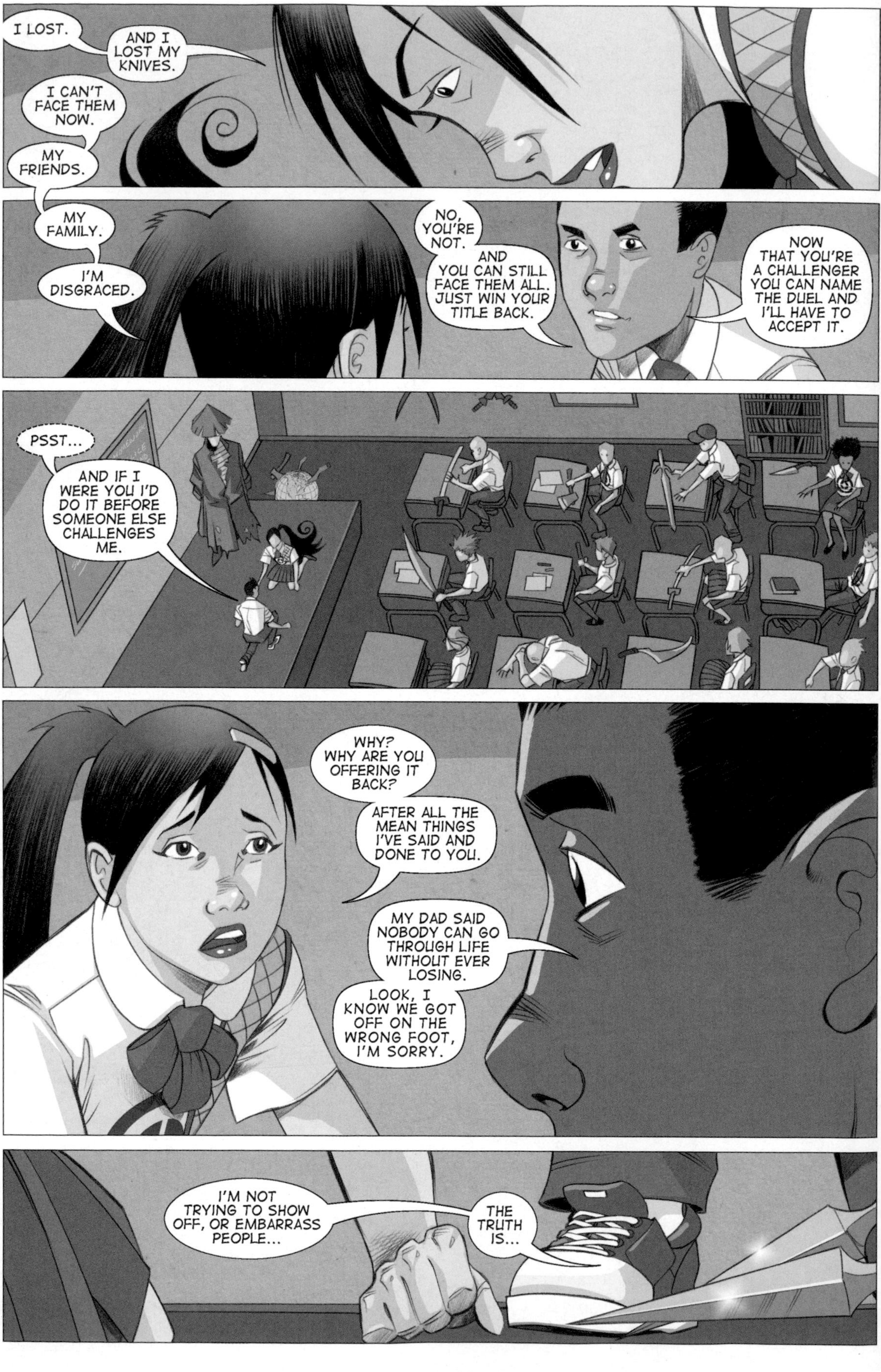
I LOST.
AND I LOST MY KNIVES.
I CAN'T FACE THEM NOW.
MY FRIENDS.
MY FAMILY.
I'M DISGRACED.
NO, YOU'RE NOT.
AND YOU CAN STILL FACE THEM ALL. JUST WIN YOUR TITLE BACK.
NOW THAT YOU'RE A CHALLENGER YOU CAN NAME THE DUEL AND I'LL HAVE TO ACCEPT IT.
PSST...
AND IF I WERE YOU I'D DO IT BEFORE SOMEONE ELSE CHALLENGES ME.
WHY? WHY ARE YOU OFFERING IT BACK?
AFTER ALL THE MEAN THINGS I'VE SAID AND DONE TO YOU.
MY DAD SAID NOBODY CAN GO THROUGH LIFE WITHOUT EVER LOSING.
LOOK, I KNOW WE GOT OFF ON THE WRONG FOOT, I'M SORRY.
I'M NOT TRYING TO SHOW OFF, OR EMBARRASS PEOPLE...
THE TRUTH IS...

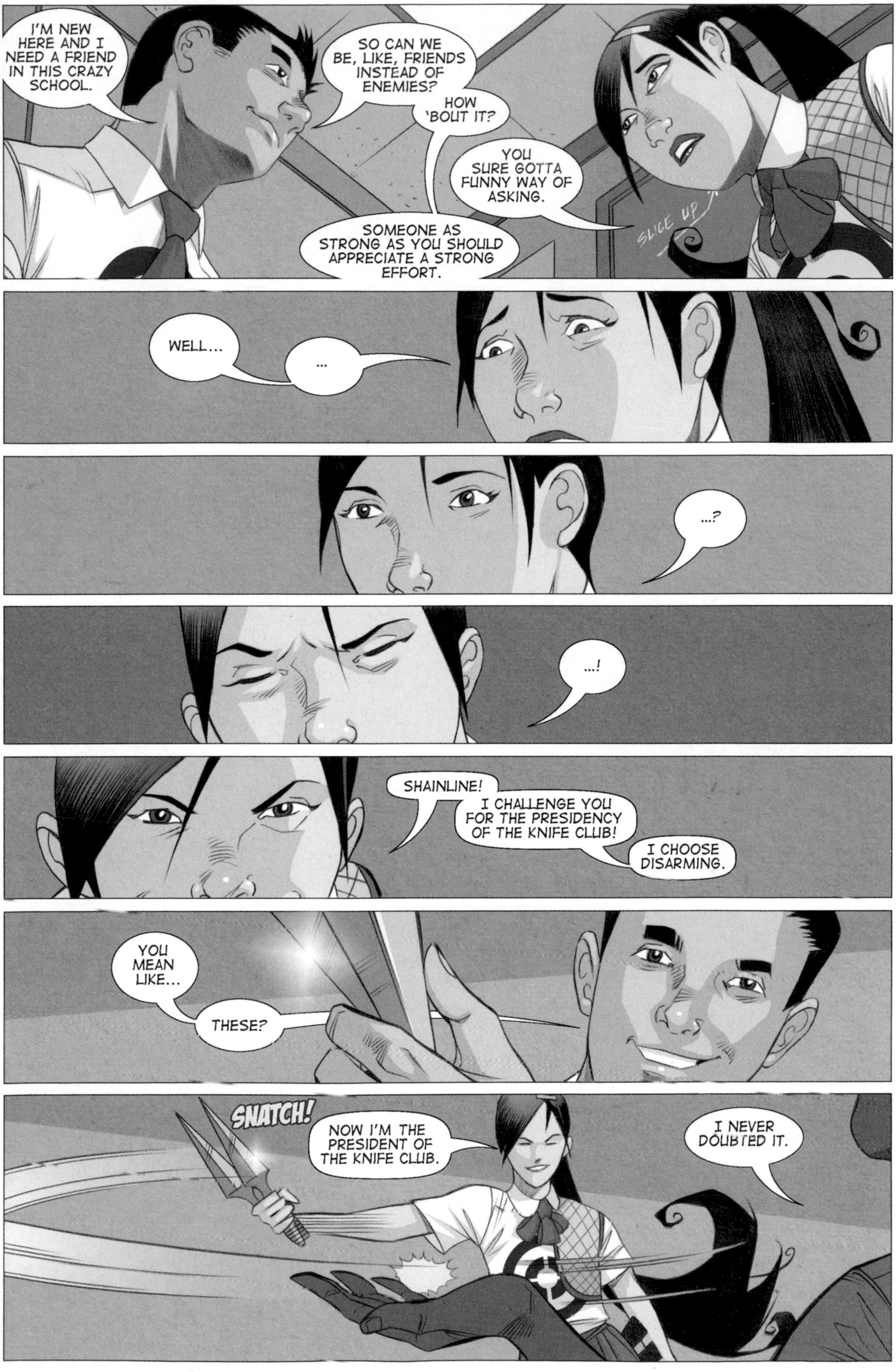
I'M NEW HERE AND I NEED A FRIEND IN THIS CRAZY SCHOOL.
SO CAN WE BE, LIKE, FRIENDS INSTEAD OF ENEMIES?
HOW 'BOUT IT?
YOU SURE GOTTA FUNNY WAY OF ASKING.
SOMEONE AS STRONG AS YOU SHOULD APPRECIATE A STRONG EFFORT.
SLICE UP
WELL...
...
...?
...!
SHAINLINE!
I CHALLENGE YOU FOR THE PRESIDENCY OF THE KNIFE CLUB!
I CHOOSE DISARMING.
YOU MEAN LIKE...
THESE?
SNATCH!
NOW I'M THE PRESIDENT OF THE KNIFE CLUB.
I NEVER DOUBTED IT.

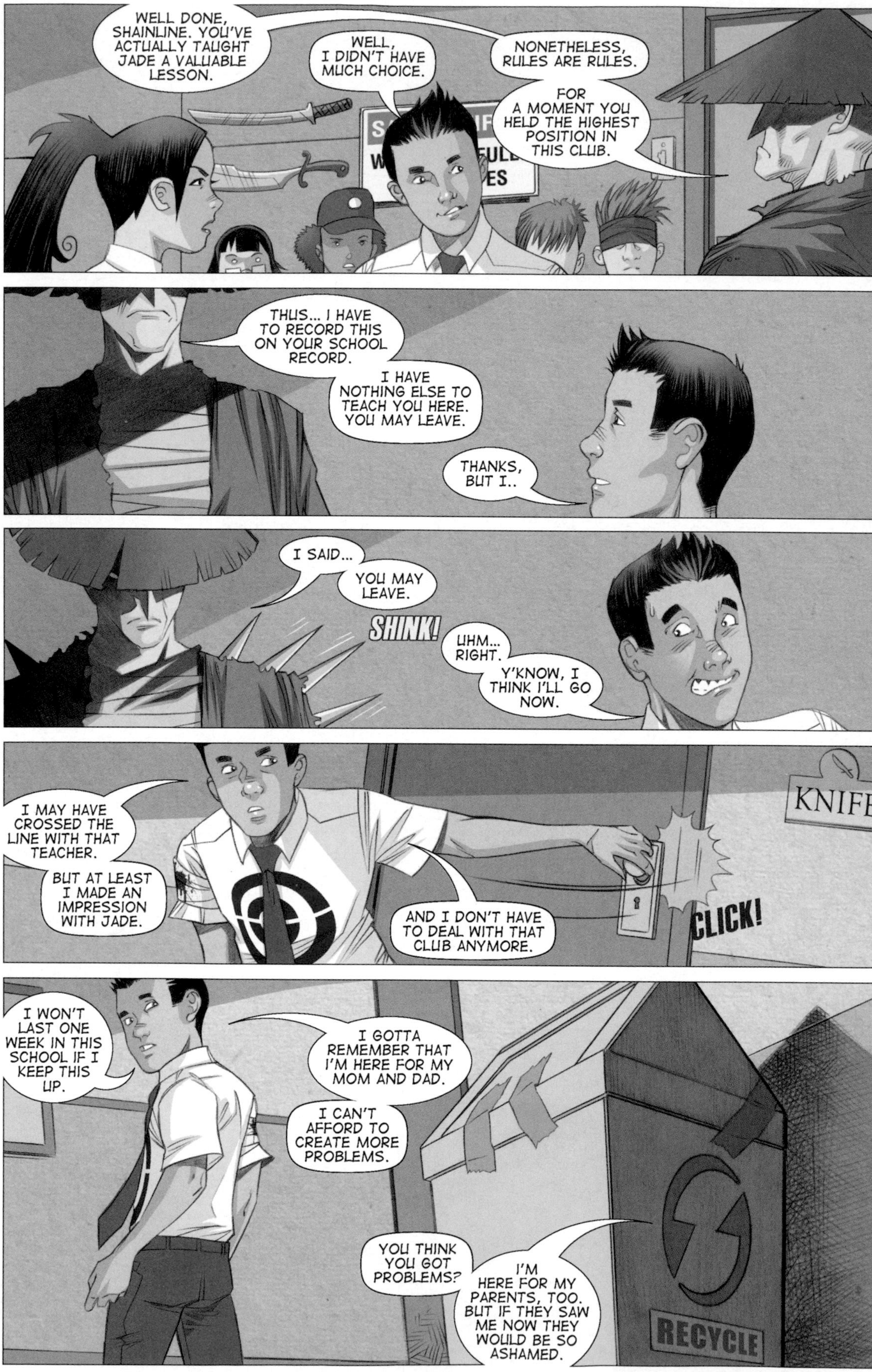
WELL DONE, SHAINLINE. YOU'VE ACTUALLY TAUGHT JADE A VALUABLE LESSON.
WELL, I DIDN'T HAVE MUCH CHOICE.
NONETHELESS, RULES ARE RULES.
FOR A MOMENT YOU HELD THE HIGHEST POSITION IN THIS CLUB.
THUS... I HAVE TO RECORD THIS ON YOUR SCHOOL RECORD.
I HAVE NOTHING ELSE TO TEACH YOU HERE. YOU MAY LEAVE.
THANKS, BUT I..
I SAID...
YOU MAY LEAVE.
SHINK!
UHM... RIGHT.
Y'KNOW, I THINK I'LL GO NOW.
KNIFE
I MAY HAVE CROSSED THE LINE WITH THAT TEACHER.
BUT AT LEAST I MADE AN IMPRESSION WITH JADE.
AND I DON'T HAVE TO DEAL WITH THAT CLUB ANYMORE.
CLICK!
I WON'T LAST ONE WEEK IN THIS SCHOOL IF I KEEP THIS UP.
I GOTTA REMEMBER THAT I'M HERE FOR MY MOM AND DAD.
I CAN'T AFFORD TO CREATE MORE PROBLEMS.
YOU THINK YOU GOT PROBLEMS?
I'M HERE FOR MY PARENTS, TOO. BUT IF THEY SAW ME NOW THEY WOULD BE SO ASHAMED.
RECYCLE

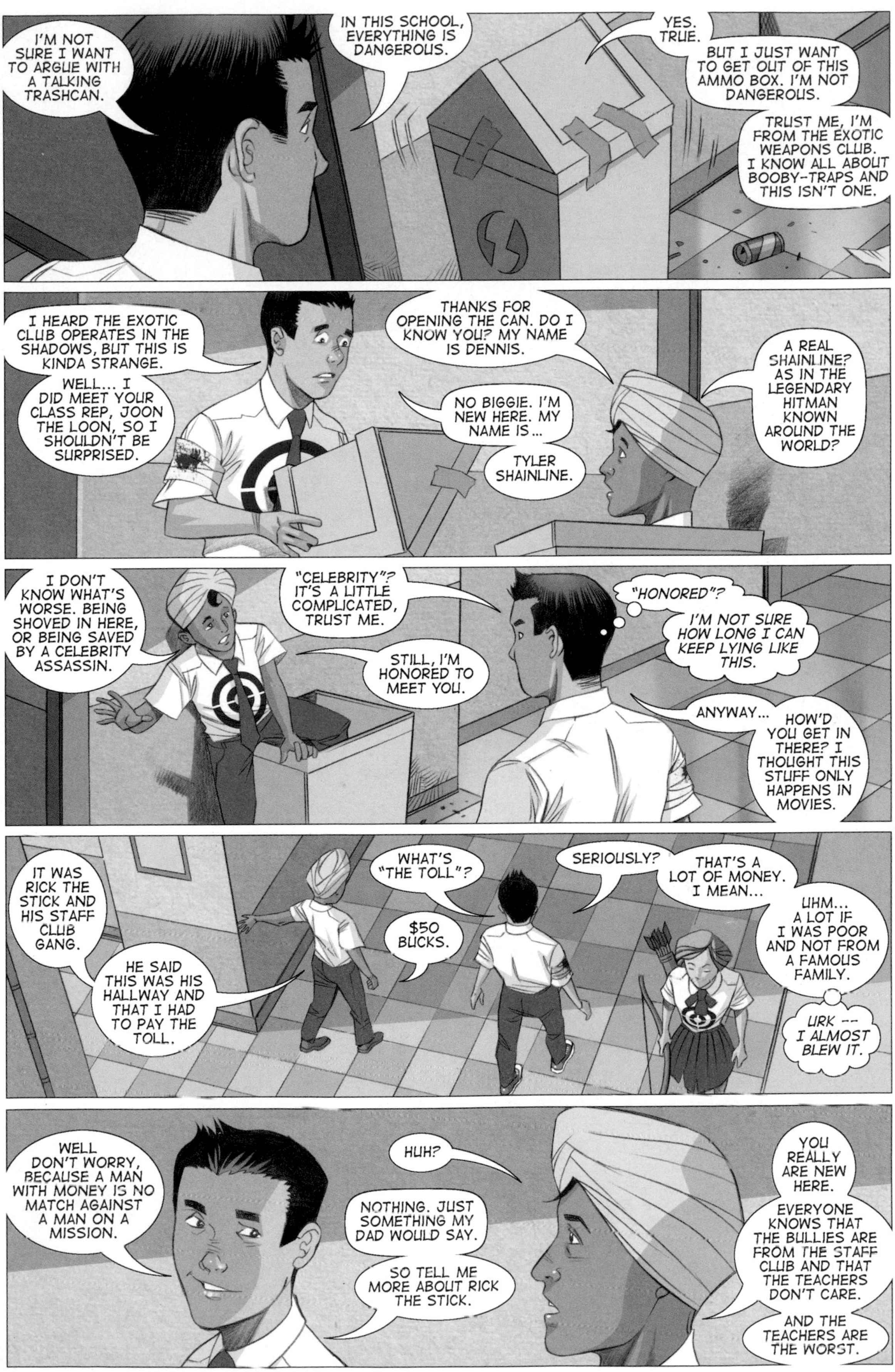
I'M NOT SURE I WANT TO ARGUE WITH A TALKING TRASHCAN.
IN THIS SCHOOL, EVERYTHING IS DANGEROUS.
YES. TRUE.
BUT I JUST WANT TO GET OUT OF THIS AMMO BOX. I'M NOT DANGEROUS.
TRUST ME, I'M FROM THE EXOTIC WEAPONS CLUB. I KNOW ALL ABOUT BOOBY-TRAPS AND THIS ISN'T ONE.
I HEARD THE EXOTIC CLUB OPERATES IN THE SHADOWS, BUT THIS IS KINDA STRANGE.
WELL... I DID MEET YOUR CLASS REP, JOON THE LOON, SO I SHOULDN'T BE SURPRISED.
THANKS FOR OPENING THE CAN. DO I KNOW YOU? MY NAME IS DENNIS.
NO BIGGIE. I'M NEW HERE. MY NAME IS...
TYLER SHAINLINE.
A REAL SHAINLINE? AS IN THE LEGENDARY HITMAN KNOWN AROUND THE WORLD?
I DON'T KNOW WHAT'S WORSE. BEING SHOVED IN HERE, OR BEING SAVED BY A CELEBRITY ASSASSIN.
"CELEBRITY"? IT'S A LITTLE COMPLICATED, TRUST ME.
STILL, I'M HONORED TO MEET YOU.
"HONORED"?
I'M NOT SURE HOW LONG I CAN KEEP LYING LIKE THIS.
ANYWAY...
HOW'D YOU GET IN THERE? I THOUGHT THIS STUFF ONLY HAPPENS IN MOVIES.
IT WAS RICK THE STICK AND HIS STAFF CLUB GANG.
HE SAID THIS WAS HIS HALLWAY AND THAT I HAD TO PAY THE TOLL.
WHAT'S "THE TOLL"?
$50 BUCKS.
SERIOUSLY?
THAT'S A LOT OF MONEY. I MEAN...
UHM... A LOT IF I WAS POOR AND NOT FROM A FAMOUS FAMILY.
URK -- I ALMOST BLEW IT.
WELL DON'T WORRY, BECAUSE A MAN WITH MONEY IS NO MATCH AGAINST A MAN ON A MISSION.
HUH?
NOTHING. JUST SOMETHING MY DAD WOULD SAY.
SO TELL ME MORE ABOUT RICK THE STICK.
YOU REALLY ARE NEW HERE.
EVERYONE KNOWS THAT THE BULLIES ARE FROM THE STAFF CLUB AND THAT THE TEACHERS DON'T CARE.
AND THE TEACHERS ARE THE WORST.

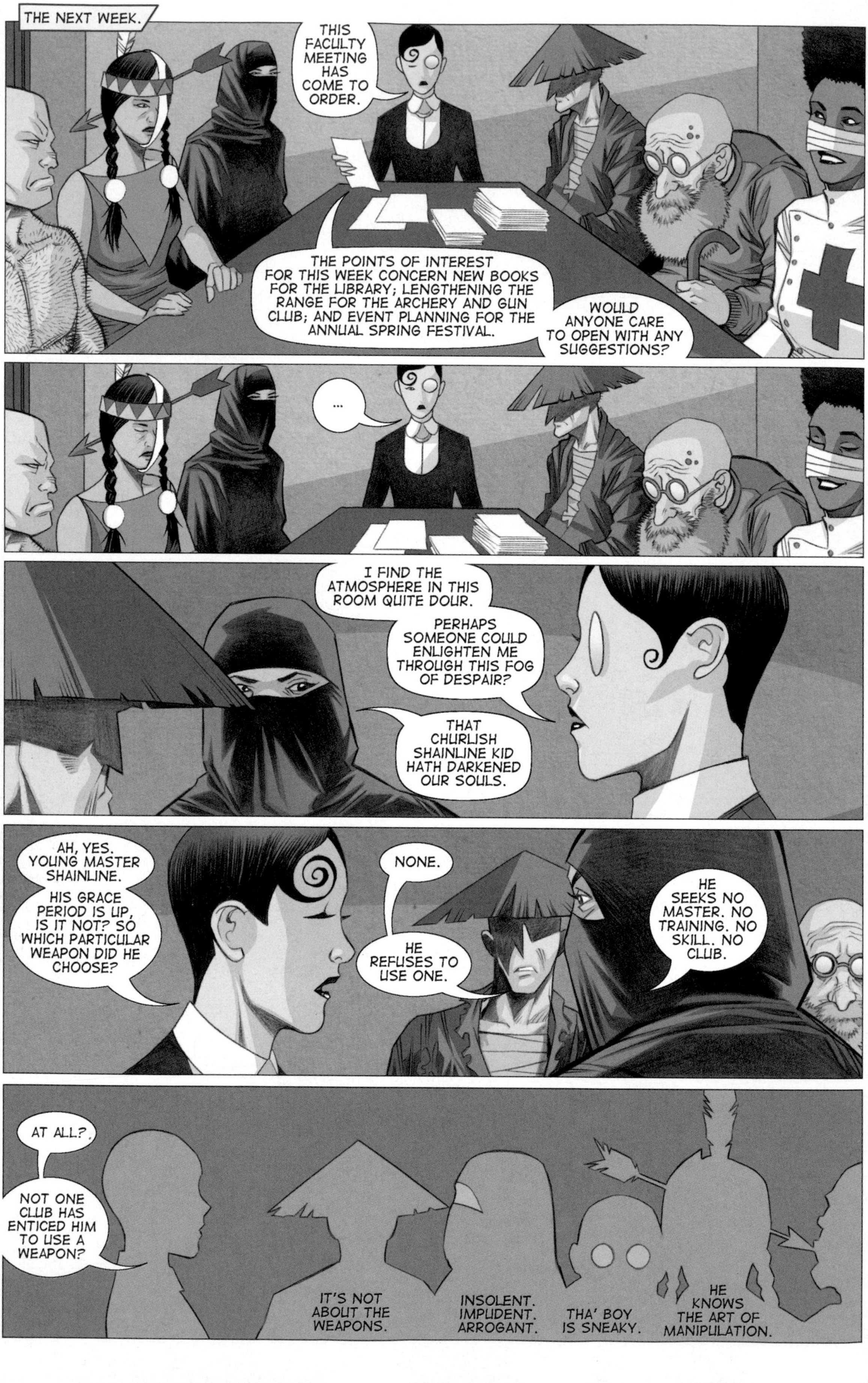
THE NEXT WEEK.
THIS FACULTY MEETING HAS COME TO ORDER.
THE POINTS OF INTEREST FOR THIS WEEK CONCERN NEW BOOKS FOR THE LIBRARY; LENGTHENING THE RANGE FOR THE ARCHERY AND GUN CLUB; AND EVENT PLANNING FOR THE ANNUAL SPRING FESTIVAL.
WOULD ANYONE CARE TO OPEN WITH ANY SUGGESTIONS?
...
I FIND THE ATMOSPHERE IN THIS ROOM QUITE DOUR.
PERHAPS SOMEONE COULD ENLIGHTEN ME THROUGH THIS FOG OF DESPAIR?
THAT CHURLISH SHAINLINE KID HATH DARKENED OUR SOULS.
AH, YES. YOUNG MASTER SHAINLINE.
HIS GRACE PERIOD IS UP, IS IT NOT? SO WHICH PARTICULAR WEAPON DID HE CHOOSE?
NONE.
HE REFUSES TO USE ONE.
HE SEEKS NO MASTER. NO TRAINING. NO SKILL. NO CLUB.
AT ALL?.
NOT ONE CLUB HAS ENTICED HIM TO USE A WEAPON?
IT'S NOT ABOUT THE WEAPONS.
INSOLENT. IMPUDENT. ARROGANT.
THA' BOY IS SNEAKY.
HE KNOWS THE ART OF MANIPULATION.

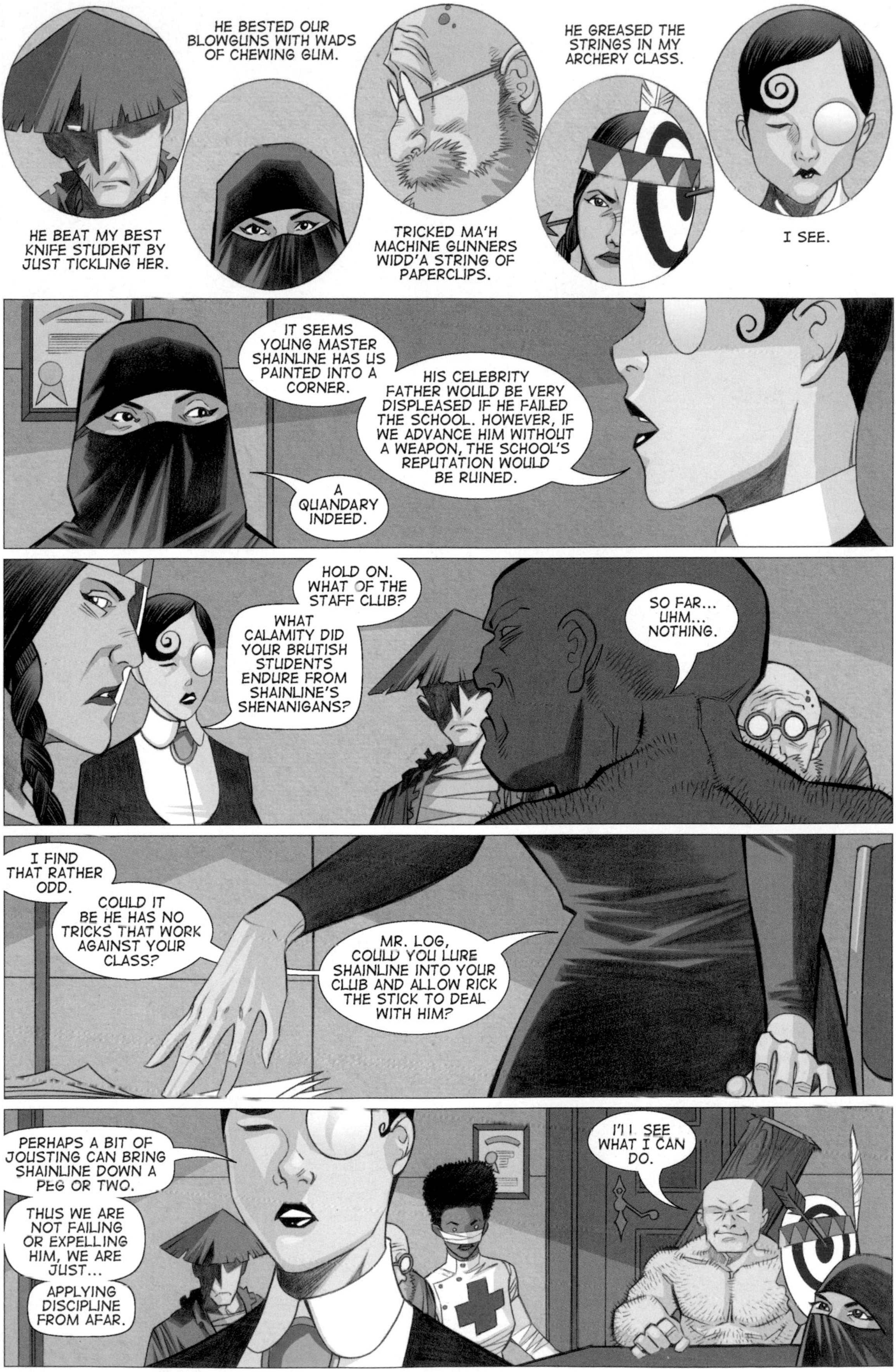
HE BEAT MY BEST KNIFE STUDENT BY JUST TICKLING HER.
HE BESTED OUR BLOWGUNS WITH WADS OF CHEWING GUM.
TRICKED MA'H MACHINE GUNNERS WIDD'A STRING OF PAPERCLIPS.
HE GREASED THE STRINGS IN MY ARCHERY CLASS.
I SEE.
IT SEEMS YOUNG MASTER SHAINLINE HAS US PAINTED INTO A CORNER.
HIS CELEBRITY FATHER WOULD BE VERY DISPLEASED IF HE FAILED THE SCHOOL. HOWEVER, IF WE ADVANCE HIM WITHOUT A WEAPON, THE SCHOOL'S REPUTATION WOULD BE RUINED.
A QUANDARY INDEED.
HOLD ON. WHAT OF THE STAFF CLUB?
WHAT CALAMITY DID YOUR BRUTISH STUDENTS ENDURE FROM SHAINLINE'S SHENANIGANS?
SO FAR... UHM... NOTHING.
I FIND THAT RATHER ODD.
COULD IT BE HE HAS NO TRICKS THAT WORK AGAINST YOUR CLASS?
MR. LOG, COULD YOU LURE SHAINLINE INTO YOUR CLUB AND ALLOW RICK THE STICK TO DEAL WITH HIM?
PERHAPS A BIT OF JOUSTING CAN BRING SHAINLINE DOWN A PEG OR TWO.
THUS WE ARE NOT FAILING OR EXPELLING HIM, WE ARE JUST...
APPLYING DISCIPLINE FROM AFAR.
I'LL SEE WHAT I CAN DO.

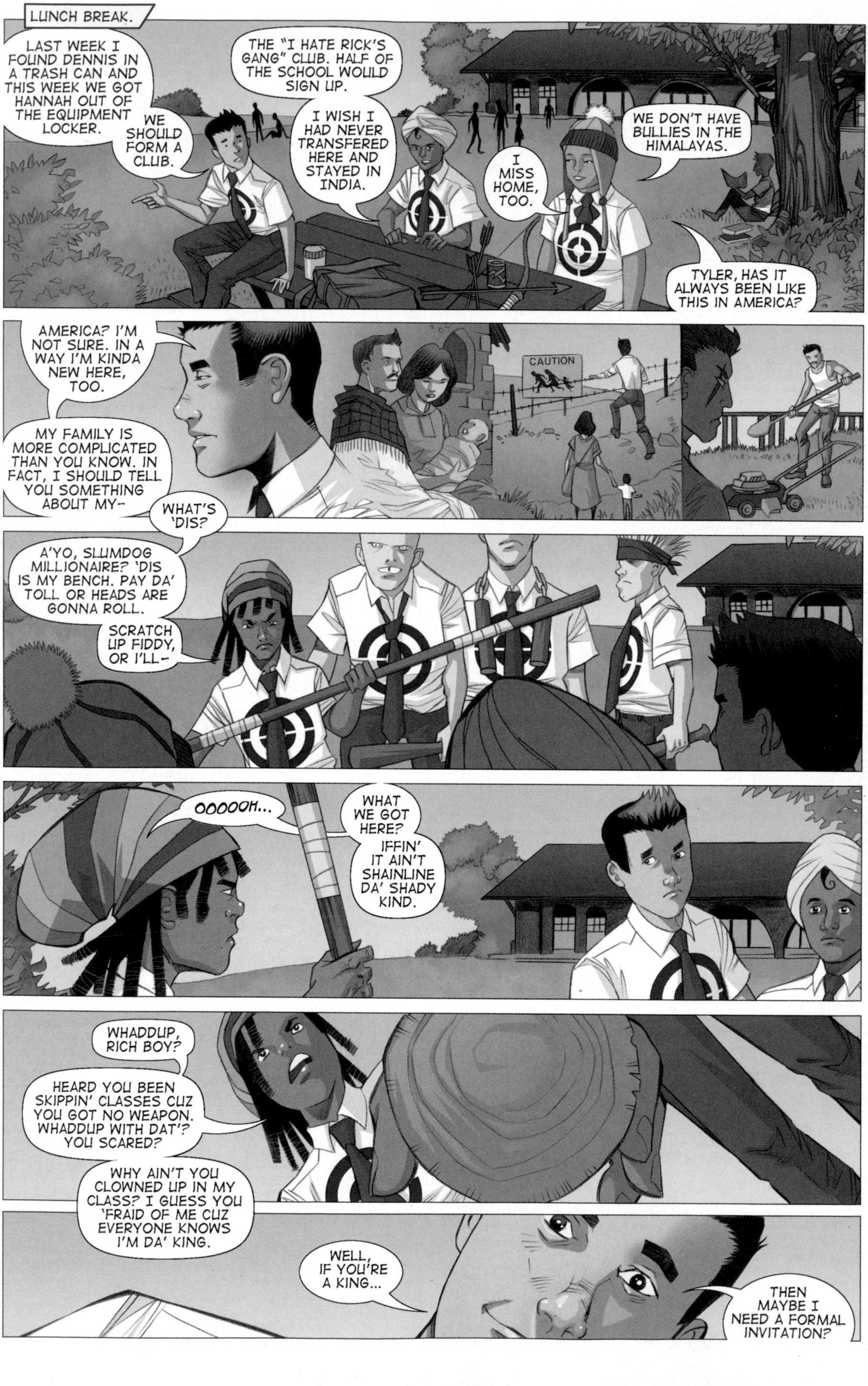
LUNCH BREAK.
LAST WEEK I FOUND DENNIS IN A TRASH CAN AND THIS WEEK WE GOT HANNAH OUT OF THE EQUIPMENT LOCKER.
WE SHOULD FORM A CLUB.
THE "I HATE RICK'S GANG" CLUB. HALF OF THE SCHOOL WOULD SIGN UP.
I WISH I HAD NEVER TRANSFERED HERE AND STAYED IN INDIA.
I MISS HOME, TOO.
WE DON'T HAVE BULLIES IN THE HIMALAYAS.
TYLER, HAS IT ALWAYS BEEN LIKE THIS IN AMERICA?
AMERICA? I'M NOT SURE. IN A WAY I'M KINDA NEW HERE, TOO.
MY FAMILY IS MORE COMPLICATED THAN YOU KNOW. IN FACT, I SHOULD TELL YOU SOMETHING ABOUT MY--
CAUTION
WHAT'S 'DIS?
A'YO, SLUMDOG MILLIONAIRE? 'DIS IS MY BENCH. PAY DA' TOLL OR HEADS ARE GONNA ROLL.
SCRATCH UP FIDDY, OR I'LL--
OOOOOH...
WHAT WE GOT HERE?
IFFIN' IT AIN'T SHAINLINE DA' SHADY KIND.
WHADDUP, RICH BOY?
HEARD YOU BEEN SKIPPIN' CLASSES CUZ YOU GOT NO WEAPON. WHADDUP WITH DAT'? YOU SCARED?
WHY AIN'T YOU CLOWNED UP IN MY CLASS? I GUESS YOU 'FRAID OF ME CUZ EVERYONE KNOWS I'M DA' KING.
WELL, IF YOU'RE A KING...
THEN MAYBE I NEED A FORMAL INVITATION?

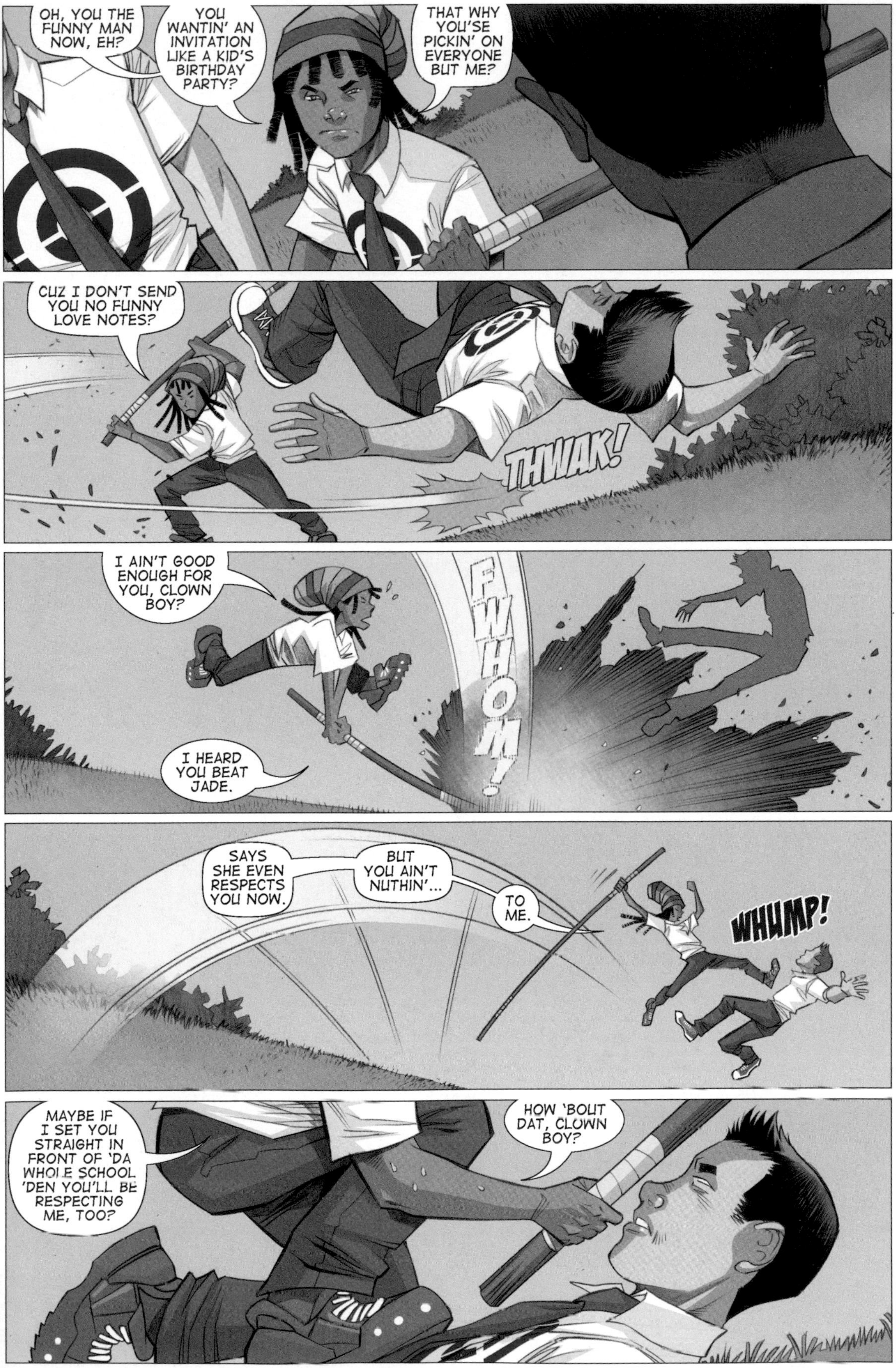
OH, YOU THE FUNNY MAN NOW, EH?
YOU WANTIN' AN INVITATION LIKE A KID'S BIRTHDAY PARTY?
THAT WHY YOU'SE PICKIN' ON EVERYONE BUT ME?
CUZ I DON'T SEND YOU NO FUNNY LOVE NOTES?
THWAK!
I AIN'T GOOD ENOUGH FOR YOU, CLOWN BOY?
PWHOM!
I HEARD YOU BEAT JADE.
SAYS SHE EVEN RESPECTS YOU NOW.
BUT YOU AIN'T NUTHIN'...
TO ME.
WHUMP!
MAYBE IF I SET YOU STRAIGHT IN FRONT OF 'DA WHOLE SCHOOL 'DEN YOU'LL BE RESPECTING ME, TOO?
HOW 'BOUT DAT, CLOWN BOY?

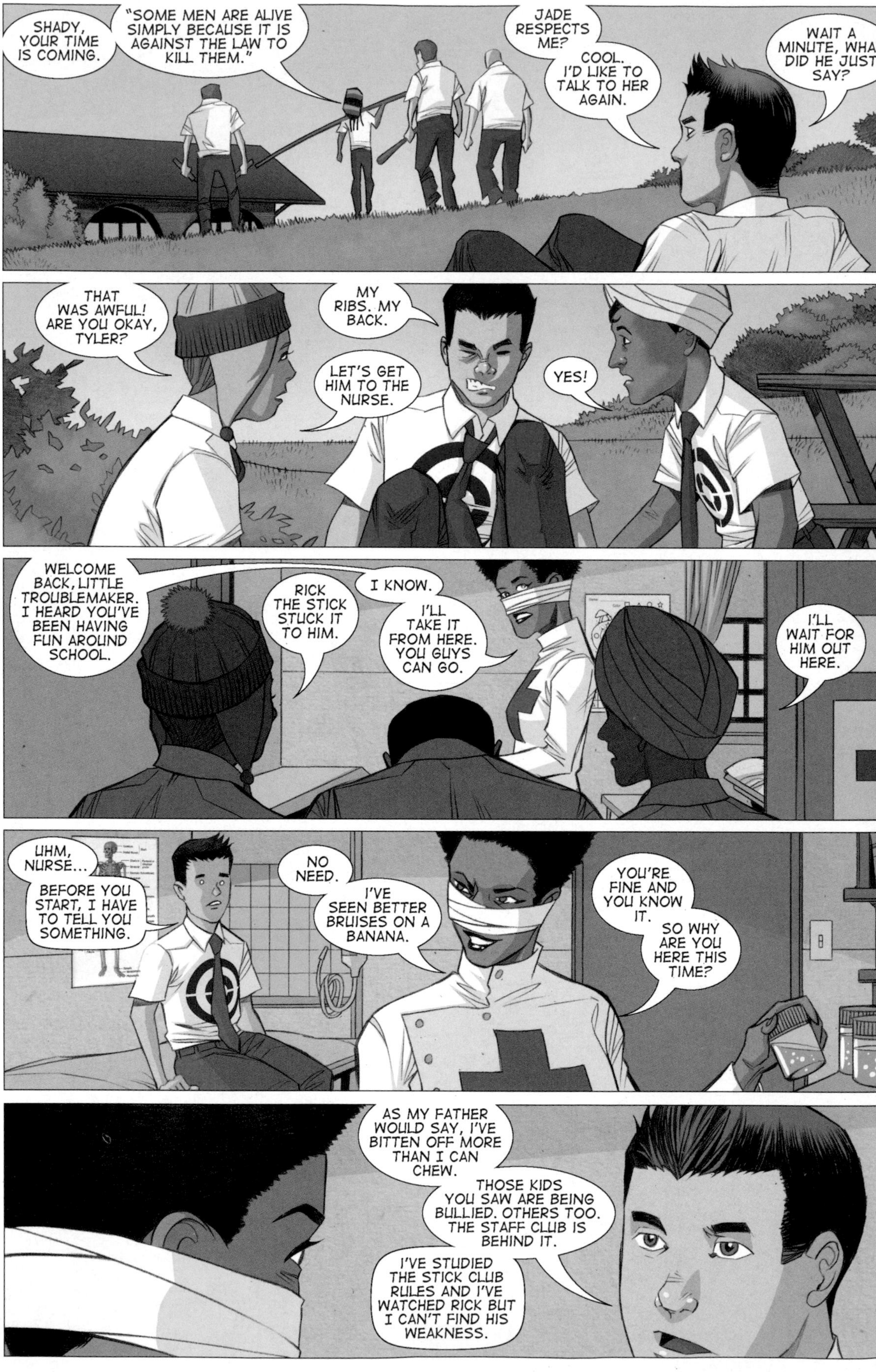

SHADY, YOUR TIME IS COMING.
"SOME MEN ARE ALIVE SIMPLY BECAUSE IT IS AGAINST THE LAW TO KILL THEM."
JADE RESPECTS ME?
COOL. I'D LIKE TO TALK TO HER AGAIN.
WAIT A MINUTE, WHAT DID HE JUST SAY?
THAT WAS AWFUL! ARE YOU OKAY, TYLER?
MY RIBS. MY BACK.
LET'S GET HIM TO THE NURSE.
YES!
WELCOME BACK, LITTLE TROUBLEMAKER. I HEARD YOU'VE BEEN HAVING FUN AROUND SCHOOL.
RICK THE STICK STUCK IT TO HIM.
I KNOW.
I'LL TAKE IT FROM HERE. YOU GUYS CAN GO.
I'LL WAIT FOR HIM OUT HERE.
UHM, NURSE...
BEFORE YOU START, I HAVE TO TELL YOU SOMETHING.
NO NEED.
I'VE SEEN BETTER BRUISES ON A BANANA.
YOU'RE FINE AND YOU KNOW IT.
SO WHY ARE YOU HERE THIS TIME?
AS MY FATHER WOULD SAY, I'VE BITTEN OFF MORE THAN I CAN CHEW.
THOSE KIDS YOU SAW ARE BEING BULLIED. OTHERS TOO. THE STAFF CLUB IS BEHIND IT.
I'VE STUDIED THE STICK CLUB RULES AND I'VE WATCHED RICK BUT I CAN'T FIND HIS WEAKNESS.

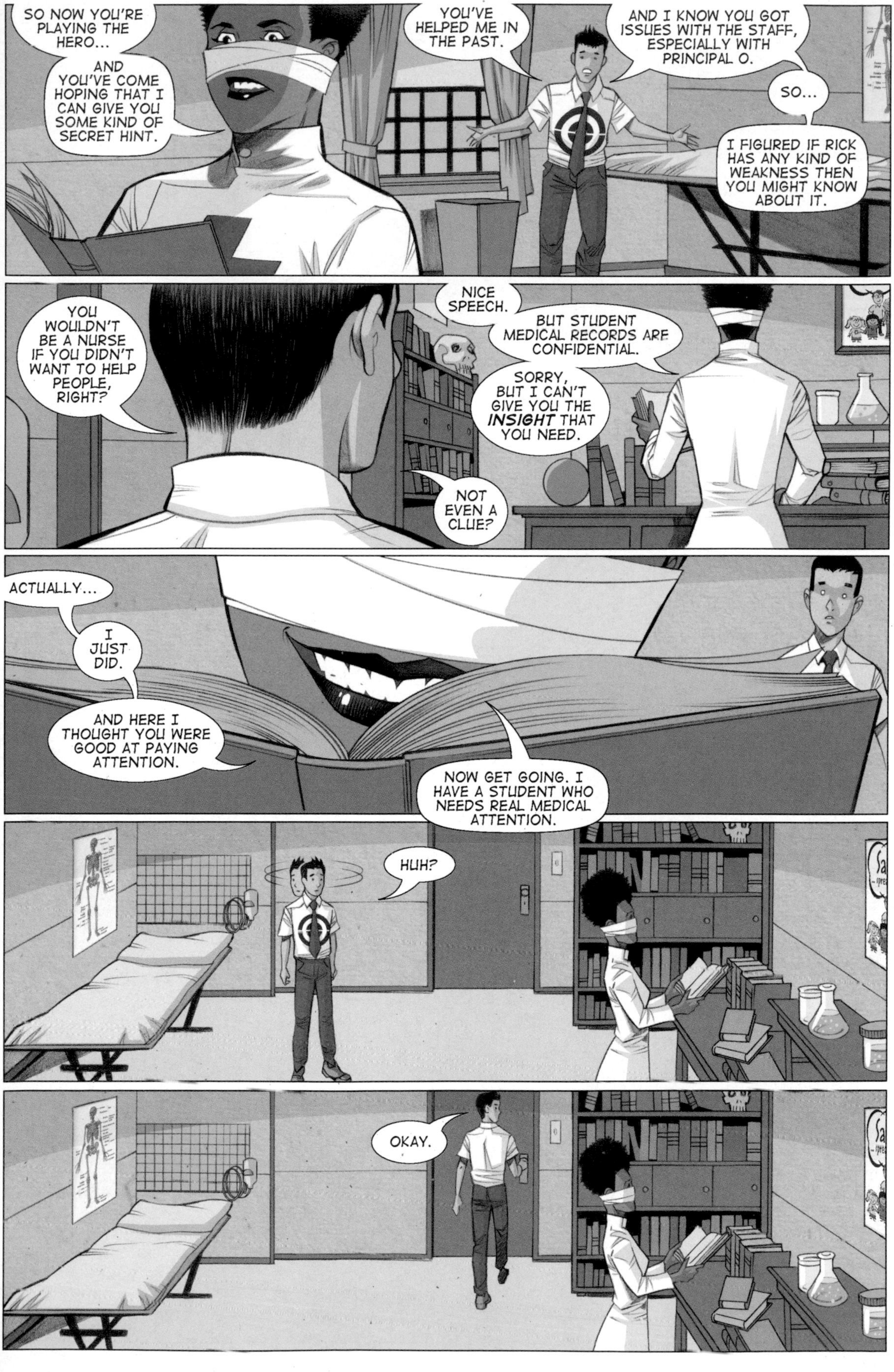
SO NOW YOU'RE PLAYING THE HERO...
AND YOU'VE COME HOPING THAT I CAN GIVE YOU SOME KIND OF SECRET HINT.
YOU'VE HELPED ME IN THE PAST.
AND I KNOW YOU GOT ISSUES WITH THE STAFF, ESPECIALLY WITH PRINCIPAL O.
SO...
I FIGURED IF RICK HAS ANY KIND OF WEAKNESS THEN YOU MIGHT KNOW ABOUT IT.
YOU WOULDN'T BE A NURSE IF YOU DIDN'T WANT TO HELP PEOPLE, RIGHT?
NICE SPEECH.
BUT STUDENT MEDICAL RECORDS ARE CONFIDENTIAL.
SORRY, BUT I CAN'T GIVE YOU THE ***INSIGHT*** THAT YOU NEED.
NOT EVEN A CLUE?
ACTUALLY...
I JUST DID.
AND HERE I THOUGHT YOU WERE GOOD AT PAYING ATTENTION.
NOW GET GOING. I HAVE A STUDENT WHO NEEDS REAL MEDICAL ATTENTION.
HUH?
OKAY.

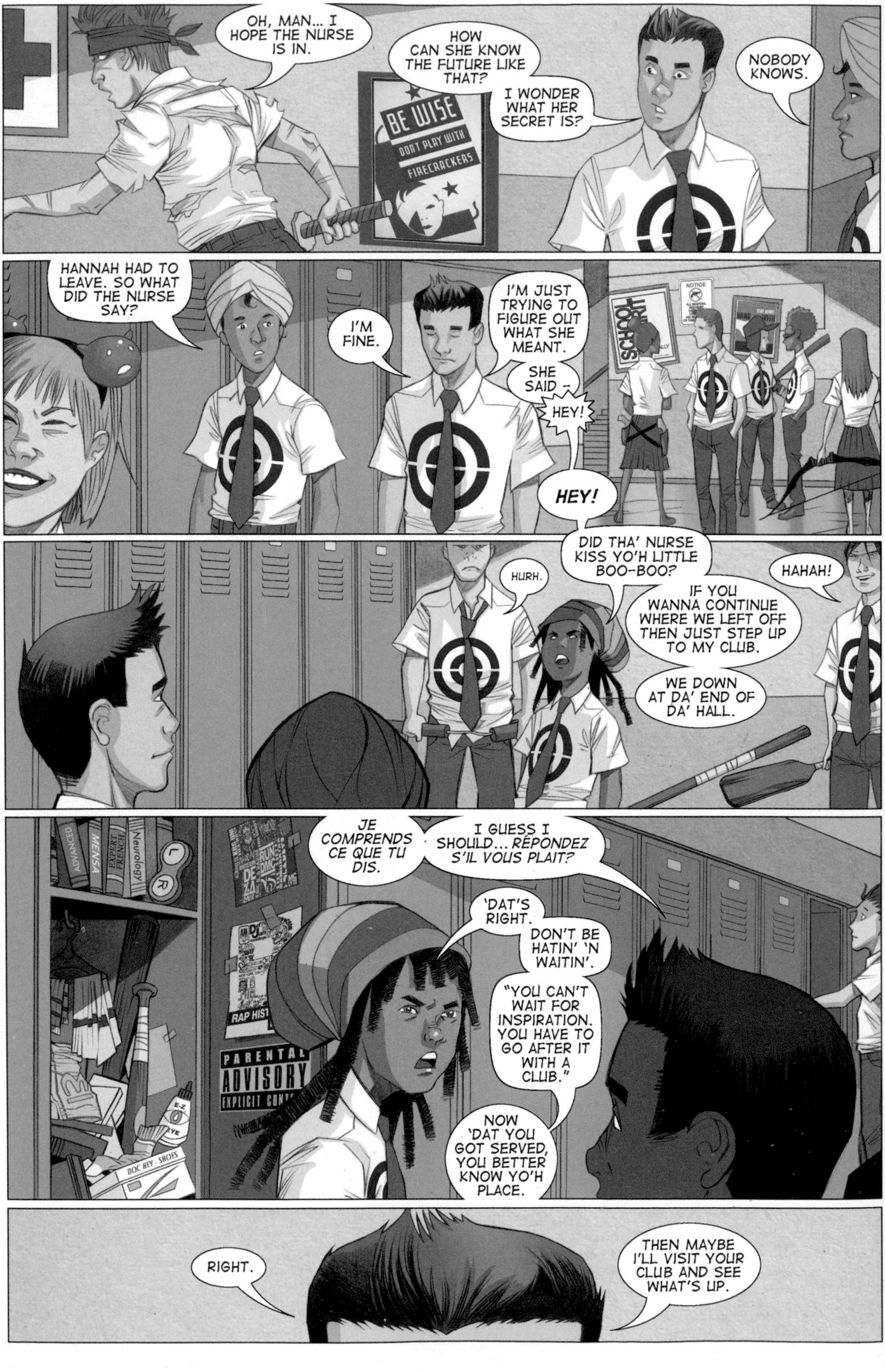
OH, MAN... I HOPE THE NURSE IS IN.
HOW CAN SHE KNOW THE FUTURE LIKE THAT?
I WONDER WHAT HER SECRET IS?
NOBODY KNOWS.
BE WISE
DON'T PLAY WITH FIRECRACKERS
HANNAH HAD TO LEAVE. SO WHAT DID THE NURSE SAY?
I'M FINE.
I'M JUST TRYING TO FIGURE OUT WHAT SHE MEANT.
SHE SAID --
HEY!
HEY!
DID THA' NURSE KISS YO'H LITTLE BOO-BOO?
HURH.
HAHAH!
IF YOU WANNA CONTINUE WHERE WE LEFT OFF THEN JUST STEP UP TO MY CLUB.
WE DOWN AT DA' END OF DA' HALL.
I GUESS I SHOULD... RÉPONDEZ S'IL VOUS PLAIT?
JE COMPRENDS CE QUE TU DIS.
'DAT'S RIGHT.
DON'T BE HATIN' 'N WAITIN'.
"YOU CAN'T WAIT FOR INSPIRATION. YOU HAVE TO GO AFTER IT WITH A CLUB."
NOW 'DAT YOU GOT SERVED, YOU BETTER KNOW YO'H PLACE.
PARENTAL ADVISORY
RIGHT.
THEN MAYBE I'LL VISIT YOUR CLUB AND SEE WHAT'S UP.

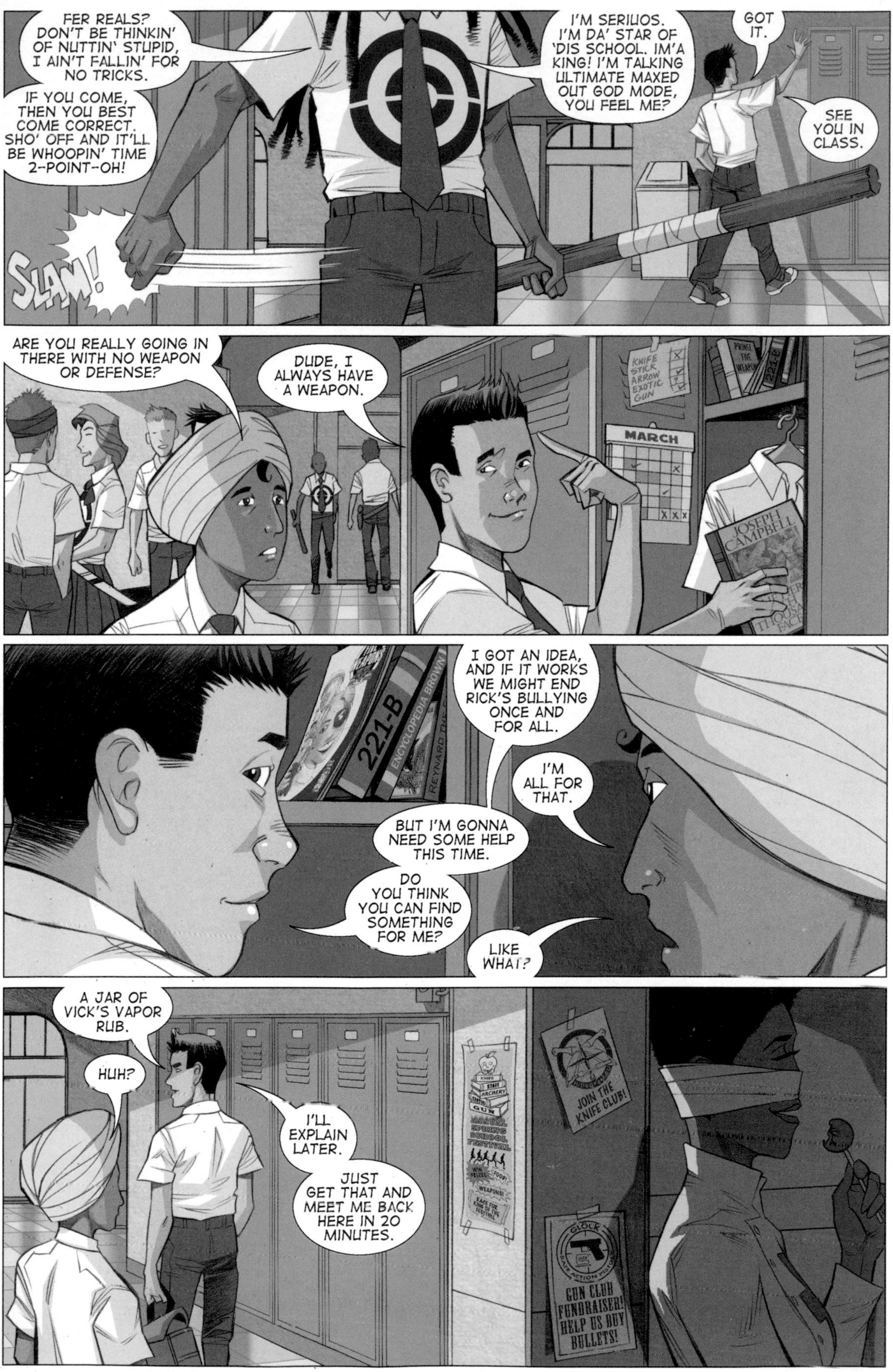
FER REALS? DON'T BE THINKIN' OF NUTTIN' STUPID, I AIN'T FALLIN' FOR NO TRICKS.
IF YOU COME, THEN YOU BEST COME CORRECT. SHO' OFF AND IT'LL BE WHOOPIN' TIME 2-POINT-OH!
SLAM!
I'M SERIUOS. I'M DA' STAR OF 'DIS SCHOOL. IM'A KING! I'M TALKING ULTIMATE MAXED OUT GOD MODE, YOU FEEL ME?
GOT IT.
SEE YOU IN CLASS.
ARE YOU REALLY GOING IN THERE WITH NO WEAPON OR DEFENSE?
DUDE, I ALWAYS HAVE A WEAPON.
KNIFE
STICK
ARROW
EXOTIC
GUN
MARCH
221-B
JOSEPH CAMPBELL
I GOT AN IDEA, AND IF IT WORKS WE MIGHT END RICK'S BULLYING ONCE AND FOR ALL.
I'M ALL FOR THAT.
BUT I'M GONNA NEED SOME HELP THIS TIME.
DO YOU THINK YOU CAN FIND SOMETHING FOR ME?
LIKE WHAT?
221-B
ENCYCLOPEDIA BROWN
A JAR OF VICK'S VAPOR RUB.
HUH?
I'LL EXPLAIN LATER.
JUST GET THAT AND MEET ME BACK HERE IN 20 MINUTES.
JOIN THE KNIFE CLUB!
GLOCK
GUN CLUB FUNDRAISER! HELP US BUY BULLETS!

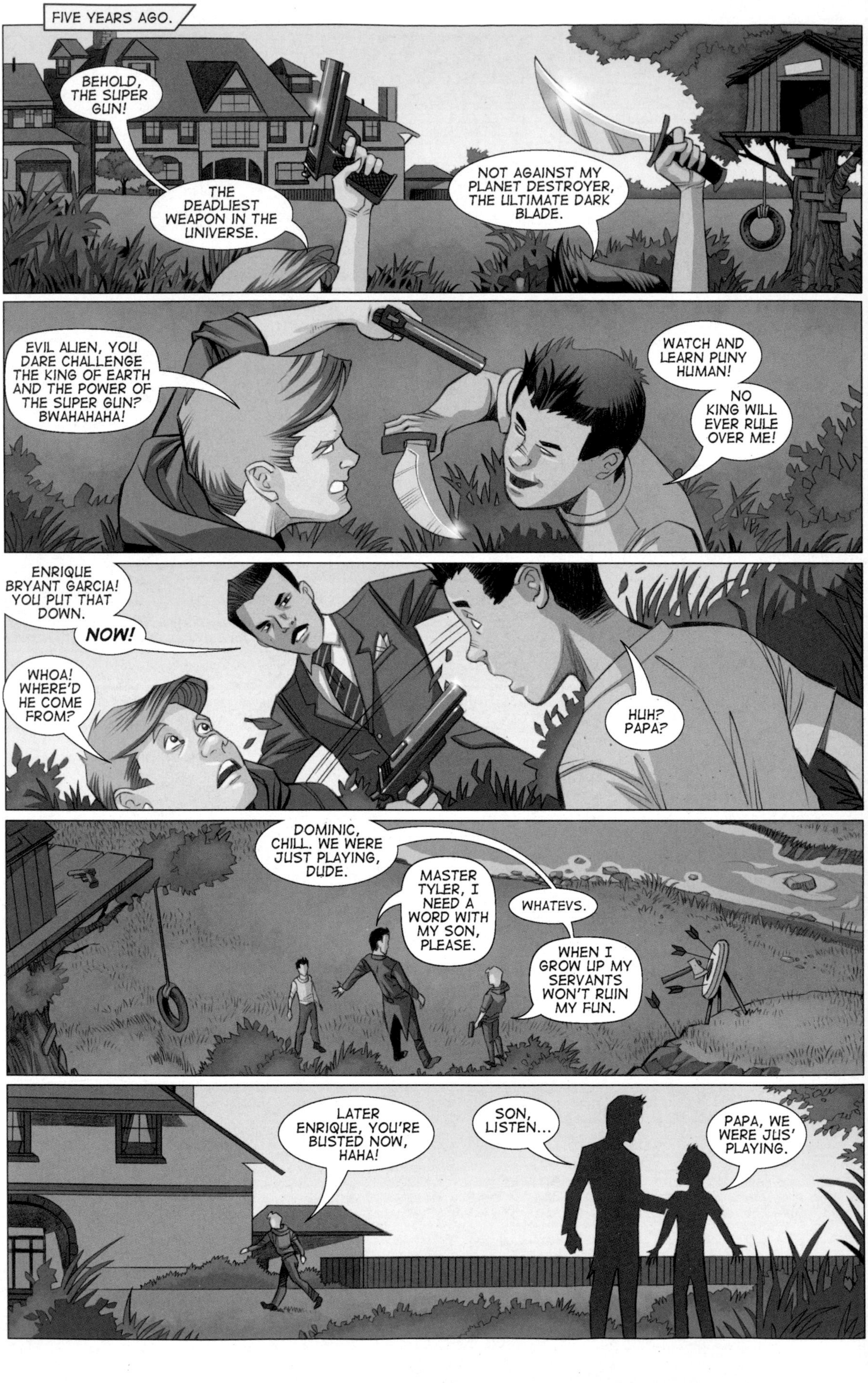
FIVE YEARS AGO.
BEHOLD, THE SUPER GUN!
THE DEADLIEST WEAPON IN THE UNIVERSE.
NOT AGAINST MY PLANET DESTROYER, THE ULTIMATE DARK BLADE.
EVIL ALIEN, YOU DARE CHALLENGE THE KING OF EARTH AND THE POWER OF THE SUPER GUN? BWAHAHAHA!
WATCH AND LEARN PUNY HUMAN!
NO KING WILL EVER RULE OVER ME!
ENRIQUE BRYANT GARCIA! YOU PUT THAT DOWN.
NOW!
WHOA! WHERE'D HE COME FROM?
HUH? PAPA?
DOMINIC, CHILL. WE WERE JUST PLAYING, DUDE.
MASTER TYLER, I NEED A WORD WITH MY SON, PLEASE.
WHATEVS.
WHEN I GROW UP MY SERVANTS WON'T RUIN MY FUN.
LATER ENRIQUE, YOU'RE BUSTED NOW, HAHA!
SON, LISTEN...
PAPA, WE WERE JUS' PLAYING.

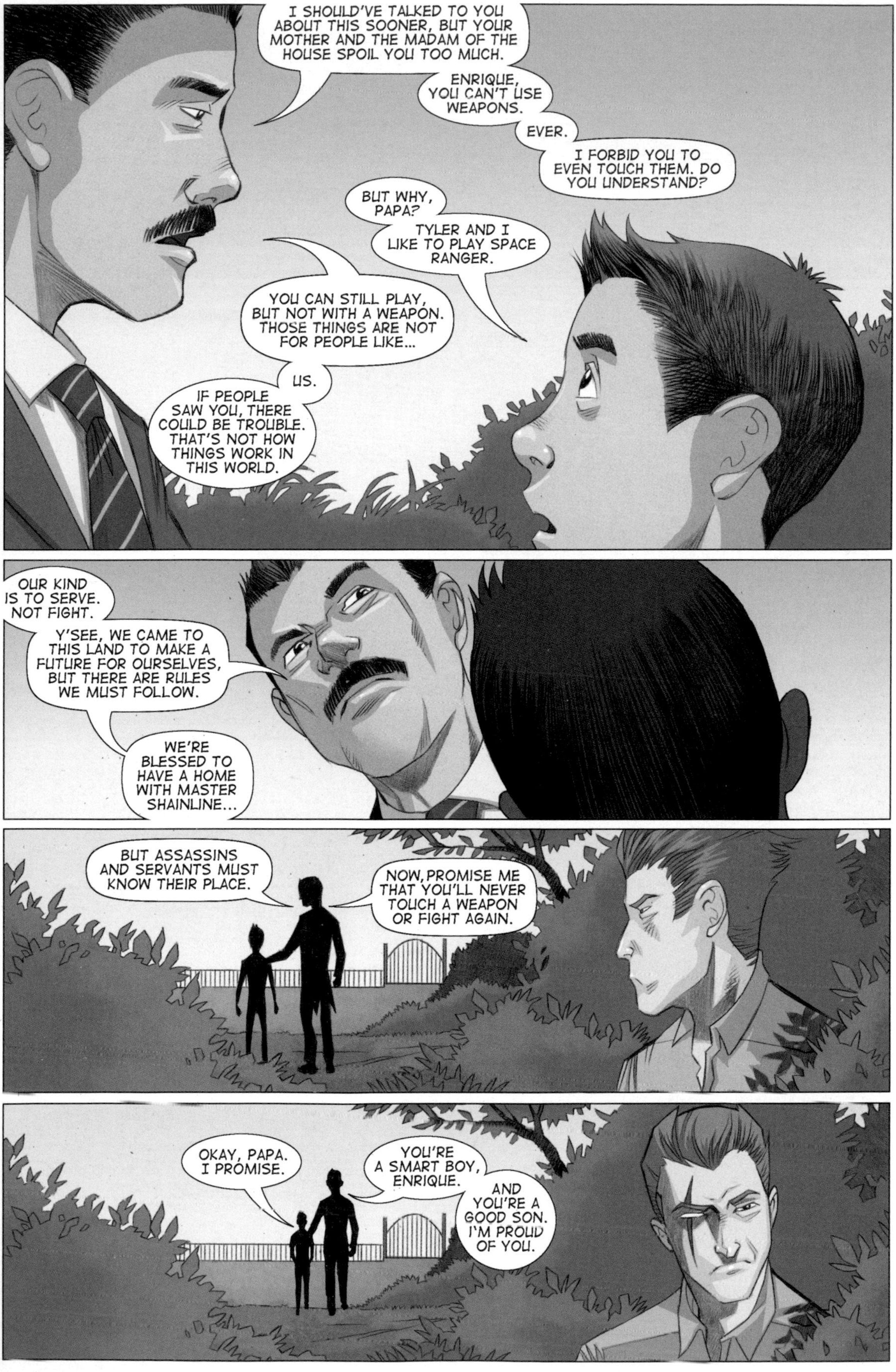
I SHOULD'VE TALKED TO YOU ABOUT THIS SOONER, BUT YOUR MOTHER AND THE MADAM OF THE HOUSE SPOIL YOU TOO MUCH.
ENRIQUE, YOU CAN'T USE WEAPONS.
EVER.
I FORBID YOU TO EVEN TOUCH THEM. DO YOU UNDERSTAND?
BUT WHY, PAPA?
TYLER AND I LIKE TO PLAY SPACE RANGER.
YOU CAN STILL PLAY, BUT NOT WITH A WEAPON. THOSE THINGS ARE NOT FOR PEOPLE LIKE...
US.
IF PEOPLE SAW YOU, THERE COULD BE TROUBLE. THAT'S NOT HOW THINGS WORK IN THIS WORLD.
OUR KIND IS TO SERVE. NOT FIGHT.
Y'SEE, WE CAME TO THIS LAND TO MAKE A FUTURE FOR OURSELVES, BUT THERE ARE RULES WE MUST FOLLOW.
WE'RE BLESSED TO HAVE A HOME WITH MASTER SHAINLINE...
BUT ASSASSINS AND SERVANTS MUST KNOW THEIR PLACE.
NOW, PROMISE ME THAT YOU'LL NEVER TOUCH A WEAPON OR FIGHT AGAIN.
OKAY, PAPA. I PROMISE.
YOU'RE A SMART BOY, ENRIQUE.
AND YOU'RE A GOOD SON. I'M PROUD OF YOU.

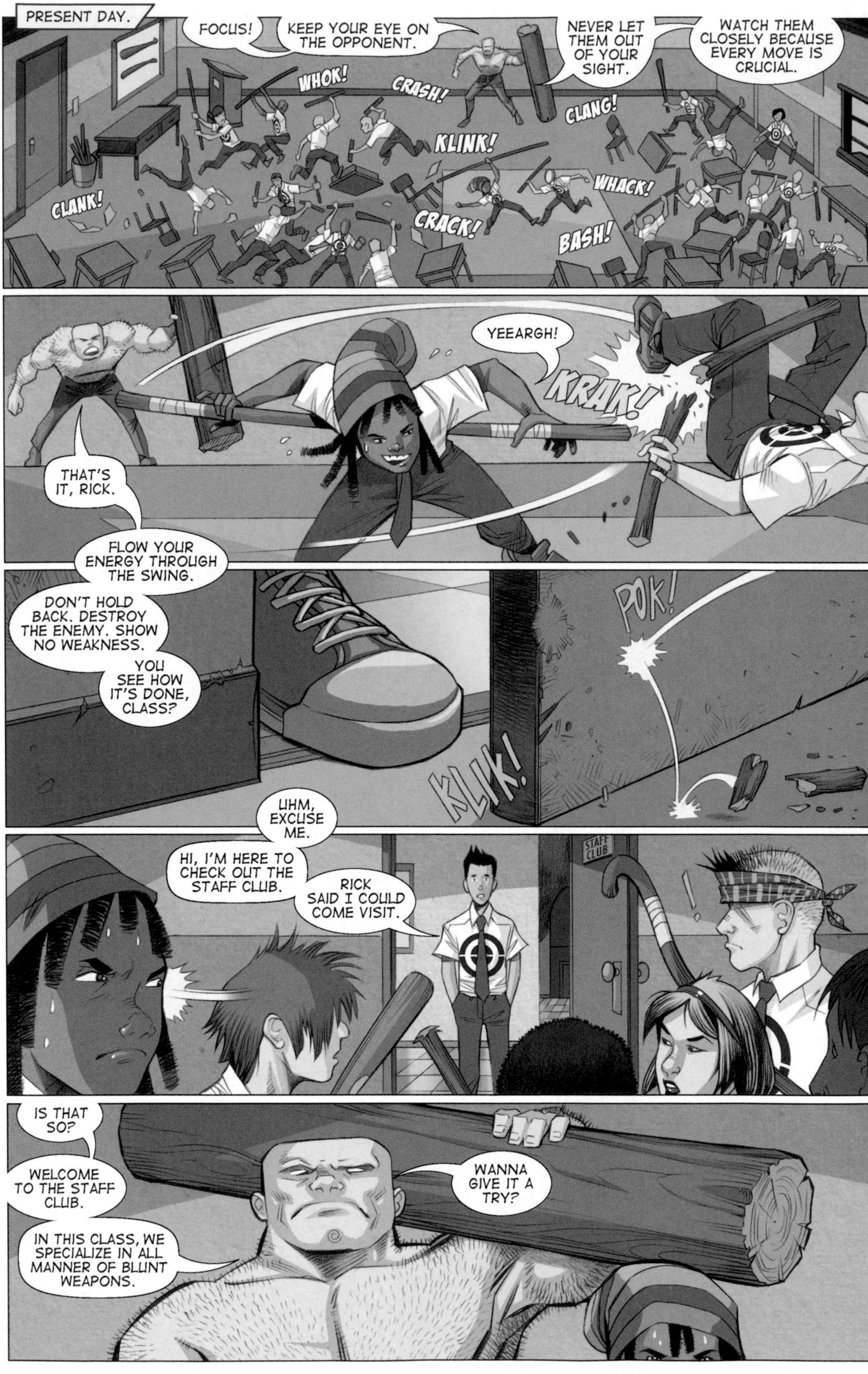
PRESENT DAY.
FOCUS!
KEEP YOUR EYE ON THE OPPONENT.
NEVER LET THEM OUT OF YOUR SIGHT.
WATCH THEM CLOSELY BECAUSE EVERY MOVE IS CRUCIAL.
WHOK!
CRASH!
CLANG!
KLINK!
CLANK!
WHACK!
CRACK!
BASH!
YEEARGH!
KRAK!
THAT'S IT, RICK.
FLOW YOUR ENERGY THROUGH THE SWING.
DON'T HOLD BACK. DESTROY THE ENEMY. SHOW NO WEAKNESS.
YOU SEE HOW IT'S DONE, CLASS?
POK!
KLIK!
UHM, EXCUSE ME.
HI, I'M HERE TO CHECK OUT THE STAFF CLUB.
RICK SAID I COULD COME VISIT.
STAFF CLUB
!
IS THAT SO?
WELCOME TO THE STAFF CLUB.
IN THIS CLASS, WE SPECIALIZE IN ALL MANNER OF BLUNT WEAPONS.
WANNA GIVE IT A TRY?

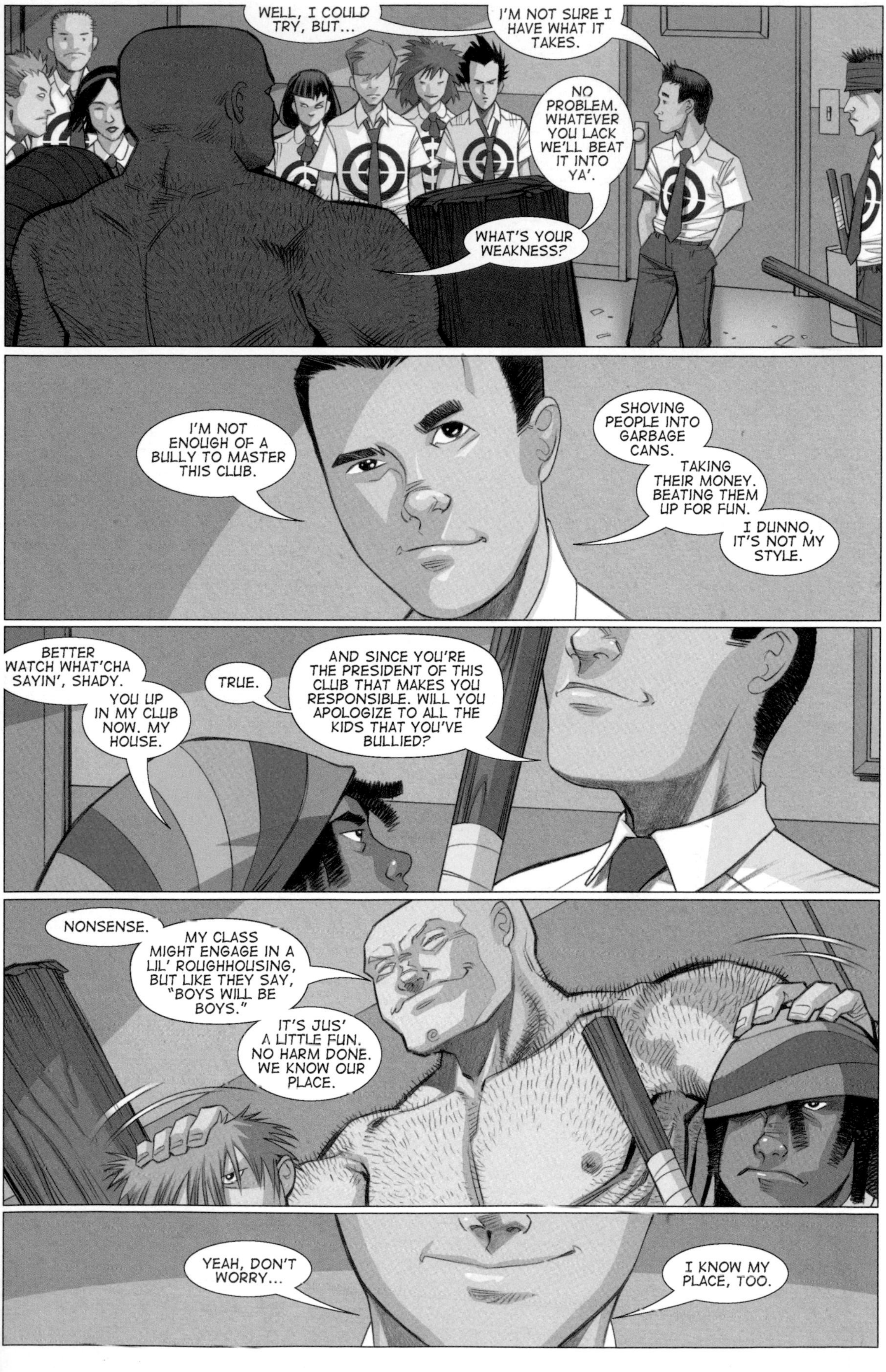
WELL, I COULD TRY, BUT...
I'M NOT SURE I HAVE WHAT IT TAKES.
NO PROBLEM. WHATEVER YOU LACK WE'LL BEAT IT INTO YA'.
WHAT'S YOUR WEAKNESS?
I'M NOT ENOUGH OF A BULLY TO MASTER THIS CLUB.
SHOVING PEOPLE INTO GARBAGE CANS.
TAKING THEIR MONEY. BEATING THEM UP FOR FUN.
I DUNNO, IT'S NOT MY STYLE.
BETTER WATCH WHAT'CHA SAYIN', SHADY.
YOU UP IN MY CLUB NOW. MY HOUSE.
TRUE.
AND SINCE YOU'RE THE PRESIDENT OF THIS CLUB THAT MAKES YOU RESPONSIBLE. WILL YOU APOLOGIZE TO ALL THE KIDS THAT YOU'VE BULLIED?
NONSENSE.
MY CLASS MIGHT ENGAGE IN A LIL' ROUGHHOUSING, BUT LIKE THEY SAY, "BOYS WILL BE BOYS."
IT'S JUS' A LITTLE FUN. NO HARM DONE. WE KNOW OUR PLACE.
YEAH, DON'T WORRY...
I KNOW MY PLACE, TOO.

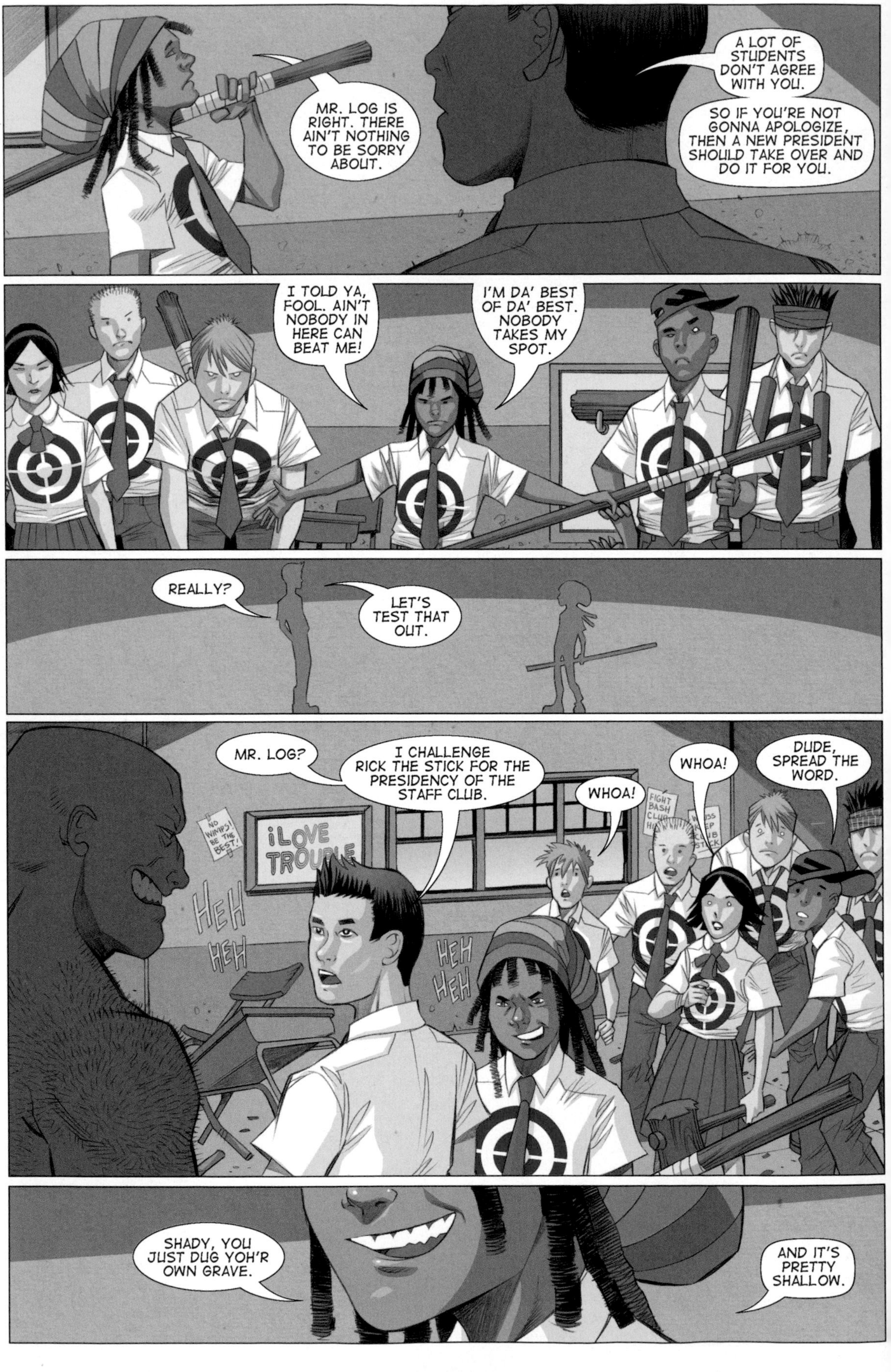
MR. LOG IS RIGHT. THERE AIN'T NOTHING TO BE SORRY ABOUT.
A LOT OF STUDENTS DON'T AGREE WITH YOU.
SO IF YOU'RE NOT GONNA APOLOGIZE, THEN A NEW PRESIDENT SHOULD TAKE OVER AND DO IT FOR YOU.
I TOLD YA, FOOL. AIN'T NOBODY IN HERE CAN BEAT ME!
I'M DA' BEST OF DA' BEST. NOBODY TAKES MY SPOT.
REALLY?
LET'S TEST THAT OUT.
MR. LOG?
I CHALLENGE RICK THE STICK FOR THE PRESIDENCY OF THE STAFF CLUB.
NO WIMPS! BE THE BEST!
iLOVE TROUBLE
HEH
HEH
HEH
HEH
WHOA!
WHOA!
DUDE, SPREAD THE WORD.
SHADY, YOU JUST DUG YOH'R OWN GRAVE.
AND IT'S PRETTY SHALLOW.

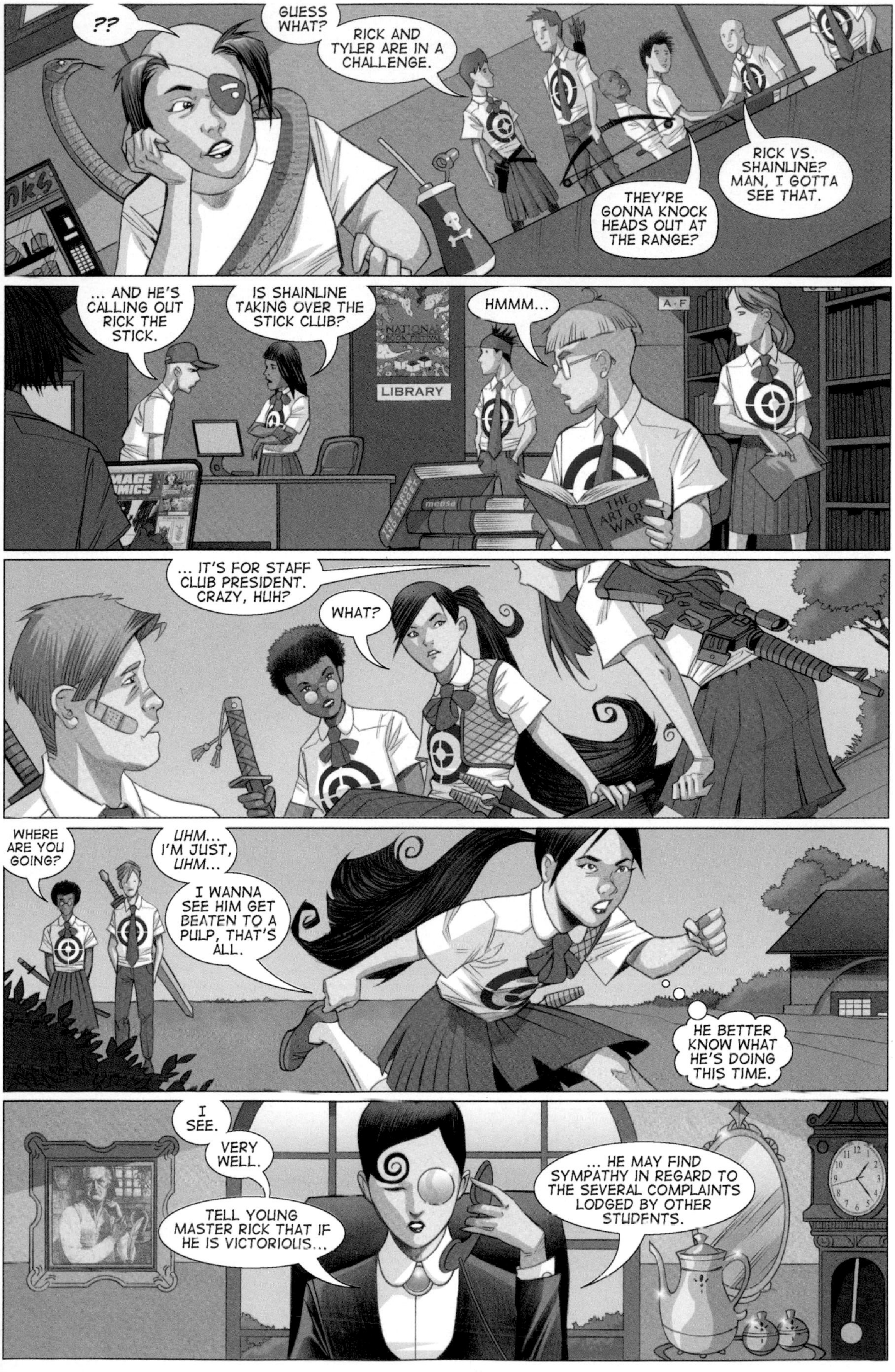
??
GUESS WHAT?
RICK AND TYLER ARE IN A CHALLENGE.
THEY'RE GONNA KNOCK HEADS OUT AT THE RANGE?
RICK VS. SHAINLINE? MAN, I GOTTA SEE THAT.
... AND HE'S CALLING OUT RICK THE STICK.
IS SHAINLINE TAKING OVER THE STICK CLUB?
NATIONAL BOOK FESTIVAL
LIBRARY
HMMM...
A-F
THE ART OF WAR
mensa
... IT'S FOR STAFF CLUB PRESIDENT. CRAZY, HUH?
WHAT?
WHERE ARE YOU GOING?
UHM... I'M JUST, UHM...
I WANNA SEE HIM GET BEATEN TO A PULP, THAT'S ALL.
HE BETTER KNOW WHAT HE'S DOING THIS TIME.
I SEE.
VERY WELL.
TELL YOUNG MASTER RICK THAT IF HE IS VICTORIOUS...
... HE MAY FIND SYMPATHY IN REGARD TO THE SEVERAL COMPLAINTS LODGED BY OTHER STUDENTS.

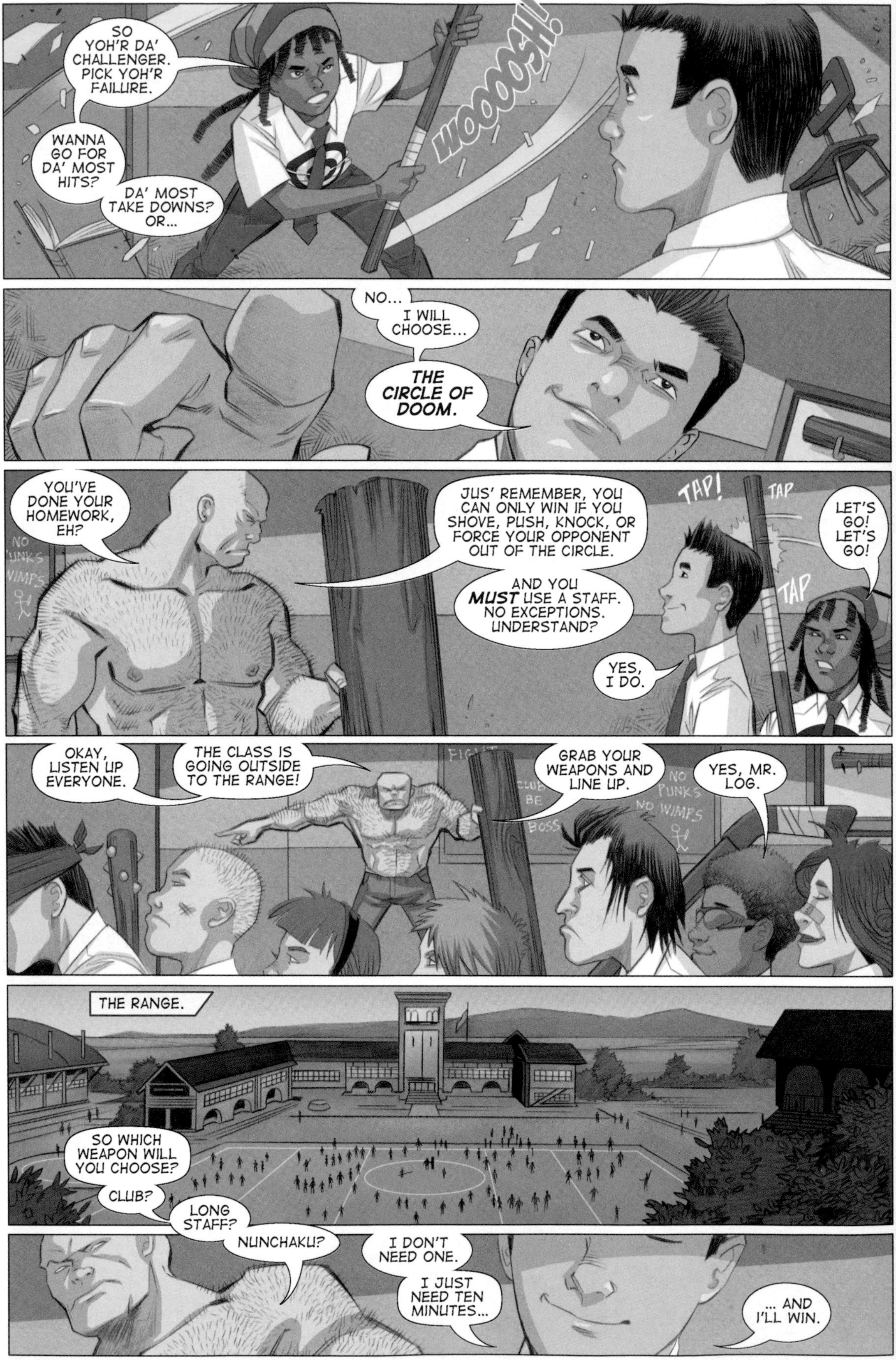
SO YOH'R DA' CHALLENGER. PICK YOH'R FAILURE.
WANNA GO FOR DA' MOST HITS?
DA' MOST TAKE DOWNS? OR...
WOOOOSH!
NO... I WILL CHOOSE...
THE CIRCLE OF DOOM.
YOU'VE DONE YOUR HOMEWORK, EH?
JUS' REMEMBER, YOU CAN ONLY WIN IF YOU SHOVE, PUSH, KNOCK, OR FORCE YOUR OPPONENT OUT OF THE CIRCLE.
AND YOU MUST USE A STAFF. NO EXCEPTIONS. UNDERSTAND?
TAP! TAP TAP
LET'S GO! LET'S GO!
YES, I DO.
OKAY, LISTEN UP EVERYONE.
THE CLASS IS GOING OUTSIDE TO THE RANGE!
GRAB YOUR WEAPONS AND LINE UP.
YES, MR. LOG.
NO PUNKS NO WIMPS
THE RANGE.
SO WHICH WEAPON WILL YOU CHOOSE?
CLUB?
LONG STAFF?
NUNCHAKU?
I DON'T NEED ONE.
I JUST NEED TEN MINUTES...
... AND I'LL WIN.

BOOK THREE
JOON THE LOON AND
DARRYL THE ARROW

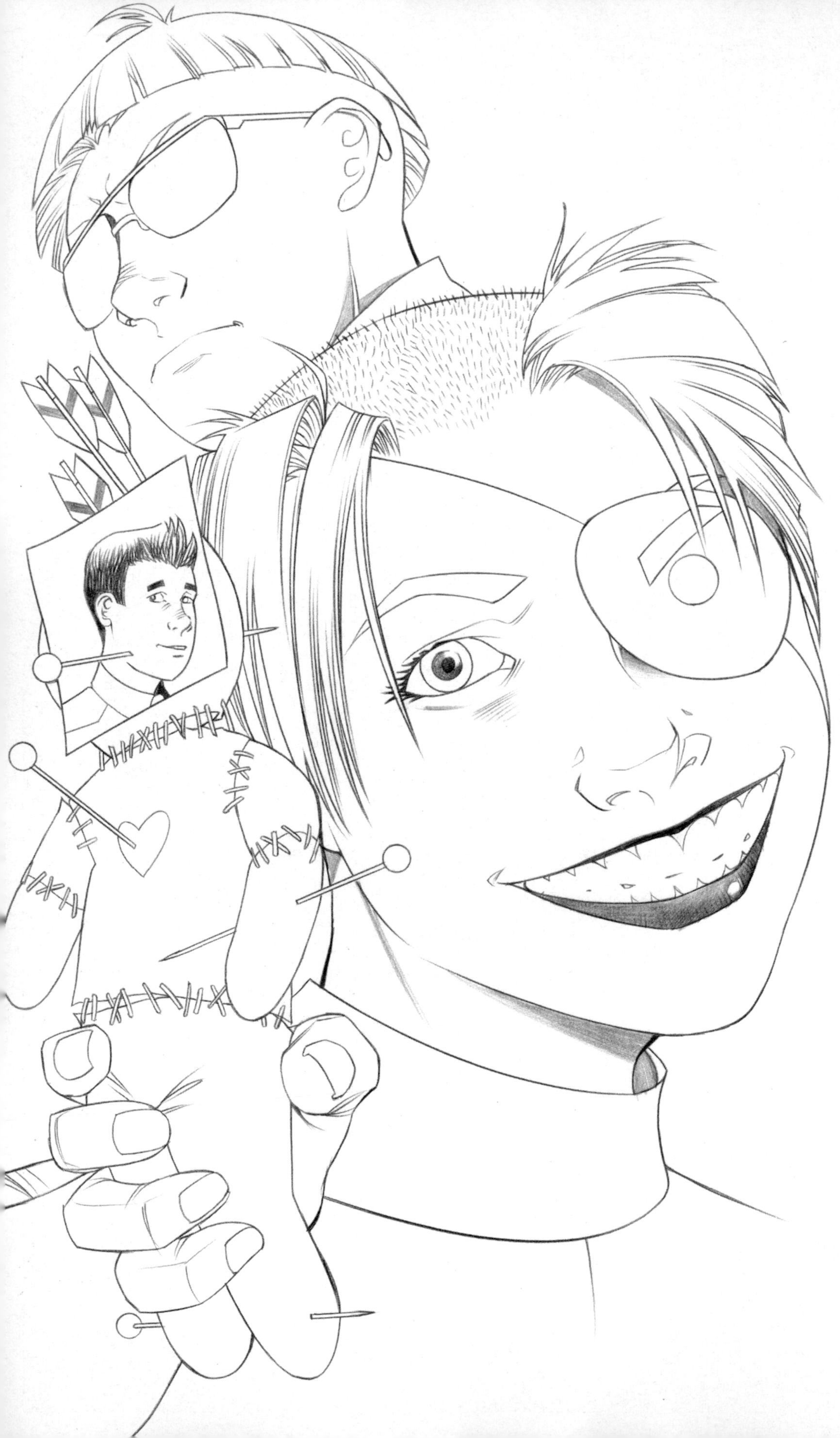

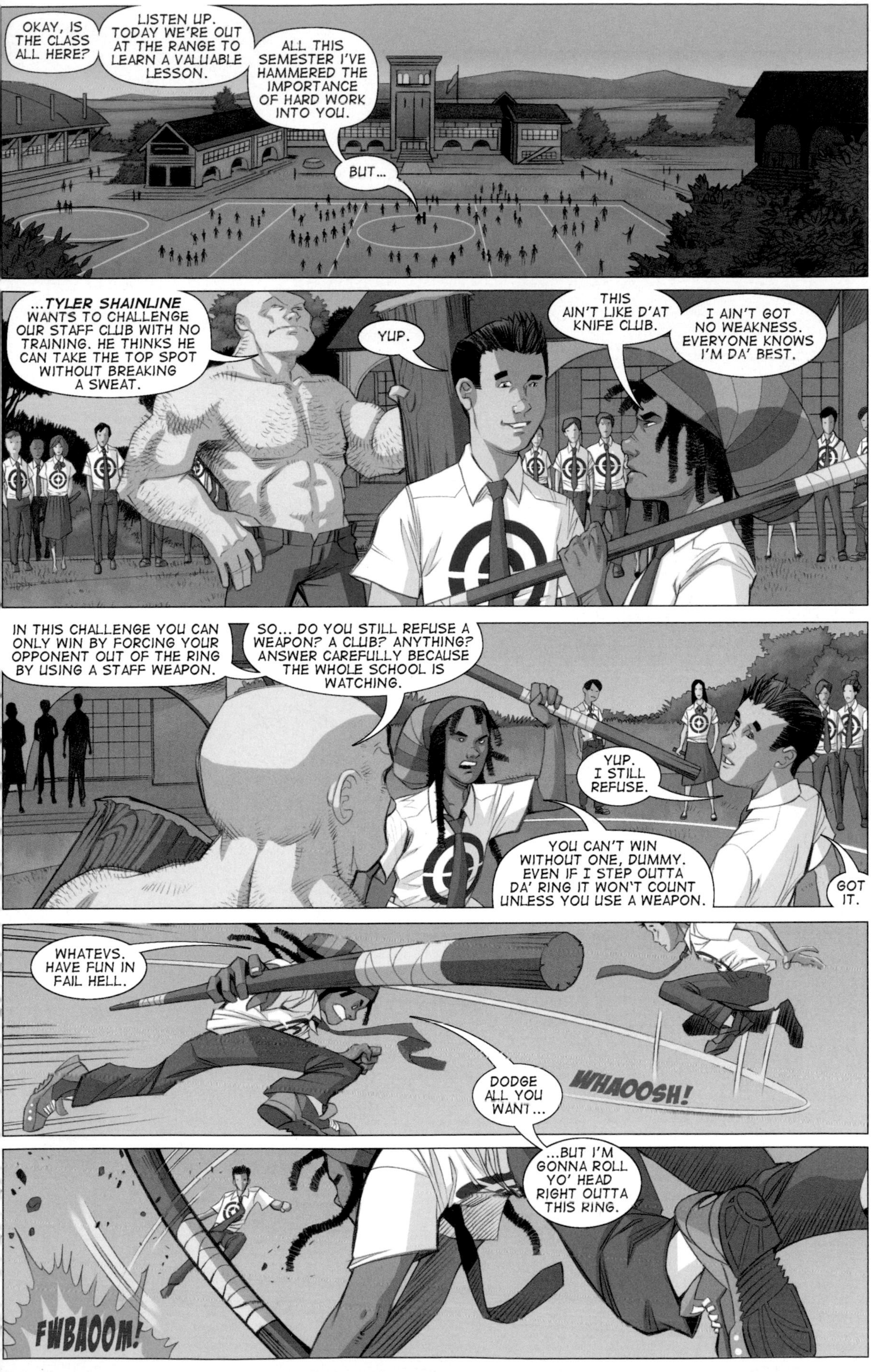
OKAY, IS THE CLASS ALL HERE?
LISTEN UP. TODAY WE'RE OUT AT THE RANGE TO LEARN A VALUABLE LESSON.
ALL THIS SEMESTER I'VE HAMMERED THE IMPORTANCE OF HARD WORK INTO YOU.
BUT...
...TYLER SHAINLINE WANTS TO CHALLENGE OUR STAFF CLUB WITH NO TRAINING. HE THINKS HE CAN TAKE THE TOP SPOT WITHOUT BREAKING A SWEAT.
YUP.
THIS AIN'T LIKE D'AT KNIFE CLUB.
I AIN'T GOT NO WEAKNESS. EVERYONE KNOWS I'M DA' BEST.
IN THIS CHALLENGE YOU CAN ONLY WIN BY FORCING YOUR OPPONENT OUT OF THE RING BY USING A STAFF WEAPON.
SO... DO YOU STILL REFUSE A WEAPON? A CLUB? ANYTHING? ANSWER CAREFULLY BECAUSE THE WHOLE SCHOOL IS WATCHING.
YUP. I STILL REFUSE.
YOU CAN'T WIN WITHOUT ONE, DUMMY. EVEN IF I STEP OUTTA DA' RING IT WON'T COUNT UNLESS YOU USE A WEAPON.
GOT IT.
WHATEVS. HAVE FUN IN FAIL HELL.
WHAOOSH!
DODGE ALL YOU WANT...
...BUT I'M GONNA ROLL YO' HEAD RIGHT OUTTA THIS RING.
FWBAOOM!

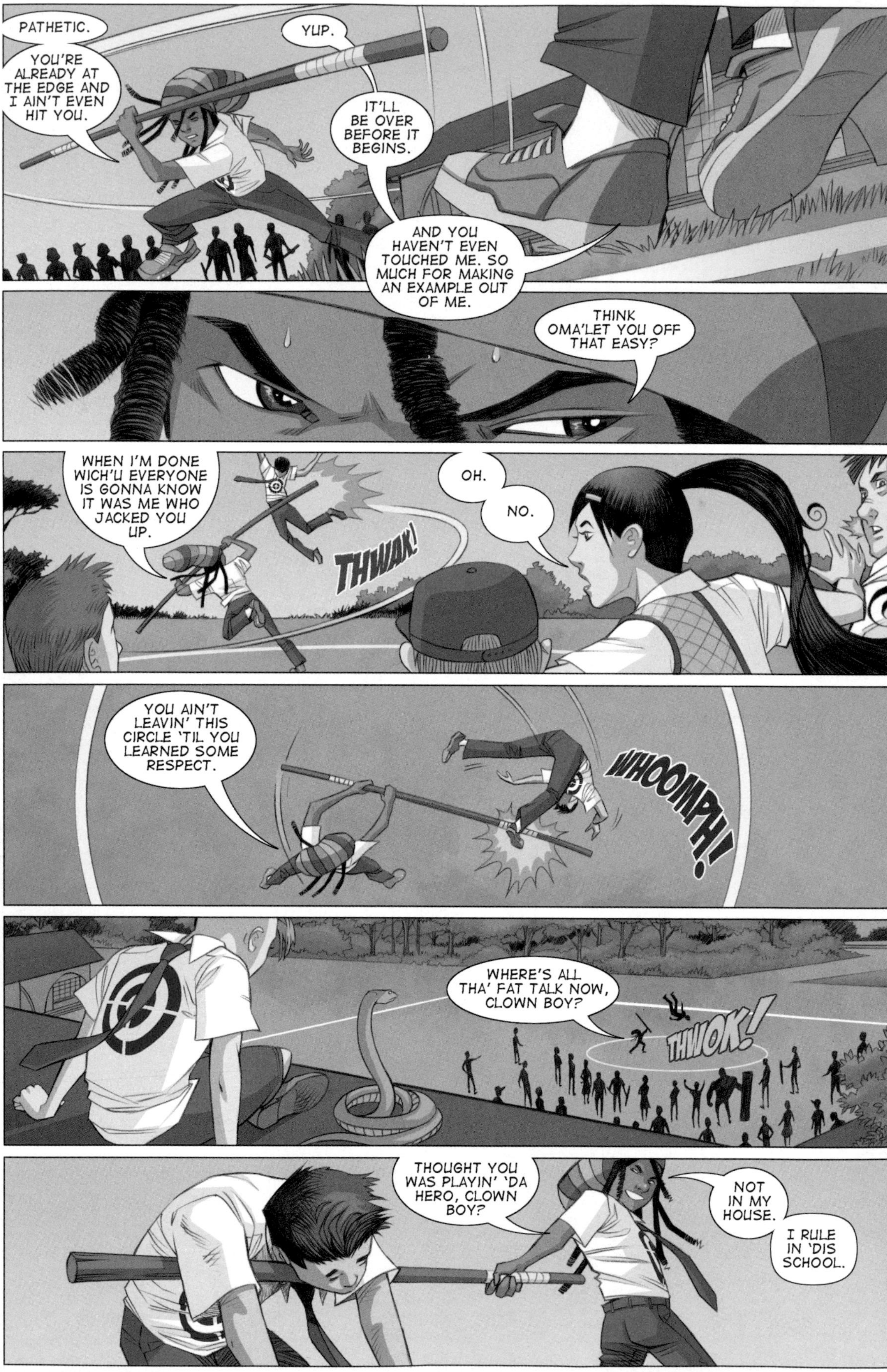
PATHETIC.
YOU'RE ALREADY AT THE EDGE AND I AIN'T EVEN HIT YOU.
YUP.
IT'LL BE OVER BEFORE IT BEGINS.
AND YOU HAVEN'T EVEN TOUCHED ME. SO MUCH FOR MAKING AN EXAMPLE OUT OF ME.
THINK OMA'LET YOU OFF THAT EASY?
WHEN I'M DONE WICH'U EVERYONE IS GONNA KNOW IT WAS ME WHO JACKED YOU UP.
THWAK!
OH.
NO.
YOU AIN'T LEAVIN' THIS CIRCLE 'TIL YOU LEARNED SOME RESPECT.
WHOOMPH!
WHERE'S ALL THA' FAT TALK NOW, CLOWN BOY?
THWOK!
THOUGHT YOU WAS PLAYIN' 'DA HERO, CLOWN BOY?
NOT IN MY HOUSE.
I RULE IN 'DIS SCHOOL.

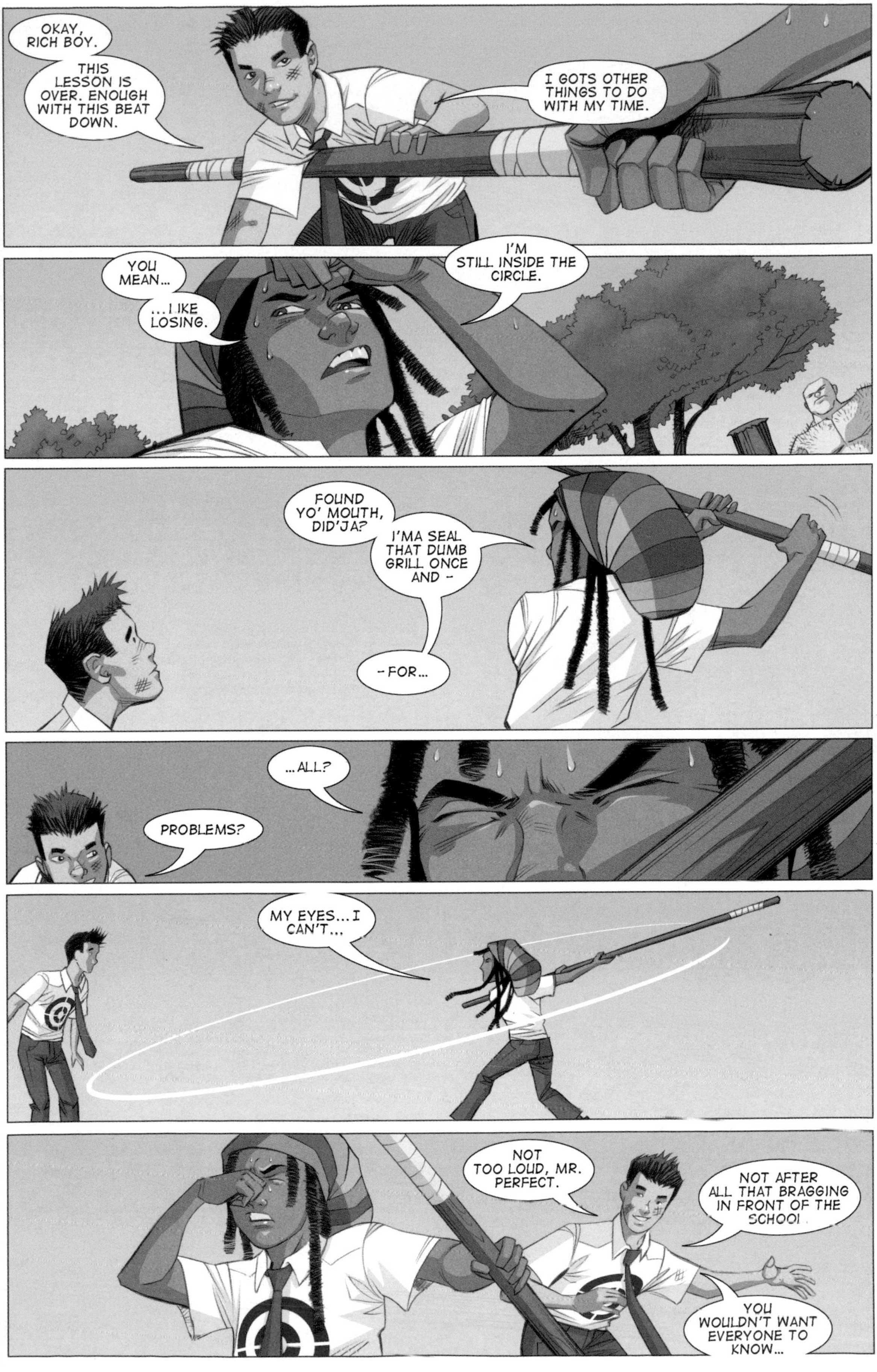
OKAY, RICH BOY.
THIS LESSON IS OVER. ENOUGH WITH THIS BEAT DOWN.
I GOTS OTHER THINGS TO DO WITH MY TIME.
YOU MEAN...
...LIKE LOSING.
I'M STILL INSIDE THE CIRCLE.
FOUND YO' MOUTH, DID'JA?
I'MA SEAL THAT DUMB GRILL ONCE AND -
- FOR...
...ALL?
PROBLEMS?
MY EYES... I CAN'T...
NOT TOO LOUD, MR. PERFECT.
NOT AFTER ALL THAT BRAGGING IN FRONT OF THE SCHOOL
YOU WOULDN'T WANT EVERYONE TO KNOW...

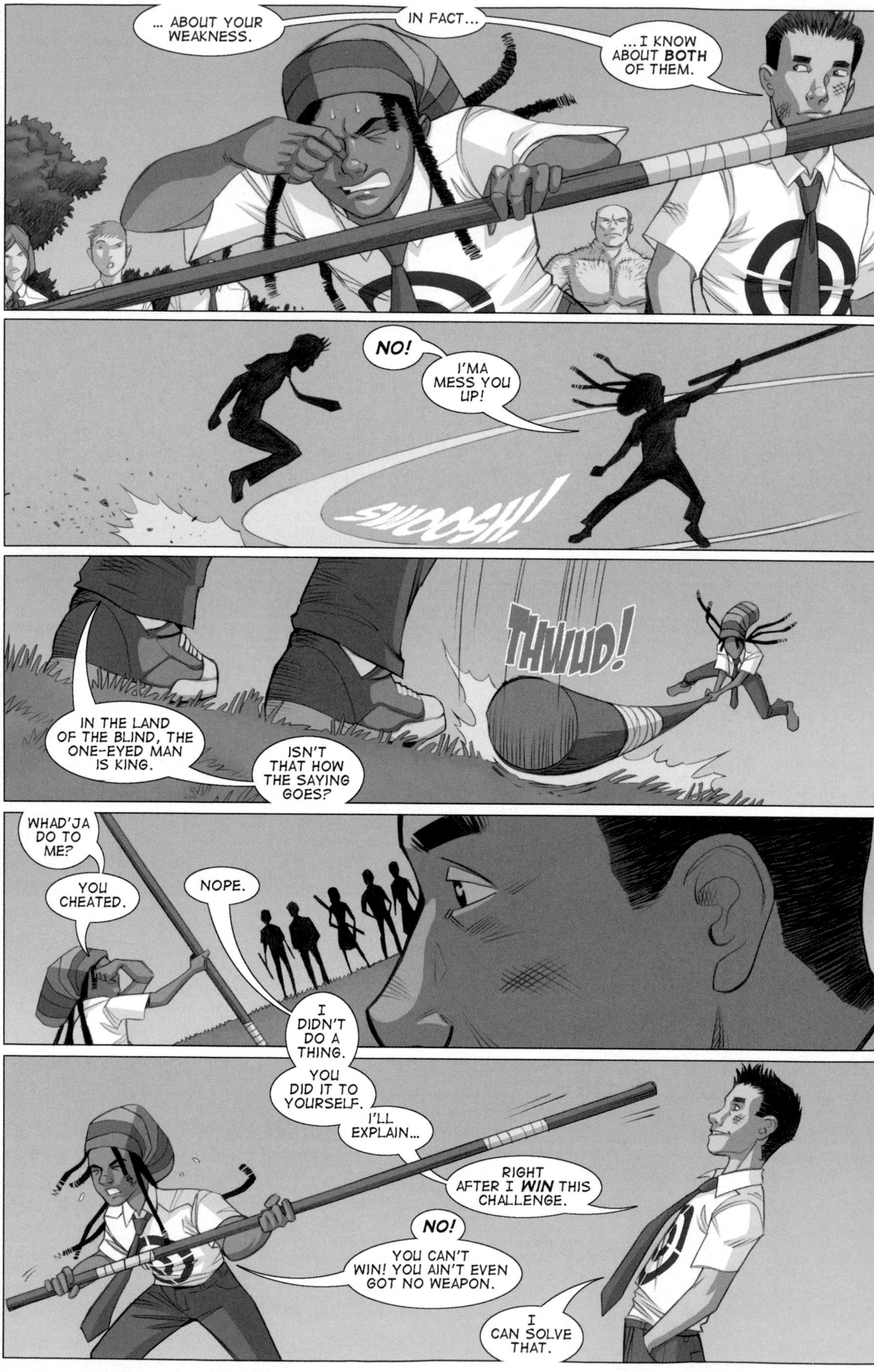

... ABOUT YOUR WEAKNESS.
IN FACT...
...I KNOW ABOUT **BOTH** OF THEM.
NO!
I'MA MESS YOU UP!
SHOOOSH!
THWUD!
IN THE LAND OF THE BLIND, THE ONE-EYED MAN IS KING.
ISN'T THAT HOW THE SAYING GOES?
WHAD'JA DO TO ME?
YOU CHEATED.
NOPE.
I DIDN'T DO A THING.
YOU DID IT TO YOURSELF.
I'LL EXPLAIN...
RIGHT AFTER I ***WIN*** THIS CHALLENGE.
NO!
YOU CAN'T WIN! YOU AIN'T EVEN GOT NO WEAPON.
I CAN SOLVE THAT.

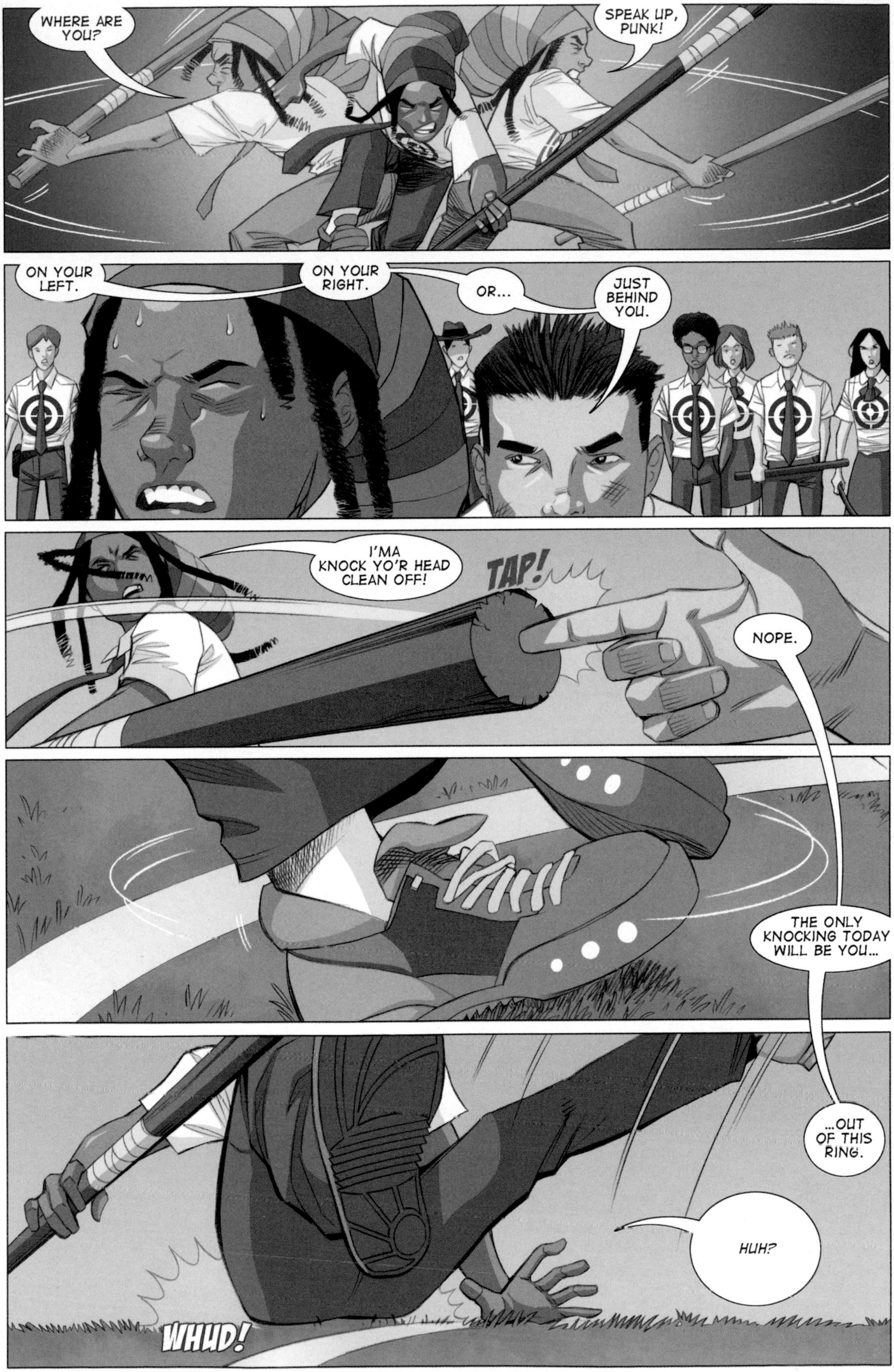
WHERE ARE YOU?
SPEAK UP, PUNK!
ON YOUR LEFT.
ON YOUR RIGHT.
OR...
JUST BEHIND YOU.
I'MA KNOCK YO'R HEAD CLEAN OFF!
TAP!
NOPE.
THE ONLY KNOCKING TODAY WILL BE YOU...
...OUT OF THIS RING.
HUH?
WHUD!

RICK IS OUT!

SHAINLINE WON?

WHA?

THAT'S ONE COLD DUDE.

DID IT WITH ONE FINGER!

HOW?

WHAT? YOU CAN'T DO THAT.

SURE I CAN. I JUST USED HIS STAFF TO PUSH HIM OUT OF THE CIRCLE.

BUT THAT DOESN'T COUNT!

WHY NOT?

NOTHING IN THE RULES SAYS IT HAS TO BE *MY* WEAPON.

NOW STAY DOWN, RICK. YOUR SECRETS ARE SAFE WITH ME.

BUT IF YOU DON'T STOP BULLYING MY FRIENDS...

I'LL TELL EVERYONE IN SCHOOL JUST HOW BLIND AS A BAT THE SO-CALLED PERFECT KING REALLY IS.

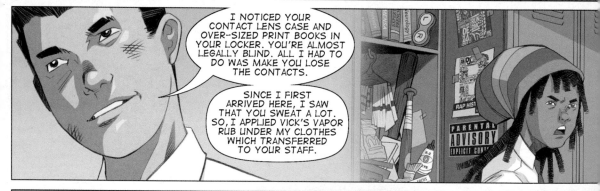

I NOTICED YOUR CONTACT LENS CASE AND OVER-SIZED PRINT BOOKS IN YOUR LOCKER. YOU'RE ALMOST LEGALLY BLIND. ALL I HAD TO DO WAS MAKE YOU LOSE THE CONTACTS.

SINCE I FIRST ARRIVED HERE, I SAW THAT YOU SWEAT A LOT. SO, I APPLIED VICK'S VAPOR RUB UNDER MY CLOTHES WHICH TRANSFERRED TO YOUR STAFF.

I KNEW I'D TAKE A BEATING, BUT YOUR DEFEAT WAS SEALED ONCE YOU WIPED THE SWEAT OUT YOUR EYES FROM ALL THAT FANCY STICK WORK.

AS FOR YOUR OTHER SECRET...

YOU CAN DROP THE WHOLE STREET THUG ACT.

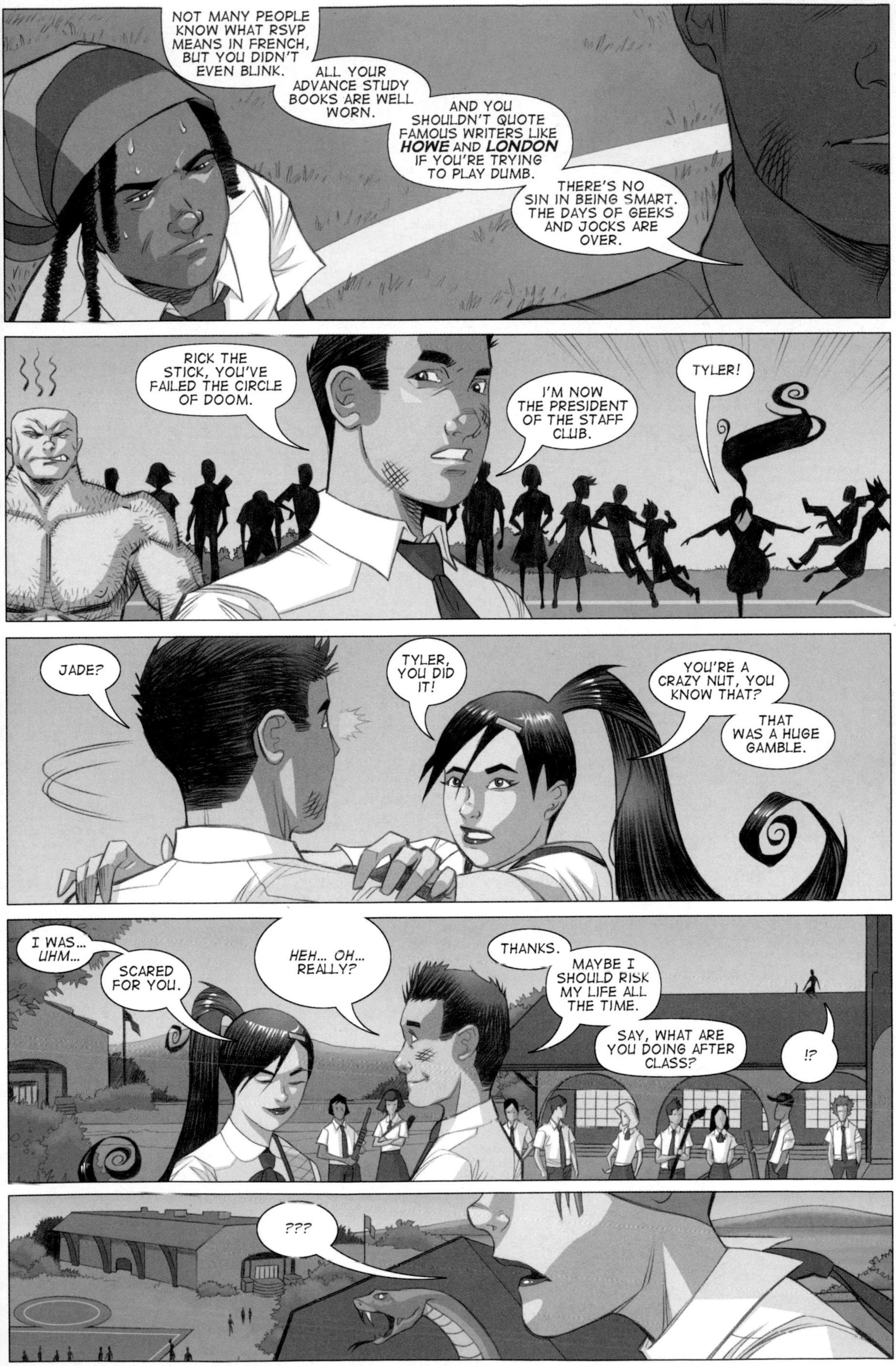
NOT MANY PEOPLE KNOW WHAT RSVP MEANS IN FRENCH, BUT YOU DIDN'T EVEN BLINK.
ALL YOUR ADVANCE STUDY BOOKS ARE WELL WORN.
AND YOU SHOULDN'T QUOTE FAMOUS WRITERS LIKE **HOWE** AND **LONDON** IF YOU'RE TRYING TO PLAY DUMB.
THERE'S NO SIN IN BEING SMART. THE DAYS OF GEEKS AND JOCKS ARE OVER.
RICK THE STICK, YOU'VE FAILED THE CIRCLE OF DOOM.
I'M NOW THE PRESIDENT OF THE STAFF CLUB.
TYLER!
JADE?
TYLER, YOU DID IT!
YOU'RE A CRAZY NUT, YOU KNOW THAT?
THAT WAS A HUGE GAMBLE.
I WAS... UHM...
SCARED FOR YOU.
HEH... OH... REALLY?
THANKS.
MAYBE I SHOULD RISK MY LIFE ALL THE TIME.
SAY, WHAT ARE YOU DOING AFTER CLASS?
!?
???

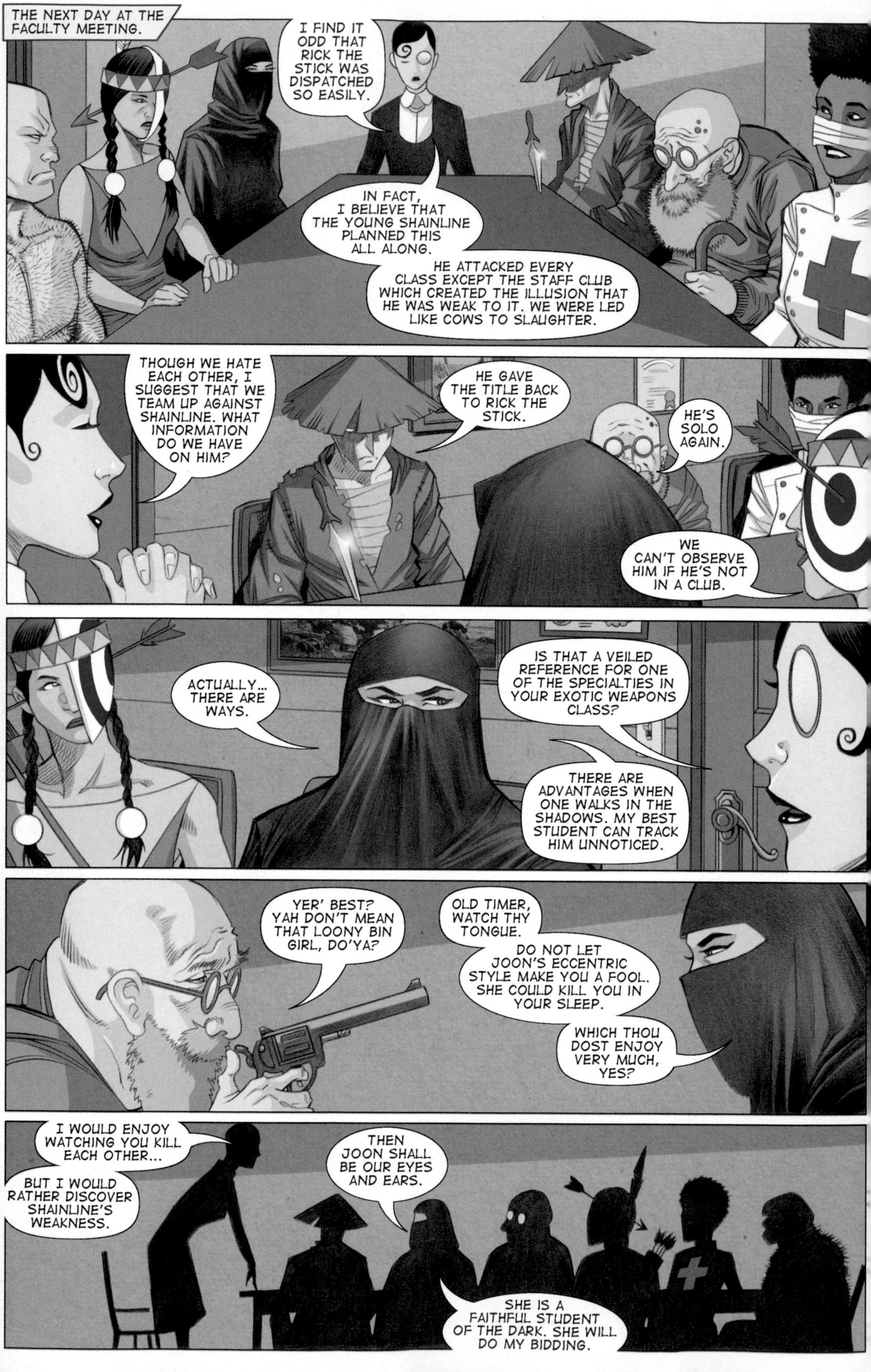
THE NEXT DAY AT THE FACULTY MEETING.
I FIND IT ODD THAT RICK THE STICK WAS DISPATCHED SO EASILY.
IN FACT, I BELIEVE THAT THE YOUNG SHAINLINE PLANNED THIS ALL ALONG.
HE ATTACKED EVERY CLASS EXCEPT THE STAFF CLUB WHICH CREATED THE ILLUSION THAT HE WAS WEAK TO IT. WE WERE LED LIKE COWS TO SLAUGHTER.
THOUGH WE HATE EACH OTHER, I SUGGEST THAT WE TEAM UP AGAINST SHAINLINE. WHAT INFORMATION DO WE HAVE ON HIM?
HE GAVE THE TITLE BACK TO RICK THE STICK.
HE'S SOLO AGAIN.
WE CAN'T OBSERVE HIM IF HE'S NOT IN A CLUB.
ACTUALLY... THERE ARE WAYS.
IS THAT A VEILED REFERENCE FOR ONE OF THE SPECIALTIES IN YOUR EXOTIC WEAPONS CLASS?
THERE ARE ADVANTAGES WHEN ONE WALKS IN THE SHADOWS. MY BEST STUDENT CAN TRACK HIM UNNOTICED.
YER' BEST? YAH DON'T MEAN THAT LOONY BIN GIRL, DO'YA?
OLD TIMER, WATCH THY TONGUE.
DO NOT LET JOON'S ECCENTRIC STYLE MAKE YOU A FOOL. SHE COULD KILL YOU IN YOUR SLEEP.
WHICH THOU DOST ENJOY VERY MUCH, YES?
I WOULD ENJOY WATCHING YOU KILL EACH OTHER...
BUT I WOULD RATHER DISCOVER SHAINLINE'S WEAKNESS.
THEN JOON SHALL BE OUR EYES AND EARS.
SHE IS A FAITHFUL STUDENT OF THE DARK. SHE WILL DO MY BIDDING.

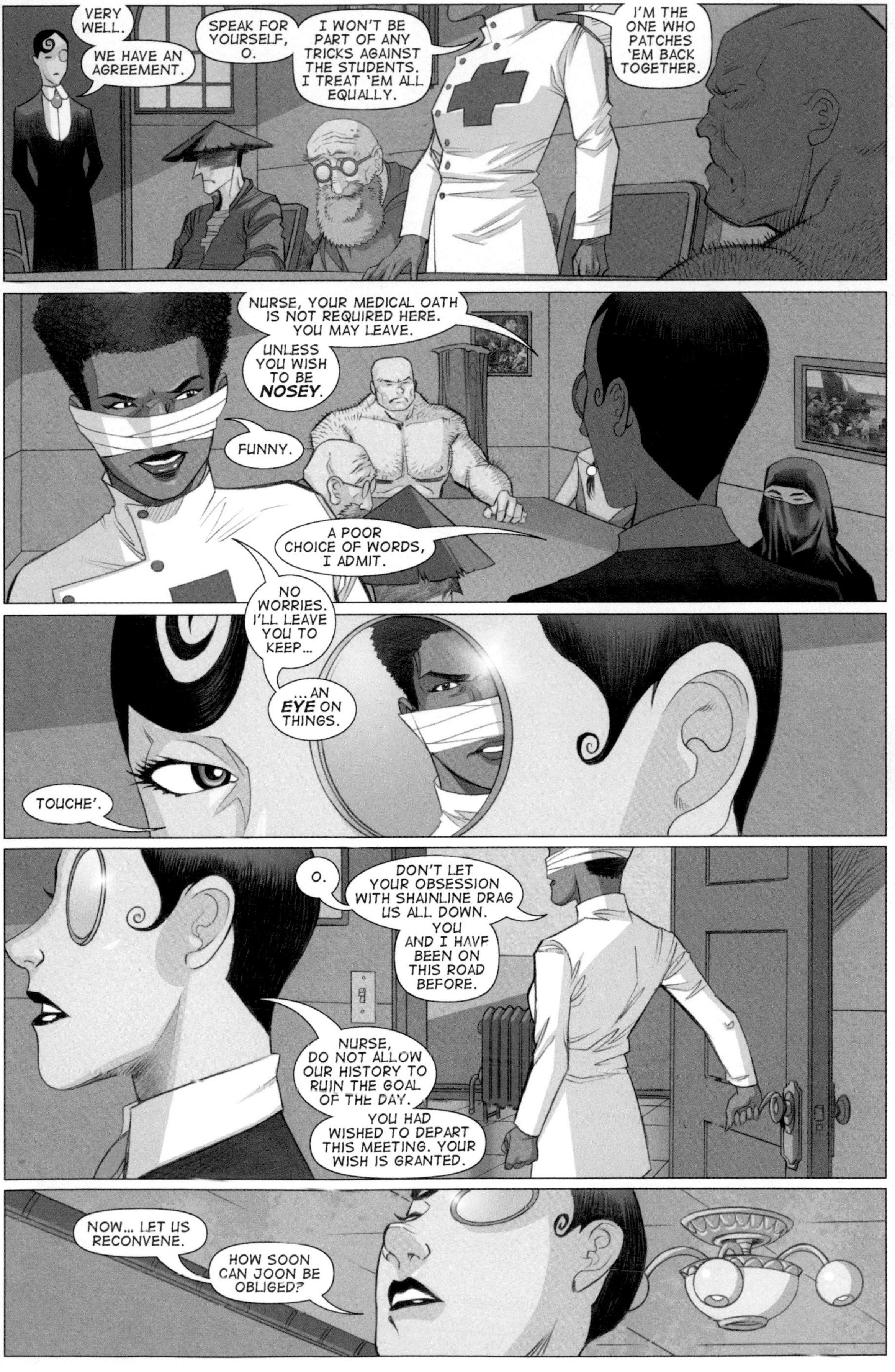
VERY WELL.
WE HAVE AN AGREEMENT.
SPEAK FOR YOURSELF, O.
I WON'T BE PART OF ANY TRICKS AGAINST THE STUDENTS. I TREAT 'EM ALL EQUALLY.
I'M THE ONE WHO PATCHES 'EM BACK TOGETHER.
NURSE, YOUR MEDICAL OATH IS NOT REQUIRED HERE. YOU MAY LEAVE.
UNLESS YOU WISH TO BE ***NOSEY***.
FUNNY.
A POOR CHOICE OF WORDS, I ADMIT.
NO WORRIES. I'LL LEAVE YOU TO KEEP...
...AN ***EYE*** ON THINGS.
TOUCHE'.
O.
DON'T LET YOUR OBSESSION WITH SHAINLINE DRAG US ALL DOWN.
YOU AND I HAVE BEEN ON THIS ROAD BEFORE.
NURSE, DO NOT ALLOW OUR HISTORY TO RUIN THE GOAL OF THE DAY.
YOU HAD WISHED TO DEPART THIS MEETING. YOUR WISH IS GRANTED.
NOW... LET US RECONVENE.
HOW SOON CAN JOON BE OBLIGED?

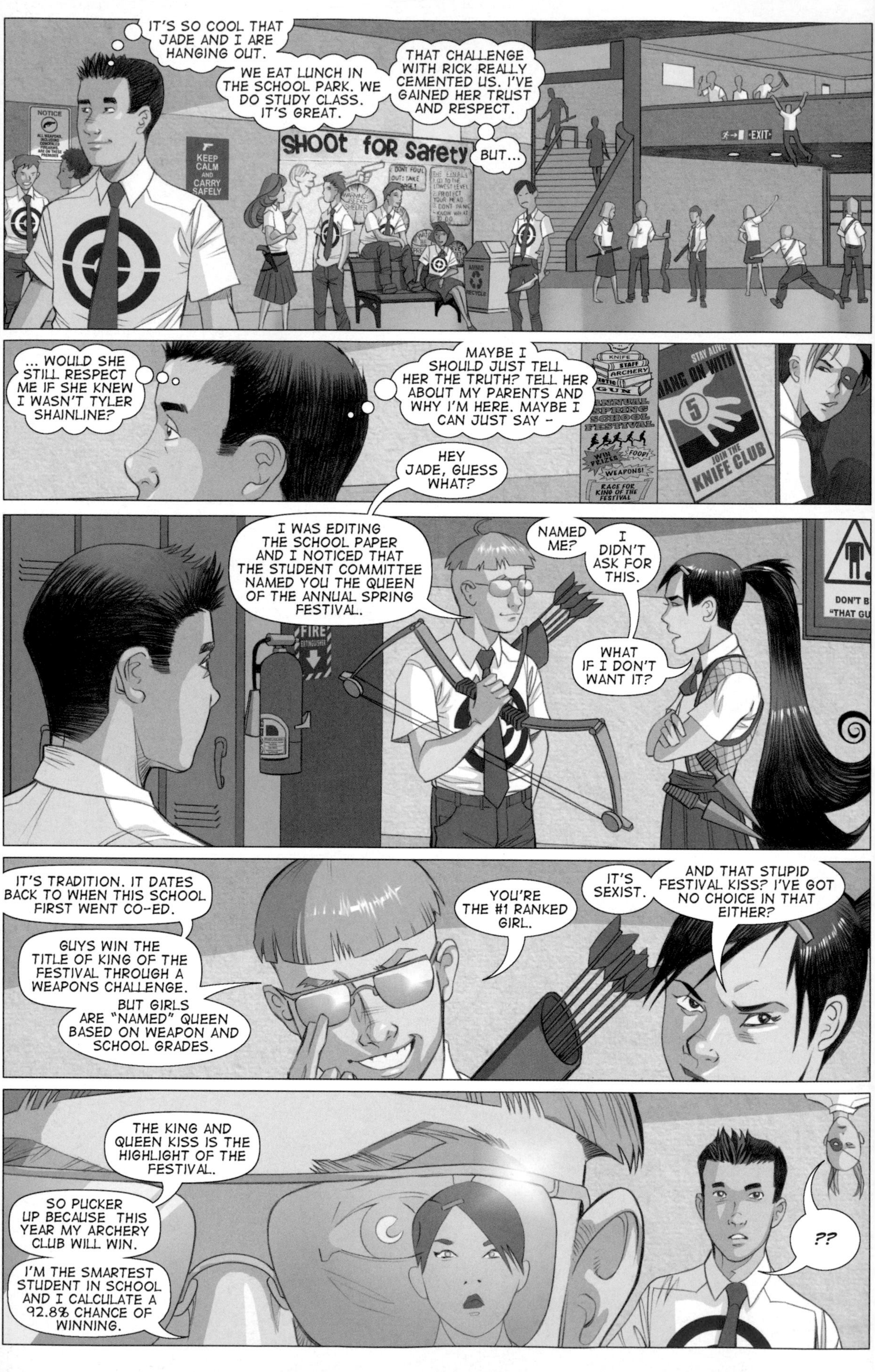
IT'S SO COOL THAT JADE AND I ARE HANGING OUT.
WE EAT LUNCH IN THE SCHOOL PARK. WE DO STUDY CLASS. IT'S GREAT.
THAT CHALLENGE WITH RICK REALLY CEMENTED US. I'VE GAINED HER TRUST AND RESPECT.
BUT...
KEEP CALM AND CARRY SAFELY
SHOOt for Safety
EXIT
AMMO RECYCLE
... WOULD SHE STILL RESPECT ME IF SHE KNEW I WASN'T TYLER SHAINLINE?
MAYBE I SHOULD JUST TELL HER THE TRUTH? TELL HER ABOUT MY PARENTS AND WHY I'M HERE. MAYBE I CAN JUST SAY -
HEY JADE, GUESS WHAT?
KNIFE
STAFF
ARCHERY
GUN
ANNUAL SPRING SCHOOL FESTIVAL
WIN PRIZES
FOOD!
WEAPONS!
RACE FOR KING OF THE FESTIVAL
STAY ALIVE!
HANG ON WITH 5
JOIN THE KNIFE CLUB
I WAS EDITING THE SCHOOL PAPER AND I NOTICED THAT THE STUDENT COMMITTEE NAMED YOU THE QUEEN OF THE ANNUAL SPRING FESTIVAL.
NAMED ME?
I DIDN'T ASK FOR THIS.
WHAT IF I DON'T WANT IT?
FIRE EXTINGUISHER
IT'S TRADITION. IT DATES BACK TO WHEN THIS SCHOOL FIRST WENT CO-ED.
GUYS WIN THE TITLE OF KING OF THE FESTIVAL THROUGH A WEAPONS CHALLENGE.
BUT GIRLS ARE "NAMED" QUEEN BASED ON WEAPON AND SCHOOL GRADES.
YOU'RE THE #1 RANKED GIRL.
IT'S SEXIST.
AND THAT STUPID FESTIVAL KISS? I'VE GOT NO CHOICE IN THAT EITHER?
THE KING AND QUEEN KISS IS THE HIGHLIGHT OF THE FESTIVAL.
SO PUCKER UP BECAUSE THIS YEAR MY ARCHERY CLUB WILL WIN.
I'M THE SMARTEST STUDENT IN SCHOOL AND I CALCULATE A 92.8% CHANCE OF WINNING.
??

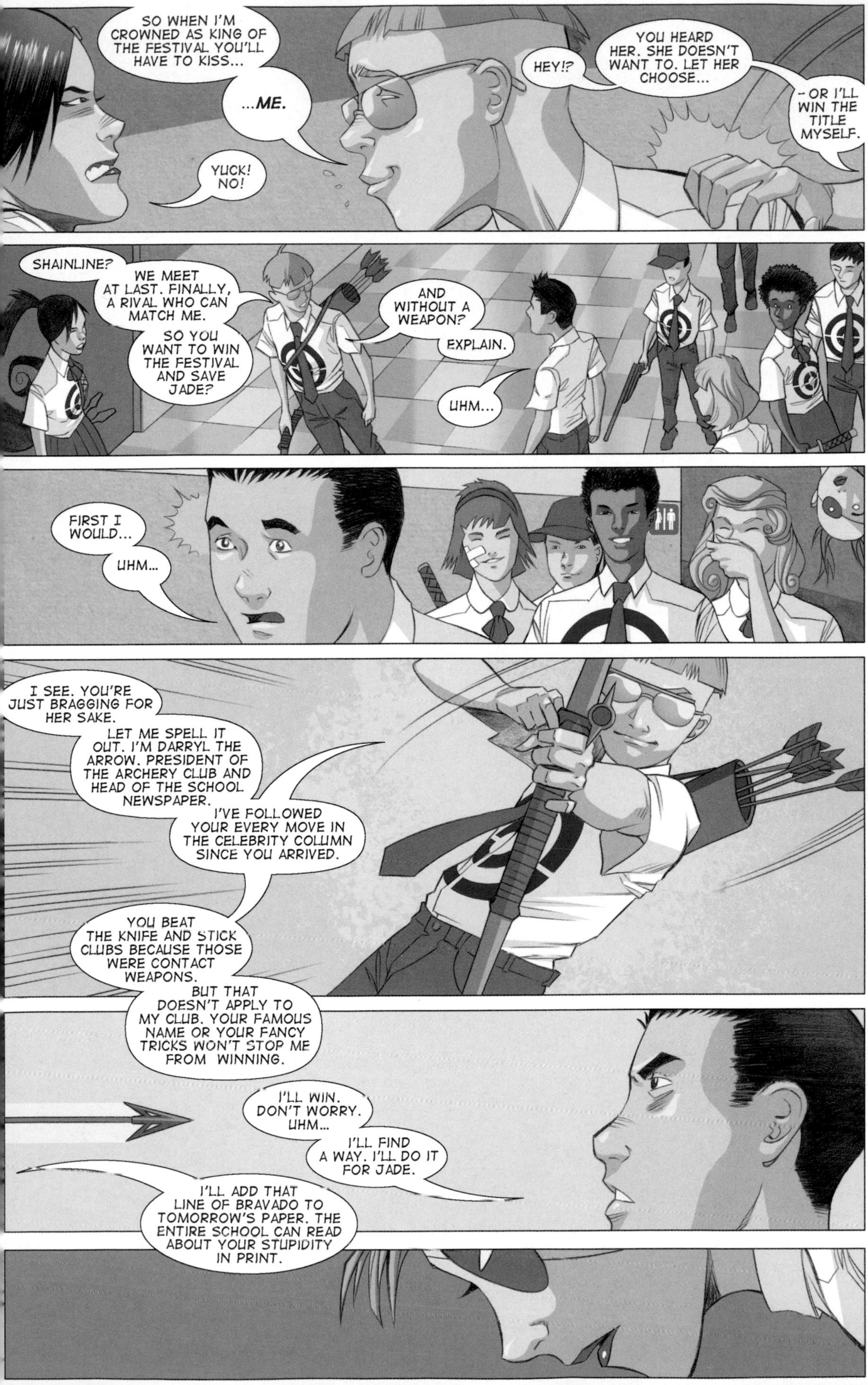
SO WHEN I'M CROWNED AS KING OF THE FESTIVAL YOU'LL HAVE TO KISS...
...ME.
YUCK! NO!
HEY!?
YOU HEARD HER. SHE DOESN'T WANT TO. LET HER CHOOSE...
-OR I'LL WIN THE TITLE MYSELF.
SHAINLINE?
WE MEET AT LAST. FINALLY, A RIVAL WHO CAN MATCH ME.
SO YOU WANT TO WIN THE FESTIVAL AND SAVE JADE?
AND WITHOUT A WEAPON?
EXPLAIN.
UHM...
FIRST I WOULD...
UHM...
I SEE. YOU'RE JUST BRAGGING FOR HER SAKE.
LET ME SPELL IT OUT. I'M DARRYL THE ARROW. PRESIDENT OF THE ARCHERY CLUB AND HEAD OF THE SCHOOL NEWSPAPER.
I'VE FOLLOWED YOUR EVERY MOVE IN THE CELEBRITY COLUMN SINCE YOU ARRIVED.
YOU BEAT THE KNIFE AND STICK CLUBS BECAUSE THOSE WERE CONTACT WEAPONS.
BUT THAT DOESN'T APPLY TO MY CLUB. YOUR FAMOUS NAME OR YOUR FANCY TRICKS WON'T STOP ME FROM WINNING.
I'LL WIN. DON'T WORRY. UHM...
I'LL FIND A WAY. I'LL DO IT FOR JADE.
I'LL ADD THAT LINE OF BRAVADO TO TOMORROW'S PAPER. THE ENTIRE SCHOOL CAN READ ABOUT YOUR STUPIDITY IN PRINT.

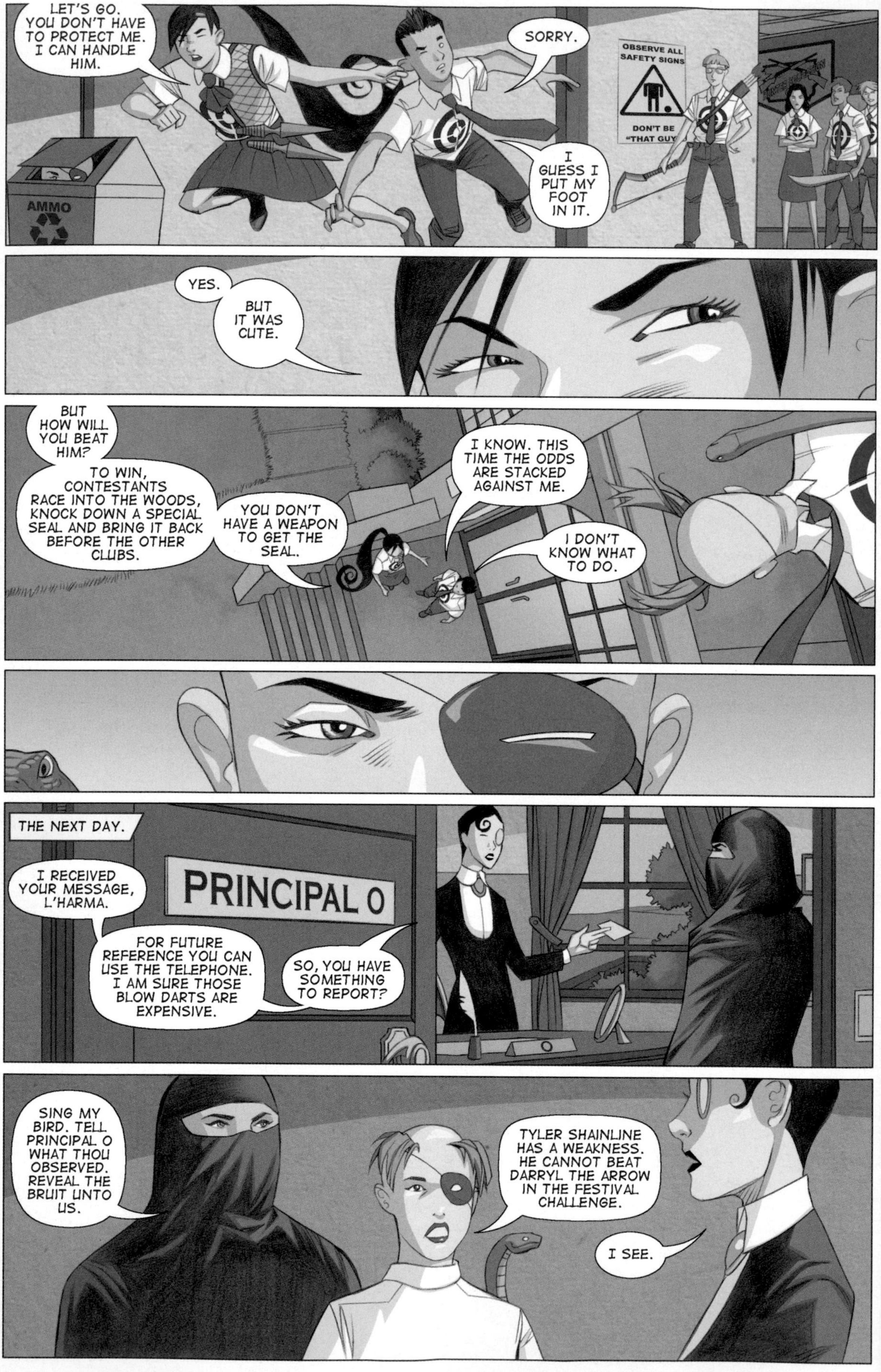
LET'S GO. YOU DON'T HAVE TO PROTECT ME. I CAN HANDLE HIM.
SORRY.
OBSERVE ALL SAFETY SIGNS
DON'T BE "THAT GUY"
I GUESS I PUT MY FOOT IN IT.
AMMO
YES.
BUT IT WAS CUTE.
BUT HOW WILL YOU BEAT HIM?
TO WIN, CONTESTANTS RACE INTO THE WOODS, KNOCK DOWN A SPECIAL SEAL AND BRING IT BACK BEFORE THE OTHER CLUBS.
YOU DON'T HAVE A WEAPON TO GET THE SEAL.
I KNOW. THIS TIME THE ODDS ARE STACKED AGAINST ME.
I DON'T KNOW WHAT TO DO.
THE NEXT DAY.
PRINCIPAL O
I RECEIVED YOUR MESSAGE, L'HARMA.
FOR FUTURE REFERENCE YOU CAN USE THE TELEPHONE. I AM SURE THOSE BLOW DARTS ARE EXPENSIVE.
SO, YOU HAVE SOMETHING TO REPORT?
SING MY BIRD. TELL PRINCIPAL O WHAT THOU OBSERVED. REVEAL THE BRUIT UNTO US.
TYLER SHAINLINE HAS A WEAKNESS. HE CANNOT BEAT DARRYL THE ARROW IN THE FESTIVAL CHALLENGE.
I SEE.

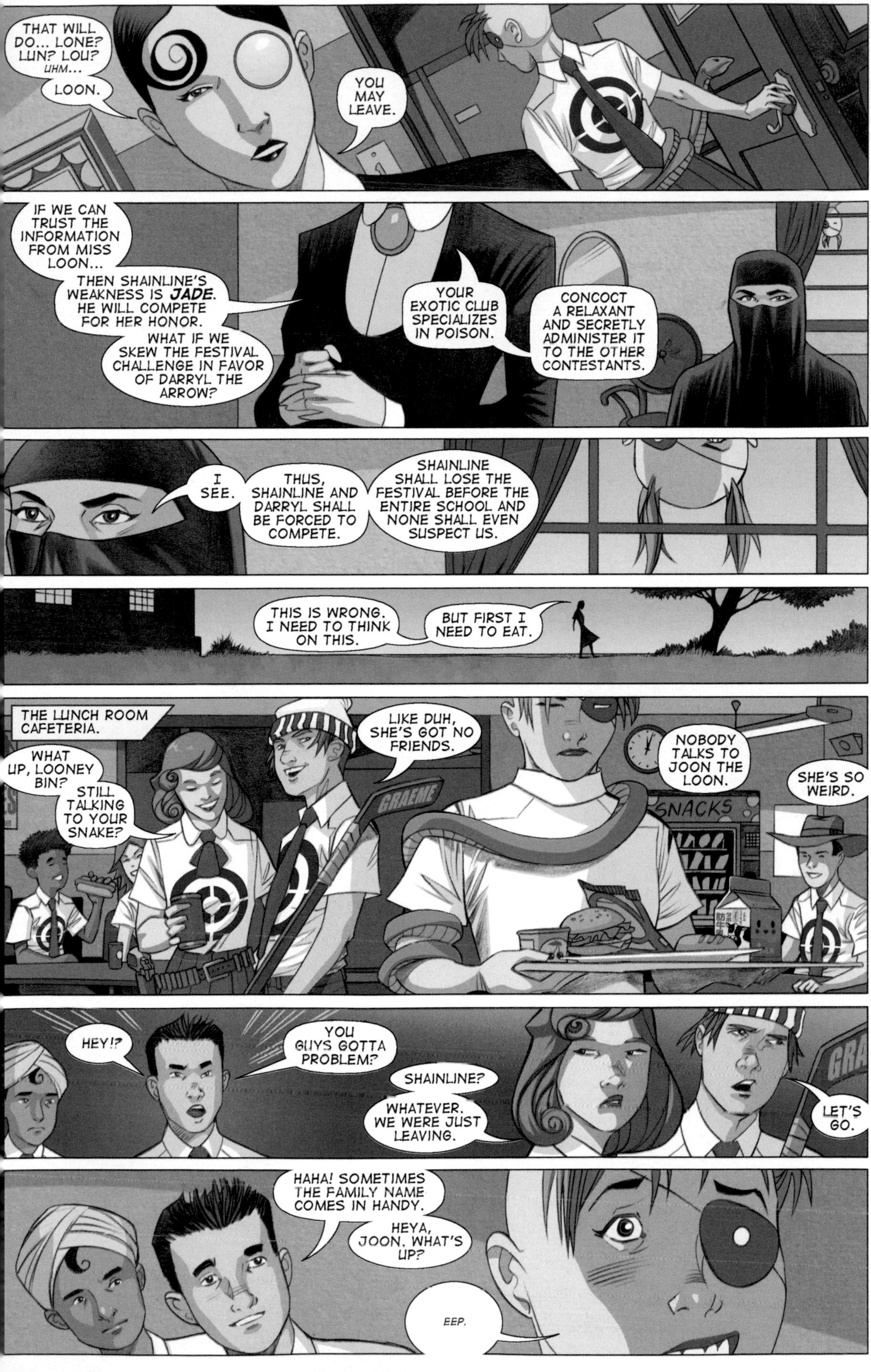
THAT WILL DO... LONE? LUN? LOU? UHM...
LOON.
YOU MAY LEAVE.
IF WE CAN TRUST THE INFORMATION FROM MISS LOON...
THEN SHAINLINE'S WEAKNESS IS JADE. HE WILL COMPETE FOR HER HONOR.
WHAT IF WE SKEW THE FESTIVAL CHALLENGE IN FAVOR OF DARRYL THE ARROW?
YOUR EXOTIC CLUB SPECIALIZES IN POISON.
CONCOCT A RELAXANT AND SECRETLY ADMINISTER IT TO THE OTHER CONTESTANTS.
I SEE.
THUS, SHAINLINE AND DARRYL SHALL BE FORCED TO COMPETE.
SHAINLINE SHALL LOSE THE FESTIVAL BEFORE THE ENTIRE SCHOOL AND NONE SHALL EVEN SUSPECT US.
THIS IS WRONG. I NEED TO THINK ON THIS.
BUT FIRST I NEED TO EAT.
THE LUNCH ROOM CAFETERIA.
WHAT UP, LOONEY BIN?
STILL TALKING TO YOUR SNAKE?
LIKE DUH, SHE'S GOT NO FRIENDS.
GRAEME
NOBODY TALKS TO JOON THE LOON.
SNACKS
SHE'S SO WEIRD.
HEY!?
YOU GUYS GOTTA PROBLEM?
SHAINLINE?
WHATEVER. WE WERE JUST LEAVING.
LET'S GO.
HAHA! SOMETIMES THE FAMILY NAME COMES IN HANDY.
HEYA, JOON. WHAT'S UP?
EEP.

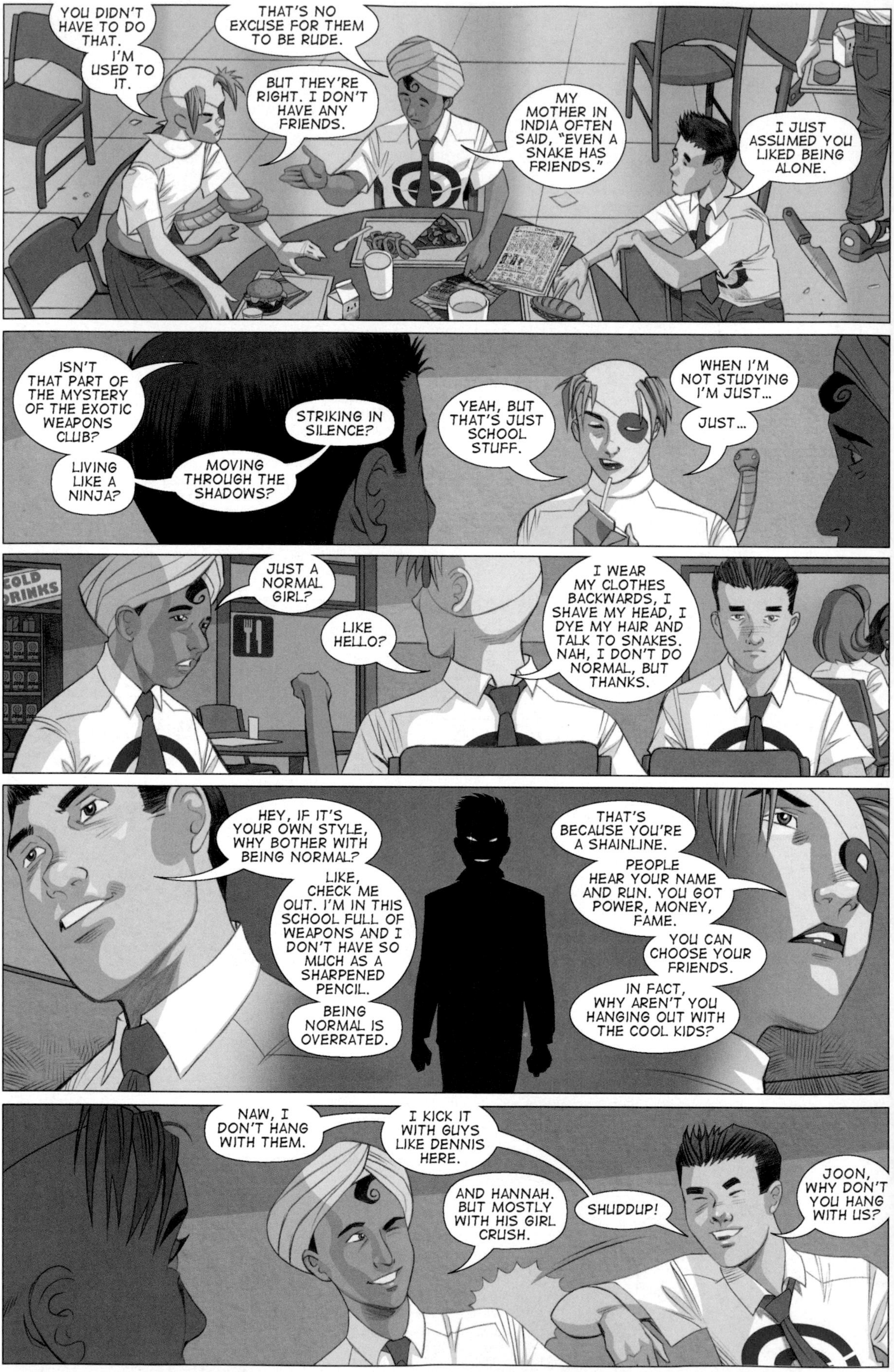
YOU DIDN'T HAVE TO DO THAT.
I'M USED TO IT.
THAT'S NO EXCUSE FOR THEM TO BE RUDE.
BUT THEY'RE RIGHT. I DON'T HAVE ANY FRIENDS.
MY MOTHER IN INDIA OFTEN SAID, "EVEN A SNAKE HAS FRIENDS."
I JUST ASSUMED YOU LIKED BEING ALONE.
ISN'T THAT PART OF THE MYSTERY OF THE EXOTIC WEAPONS CLUB?
LIVING LIKE A NINJA?
MOVING THROUGH THE SHADOWS?
STRIKING IN SILENCE?
YEAH, BUT THAT'S JUST SCHOOL STUFF.
WHEN I'M NOT STUDYING I'M JUST...
JUST...
JUST A NORMAL GIRL?
LIKE HELLO?
I WEAR MY CLOTHES BACKWARDS, I SHAVE MY HEAD, I DYE MY HAIR AND TALK TO SNAKES. NAH, I DON'T DO NORMAL, BUT THANKS.
HEY, IF IT'S YOUR OWN STYLE, WHY BOTHER WITH BEING NORMAL?
LIKE, CHECK ME OUT. I'M IN THIS SCHOOL FULL OF WEAPONS AND I DON'T HAVE SO MUCH AS A SHARPENED PENCIL.
BEING NORMAL IS OVERRATED.
THAT'S BECAUSE YOU'RE A SHAINLINE.
PEOPLE HEAR YOUR NAME AND RUN. YOU GOT POWER, MONEY, FAME.
YOU CAN CHOOSE YOUR FRIENDS.
IN FACT, WHY AREN'T YOU HANGING OUT WITH THE COOL KIDS?
NAW, I DON'T HANG WITH THEM.
I KICK IT WITH GUYS LIKE DENNIS HERE.
AND HANNAH. BUT MOSTLY WITH HIS GIRL CRUSH.
SHUDDUP!
JOON, WHY DON'T YOU HANG WITH US?

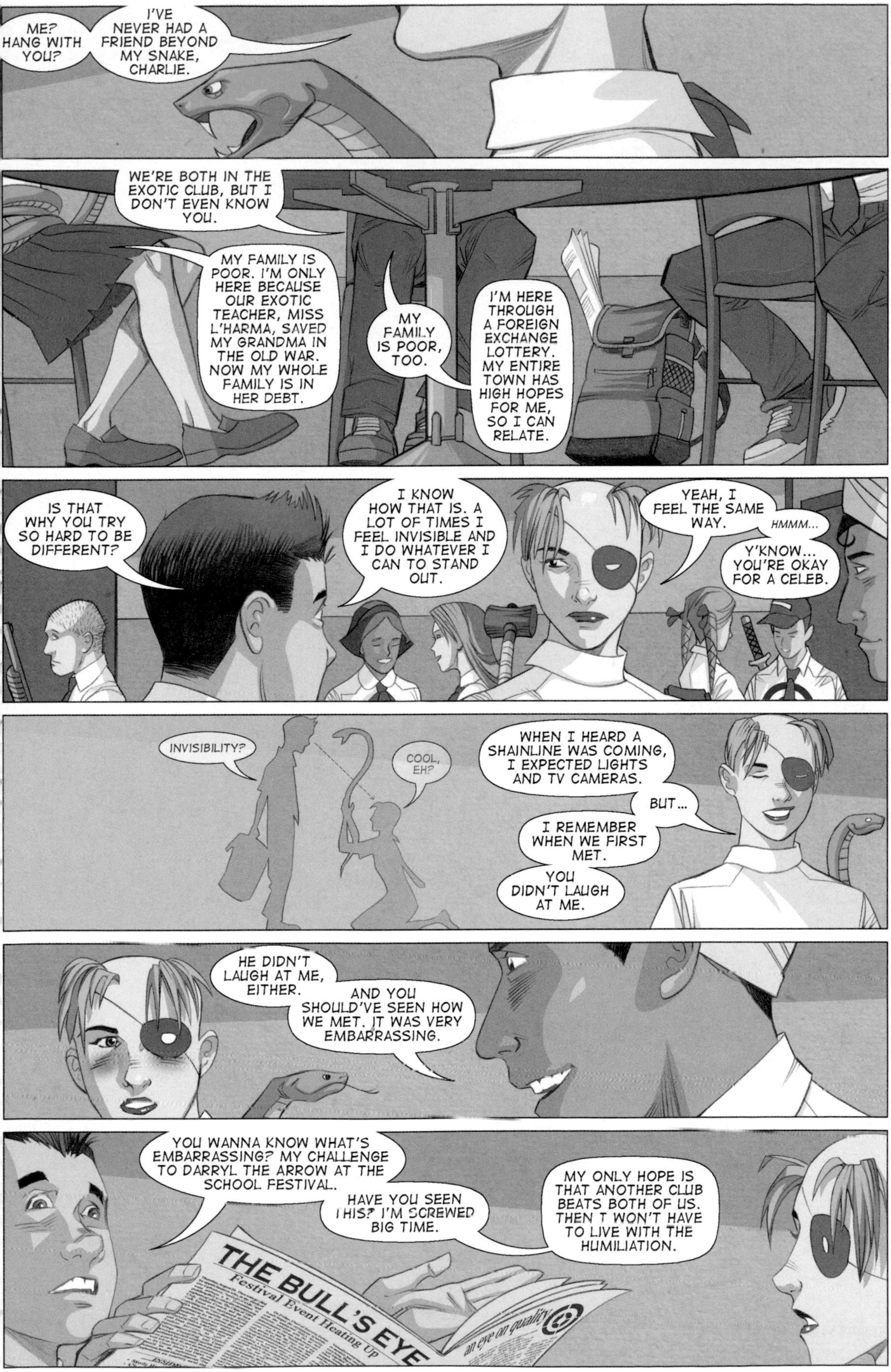
ME? HANG WITH YOU?
I'VE NEVER HAD A FRIEND BEYOND MY SNAKE, CHARLIE.
WE'RE BOTH IN THE EXOTIC CLUB, BUT I DON'T EVEN KNOW YOU.
MY FAMILY IS POOR. I'M ONLY HERE BECAUSE OUR EXOTIC TEACHER, MISS L'HARMA, SAVED MY GRANDMA IN THE OLD WAR. NOW MY WHOLE FAMILY IS IN HER DEBT.
MY FAMILY IS POOR, TOO.
I'M HERE THROUGH A FOREIGN EXCHANGE LOTTERY. MY ENTIRE TOWN HAS HIGH HOPES FOR ME, SO I CAN RELATE.
IS THAT WHY YOU TRY SO HARD TO BE DIFFERENT?
I KNOW HOW THAT IS. A LOT OF TIMES I FEEL INVISIBLE AND I DO WHATEVER I CAN TO STAND OUT.
YEAH, I FEEL THE SAME WAY.
HMMM...
Y'KNOW... YOU'RE OKAY FOR A CELEB.
INVISIBILITY?
COOL, EH?
WHEN I HEARD A SHAINLINE WAS COMING, I EXPECTED LIGHTS AND TV CAMERAS.
BUT...
I REMEMBER WHEN WE FIRST MET.
YOU DIDN'T LAUGH AT ME.
HE DIDN'T LAUGH AT ME, EITHER.
AND YOU SHOULD'VE SEEN HOW WE MET. IT WAS VERY EMBARRASSING.
YOU WANNA KNOW WHAT'S EMBARRASSING? MY CHALLENGE TO DARRYL THE ARROW AT THE SCHOOL FESTIVAL.
HAVE YOU SEEN THIS? I'M SCREWED BIG TIME.
MY ONLY HOPE IS THAT ANOTHER CLUB BEATS BOTH OF US. THEN I WON'T HAVE TO LIVE WITH THE HUMILIATION.
THE BULL'S EYE
Festival Event Heating Up
an eye on quality

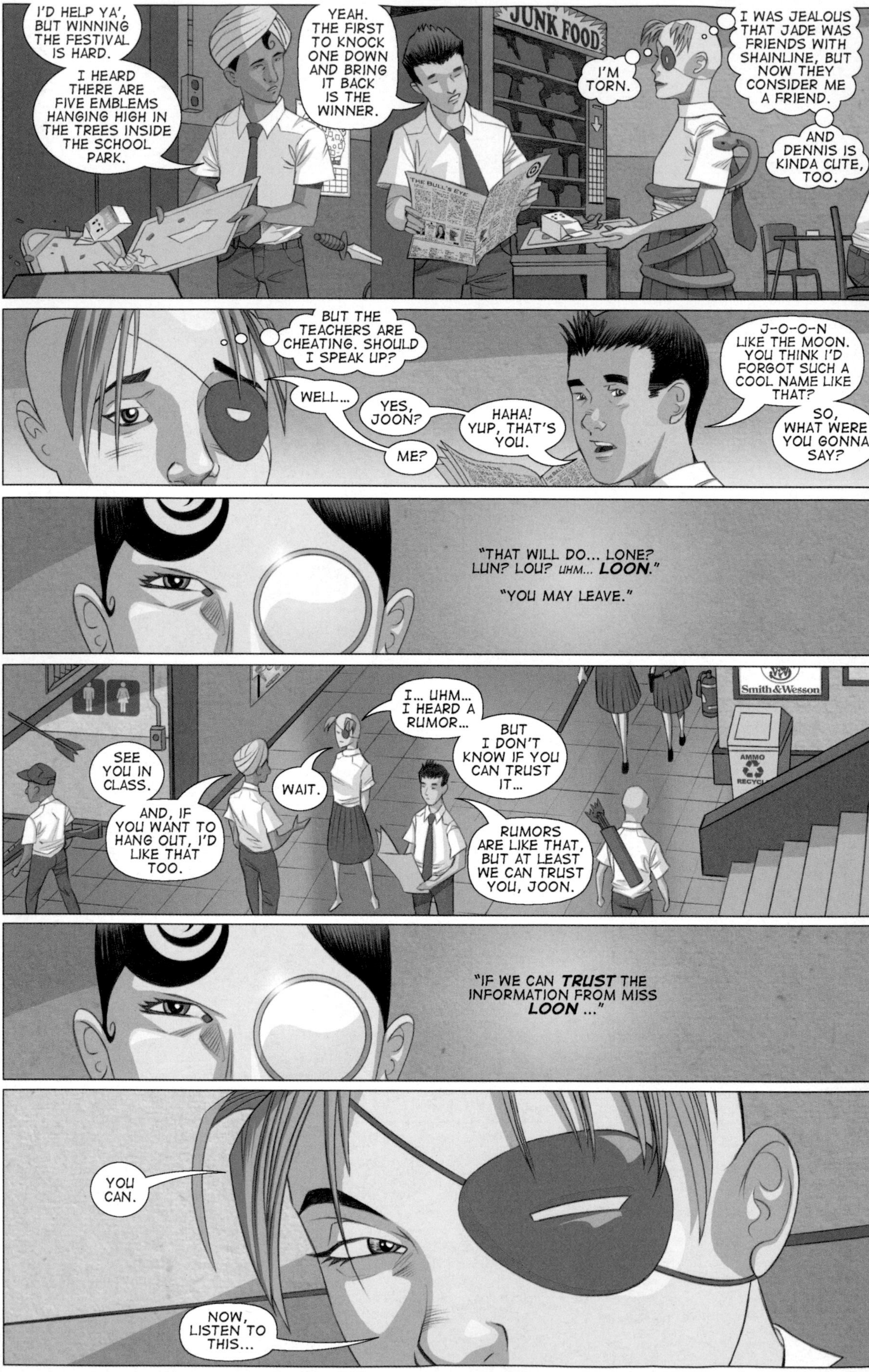
I'D HELP YA', BUT WINNING THE FESTIVAL IS HARD.
I HEARD THERE ARE FIVE EMBLEMS HANGING HIGH IN THE TREES INSIDE THE SCHOOL PARK.
YEAH. THE FIRST TO KNOCK ONE DOWN AND BRING IT BACK IS THE WINNER.
JUNK FOOD
I'M TORN.
I WAS JEALOUS THAT JADE WAS FRIENDS WITH SHAINLINE, BUT NOW THEY CONSIDER ME A FRIEND.
AND DENNIS IS KINDA CUTE, TOO.
THE BULL'S EYE
BUT THE TEACHERS ARE CHEATING. SHOULD I SPEAK UP?
WELL...
YES, JOON?
ME?
HAHA! YUP, THAT'S YOU.
J-O-O-N LIKE THE MOON. YOU THINK I'D FORGOT SUCH A COOL NAME LIKE THAT?
SO, WHAT WERE YOU GONNA SAY?
"THAT WILL DO... LONE? LUN? LOU? UHM... LOON."
"YOU MAY LEAVE."
Smith&Wesson
AMMO RECYCL
SEE YOU IN CLASS.
AND, IF YOU WANT TO HANG OUT, I'D LIKE THAT TOO.
WAIT.
I... UHM... I HEARD A RUMOR...
BUT I DON'T KNOW IF YOU CAN TRUST IT...
RUMORS ARE LIKE THAT, BUT AT LEAST WE CAN TRUST YOU, JOON.
"IF WE CAN TRUST THE INFORMATION FROM MISS LOON ..."
YOU CAN.
NOW, LISTEN TO THIS...

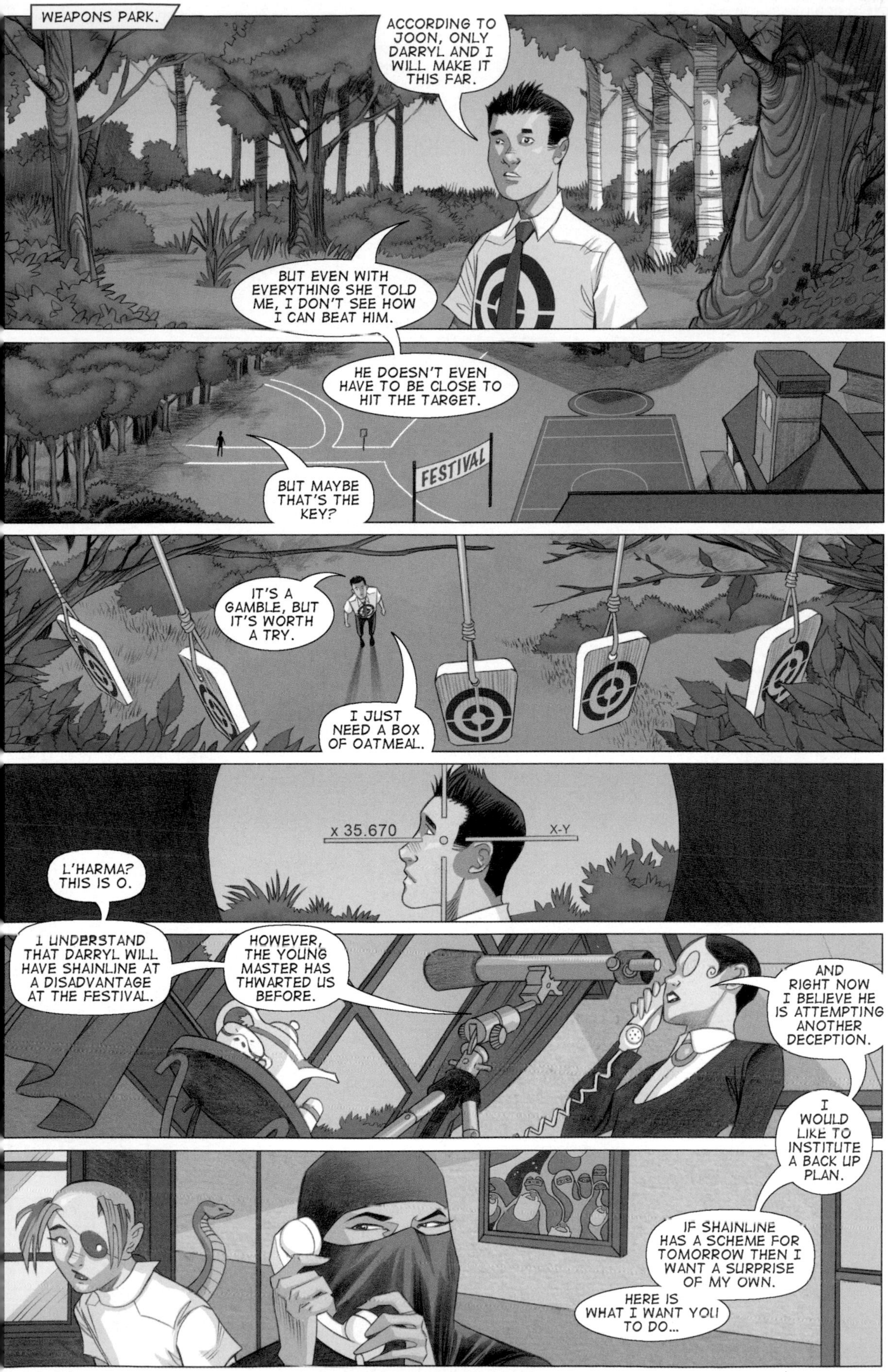
WEAPONS PARK.
ACCORDING TO JOON, ONLY DARRYL AND I WILL MAKE IT THIS FAR.
BUT EVEN WITH EVERYTHING SHE TOLD ME, I DON'T SEE HOW I CAN BEAT HIM.
HE DOESN'T EVEN HAVE TO BE CLOSE TO HIT THE TARGET.
FESTIVAL
BUT MAYBE THAT'S THE KEY?
IT'S A GAMBLE, BUT IT'S WORTH A TRY.
I JUST NEED A BOX OF OATMEAL.
x 35.670
X-Y
L'HARMA? THIS IS O.
I UNDERSTAND THAT DARRYL WILL HAVE SHAINLINE AT A DISADVANTAGE AT THE FESTIVAL.
HOWEVER, THE YOUNG MASTER HAS THWARTED US BEFORE.
AND RIGHT NOW I BELIEVE HE IS ATTEMPTING ANOTHER DECEPTION.
I WOULD LIKE TO INSTITUTE A BACK UP PLAN.
IF SHAINLINE HAS A SCHEME FOR TOMORROW THEN I WANT A SURPRISE OF MY OWN.
HERE IS WHAT I WANT YOU TO DO...

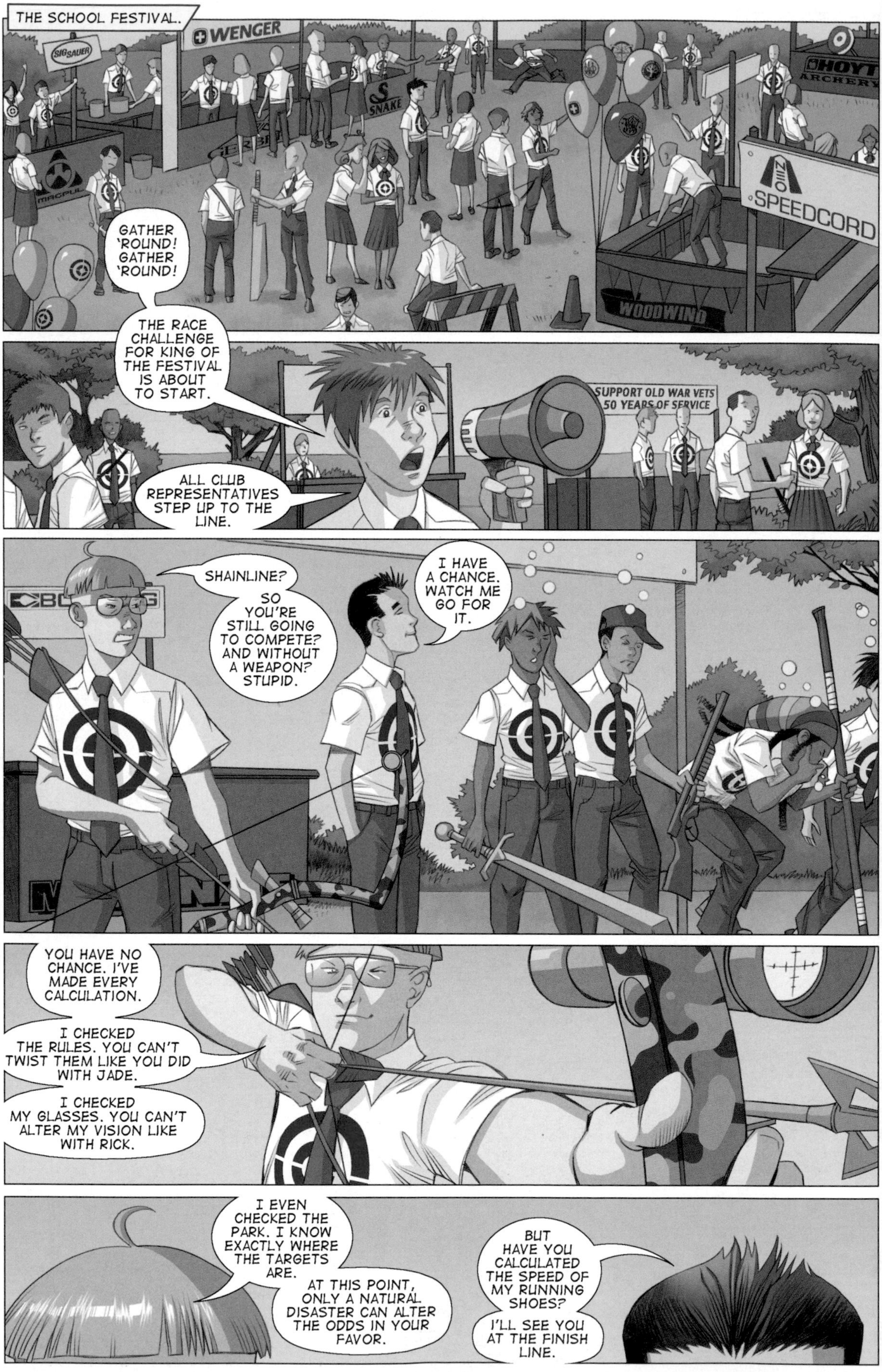
THE SCHOOL FESTIVAL.
SIG SAUER
WENGER
SNAKE
MAGPUL
HOYT
ARCHERY
NEO
SPEEDCORD
WOODWIND
GATHER 'ROUND! GATHER 'ROUND!
THE RACE CHALLENGE FOR KING OF THE FESTIVAL IS ABOUT TO START.
SUPPORT OLD WAR VETS
50 YEARS OF SERVICE
ALL CLUB REPRESENTATIVES STEP UP TO THE LINE.
SHAINLINE?
SO YOU'RE STILL GOING TO COMPETE? AND WITHOUT A WEAPON? STUPID.
I HAVE A CHANCE. WATCH ME GO FOR IT.
YOU HAVE NO CHANCE. I'VE MADE EVERY CALCULATION.
I CHECKED THE RULES. YOU CAN'T TWIST THEM LIKE YOU DID WITH JADE.
I CHECKED MY GLASSES. YOU CAN'T ALTER MY VISION LIKE WITH RICK.
I EVEN CHECKED THE PARK. I KNOW EXACTLY WHERE THE TARGETS ARE.
AT THIS POINT, ONLY A NATURAL DISASTER CAN ALTER THE ODDS IN YOUR FAVOR.
BUT HAVE YOU CALCULATED THE SPEED OF MY RUNNING SHOES?
I'LL SEE YOU AT THE FINISH LINE.

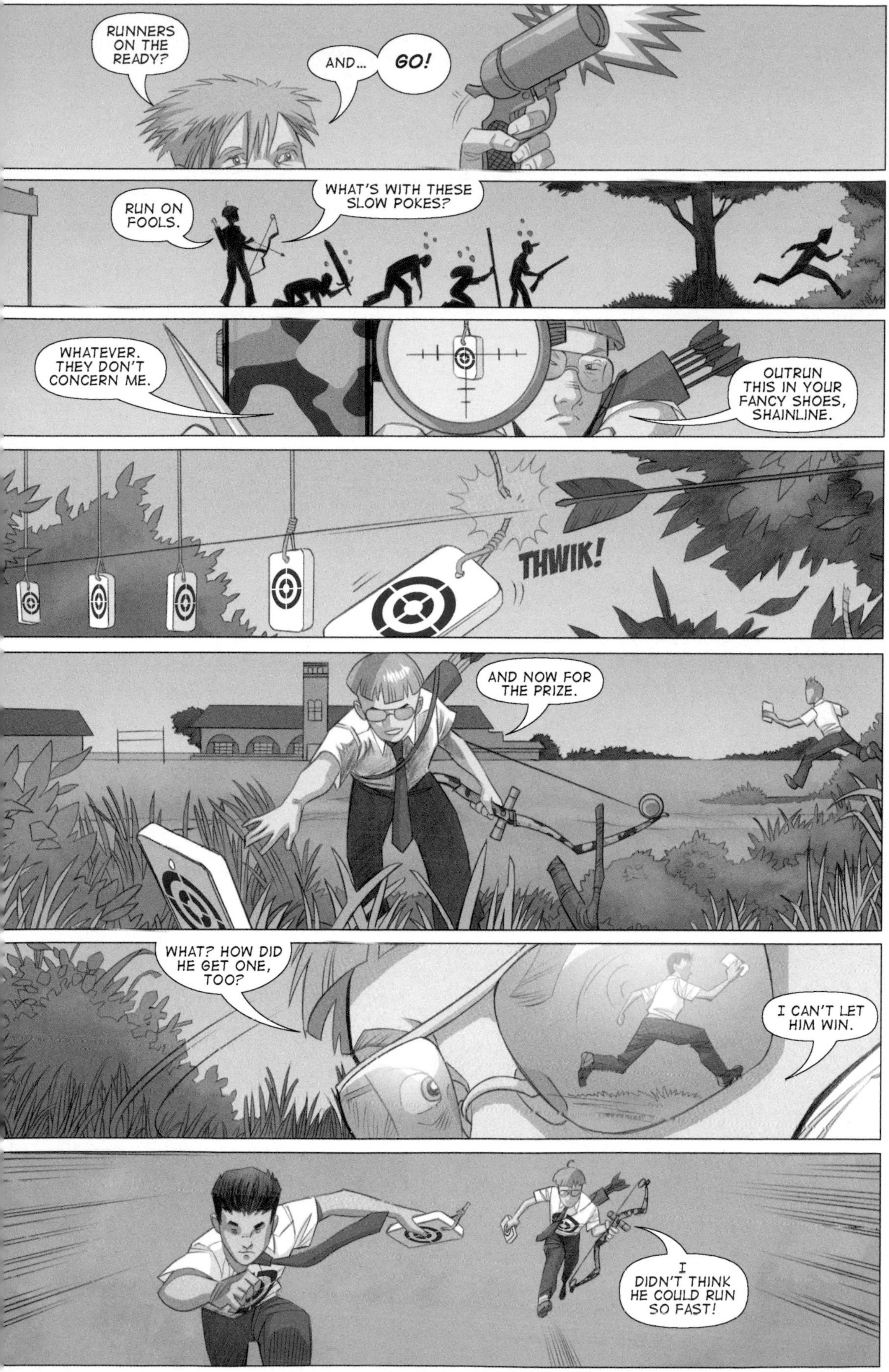
RUNNERS ON THE READY?
AND... GO!
RUN ON FOOLS.
WHAT'S WITH THESE SLOW POKES?
WHATEVER. THEY DON'T CONCERN ME.
OUTRUN THIS IN YOUR FANCY SHOES, SHAINLINE.
THWIK!
AND NOW FOR THE PRIZE.
WHAT? HOW DID HE GET ONE, TOO?
I CAN'T LET HIM WIN.
I DIDN'T THINK HE COULD RUN SO FAST!

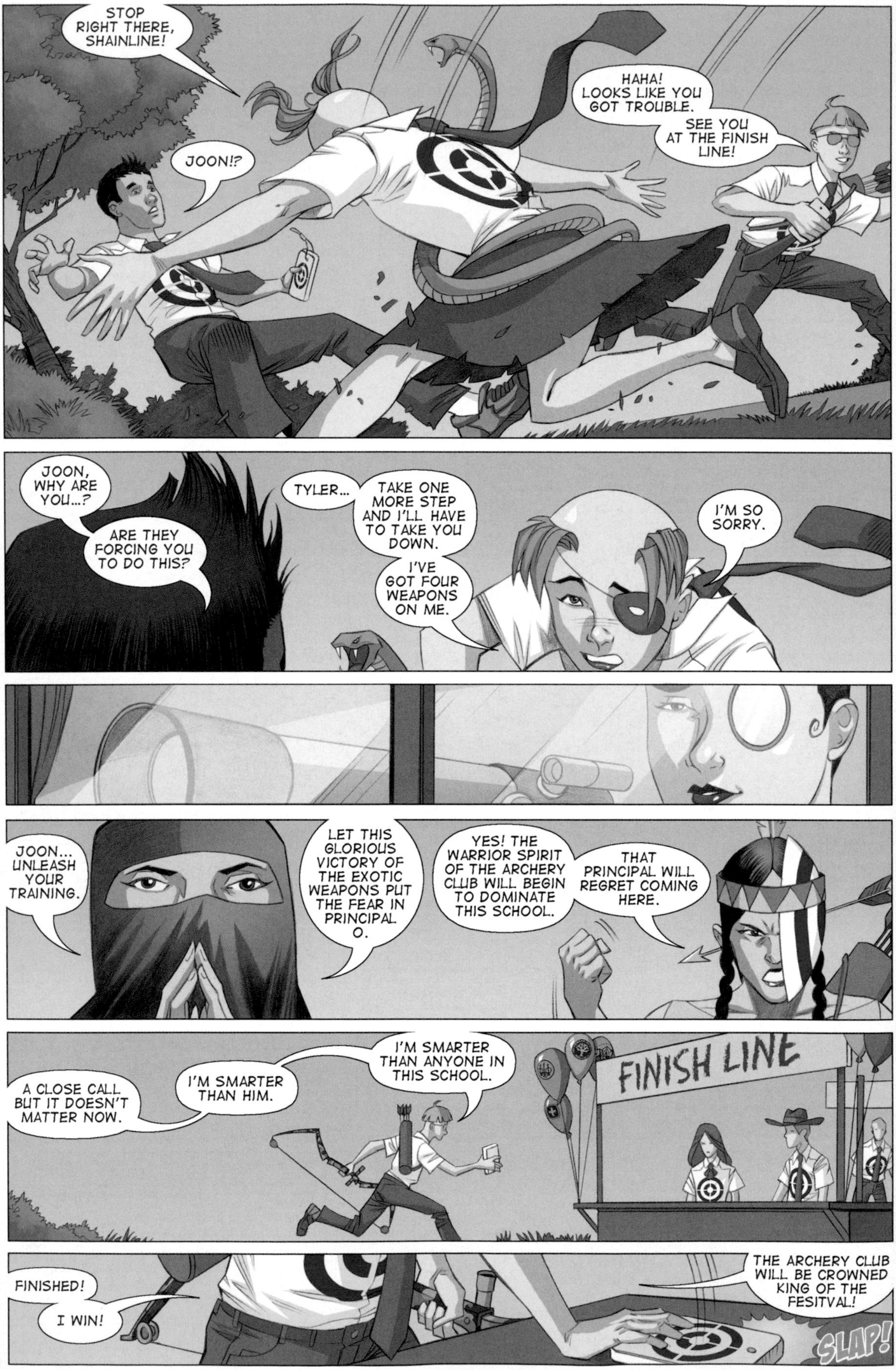
STOP RIGHT THERE, SHAINLINE!
JOON!?
HAHA! LOOKS LIKE YOU GOT TROUBLE.
SEE YOU AT THE FINISH LINE!
JOON, WHY ARE YOU...?
ARE THEY FORCING YOU TO DO THIS?
TYLER...
TAKE ONE MORE STEP AND I'LL HAVE TO TAKE YOU DOWN.
I'VE GOT FOUR WEAPONS ON ME.
I'M SO SORRY.
JOON... UNLEASH YOUR TRAINING.
LET THIS GLORIOUS VICTORY OF THE EXOTIC WEAPONS PUT THE FEAR IN PRINCIPAL O.
YES! THE WARRIOR SPIRIT OF THE ARCHERY CLUB WILL BEGIN TO DOMINATE THIS SCHOOL.
THAT PRINCIPAL WILL REGRET COMING HERE.
A CLOSE CALL BUT IT DOESN'T MATTER NOW.
I'M SMARTER THAN HIM.
I'M SMARTER THAN ANYONE IN THIS SCHOOL.
FINISH LINE
FINISHED!
I WIN!
THE ARCHERY CLUB WILL BE CROWNED KING OF THE FESITVAL!
SLAP!

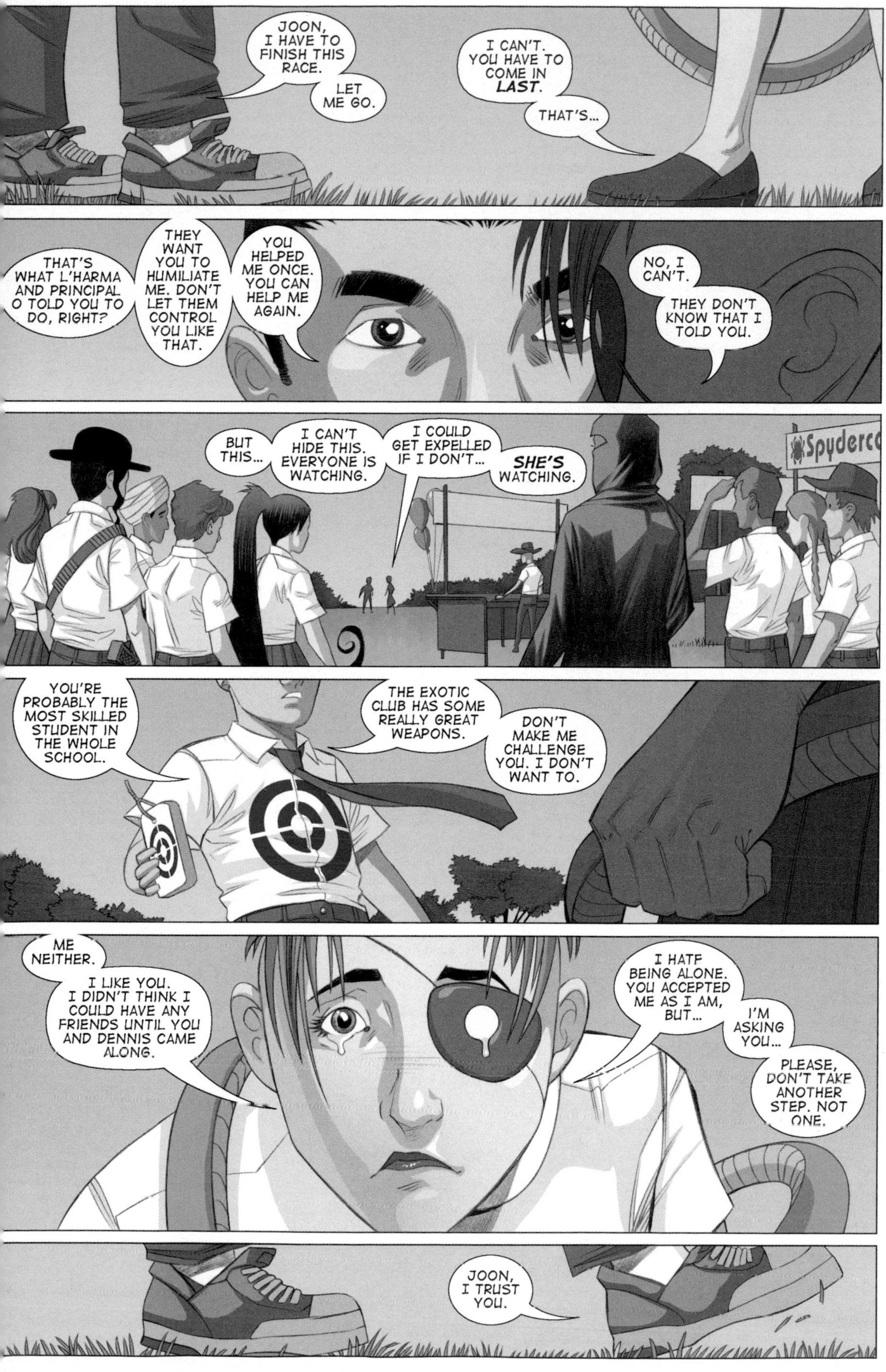

JOON, I HAVE TO FINISH THIS RACE.
LET ME GO.
I CAN'T. YOU HAVE TO COME IN LAST.
THAT'S...
THAT'S WHAT L'HARMA AND PRINCIPAL O TOLD YOU TO DO, RIGHT?
THEY WANT YOU TO HUMILIATE ME. DON'T LET THEM CONTROL YOU LIKE THAT.
YOU HELPED ME ONCE. YOU CAN HELP ME AGAIN.
NO, I CAN'T.
THEY DON'T KNOW THAT I TOLD YOU.
BUT THIS...
I CAN'T HIDE THIS. EVERYONE IS WATCHING.
I COULD GET EXPELLED IF I DON'T...
SHE'S WATCHING.
Spyderco
YOU'RE PROBABLY THE MOST SKILLED STUDENT IN THE WHOLE SCHOOL.
THE EXOTIC CLUB HAS SOME REALLY GREAT WEAPONS.
DON'T MAKE ME CHALLENGE YOU. I DON'T WANT TO.
ME NEITHER.
I LIKE YOU. I DIDN'T THINK I COULD HAVE ANY FRIENDS UNTIL YOU AND DENNIS CAME ALONG.
I HATE BEING ALONE. YOU ACCEPTED ME AS I AM, BUT...
I'M ASKING YOU...
PLEASE, DON'T TAKE ANOTHER STEP. NOT ONE.
JOON, I TRUST YOU.

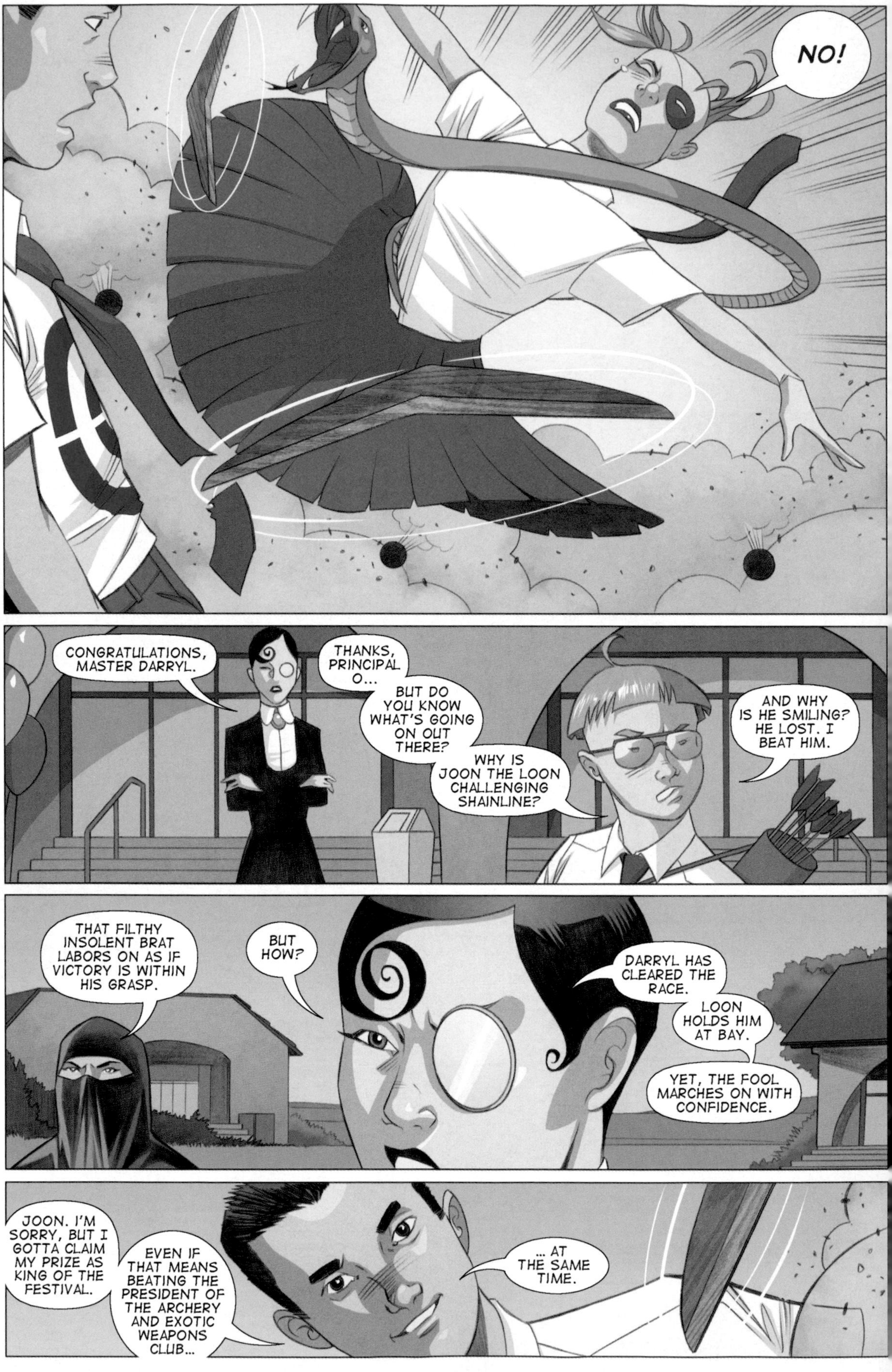
NO!
CONGRATULATIONS, MASTER DARRYL.
THANKS, PRINCIPAL O...
BUT DO YOU KNOW WHAT'S GOING ON OUT THERE?
WHY IS JOON THE LOON CHALLENGING SHAINLINE?
AND WHY IS HE SMILING? HE LOST. I BEAT HIM.
THAT FILTHY INSOLENT BRAT LABORS ON AS IF VICTORY IS WITHIN HIS GRASP.
BUT HOW?
DARRYL HAS CLEARED THE RACE.
LOON HOLDS HIM AT BAY.
YET, THE FOOL MARCHES ON WITH CONFIDENCE.
JOON. I'M SORRY, BUT I GOTTA CLAIM MY PRIZE AS KING OF THE FESTIVAL.
EVEN IF THAT MEANS BEATING THE PRESIDENT OF THE ARCHERY AND EXOTIC WEAPONS CLUB...
... AT THE SAME TIME.

BOOK FOUR
NAT THE GAT

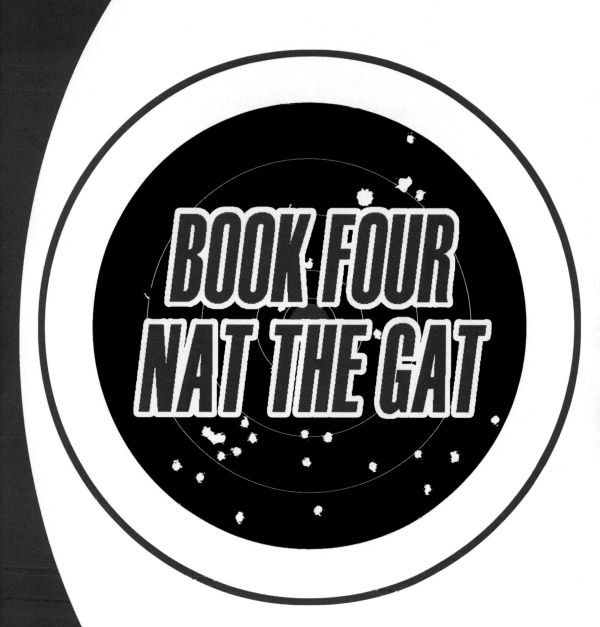

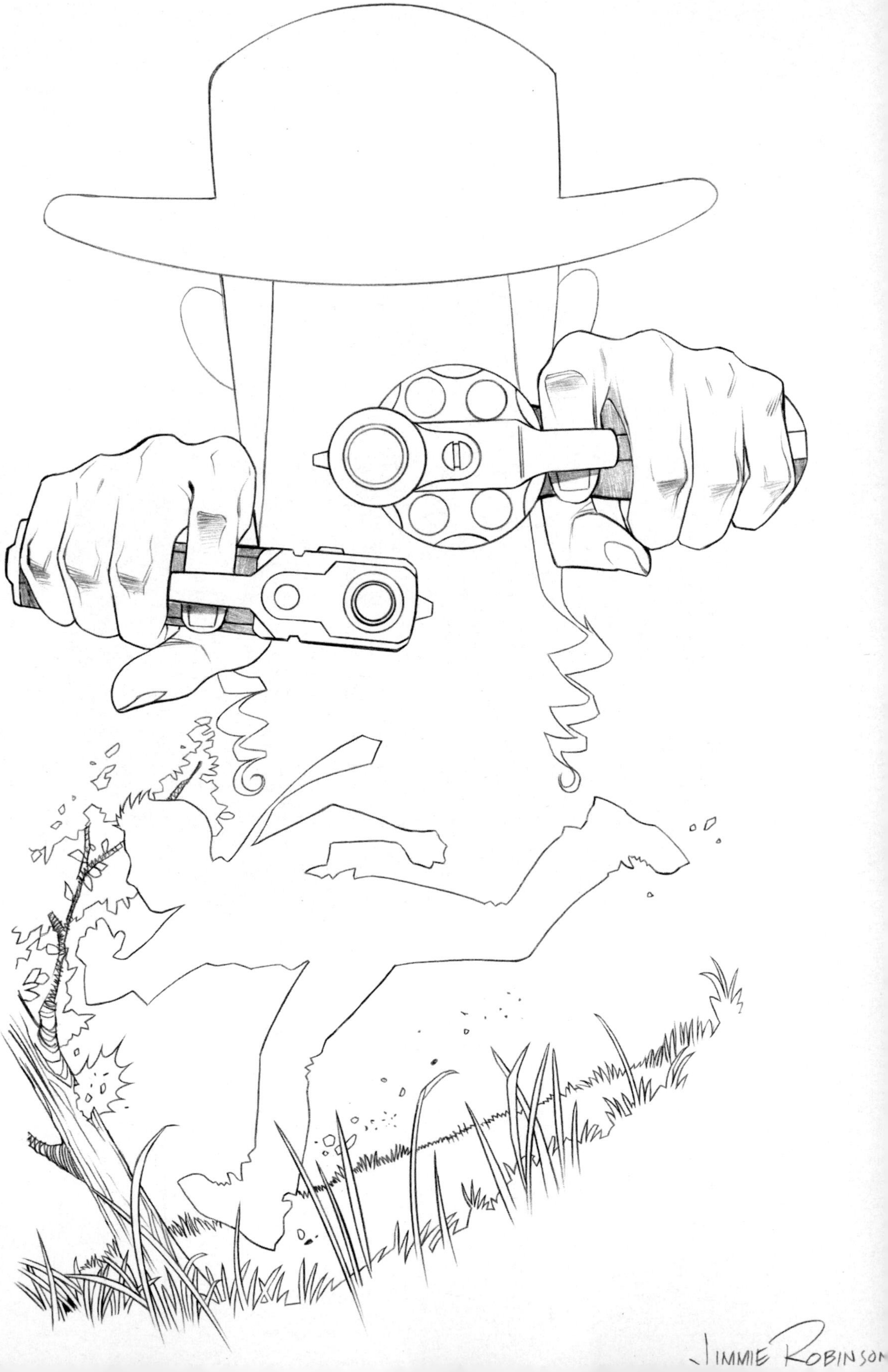
JIMMIE ROBINSON

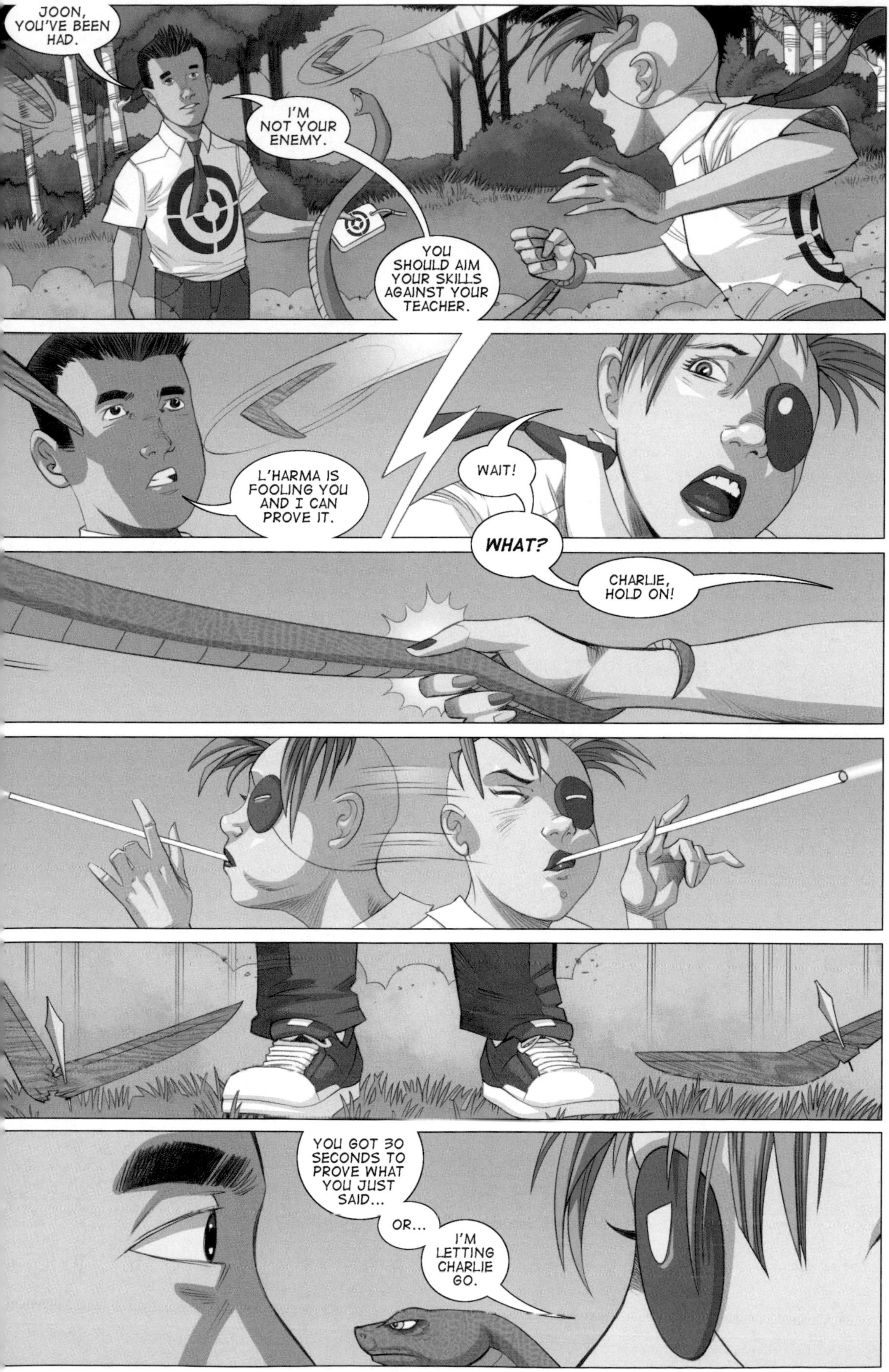
JOON, YOU'VE BEEN HAD.
I'M NOT YOUR ENEMY.
YOU SHOULD AIM YOUR SKILLS AGAINST YOUR TEACHER.
L'HARMA IS FOOLING YOU AND I CAN PROVE IT.
WAIT!
WHAT?
CHARLIE, HOLD ON!
YOU GOT 30 SECONDS TO PROVE WHAT YOU JUST SAID...
OR...
I'M LETTING CHARLIE GO.

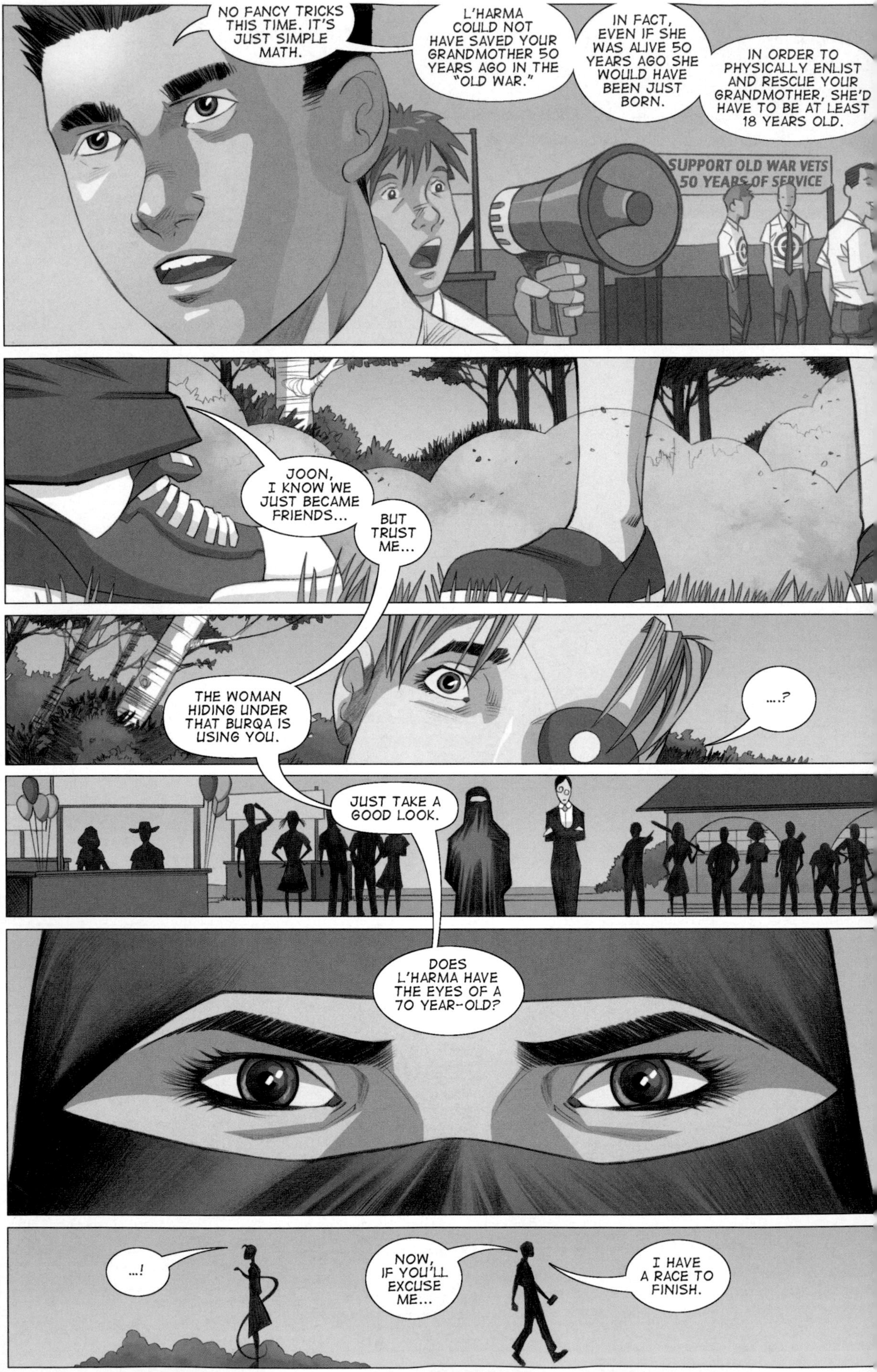
NO FANCY TRICKS THIS TIME. IT'S JUST SIMPLE MATH.
L'HARMA COULD NOT HAVE SAVED YOUR GRANDMOTHER 50 YEARS AGO IN THE "OLD WAR."
IN FACT, EVEN IF SHE WAS ALIVE 50 YEARS AGO SHE WOULD HAVE BEEN JUST BORN.
IN ORDER TO PHYSICALLY ENLIST AND RESCUE YOUR GRANDMOTHER, SHE'D HAVE TO BE AT LEAST 18 YEARS OLD.
SUPPORT OLD WAR VETS 50 YEARS OF SERVICE
JOON, I KNOW WE JUST BECAME FRIENDS...
BUT TRUST ME...
THE WOMAN HIDING UNDER THAT BURQA IS USING YOU.
....?
JUST TAKE A GOOD LOOK.
DOES L'HARMA HAVE THE EYES OF A 70 YEAR-OLD?
...!
NOW, IF YOU'LL EXCUSE ME...
I HAVE A RACE TO FINISH.

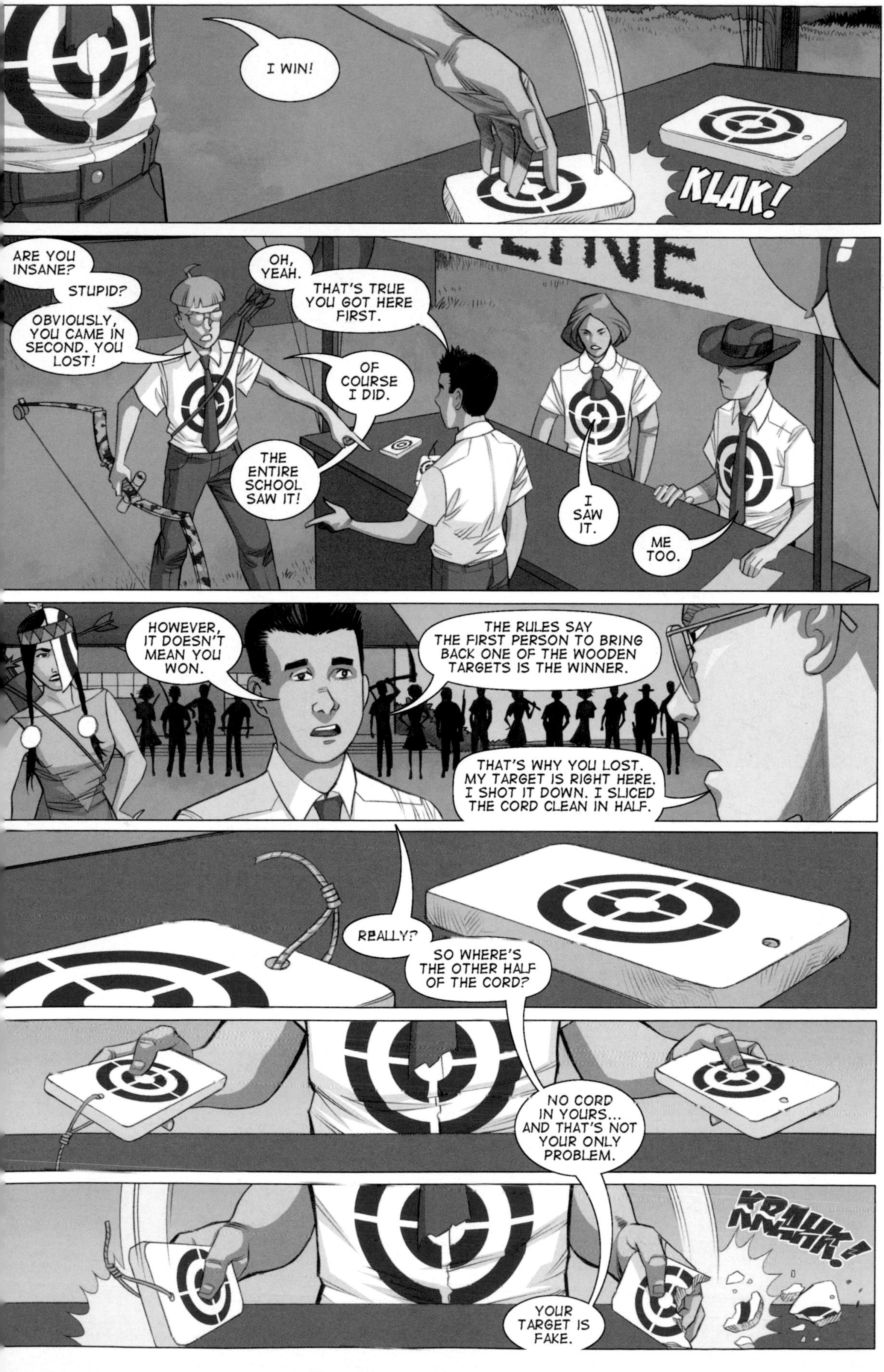
I WIN!
KLAK!
ARE YOU INSANE?
STUPID?
OBVIOUSLY, YOU CAME IN SECOND. YOU LOST!
OH, YEAH.
THAT'S TRUE YOU GOT HERE FIRST.
OF COURSE I DID.
THE ENTIRE SCHOOL SAW IT!
I SAW IT.
ME TOO.
HOWEVER, IT DOESN'T MEAN YOU WON.
THE RULES SAY THE FIRST PERSON TO BRING BACK ONE OF THE WOODEN TARGETS IS THE WINNER.
THAT'S WHY YOU LOST. MY TARGET IS RIGHT HERE. I SHOT IT DOWN. I SLICED THE CORD CLEAN IN HALF.
REALLY?
SO WHERE'S THE OTHER HALF OF THE CORD?
NO CORD IN YOURS... AND THAT'S NOT YOUR ONLY PROBLEM.
KRAUK!
YOUR TARGET IS FAKE.

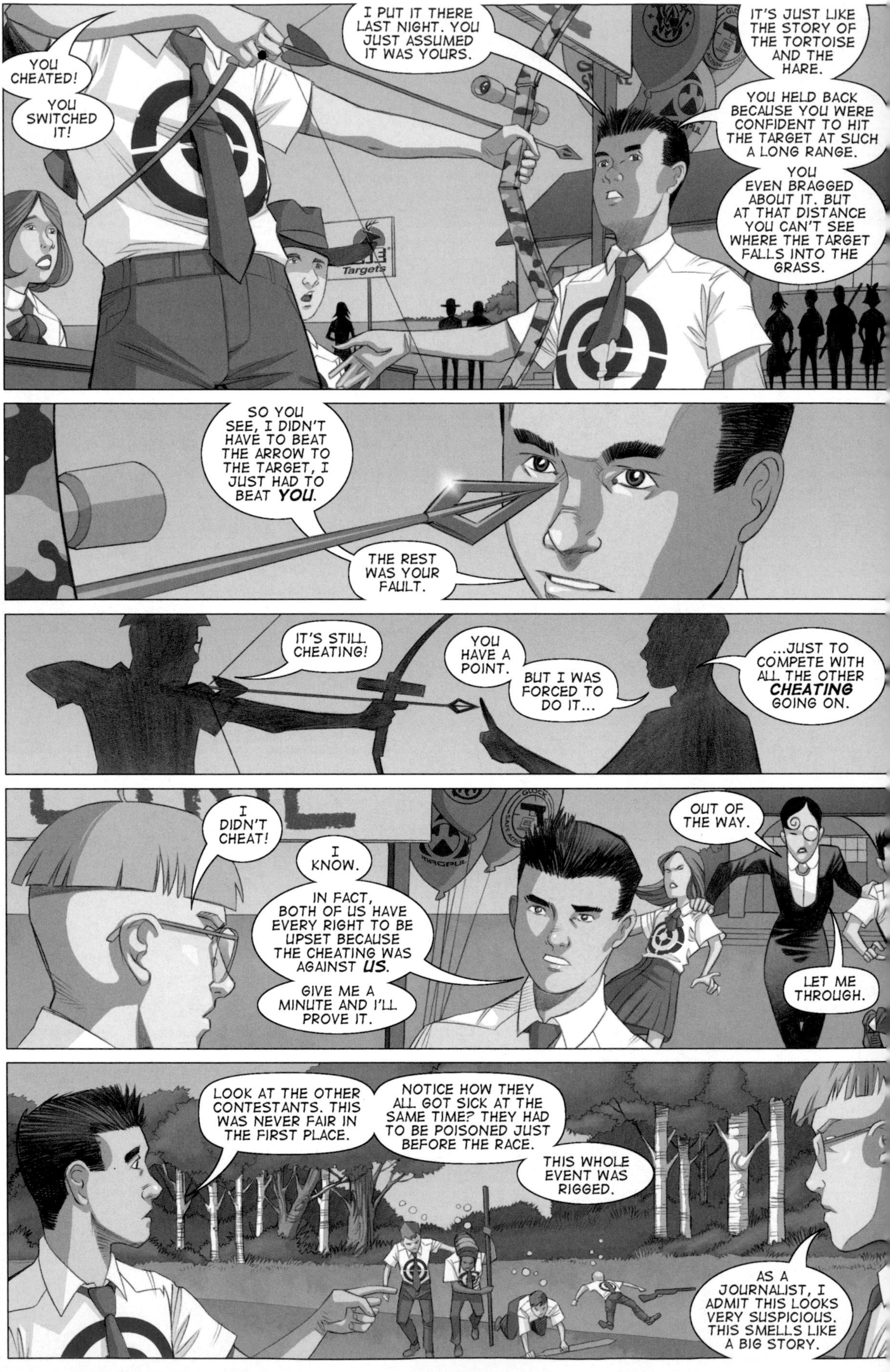
YOU CHEATED!
YOU SWITCHED IT!
I PUT IT THERE LAST NIGHT. YOU JUST ASSUMED IT WAS YOURS.
IT'S JUST LIKE THE STORY OF THE TORTOISE AND THE HARE.
YOU HELD BACK BECAUSE YOU WERE CONFIDENT TO HIT THE TARGET AT SUCH A LONG RANGE.
YOU EVEN BRAGGED ABOUT IT. BUT AT THAT DISTANCE YOU CAN'T SEE WHERE THE TARGET FALLS INTO THE GRASS.
Targets
SO YOU SEE, I DIDN'T HAVE TO BEAT THE ARROW TO THE TARGET, I JUST HAD TO BEAT YOU.
THE REST WAS YOUR FAULT.
IT'S STILL CHEATING!
YOU HAVE A POINT.
BUT I WAS FORCED TO DO IT...
...JUST TO COMPETE WITH ALL THE OTHER CHEATING GOING ON.
I DIDN'T CHEAT!
I KNOW.
IN FACT, BOTH OF US HAVE EVERY RIGHT TO BE UPSET BECAUSE THE CHEATING WAS AGAINST US.
GIVE ME A MINUTE AND I'LL PROVE IT.
OUT OF THE WAY.
LET ME THROUGH.
LOOK AT THE OTHER CONTESTANTS. THIS WAS NEVER FAIR IN THE FIRST PLACE.
NOTICE HOW THEY ALL GOT SICK AT THE SAME TIME? THEY HAD TO BE POISONED JUST BEFORE THE RACE.
THIS WHOLE EVENT WAS RIGGED.
AS A JOURNALIST, I ADMIT THIS LOOKS VERY SUSPICIOUS. THIS SMELLS LIKE A BIG STORY.

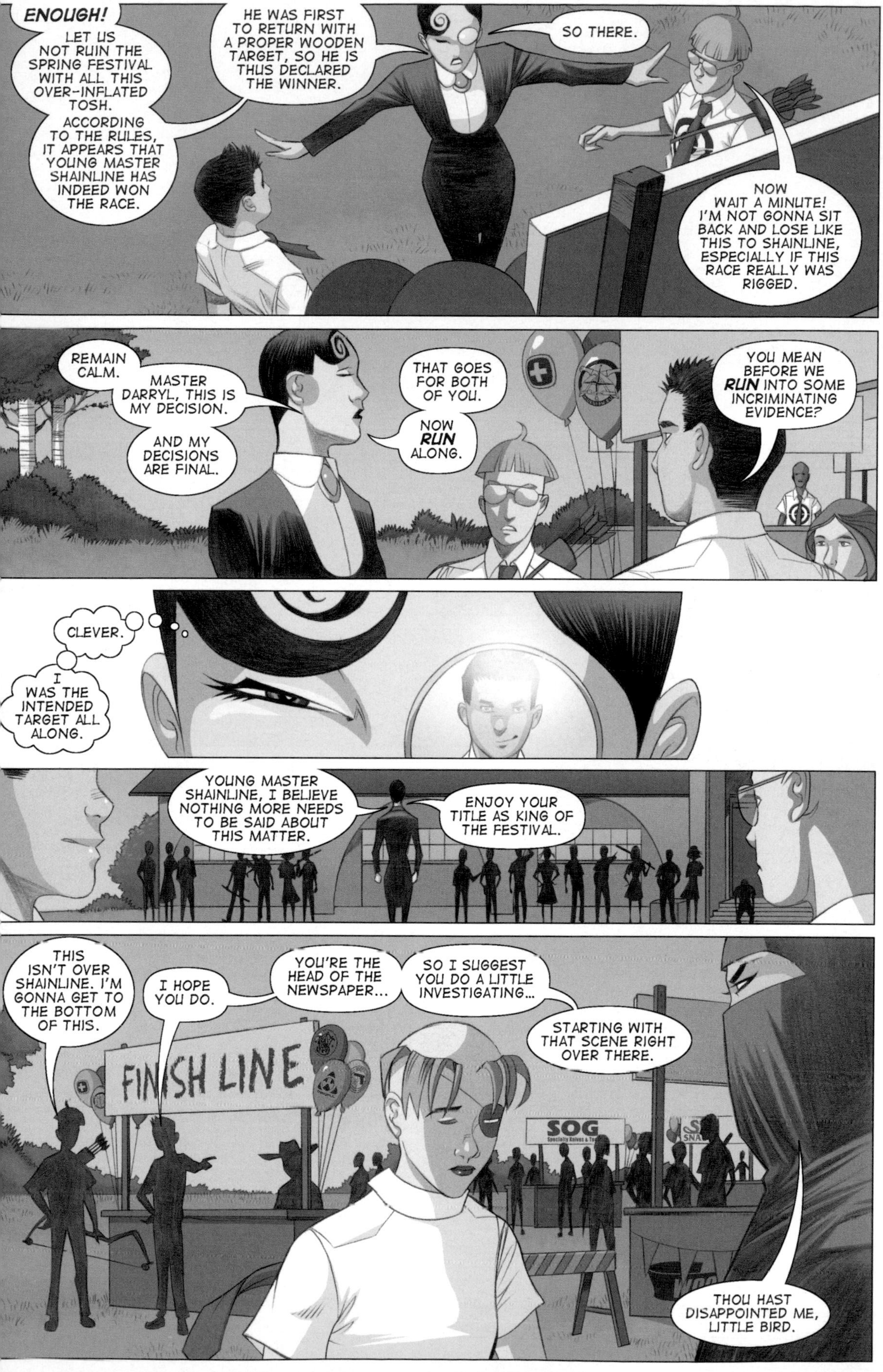
ENOUGH!
LET US NOT RUIN THE SPRING FESTIVAL WITH ALL THIS OVER-INFLATED TOSH.
ACCORDING TO THE RULES, IT APPEARS THAT YOUNG MASTER SHAINLINE HAS INDEED WON THE RACE.
HE WAS FIRST TO RETURN WITH A PROPER WOODEN TARGET, SO HE IS THUS DECLARED THE WINNER.
SO THERE.
NOW WAIT A MINUTE! I'M NOT GONNA SIT BACK AND LOSE LIKE THIS TO SHAINLINE, ESPECIALLY IF THIS RACE REALLY WAS RIGGED.
REMAIN CALM.
MASTER DARRYL, THIS IS MY DECISION.
AND MY DECISIONS ARE FINAL.
THAT GOES FOR BOTH OF YOU.
NOW RUN ALONG.
YOU MEAN BEFORE WE RUN INTO SOME INCRIMINATING EVIDENCE?
CLEVER.
I WAS THE INTENDED TARGET ALL ALONG.
YOUNG MASTER SHAINLINE, I BELIEVE NOTHING MORE NEEDS TO BE SAID ABOUT THIS MATTER.
ENJOY YOUR TITLE AS KING OF THE FESTIVAL.
THIS ISN'T OVER SHAINLINE. I'M GONNA GET TO THE BOTTOM OF THIS.
I HOPE YOU DO.
YOU'RE THE HEAD OF THE NEWSPAPER...
SO I SUGGEST YOU DO A LITTLE INVESTIGATING...
STARTING WITH THAT SCENE RIGHT OVER THERE.
FINISH LINE
SOG
THOU HAST DISAPPOINTED ME, LITTLE BIRD.

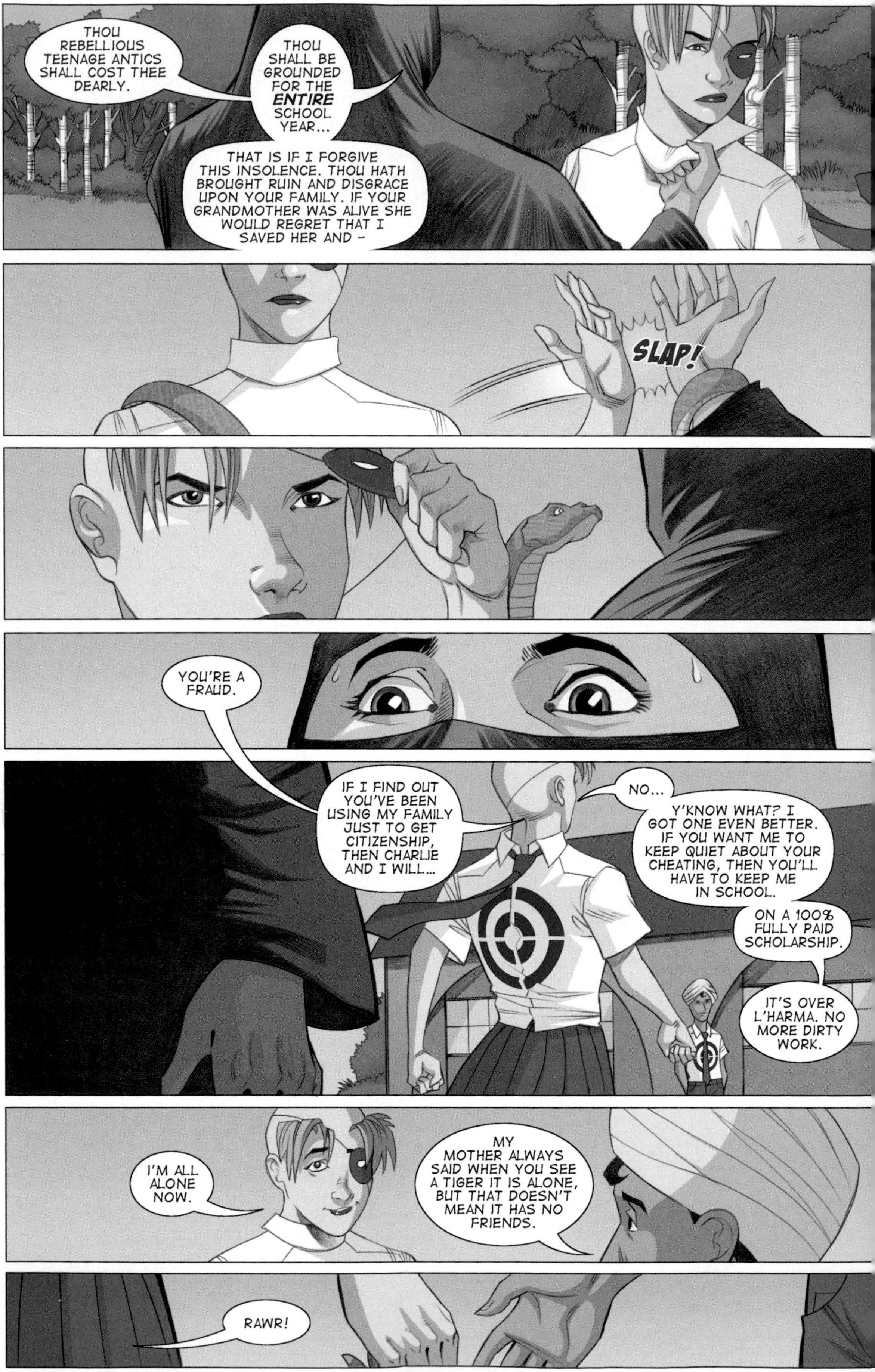
THOU REBELLIOUS TEENAGE ANTICS SHALL COST THEE DEARLY.
THOU SHALL BE GROUNDED FOR THE ENTIRE SCHOOL YEAR...
THAT IS IF I FORGIVE THIS INSOLENCE. THOU HATH BROUGHT RUIN AND DISGRACE UPON YOUR FAMILY. IF YOUR GRANDMOTHER WAS ALIVE SHE WOULD REGRET THAT I SAVED HER AND -
SLAP!
YOU'RE A FRAUD.
IF I FIND OUT YOU'VE BEEN USING MY FAMILY JUST TO GET CITIZENSHIP, THEN CHARLIE AND I WILL...
NO...
Y'KNOW WHAT? I GOT ONE EVEN BETTER. IF YOU WANT ME TO KEEP QUIET ABOUT YOUR CHEATING, THEN YOU'LL HAVE TO KEEP ME IN SCHOOL.
ON A 100% FULLY PAID SCHOLARSHIP.
IT'S OVER L'HARMA. NO MORE DIRTY WORK.
I'M ALL ALONE NOW.
MY MOTHER ALWAYS SAID WHEN YOU SEE A TIGER IT IS ALONE, BUT THAT DOESN'T MEAN IT HAS NO FRIENDS.
RAWR!

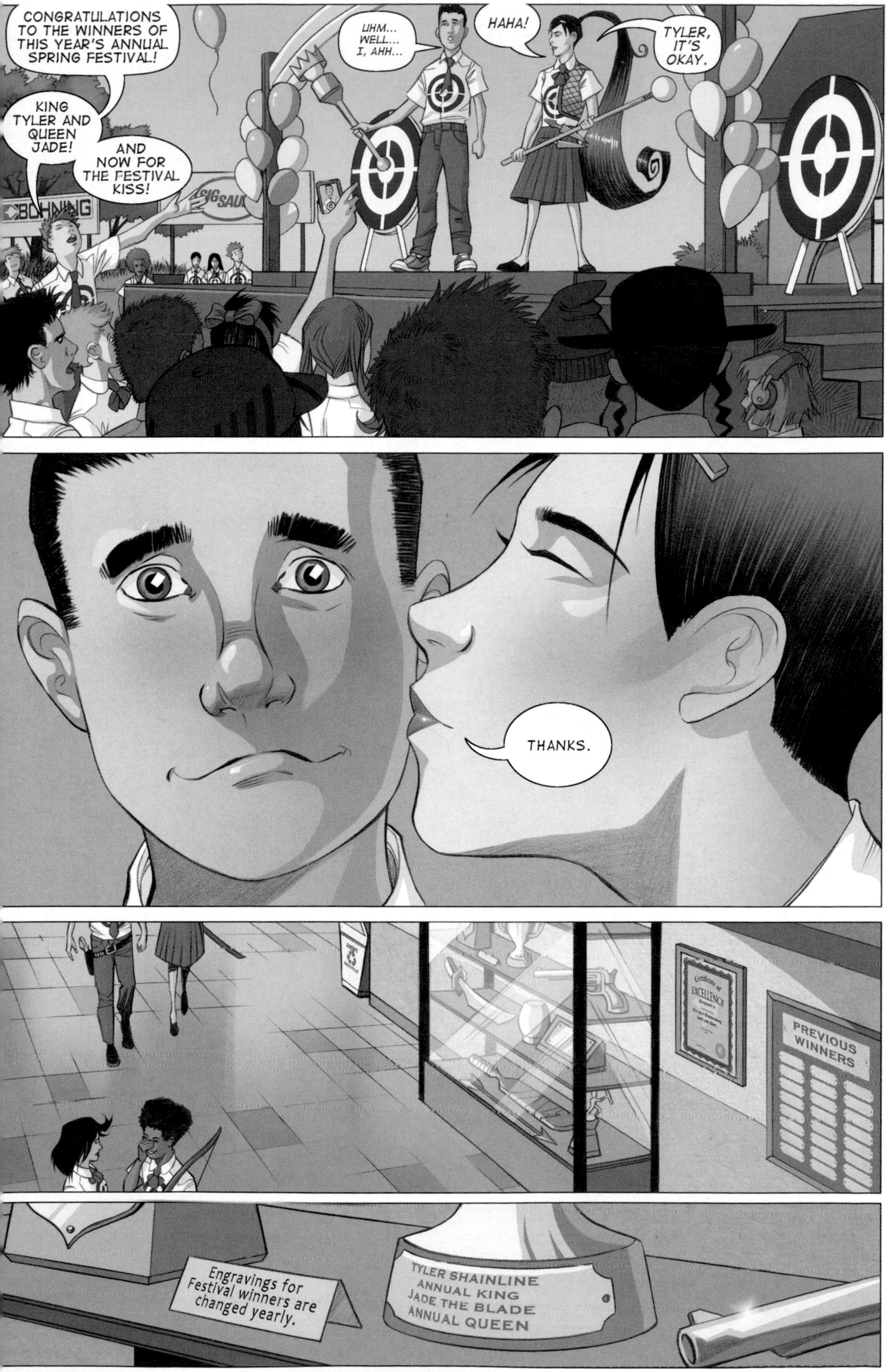
CONGRATULATIONS TO THE WINNERS OF THIS YEAR'S ANNUAL SPRING FESTIVAL!
KING TYLER AND QUEEN JADE!
AND NOW FOR THE FESTIVAL KISS!
UHM... WELL... I, AHH...
HAHA!
TYLER, IT'S OKAY.
BOHNING
THANKS.
Certificate of EXCELLENCE
PREVIOUS WINNERS
Engravings for Festival winners are changed yearly.
TYLER SHAINLINE
ANNUAL KING
JADE THE BLADE
ANNUAL QUEEN

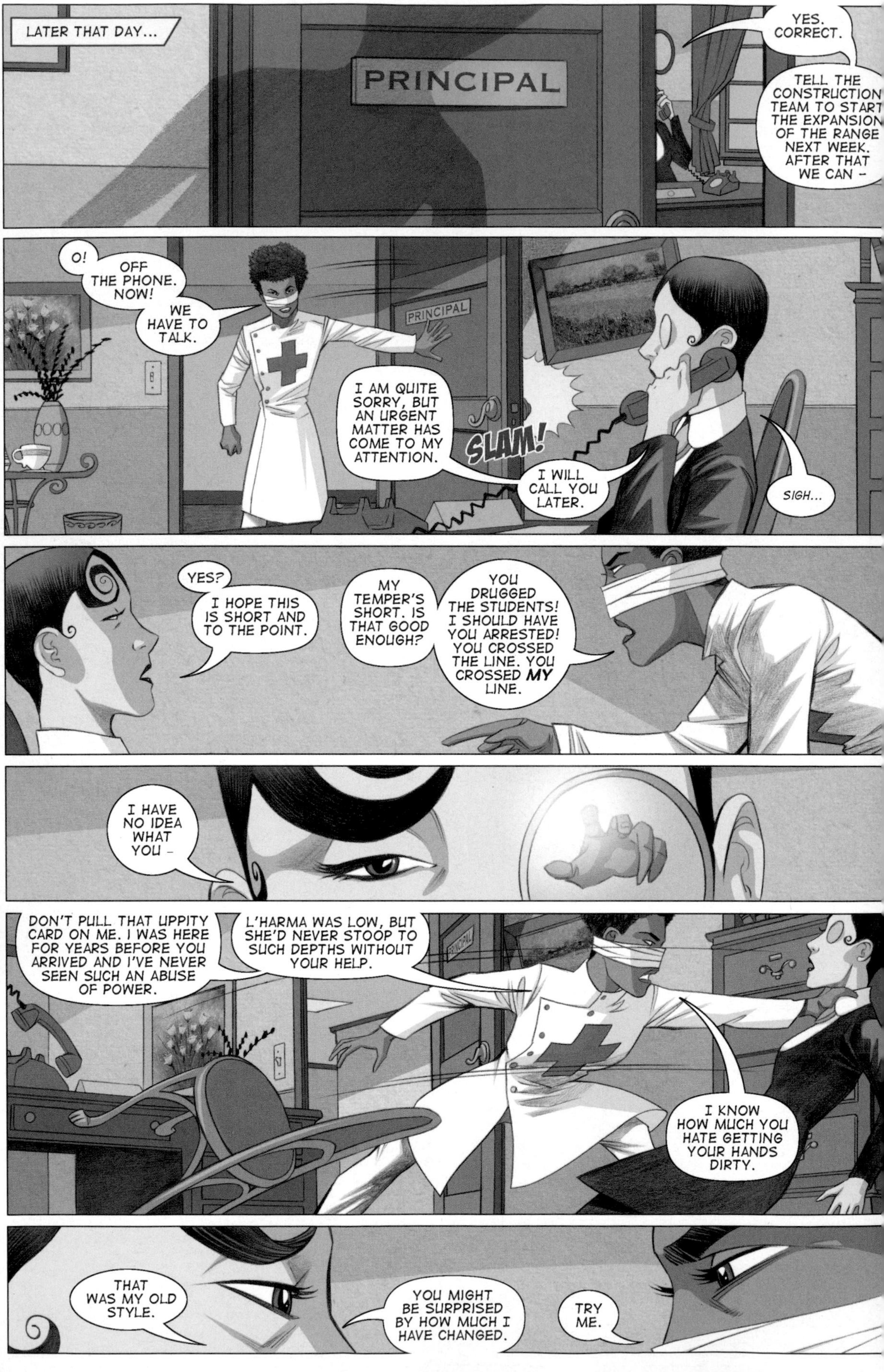
LATER THAT DAY...
PRINCIPAL
YES. CORRECT.
TELL THE CONSTRUCTION TEAM TO START THE EXPANSION OF THE RANGE NEXT WEEK. AFTER THAT WE CAN -
O!
OFF THE PHONE. NOW!
WE HAVE TO TALK.
PRINCIPAL
I AM QUITE SORRY, BUT AN URGENT MATTER HAS COME TO MY ATTENTION.
SLAM!
I WILL CALL YOU LATER.
SIGH...
YES?
I HOPE THIS IS SHORT AND TO THE POINT.
MY TEMPER'S SHORT. IS THAT GOOD ENOUGH?
YOU DRUGGED THE STUDENTS! I SHOULD HAVE YOU ARRESTED! YOU CROSSED THE LINE. YOU CROSSED MY LINE.
I HAVE NO IDEA WHAT YOU -
DON'T PULL THAT UPPITY CARD ON ME. I WAS HERE FOR YEARS BEFORE YOU ARRIVED AND I'VE NEVER SEEN SUCH AN ABUSE OF POWER.
L'HARMA WAS LOW, BUT SHE'D NEVER STOOP TO SUCH DEPTHS WITHOUT YOUR HELP.
I KNOW HOW MUCH YOU HATE GETTING YOUR HANDS DIRTY.
THAT WAS MY OLD STYLE.
YOU MIGHT BE SURPRISED BY HOW MUCH I HAVE CHANGED.
TRY ME.

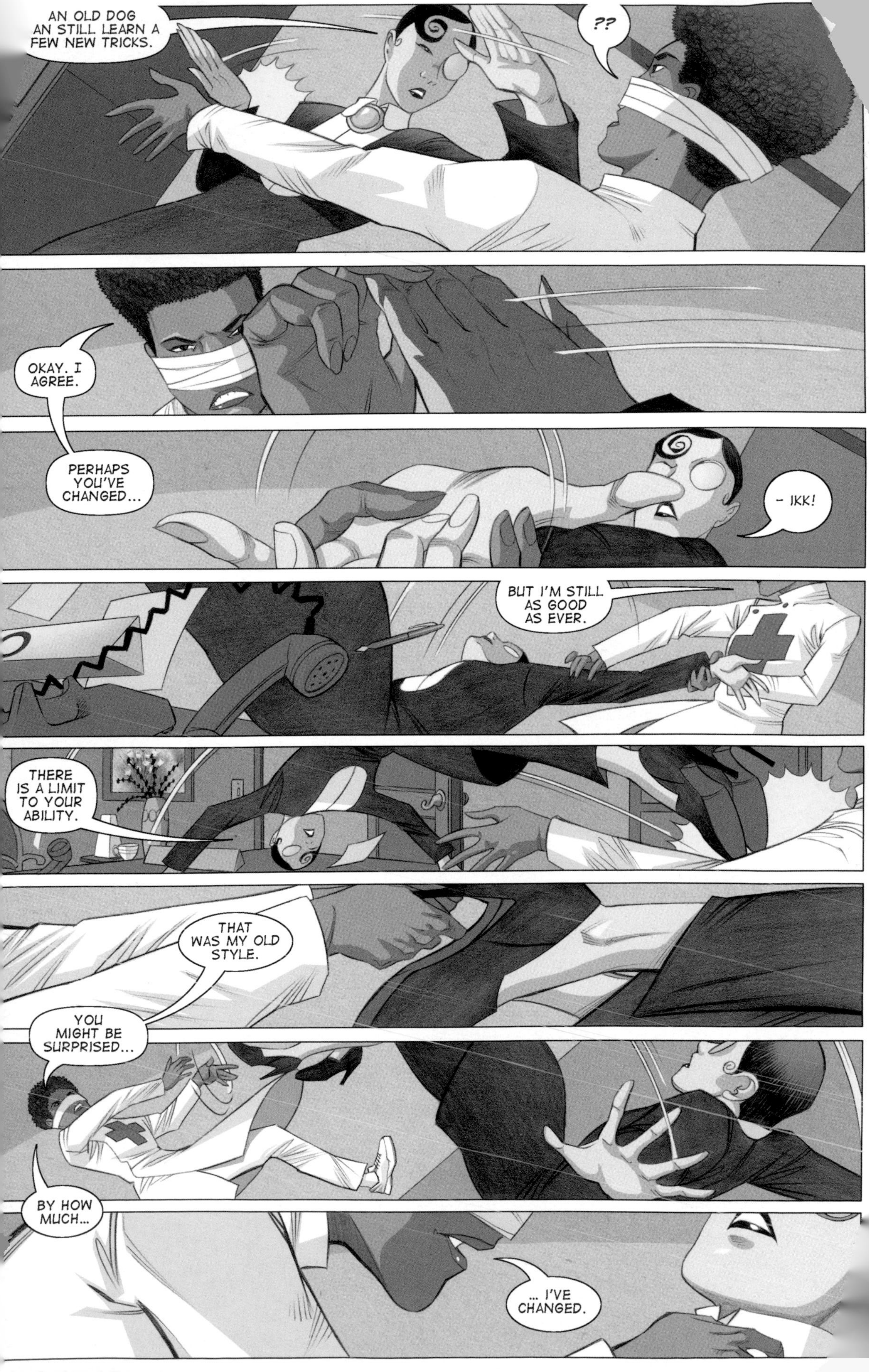
AN OLD DOG AN STILL LEARN A FEW NEW TRICKS.
??
OKAY. I AGREE.
PERHAPS YOU'VE CHANGED...
– IKK!
BUT I'M STILL AS GOOD AS EVER.
THERE IS A LIMIT TO YOUR ABILITY.
THAT WAS MY OLD STYLE.
YOU MIGHT BE SURPRISED...
BY HOW MUCH...
... I'VE CHANGED.

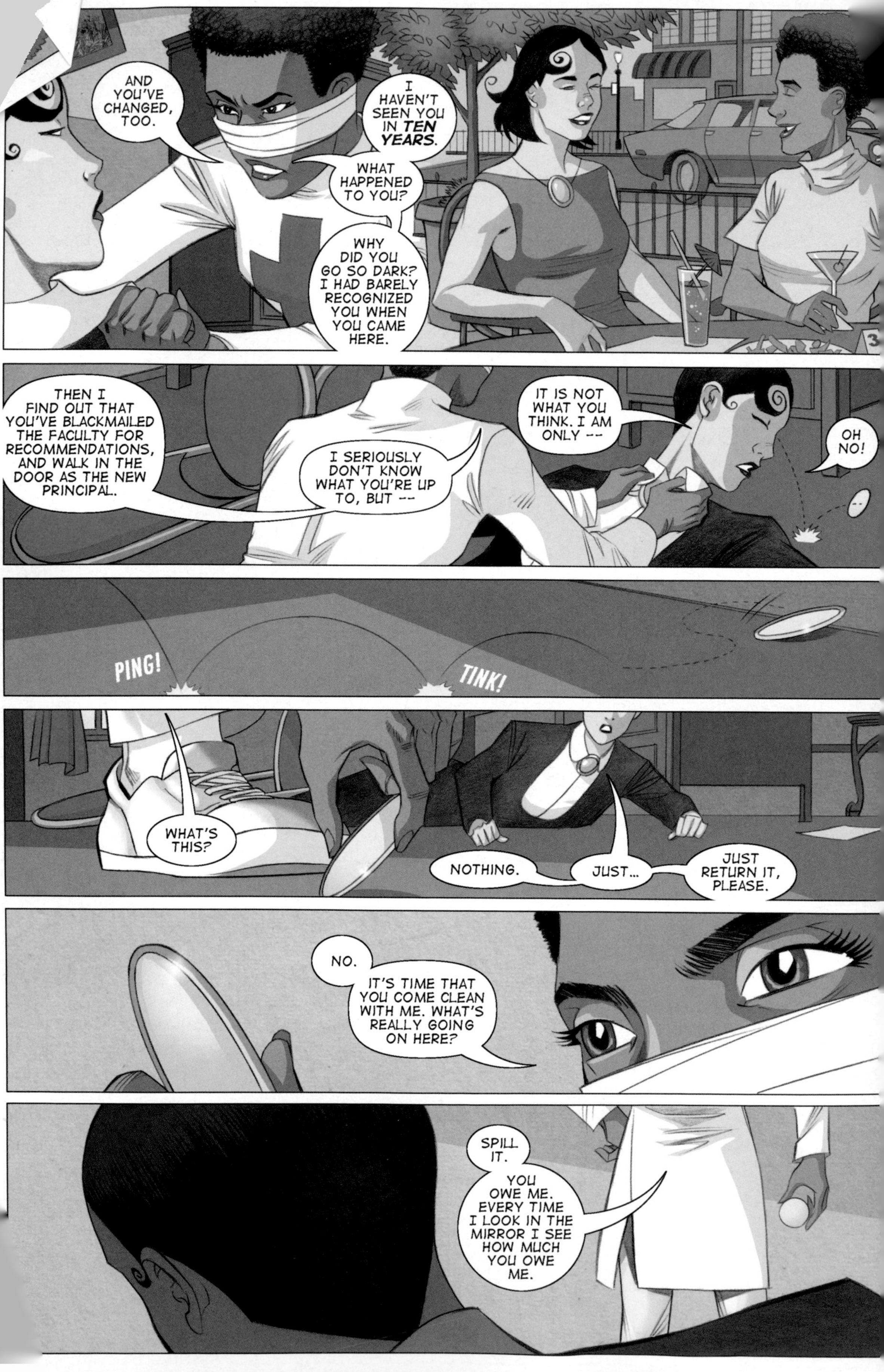
AND YOU'VE CHANGED, TOO.
I HAVEN'T SEEN YOU IN TEN YEARS.
WHAT HAPPENED TO YOU?
WHY DID YOU GO SO DARK? I HAD BARELY RECOGNIZED YOU WHEN YOU CAME HERE.
THEN I FIND OUT THAT YOU'VE BLACKMAILED THE FACULTY FOR RECOMMENDATIONS, AND WALK IN THE DOOR AS THE NEW PRINCIPAL.
I SERIOUSLY DON'T KNOW WHAT YOU'RE UP TO, BUT --
IT IS NOT WHAT YOU THINK. I AM ONLY --
OH NO!
PING!
TINK!
WHAT'S THIS?
NOTHING.
JUST...
JUST RETURN IT, PLEASE.
NO.
IT'S TIME THAT YOU COME CLEAN WITH ME. WHAT'S REALLY GOING ON HERE?
SPILL IT.
YOU OWE ME. EVERY TIME I LOOK IN THE MIRROR I SEE HOW MUCH YOU OWE ME.

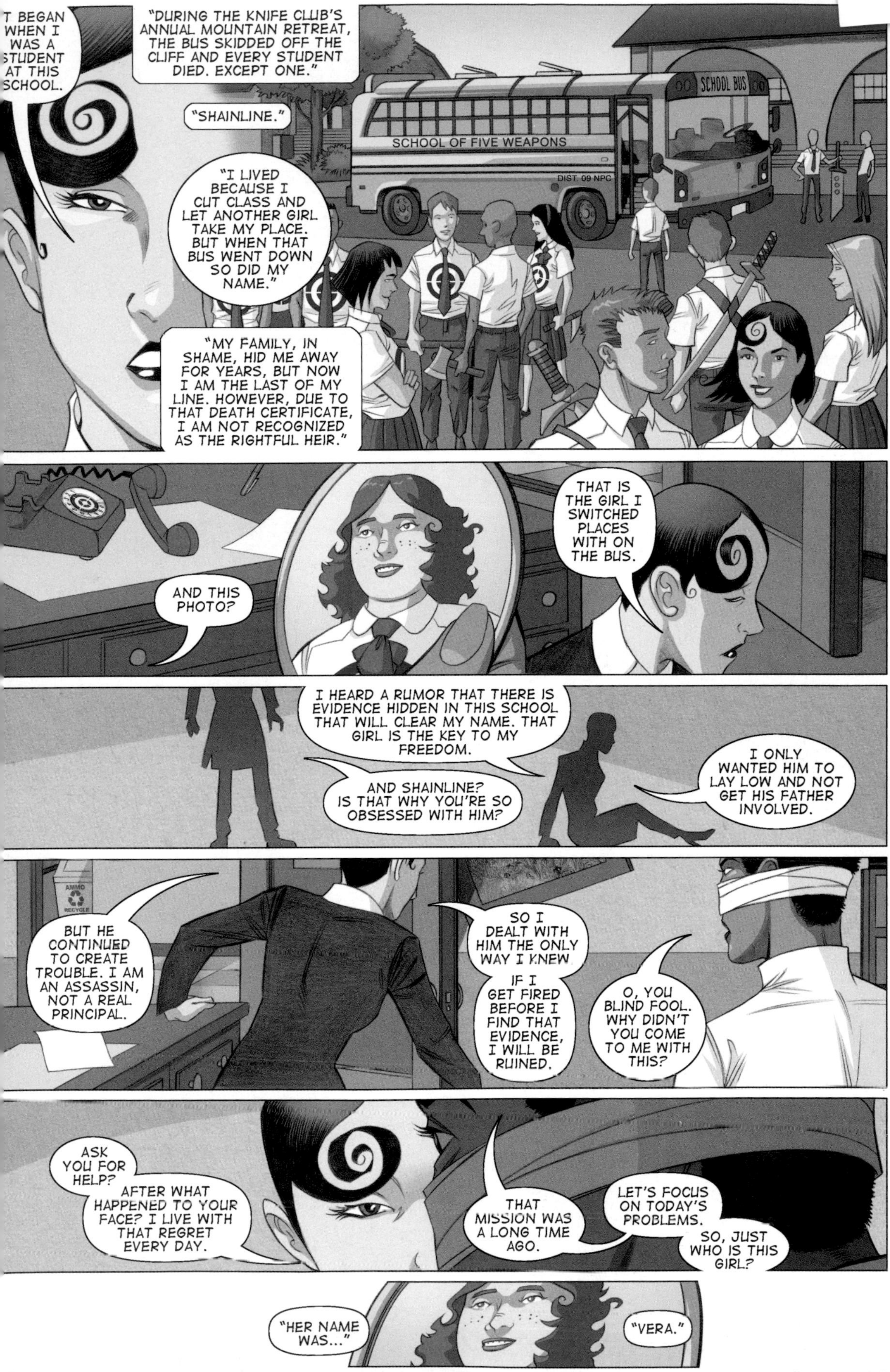
T BEGAN WHEN I WAS A STUDENT AT THIS SCHOOL.
"DURING THE KNIFE CLUB'S ANNUAL MOUNTAIN RETREAT, THE BUS SKIDDED OFF THE CLIFF AND EVERY STUDENT DIED. EXCEPT ONE."
"SHAINLINE."
SCHOOL BUS
SCHOOL OF FIVE WEAPONS
DIST. 09 NPC
"I LIVED BECAUSE I CUT CLASS AND LET ANOTHER GIRL TAKE MY PLACE. BUT WHEN THAT BUS WENT DOWN SO DID MY NAME."
"MY FAMILY, IN SHAME, HID ME AWAY FOR YEARS, BUT NOW I AM THE LAST OF MY LINE. HOWEVER, DUE TO THAT DEATH CERTIFICATE, I AM NOT RECOGNIZED AS THE RIGHTFUL HEIR."
AND THIS PHOTO?
THAT IS THE GIRL I SWITCHED PLACES WITH ON THE BUS.
I HEARD A RUMOR THAT THERE IS EVIDENCE HIDDEN IN THIS SCHOOL THAT WILL CLEAR MY NAME. THAT GIRL IS THE KEY TO MY FREEDOM.
AND SHAINLINE? IS THAT WHY YOU'RE SO OBSESSED WITH HIM?
I ONLY WANTED HIM TO LAY LOW AND NOT GET HIS FATHER INVOLVED.
AMMO RECYCLE
BUT HE CONTINUED TO CREATE TROUBLE. I AM AN ASSASSIN, NOT A REAL PRINCIPAL.
SO I DEALT WITH HIM THE ONLY WAY I KNEW.
IF I GET FIRED BEFORE I FIND THAT EVIDENCE, I WILL BE RUINED.
O, YOU BLIND FOOL. WHY DIDN'T YOU COME TO ME WITH THIS?
ASK YOU FOR HELP?
AFTER WHAT HAPPENED TO YOUR FACE? I LIVE WITH THAT REGRET EVERY DAY.
THAT MISSION WAS A LONG TIME AGO.
LET'S FOCUS ON TODAY'S PROBLEMS.
SO, JUST WHO IS THIS GIRL?
"HER NAME WAS..."
"VERA."

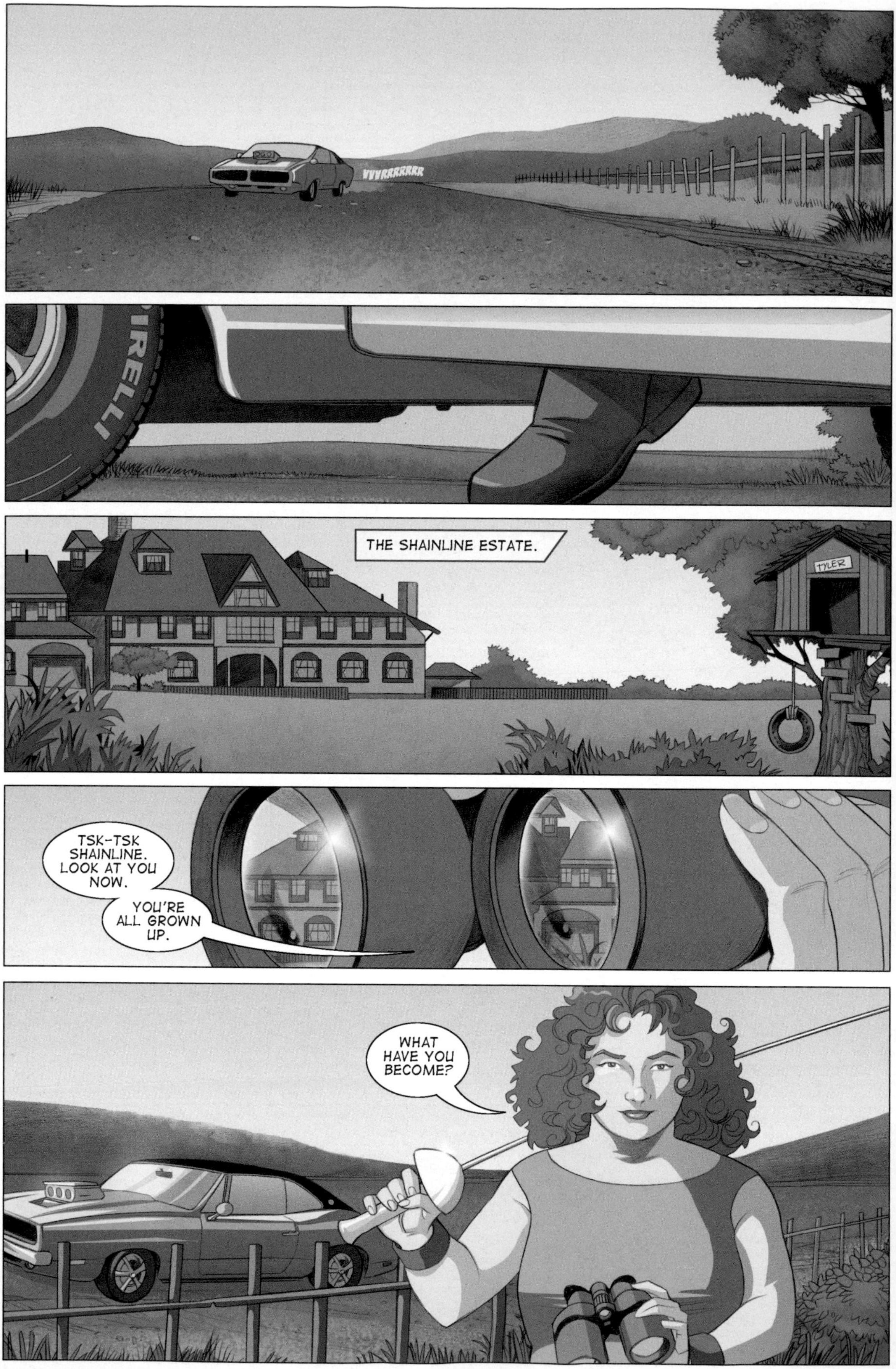
VVVRRRRRRR
PIRELLI
THE SHAINLINE ESTATE.
TYLER
TSK-TSK SHAINLINE. LOOK AT YOU NOW.
YOU'RE ALL GROWN UP.
WHAT HAVE YOU BECOME?

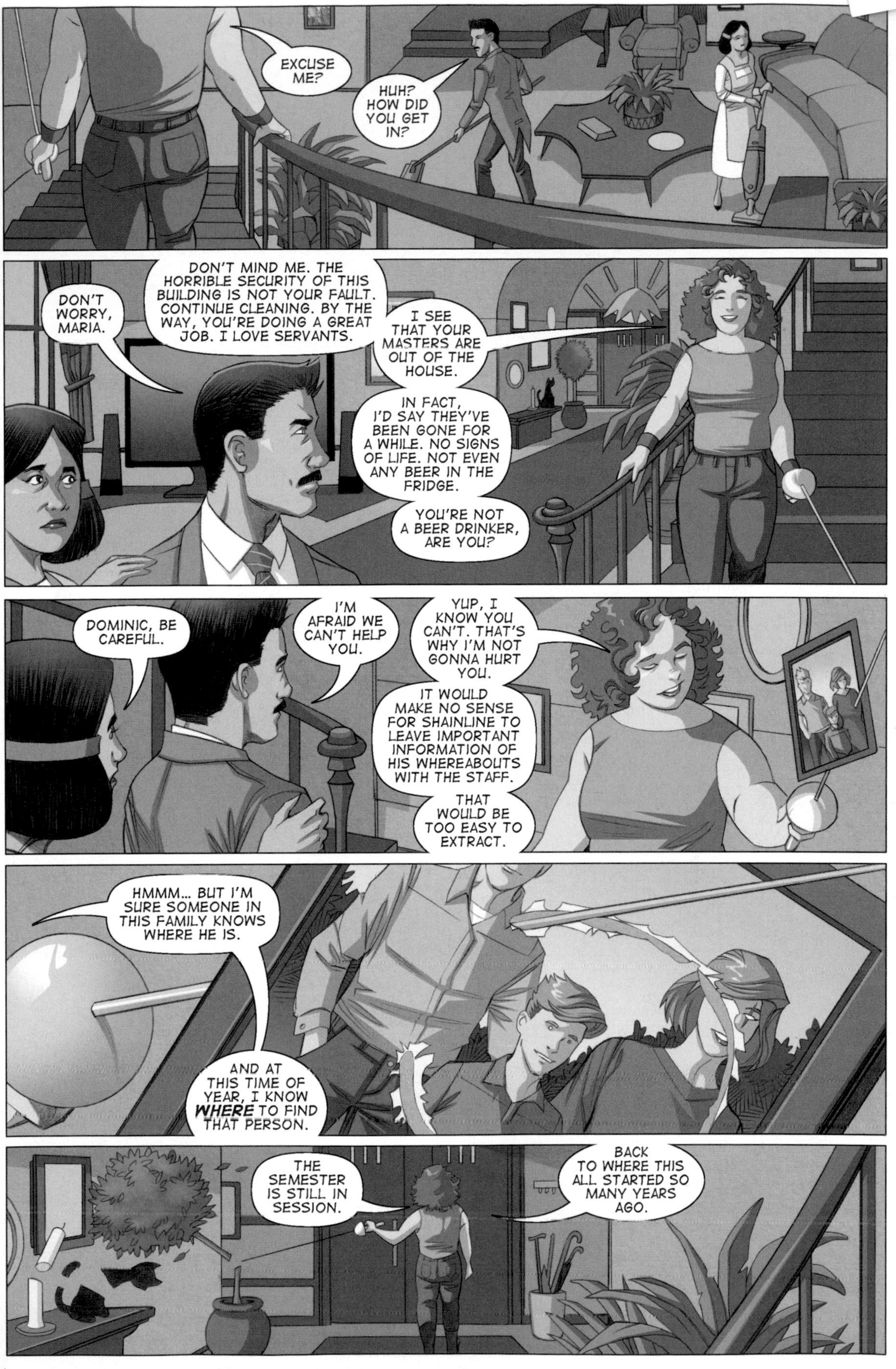

EXCUSE ME?
HUH? HOW DID YOU GET IN?
DON'T WORRY, MARIA.
DON'T MIND ME. THE HORRIBLE SECURITY OF THIS BUILDING IS NOT YOUR FAULT. CONTINUE CLEANING. BY THE WAY, YOU'RE DOING A GREAT JOB. I LOVE SERVANTS.
I SEE THAT YOUR MASTERS ARE OUT OF THE HOUSE.
IN FACT, I'D SAY THEY'VE BEEN GONE FOR A WHILE. NO SIGNS OF LIFE. NOT EVEN ANY BEER IN THE FRIDGE.
YOU'RE NOT A BEER DRINKER, ARE YOU?
DOMINIC, BE CAREFUL.
I'M AFRAID WE CAN'T HELP YOU.
YUP, I KNOW YOU CAN'T. THAT'S WHY I'M NOT GONNA HURT YOU.
IT WOULD MAKE NO SENSE FOR SHAINLINE TO LEAVE IMPORTANT INFORMATION OF HIS WHEREABOUTS WITH THE STAFF.
THAT WOULD BE TOO EASY TO EXTRACT.
HMMM... BUT I'M SURE SOMEONE IN THIS FAMILY KNOWS WHERE HE IS.
AND AT THIS TIME OF YEAR, I KNOW WHERE TO FIND THAT PERSON.
THE SEMESTER IS STILL IN SESSION.
BACK TO WHERE THIS ALL STARTED SO MANY YEARS AGO.

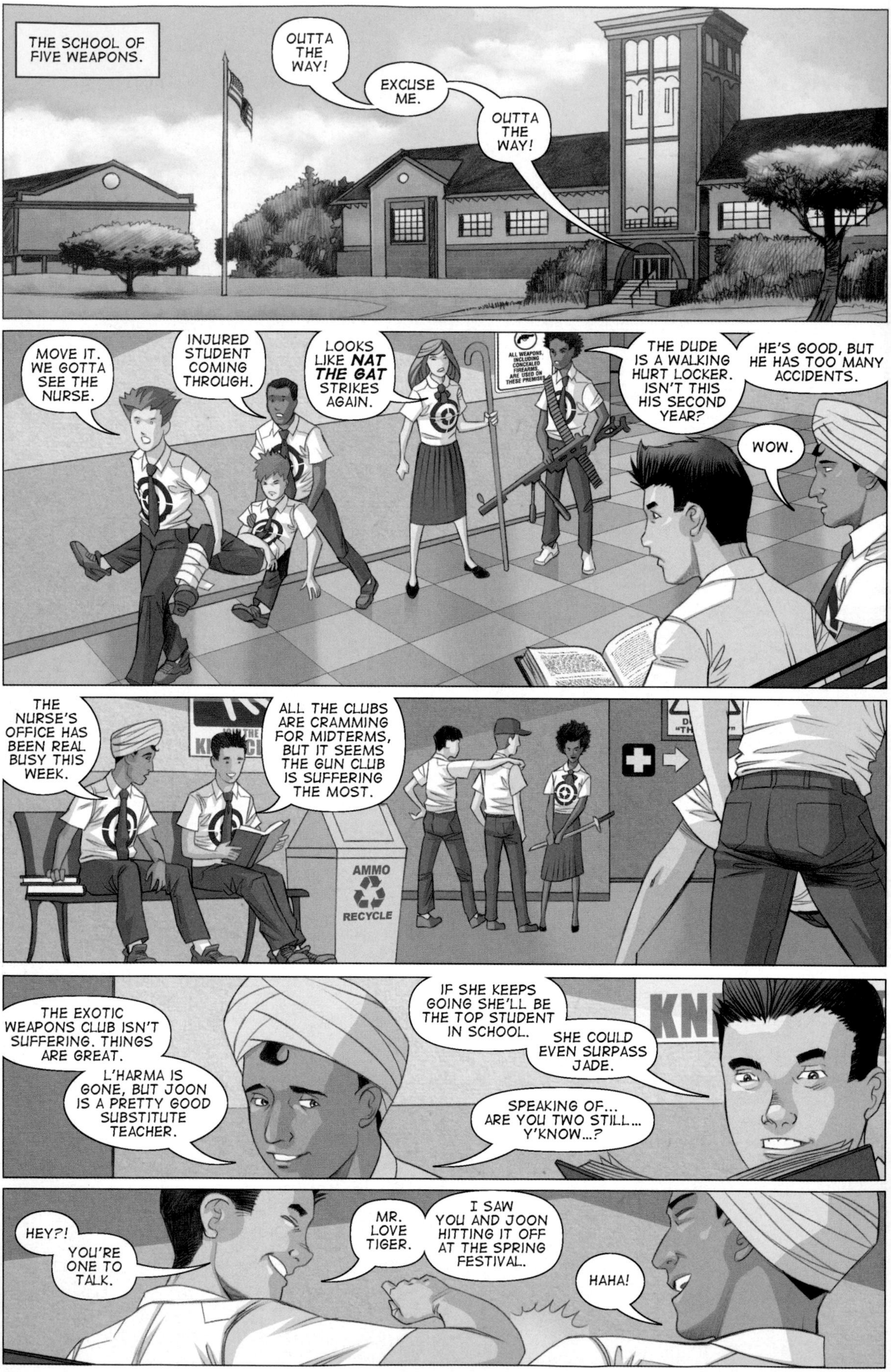

THE SCHOOL OF FIVE WEAPONS.
OUTTA THE WAY!
EXCUSE ME.
OUTTA THE WAY!
MOVE IT. WE GOTTA SEE THE NURSE.
INJURED STUDENT COMING THROUGH.
LOOKS LIKE NAT THE GAT STRIKES AGAIN.
ALL WEAPONS, INCLUDING CONCEALED FIREARMS, ARE USED ON THESE PREMISES
THE DUDE IS A WALKING HURT LOCKER. ISN'T THIS HIS SECOND YEAR?
HE'S GOOD, BUT HE HAS TOO MANY ACCIDENTS.
WOW.
THE NURSE'S OFFICE HAS BEEN REAL BUSY THIS WEEK.
ALL THE CLUBS ARE CRAMMING FOR MIDTERMS, BUT IT SEEMS THE GUN CLUB IS SUFFERING THE MOST.
AMMO RECYCLE
THE EXOTIC WEAPONS CLUB ISN'T SUFFERING. THINGS ARE GREAT.
L'HARMA IS GONE, BUT JOON IS A PRETTY GOOD SUBSTITUTE TEACHER.
IF SHE KEEPS GOING SHE'LL BE THE TOP STUDENT IN SCHOOL.
SHE COULD EVEN SURPASS JADE.
SPEAKING OF... ARE YOU TWO STILL... Y'KNOW...?
HEY?!
YOU'RE ONE TO TALK.
MR. LOVE TIGER.
I SAW YOU AND JOON HITTING IT OFF AT THE SPRING FESTIVAL.
HAHA!

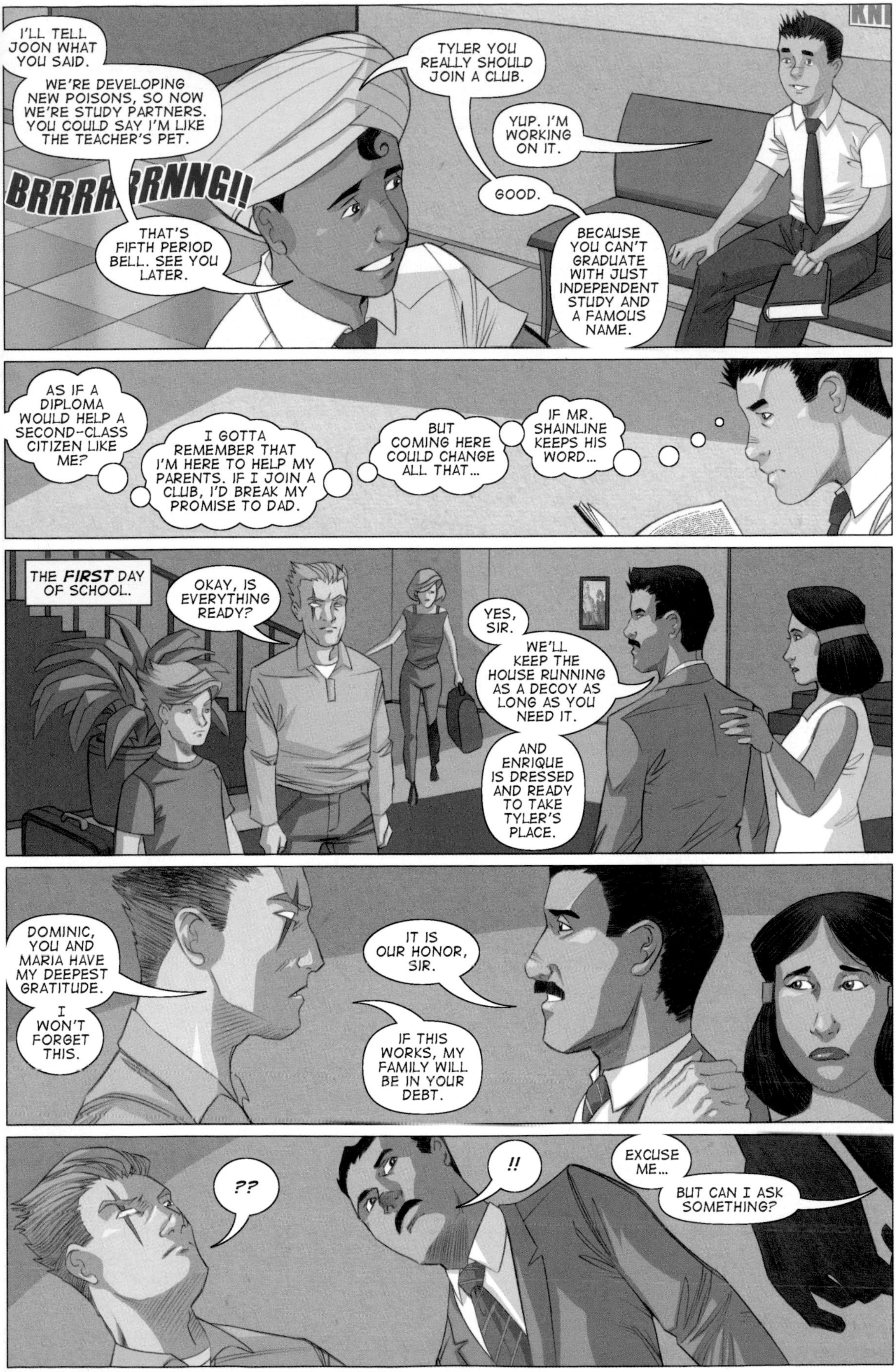
I'LL TELL JOON WHAT YOU SAID.
WE'RE DEVELOPING NEW POISONS, SO NOW WE'RE STUDY PARTNERS. YOU COULD SAY I'M LIKE THE TEACHER'S PET.
BRRRRRRNNG!!
THAT'S FIFTH PERIOD BELL. SEE YOU LATER.
TYLER YOU REALLY SHOULD JOIN A CLUB.
YUP. I'M WORKING ON IT.
GOOD.
BECAUSE YOU CAN'T GRADUATE WITH JUST INDEPENDENT STUDY AND A FAMOUS NAME.
AS IF A DIPLOMA WOULD HELP A SECOND-CLASS CITIZEN LIKE ME?
I GOTTA REMEMBER THAT I'M HERE TO HELP MY PARENTS. IF I JOIN A CLUB, I'D BREAK MY PROMISE TO DAD.
BUT COMING HERE COULD CHANGE ALL THAT...
IF MR. SHAINLINE KEEPS HIS WORD...
THE FIRST DAY OF SCHOOL.
OKAY, IS EVERYTHING READY?
YES, SIR.
WE'LL KEEP THE HOUSE RUNNING AS A DECOY AS LONG AS YOU NEED IT.
AND ENRIQUE IS DRESSED AND READY TO TAKE TYLER'S PLACE.
DOMINIC, YOU AND MARIA HAVE MY DEEPEST GRATITUDE.
I WON'T FORGET THIS.
IT IS OUR HONOR, SIR.
IF THIS WORKS, MY FAMILY WILL BE IN YOUR DEBT.
??
!!
EXCUSE ME...
BUT CAN I ASK SOMETHING?

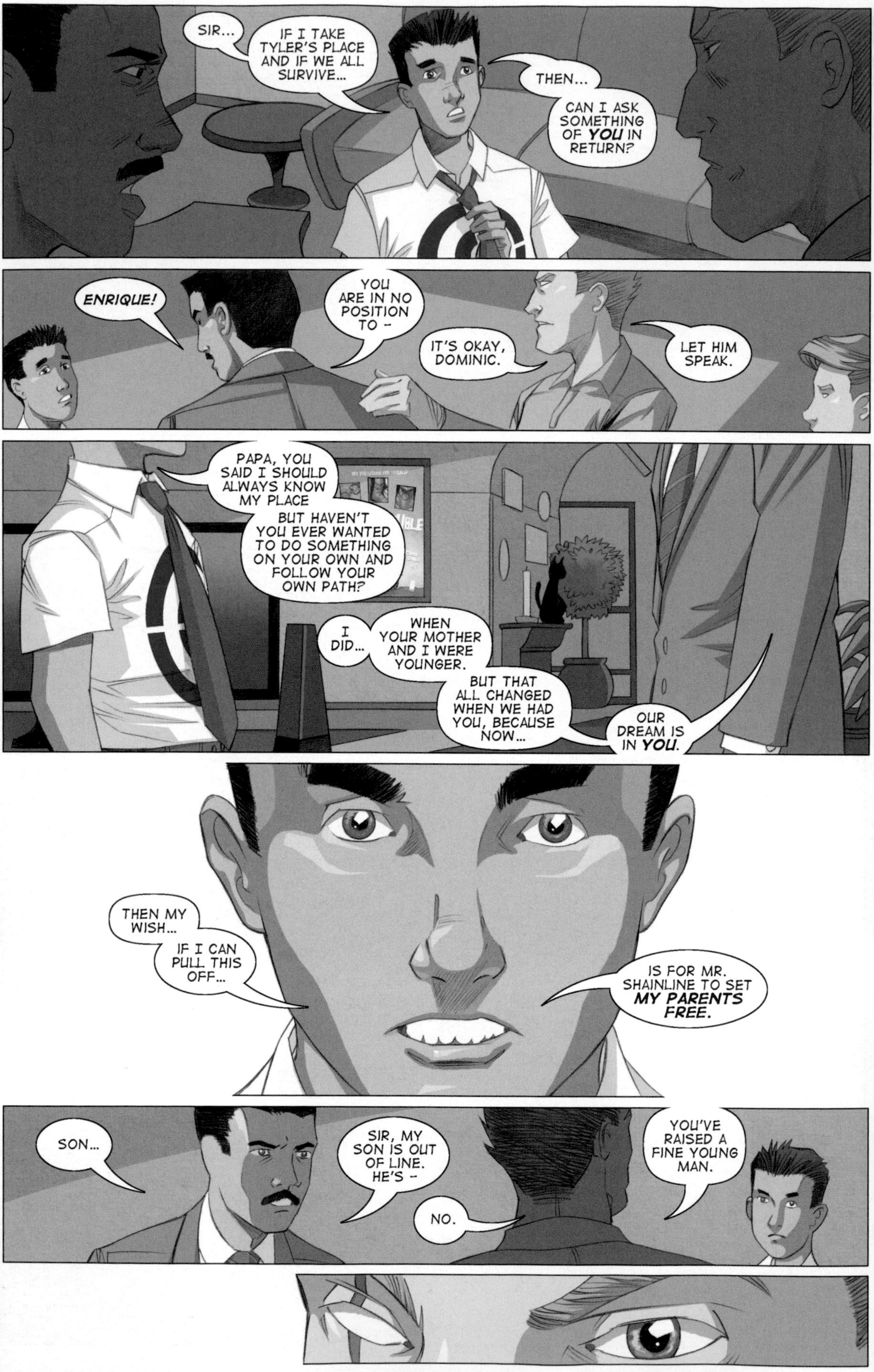
SIR...
IF I TAKE TYLER'S PLACE AND IF WE ALL SURVIVE...
THEN...
CAN I ASK SOMETHING OF YOU IN RETURN?
ENRIQUE!
YOU ARE IN NO POSITION TO -
IT'S OKAY, DOMINIC.
LET HIM SPEAK.
PAPA, YOU SAID I SHOULD ALWAYS KNOW MY PLACE
BUT HAVEN'T YOU EVER WANTED TO DO SOMETHING ON YOUR OWN AND FOLLOW YOUR OWN PATH?
I DID...
WHEN YOUR MOTHER AND I WERE YOUNGER.
BUT THAT ALL CHANGED WHEN WE HAD YOU, BECAUSE NOW...
OUR DREAM IS IN YOU.
THEN MY WISH...
IF I CAN PULL THIS OFF...
IS FOR MR. SHAINLINE TO SET MY PARENTS FREE.
SON...
SIR, MY SON IS OUT OF LINE. HE'S -
NO.
YOU'VE RAISED A FINE YOUNG MAN.

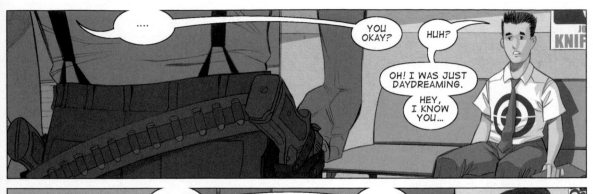

YOU OKAY?

HUH?

....

OH! I WAS JUST DAYDREAMING. HEY, I KNOW YOU...

KNIF

YOU'RE **NAT THE GAT.**

....

WHEN I FIRST CAME HERE, JADE SHOWED ME AROUND AND SHE SAID YOU WERE THE HEAD OF THE GUN CLUB.

....

HANG ON WITH 5

KNIFE

SCH

....

NOT MUCH TO SAY.

JUST GOING TO THE BATHROOM. I THOUGHT YOU WERE HURT.

AND I ALSO RECALL THAT SHE SAID YOU DIDN'T TALK MUCH.

SCH PEP RALLY

NOPE. I'M GOOD.

THOUGH I NOTICED A LOT OF KIDS FROM THE GUN CLUB ARE GETTING HURT.

WHAT'S UP WITH THAT?

ACCIDENTS.

THAT'S WHAT I HEARD, BUT I WASN'T SURE IF IT WAS A RUMOR OR NOT. SO, IT'S REALLY JUST BAD LUCK?

THE WORST.

SO YOU'RE THE SHAINLINE KID, RIGHT?

YOU BEAT ALL THOSE CLUBS?

WELL... I WOULDN'T SAY I BEAT 'EM. I JUST OBSERVED A FEW LOOPHOLES AND FIGURED OUT THEIR WEAK POINTS. BUT SOMETIMES I JUST GET LUCKY.

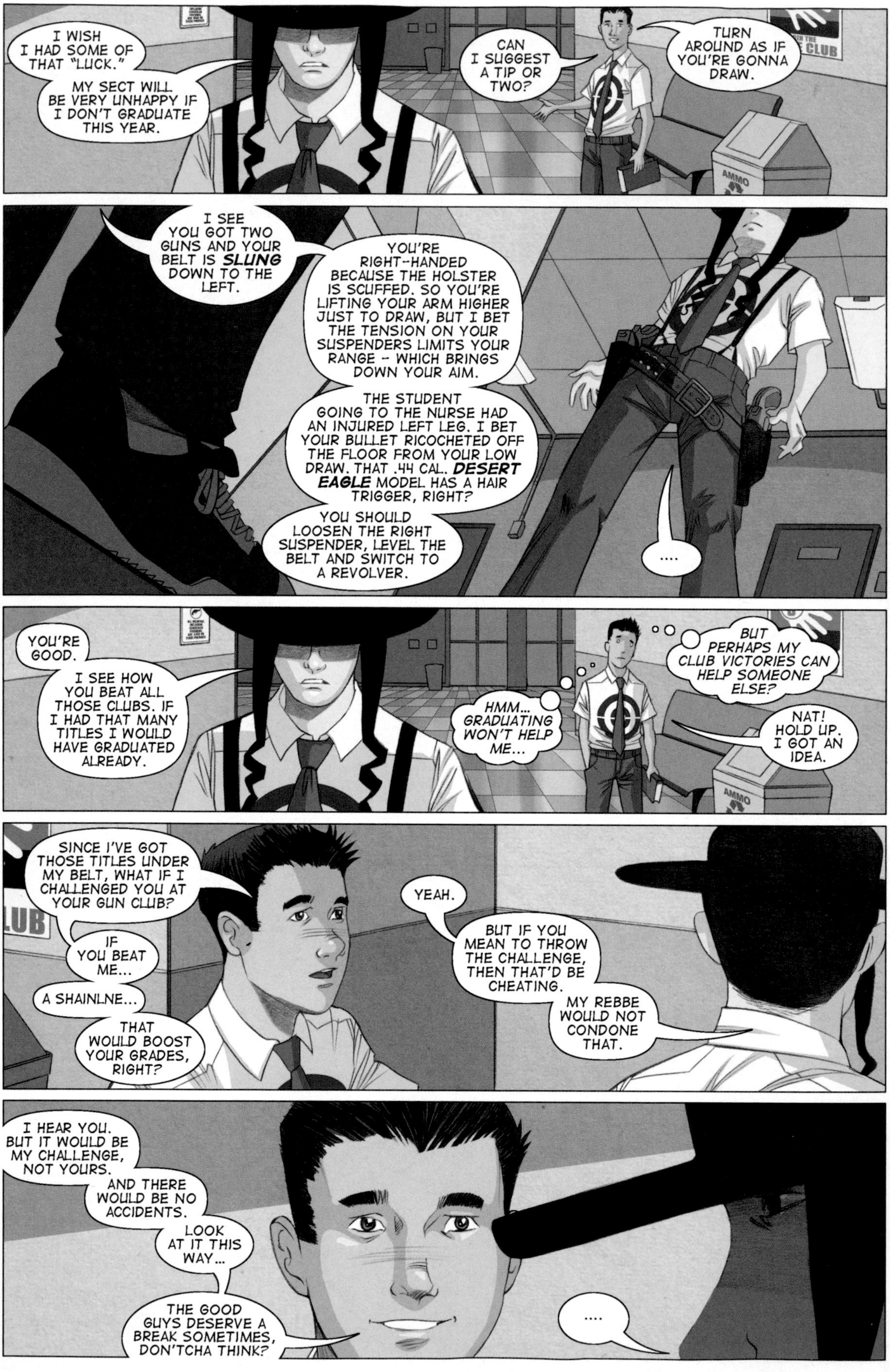
I WISH I HAD SOME OF THAT "LUCK."
MY SECT WILL BE VERY UNHAPPY IF I DON'T GRADUATE THIS YEAR.
CAN I SUGGEST A TIP OR TWO?
TURN AROUND AS IF YOU'RE GONNA DRAW.
AMMO
I SEE YOU GOT TWO GUNS AND YOUR BELT IS *SLUNG* DOWN TO THE LEFT.
YOU'RE RIGHT--HANDED BECAUSE THE HOLSTER IS SCUFFED. SO YOU'RE LIFTING YOUR ARM HIGHER JUST TO DRAW, BUT I BET THE TENSION ON YOUR SUSPENDERS LIMITS YOUR RANGE - WHICH BRINGS DOWN YOUR AIM.
THE STUDENT GOING TO THE NURSE HAD AN INJURED LEFT LEG. I BET YOUR BULLET RICOCHETED OFF THE FLOOR FROM YOUR LOW DRAW. THAT .44 CAL. ***DESERT EAGLE*** MODEL HAS A HAIR TRIGGER, RIGHT?
YOU SHOULD LOOSEN THE RIGHT SUSPENDER, LEVEL THE BELT AND SWITCH TO A REVOLVER.
....
YOU'RE GOOD.
I SEE HOW YOU BEAT ALL THOSE CLUBS. IF I HAD THAT MANY TITLES I WOULD HAVE GRADUATED ALREADY.
HMM... GRADUATING WON'T HELP ME...
BUT PERHAPS MY CLUB VICTORIES CAN HELP SOMEONE ELSE?
NAT! HOLD UP. I GOT AN IDEA.
AMMO
SINCE I'VE GOT THOSE TITLES UNDER MY BELT, WHAT IF I CHALLENGED YOU AT YOUR GUN CLUB?
IF YOU BEAT ME...
A SHAINLNE...
THAT WOULD BOOST YOUR GRADES, RIGHT?
YEAH.
BUT IF YOU MEAN TO THROW THE CHALLENGE, THEN THAT'D BE CHEATING.
MY REBBE WOULD NOT CONDONE THAT.
I HEAR YOU. BUT IT WOULD BE MY CHALLENGE, NOT YOURS.
AND THERE WOULD BE NO ACCIDENTS.
LOOK AT IT THIS WAY...
THE GOOD GUYS DESERVE A BREAK SOMETIMES, DON'TCHA THINK?
....

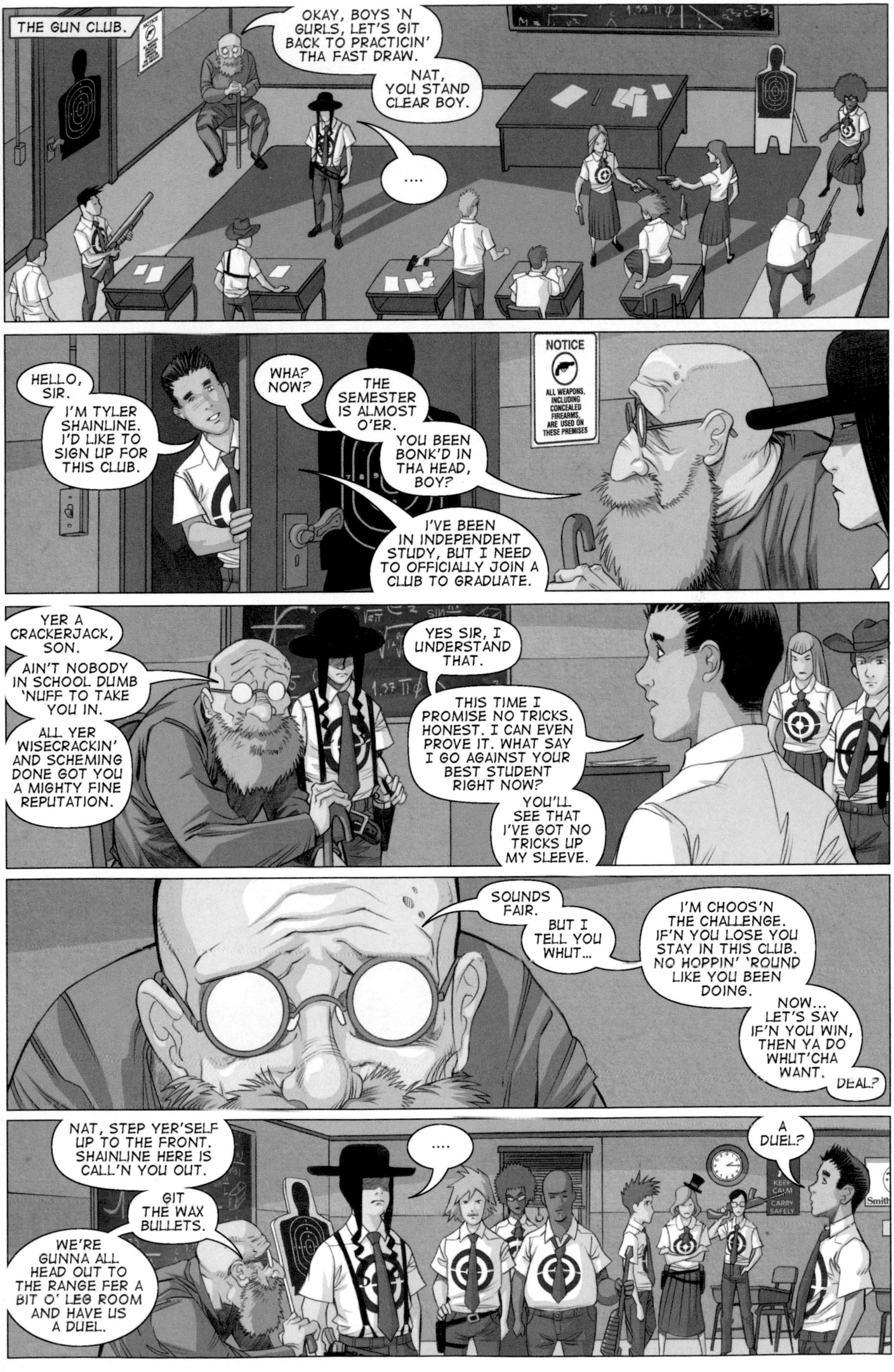
THE GUN CLUB.
OKAY, BOYS 'N GURLS, LET'S GIT BACK TO PRACTICIN' THA FAST DRAW.
NAT, YOU STAND CLEAR BOY.
....
HELLO, SIR.
I'M TYLER SHAINLINE. I'D LIKE TO SIGN UP FOR THIS CLUB.
WHA? NOW?
THE SEMESTER IS ALMOST O'ER.
YOU BEEN BONK'D IN THA HEAD, BOY?
NOTICE
ALL WEAPONS, INCLUDING CONCEALED FIREARMS, ARE USED ON THESE PREMISES
I'VE BEEN IN INDEPENDENT STUDY, BUT I NEED TO OFFICIALLY JOIN A CLUB TO GRADUATE.
YER A CRACKERJACK, SON.
AIN'T NOBODY IN SCHOOL DUMB 'NUFF TO TAKE YOU IN.
ALL YER WISECRACKIN' AND SCHEMING DONE GOT YOU A MIGHTY FINE REPUTATION.
YES SIR, I UNDERSTAND THAT.
THIS TIME I PROMISE NO TRICKS. HONEST. I CAN EVEN PROVE IT. WHAT SAY I GO AGAINST YOUR BEST STUDENT RIGHT NOW?
YOU'LL SEE THAT I'VE GOT NO TRICKS UP MY SLEEVE.
SOUNDS FAIR.
BUT I TELL YOU WHUT...
I'M CHOOS'N THE CHALLENGE. IF'N YOU LOSE YOU STAY IN THIS CLUB. NO HOPPIN' 'ROUND LIKE YOU BEEN DOING.
NOW... LET'S SAY IF'N YOU WIN, THEN YA DO WHUT'CHA WANT.
DEAL?
NAT, STEP YER'SELF UP TO THE FRONT. SHAINLINE HERE IS CALL'N YOU OUT.
GIT THE WAX BULLETS.
WE'RE GUNNA ALL HEAD OUT TO THE RANGE FER A BIT O' LEG ROOM AND HAVE US A DUEL.
....
A DUEL?
KEEP CALM CARRY SAFELY
Smith

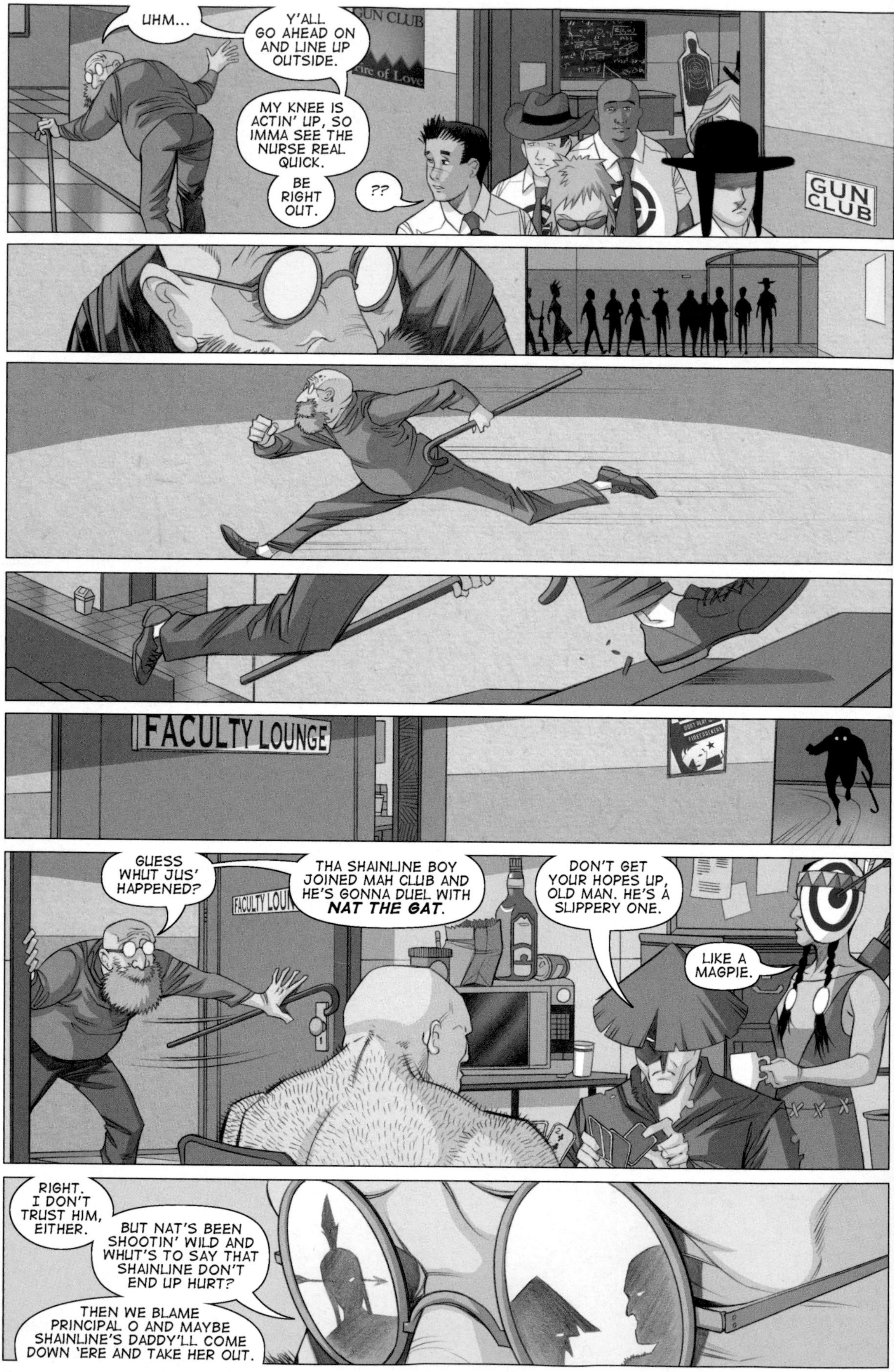
UHM...
Y'ALL GO AHEAD ON AND LINE UP OUTSIDE.
GUN CLUB
Fire of Love
MY KNEE IS ACTIN' UP, SO IMMA SEE THE NURSE REAL QUICK.
BE RIGHT OUT.
??
GUN CLUB
FACULTY LOUNGE
GUESS WHUT JUS' HAPPENED?
THA SHAINLINE BOY JOINED MAH CLUB AND HE'S GONNA DUEL WITH **NAT THE GAT**.
FACULTY LOUNGE
DON'T GET YOUR HOPES UP, OLD MAN. HE'S A SLIPPERY ONE.
LIKE A MAGPIE.
RIGHT. I DON'T TRUST HIM, EITHER.
BUT NAT'S BEEN SHOOTIN' WILD AND WHUT'S TO SAY THAT SHAINLINE DON'T END UP HURT?
THEN WE BLAME PRINCIPAL O AND MAYBE SHAINLINE'S DADDY'LL COME DOWN 'ERE AND TAKE HER OUT.

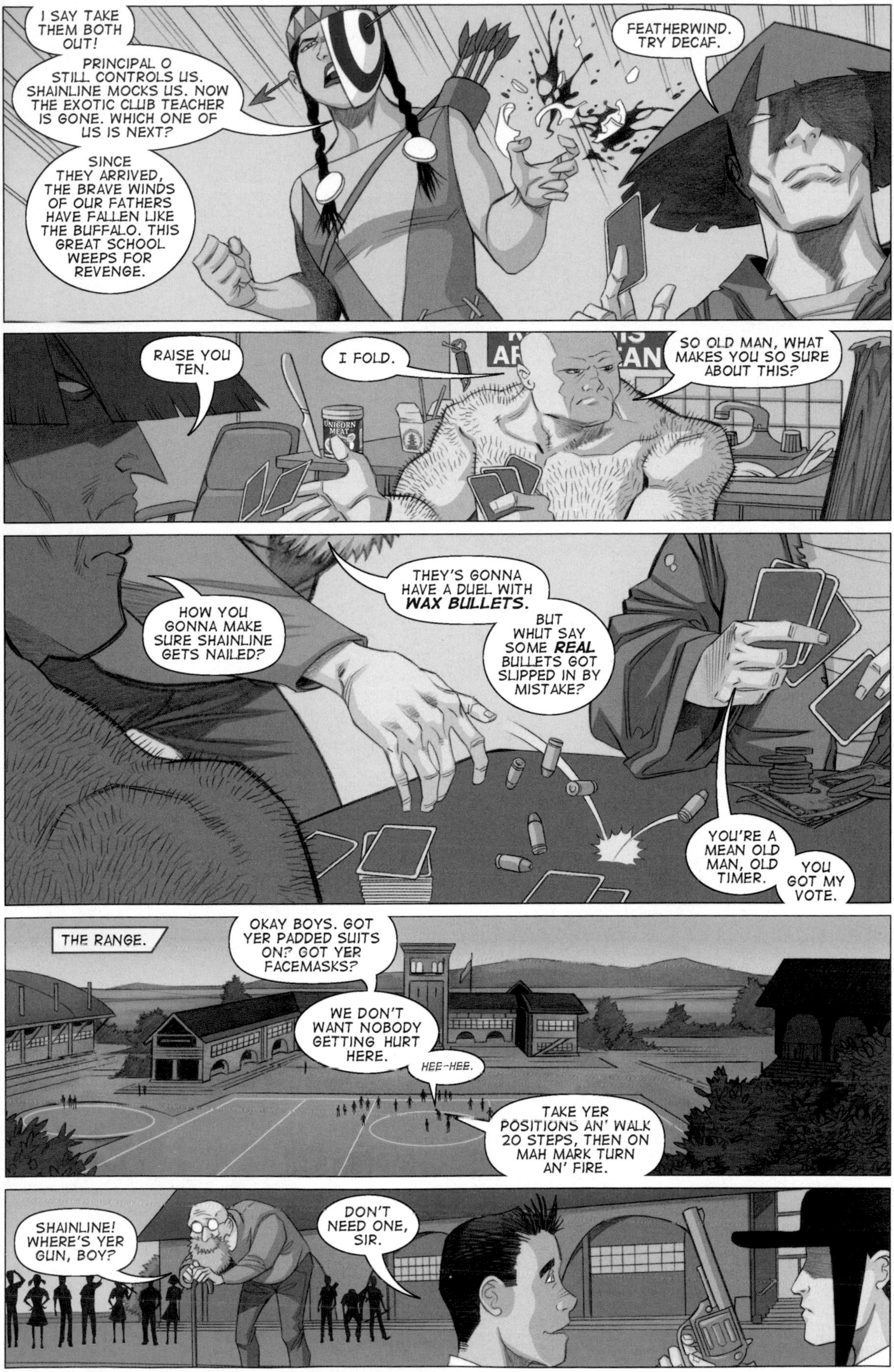
I SAY TAKE THEM BOTH OUT!
PRINCIPAL O STILL CONTROLS US. SHAINLINE MOCKS US. NOW THE EXOTIC CLUB TEACHER IS GONE. WHICH ONE OF US IS NEXT?
SINCE THEY ARRIVED, THE BRAVE WINDS OF OUR FATHERS HAVE FALLEN LIKE THE BUFFALO. THIS GREAT SCHOOL WEEPS FOR REVENGE.
FEATHERWIND. TRY DECAF.
RAISE YOU TEN.
I FOLD.
UNICORN MEAT
SO OLD MAN, WHAT MAKES YOU SO SURE ABOUT THIS?
HOW YOU GONNA MAKE SURE SHAINLINE GETS NAILED?
THEY'S GONNA HAVE A DUEL WITH **WAX BULLETS.**
BUT WHUT SAY SOME **REAL** BULLETS GOT SLIPPED IN BY MISTAKE?
YOU'RE A MEAN OLD MAN, OLD TIMER.
YOU GOT MY VOTE.
THE RANGE.
OKAY BOYS. GOT YER PADDED SUITS ON? GOT YER FACEMASKS?
WE DON'T WANT NOBODY GETTING HURT HERE.
HEE-HEE.
TAKE YER POSITIONS AN' WALK 20 STEPS, THEN ON MAH MARK TURN AN' FIRE.
SHAINLINE! WHERE'S YER GUN, BOY?
DON'T NEED ONE, SIR.

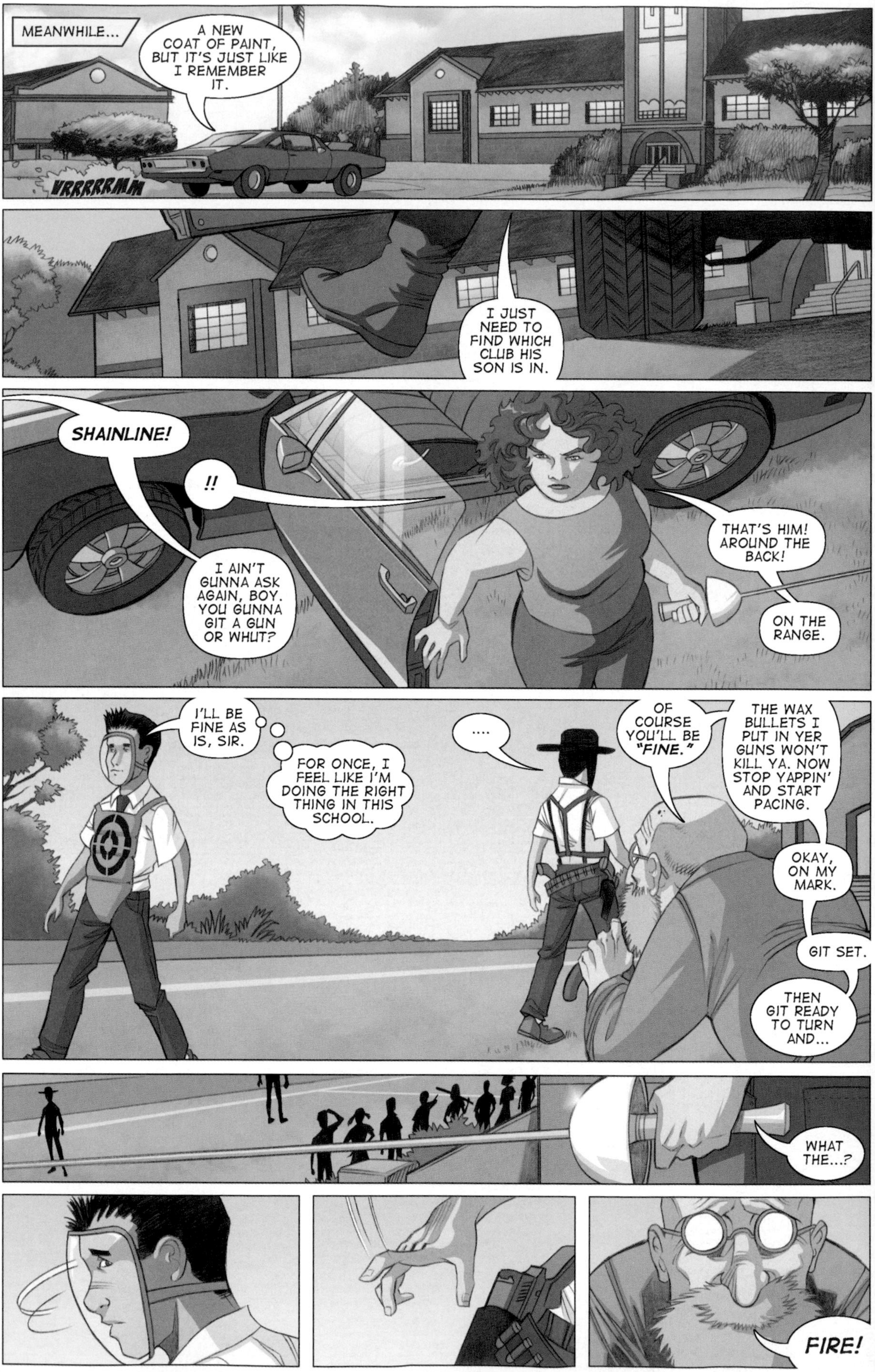
MEANWHILE...
A NEW COAT OF PAINT, BUT IT'S JUST LIKE I REMEMBER IT.
VRRRRRMM
I JUST NEED TO FIND WHICH CLUB HIS SON IS IN.
SHAINLINE!
!!
I AIN'T GUNNA ASK AGAIN, BOY. YOU GUNNA GIT A GUN OR WHUT?
THAT'S HIM! AROUND THE BACK!
ON THE RANGE.
I'LL BE FINE AS IS, SIR.
FOR ONCE, I FEEL LIKE I'M DOING THE RIGHT THING IN THIS SCHOOL.
....
OF COURSE YOU'LL BE *"FINE."*
THE WAX BULLETS I PUT IN YER GUNS WON'T KILL YA. NOW STOP YAPPIN' AND START PACING.
OKAY, ON MY MARK.
GIT SET.
THEN GIT READY TO TURN AND...
WHAT THE...?
FIRE!

BOOK FIVE
THE FINAL EXAM

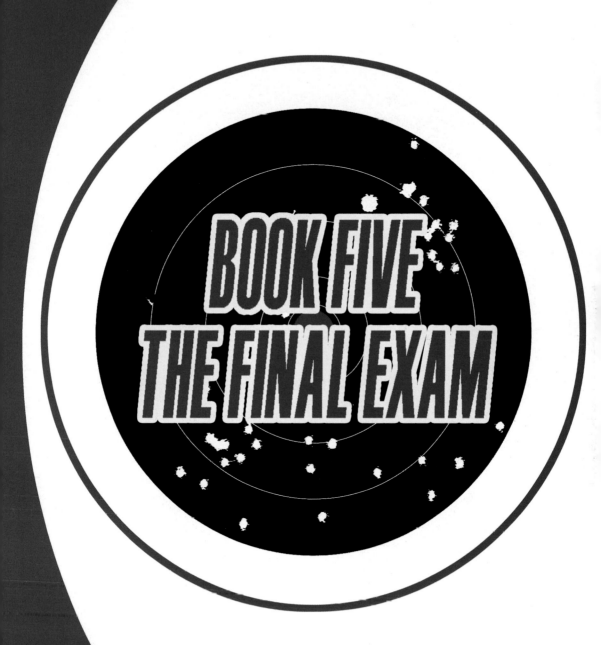

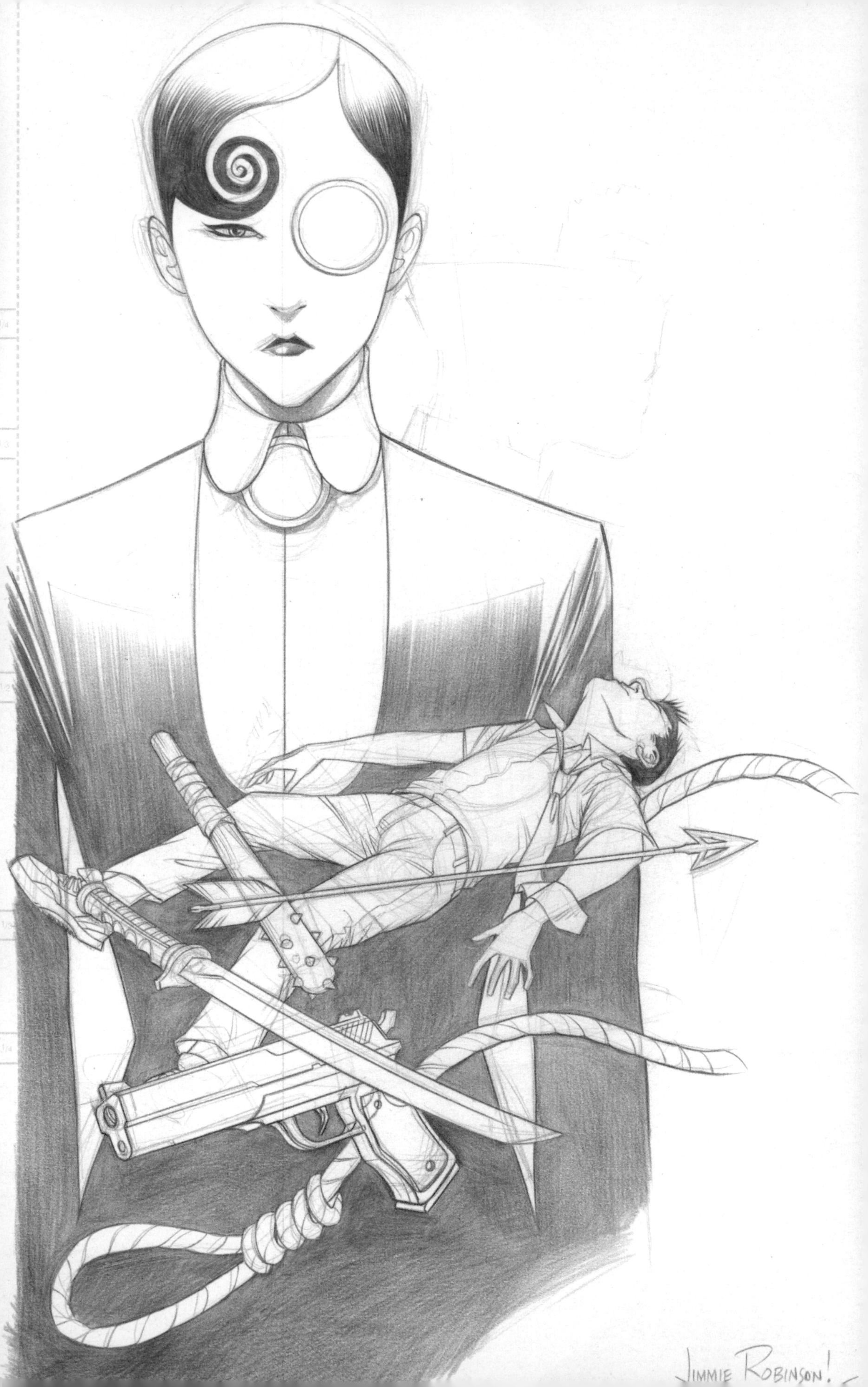
JIMMIE ROBINSON!

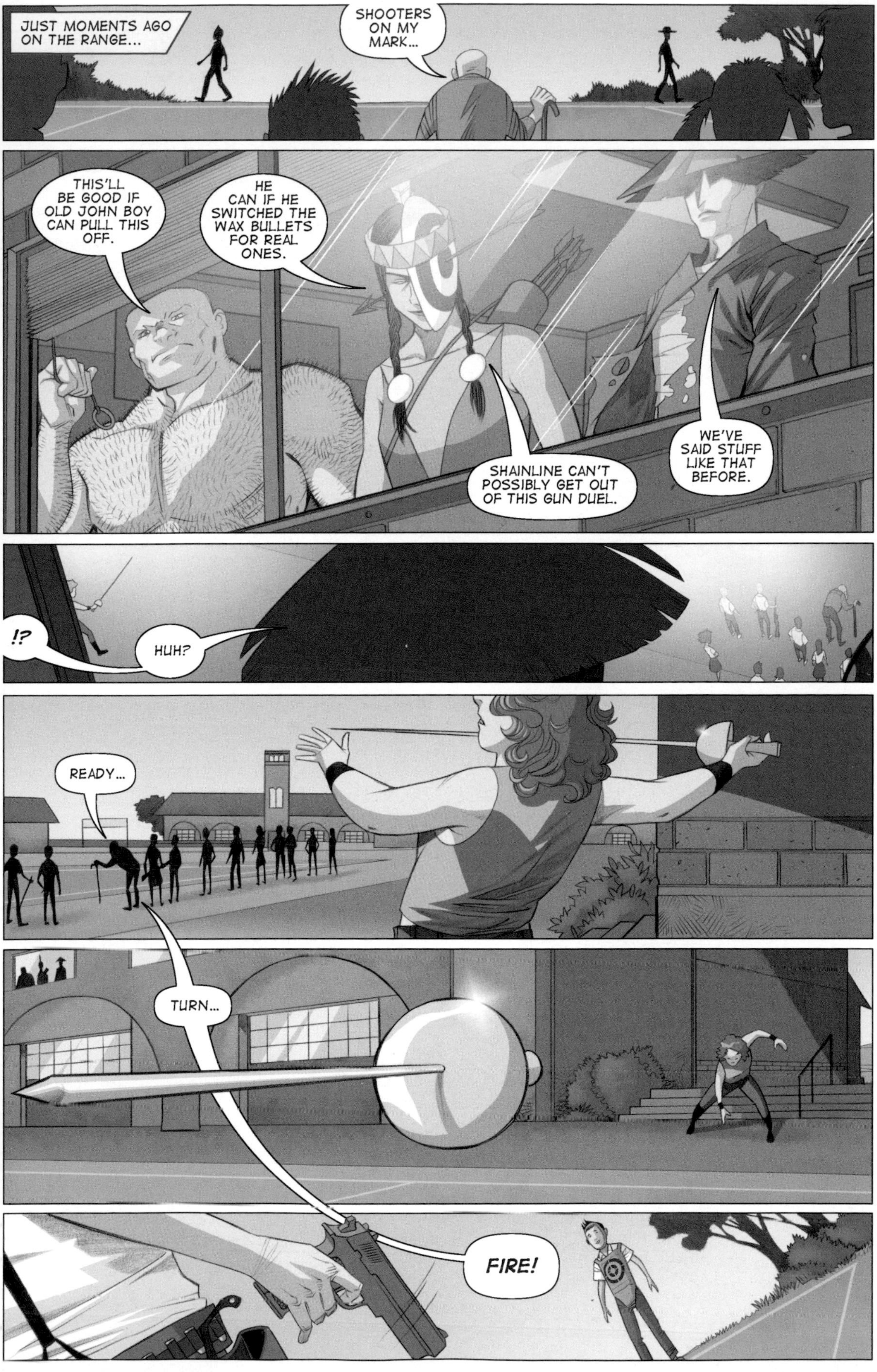
JUST MOMENTS AGO ON THE RANGE...
SHOOTERS ON MY MARK...
THIS'LL BE GOOD IF OLD JOHN BOY CAN PULL THIS OFF.
HE CAN IF HE SWITCHED THE WAX BULLETS FOR REAL ONES.
SHAINLINE CAN'T POSSIBLY GET OUT OF THIS GUN DUEL.
WE'VE SAID STUFF LIKE THAT BEFORE.
!?
HUH?
READY...
TURN...
FIRE!

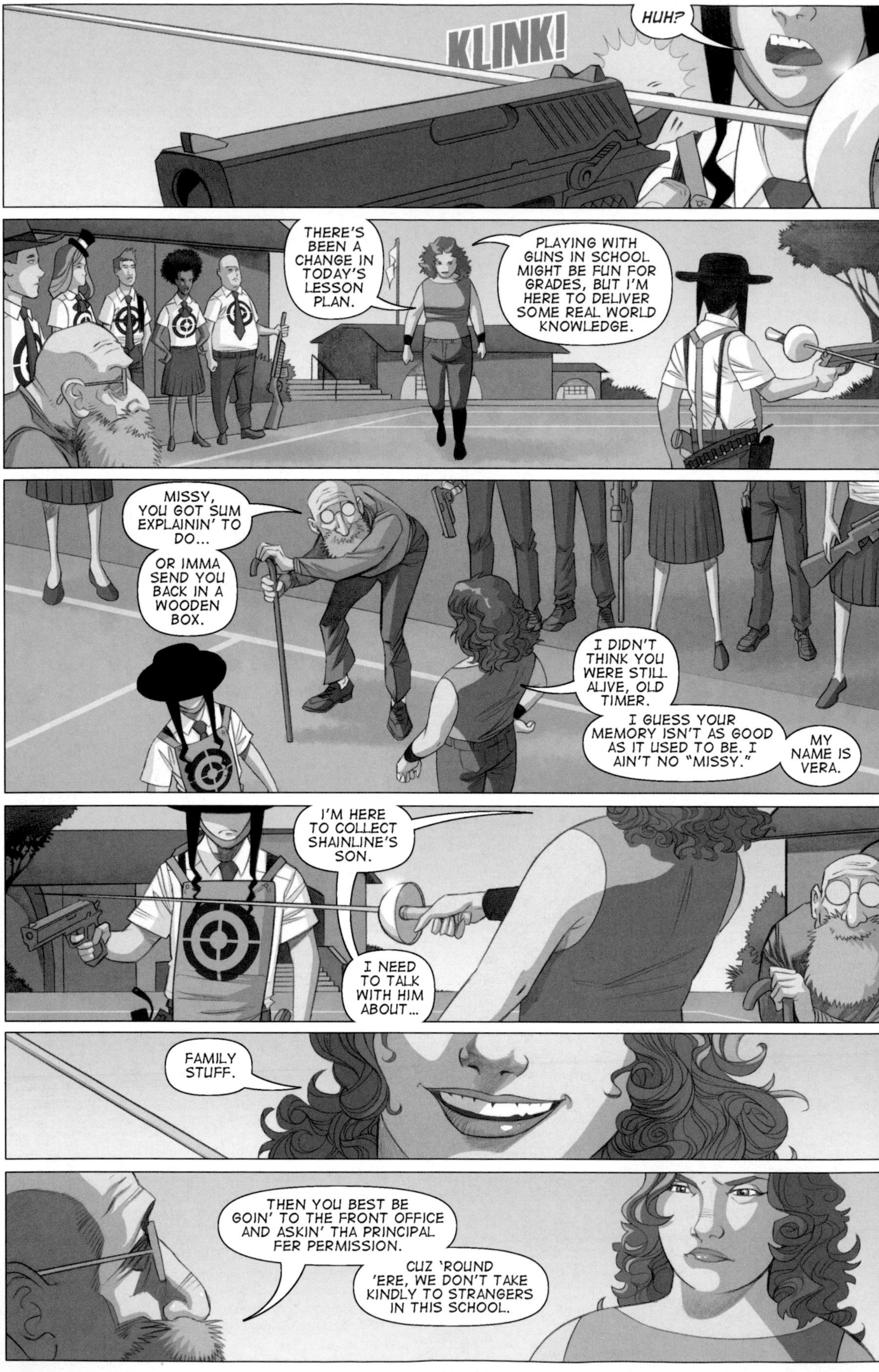
KLINK!
HUH?
THERE'S BEEN A CHANGE IN TODAY'S LESSON PLAN.
PLAYING WITH GUNS IN SCHOOL MIGHT BE FUN FOR GRADES, BUT I'M HERE TO DELIVER SOME REAL WORLD KNOWLEDGE.
MISSY, YOU GOT SUM EXPLAININ' TO DO...
OR IMMA SEND YOU BACK IN A WOODEN BOX.
I DIDN'T THINK YOU WERE STILL ALIVE, OLD TIMER.
I GUESS YOUR MEMORY ISN'T AS GOOD AS IT USED TO BE. I AIN'T NO "MISSY."
MY NAME IS VERA.
I'M HERE TO COLLECT SHAINLINE'S SON.
I NEED TO TALK WITH HIM ABOUT...
FAMILY STUFF.
THEN YOU BEST BE GOIN' TO THE FRONT OFFICE AND ASKIN' THA PRINCIPAL FER PERMISSION.
CUZ 'ROUND 'ERE, WE DON'T TAKE KINDLY TO STRANGERS IN THIS SCHOOL.

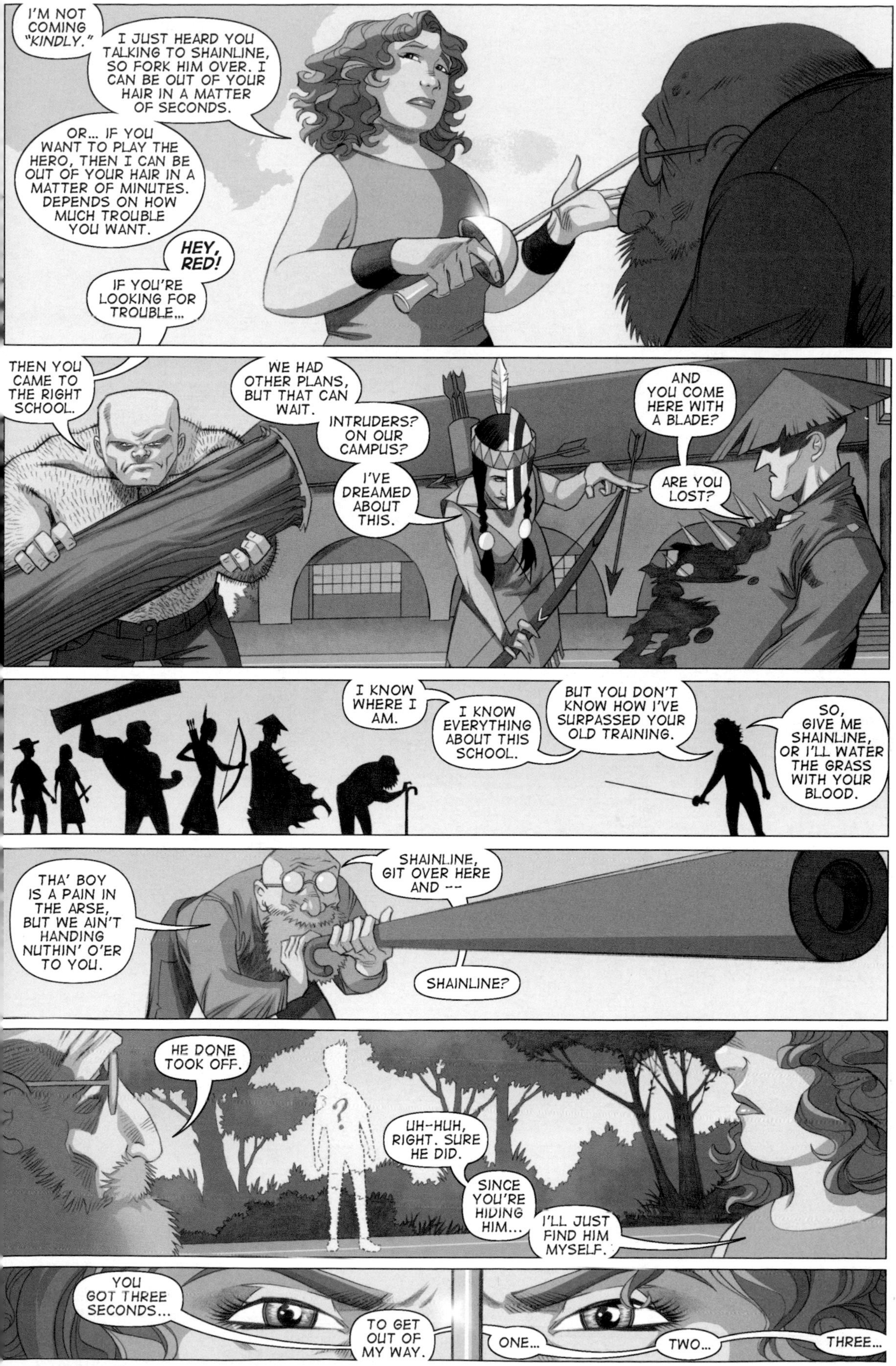
I'M NOT COMING "KINDLY."
I JUST HEARD YOU TALKING TO SHAINLINE, SO FORK HIM OVER. I CAN BE OUT OF YOUR HAIR IN A MATTER OF SECONDS.
OR... IF YOU WANT TO PLAY THE HERO, THEN I CAN BE OUT OF YOUR HAIR IN A MATTER OF MINUTES. DEPENDS ON HOW MUCH TROUBLE YOU WANT.
HEY, RED!
IF YOU'RE LOOKING FOR TROUBLE...
THEN YOU CAME TO THE RIGHT SCHOOL.
WE HAD OTHER PLANS, BUT THAT CAN WAIT.
INTRUDERS? ON OUR CAMPUS?
I'VE DREAMED ABOUT THIS.
AND YOU COME HERE WITH A BLADE?
ARE YOU LOST?
I KNOW WHERE I AM.
I KNOW EVERYTHING ABOUT THIS SCHOOL.
BUT YOU DON'T KNOW HOW I'VE SURPASSED YOUR OLD TRAINING.
SO, GIVE ME SHAINLINE, OR I'LL WATER THE GRASS WITH YOUR BLOOD.
THA' BOY IS A PAIN IN THE ARSE, BUT WE AIN'T HANDING NUTHIN' O'ER TO YOU.
SHAINLINE, GIT OVER HERE AND --
SHAINLINE?
HE DONE TOOK OFF.
UH-HUH, RIGHT. SURE HE DID.
SINCE YOU'RE HIDING HIM...
I'LL JUST FIND HIM MYSELF.
YOU GOT THREE SECONDS...
TO GET OUT OF MY WAY.
ONE...
TWO...
THREE...

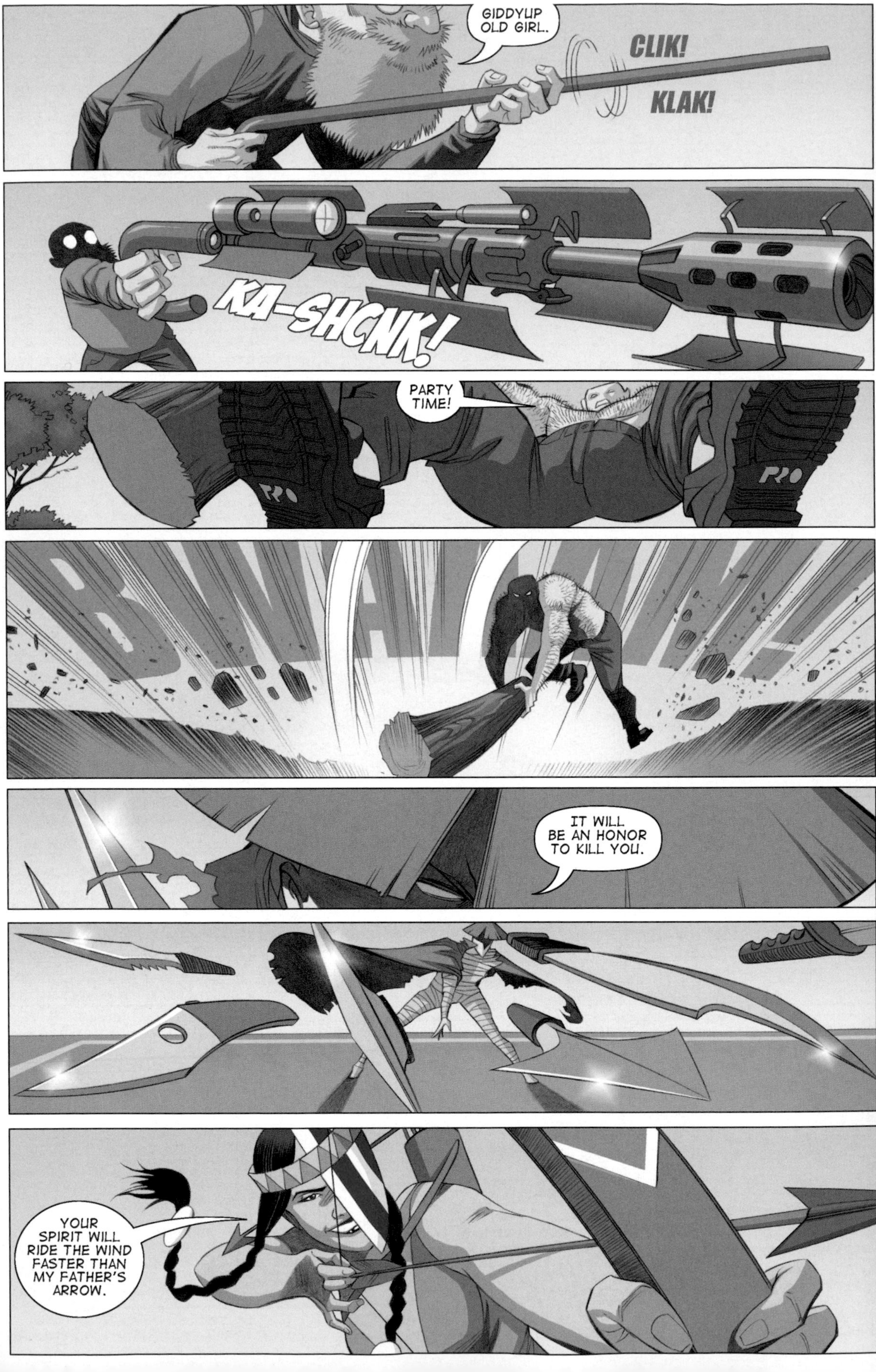
GIDDYUP OLD GIRL.
CLIK!
KLAK!
KA-SHCNK!
PARTY TIME!
IT WILL BE AN HONOR TO KILL YOU.
YOUR SPIRIT WILL RIDE THE WIND FASTER THAN MY FATHER'S ARROW.

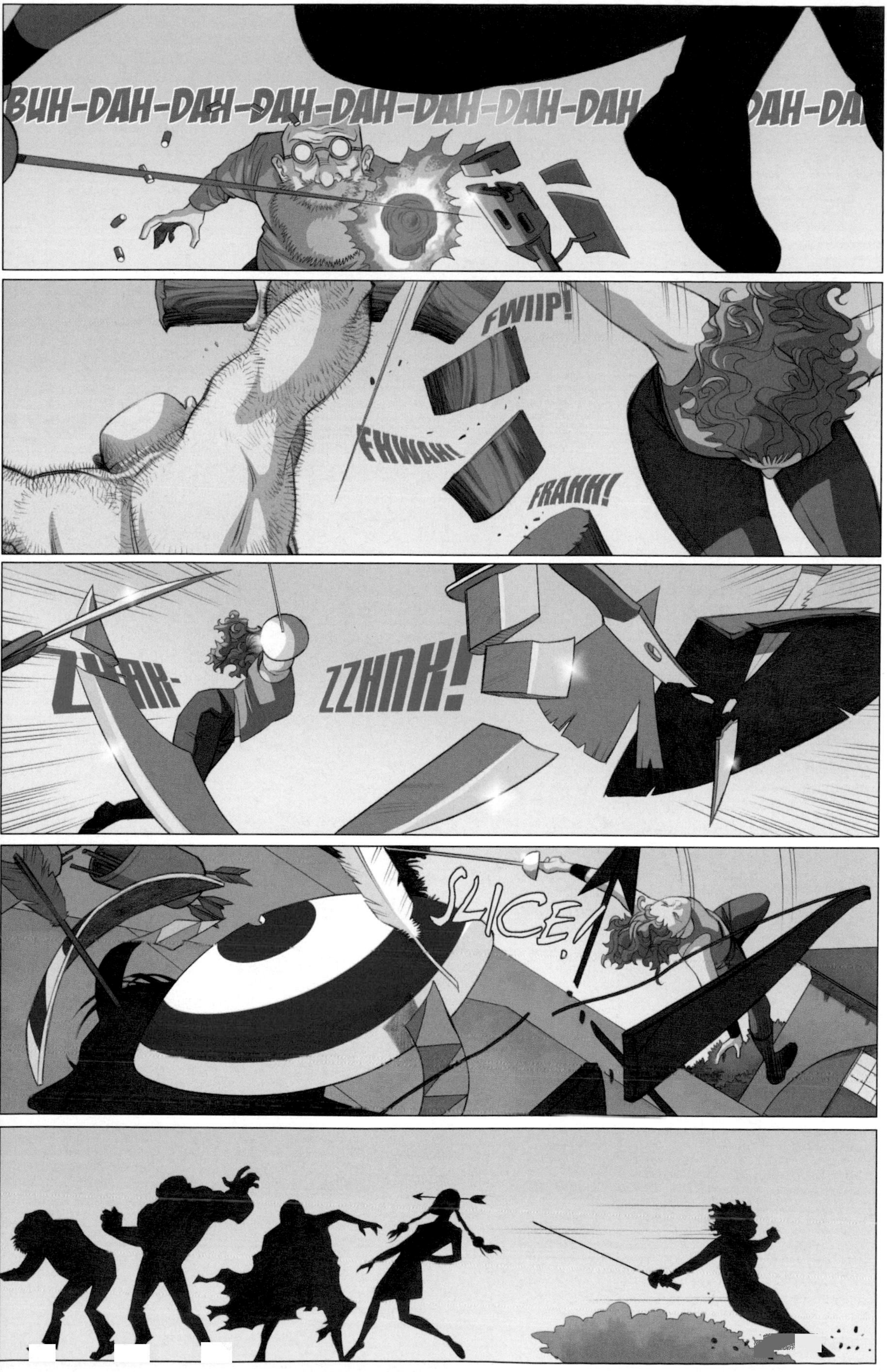

BUH-DAH-DAH-DAH-DAH-DAH-DAH-DAH-
DAH-DA
FWIIP!
FHWAK!
FRAHH!
ZZHNK!
SLICE!

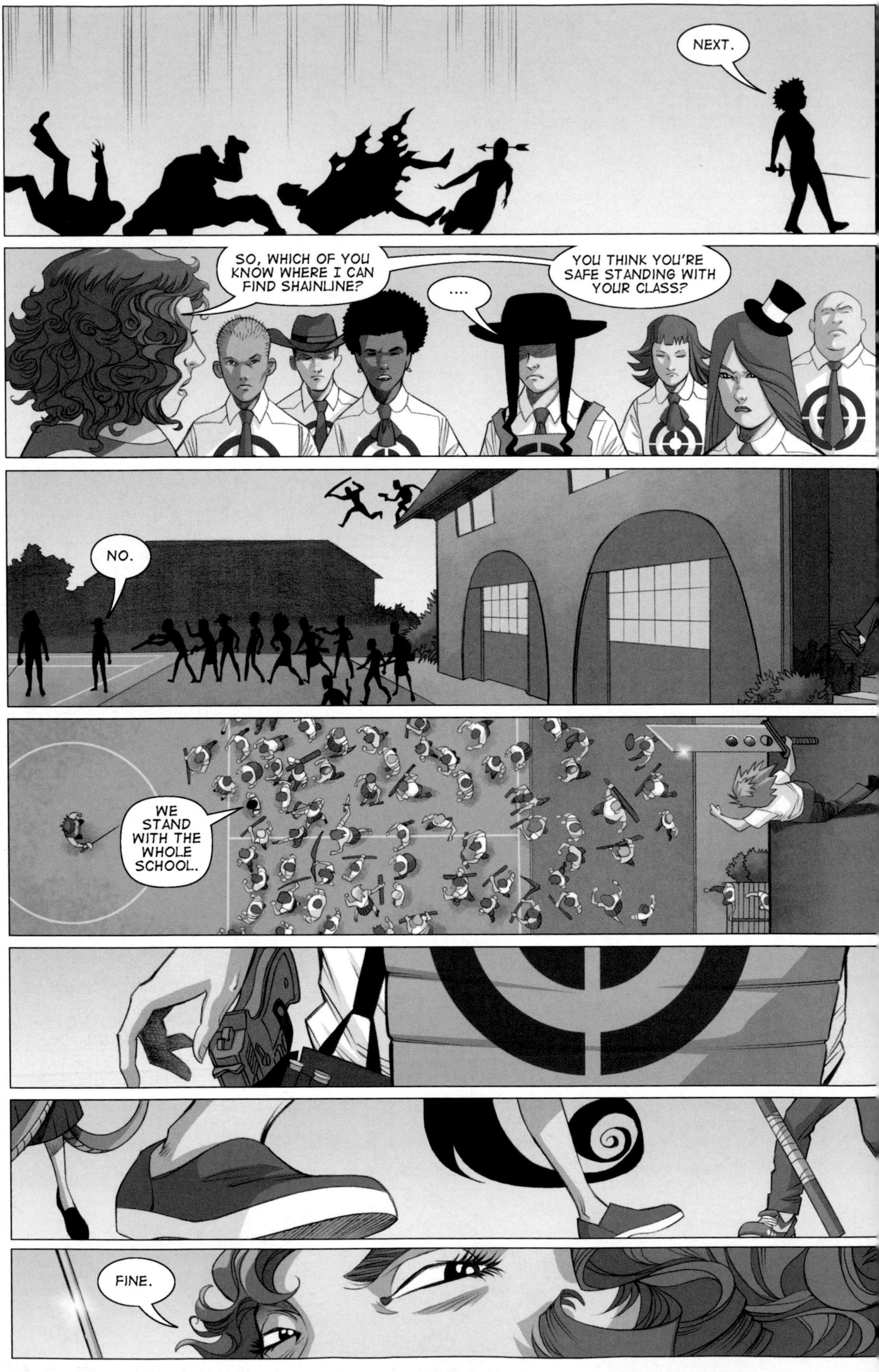
NEXT.
SO, WHICH OF YOU KNOW WHERE I CAN FIND SHAINLINE?
YOU THINK YOU'RE SAFE STANDING WITH YOUR CLASS?
....
NO.
WE STAND WITH THE WHOLE SCHOOL.
FINE.

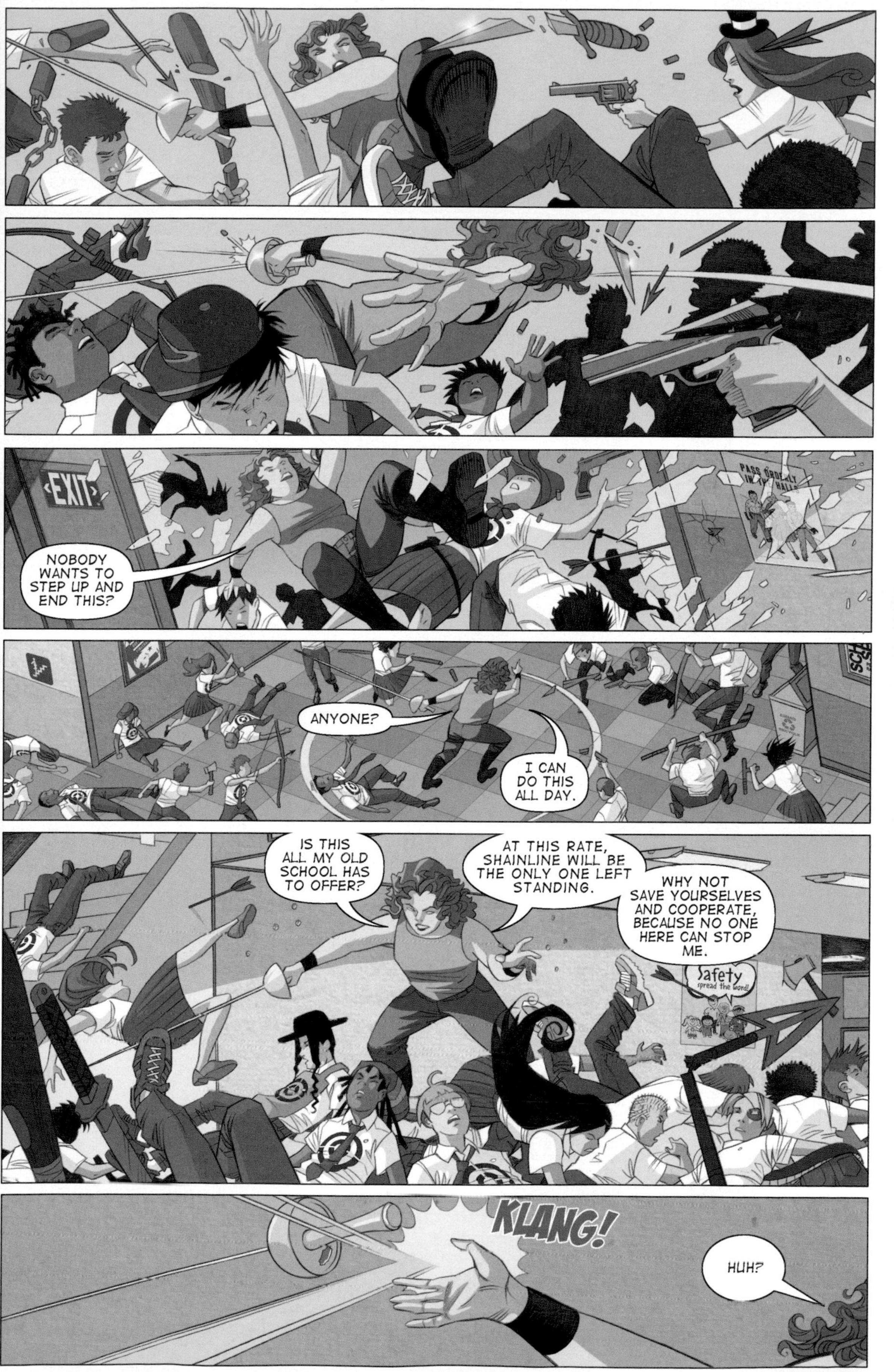
EXIT
NOBODY WANTS TO STEP UP AND END THIS?
PASS ORDERLY IN THE HALLS
ANYONE?
I CAN DO THIS ALL DAY.
IS THIS ALL MY OLD SCHOOL HAS TO OFFER?
AT THIS RATE, SHAINLINE WILL BE THE ONLY ONE LEFT STANDING.
WHY NOT SAVE YOURSELVES AND COOPERATE, BECAUSE NO ONE HERE CAN STOP ME.
Safety spread the word!
KLANG!
HUH?

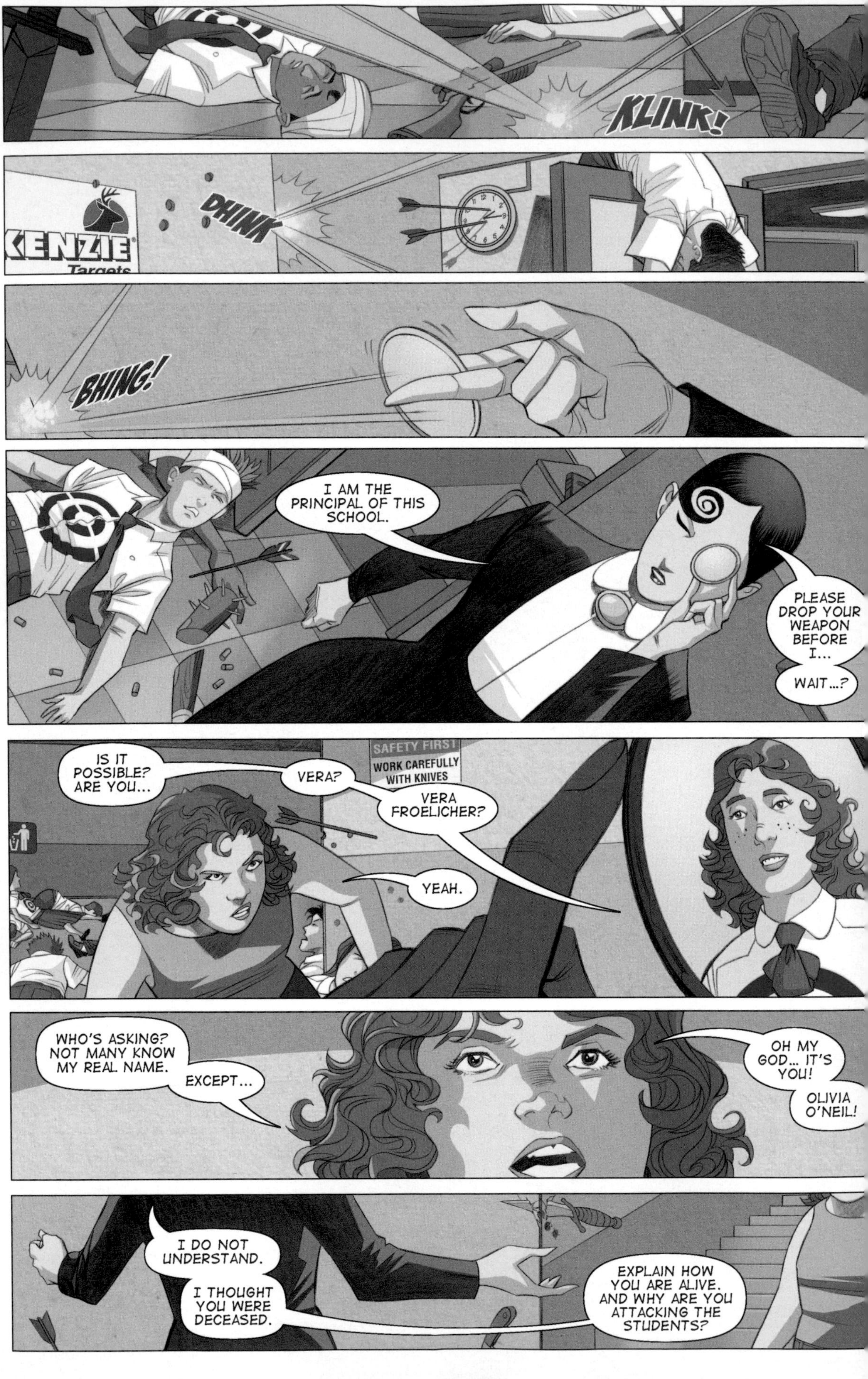
KLINK!
KENZIE
Targets
DHINK
BHING!
I AM THE PRINCIPAL OF THIS SCHOOL.
PLEASE DROP YOUR WEAPON BEFORE I...
WAIT...?
IS IT POSSIBLE? ARE YOU...
VERA?
VERA FROELICHER?
SAFETY FIRST
WORK CAREFULLY WITH KNIVES
YEAH.
WHO'S ASKING? NOT MANY KNOW MY REAL NAME.
EXCEPT...
OH MY GOD... IT'S YOU!
OLIVIA O'NEIL!
I DO NOT UNDERSTAND.
I THOUGHT YOU WERE DECEASED.
EXPLAIN HOW YOU ARE ALIVE. AND WHY ARE YOU ATTACKING THE STUDENTS?

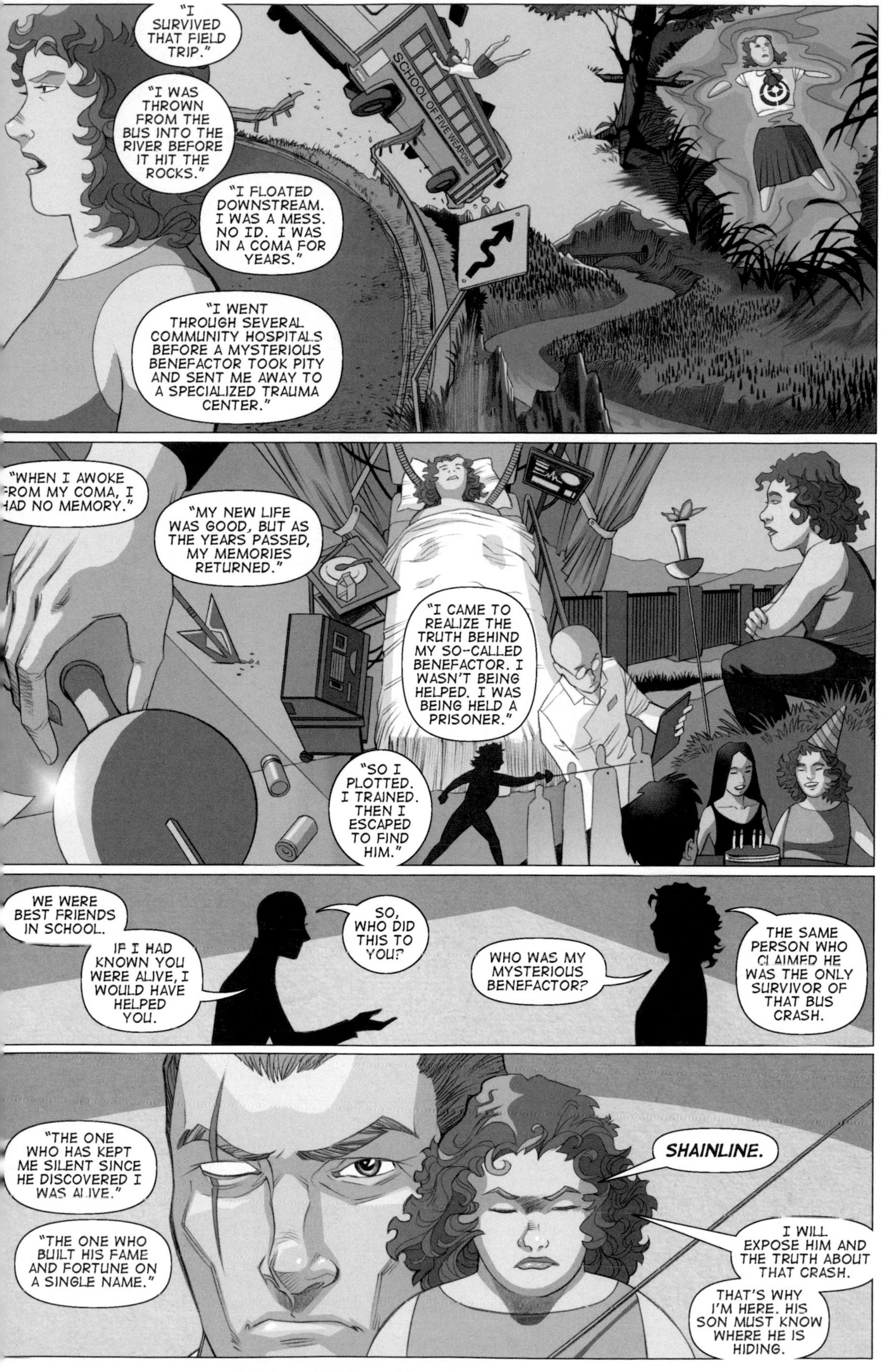
"I SURVIVED THAT FIELD TRIP."
SCHOOL OF FIVE WEAPONS
"I WAS THROWN FROM THE BUS INTO THE RIVER BEFORE IT HIT THE ROCKS."
"I FLOATED DOWNSTREAM. I WAS A MESS. NO ID. I WAS IN A COMA FOR YEARS."
"I WENT THROUGH SEVERAL COMMUNITY HOSPITALS BEFORE A MYSTERIOUS BENEFACTOR TOOK PITY AND SENT ME AWAY TO A SPECIALIZED TRAUMA CENTER."
"WHEN I AWOKE FROM MY COMA, I HAD NO MEMORY."
"MY NEW LIFE WAS GOOD, BUT AS THE YEARS PASSED, MY MEMORIES RETURNED."
"I CAME TO REALIZE THE TRUTH BEHIND MY SO-CALLED BENEFACTOR. I WASN'T BEING HELPED. I WAS BEING HELD A PRISONER."
"SO I PLOTTED. I TRAINED. THEN I ESCAPED TO FIND HIM."
WE WERE BEST FRIENDS IN SCHOOL.
IF I HAD KNOWN YOU WERE ALIVE, I WOULD HAVE HELPED YOU.
SO, WHO DID THIS TO YOU?
WHO WAS MY MYSTERIOUS BENEFACTOR?
THE SAME PERSON WHO CLAIMED HE WAS THE ONLY SURVIVOR OF THAT BUS CRASH.
"THE ONE WHO HAS KEPT ME SILENT SINCE HE DISCOVERED I WAS ALIVE."
"THE ONE WHO BUILT HIS FAME AND FORTUNE ON A SINGLE NAME."
SHAINLINE.
I WILL EXPOSE HIM AND THE TRUTH ABOUT THAT CRASH.
THAT'S WHY I'M HERE. HIS SON MUST KNOW WHERE HE IS HIDING.

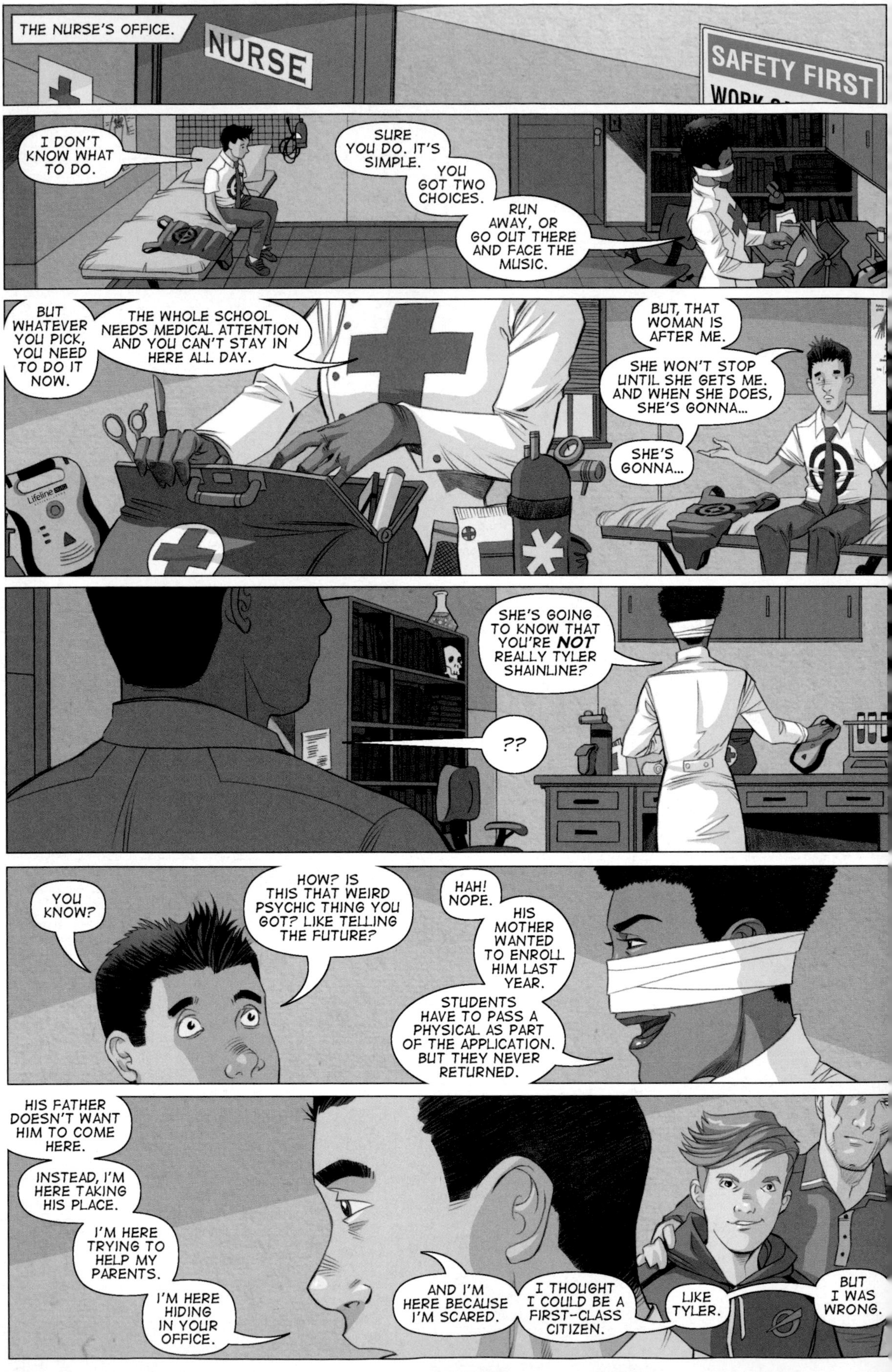
THE NURSE'S OFFICE.
NURSE
SAFETY FIRST
I DON'T KNOW WHAT TO DO.
SURE YOU DO. IT'S SIMPLE.
YOU GOT TWO CHOICES.
RUN AWAY, OR GO OUT THERE AND FACE THE MUSIC.
BUT WHATEVER YOU PICK, YOU NEED TO DO IT NOW.
THE WHOLE SCHOOL NEEDS MEDICAL ATTENTION AND YOU CAN'T STAY IN HERE ALL DAY.
BUT, THAT WOMAN IS AFTER ME.
SHE WON'T STOP UNTIL SHE GETS ME. AND WHEN SHE DOES, SHE'S GONNA...
SHE'S GONNA...
Lifeline
SHE'S GOING TO KNOW THAT YOU'RE ***NOT*** REALLY TYLER SHAINLINE?
??
YOU KNOW?
HOW? IS THIS THAT WEIRD PSYCHIC THING YOU GOT? LIKE TELLING THE FUTURE?
HAH! NOPE.
HIS MOTHER WANTED TO ENROLL HIM LAST YEAR.
STUDENTS HAVE TO PASS A PHYSICAL AS PART OF THE APPLICATION. BUT THEY NEVER RETURNED.
HIS FATHER DOESN'T WANT HIM TO COME HERE.
INSTEAD, I'M HERE TAKING HIS PLACE.
I'M HERE TRYING TO HELP MY PARENTS.
I'M HERE HIDING IN YOUR OFFICE.
AND I'M HERE BECAUSE I'M SCARED.
I THOUGHT I COULD BE A FIRST-CLASS CITIZEN.
LIKE TYLER.
BUT I WAS WRONG.

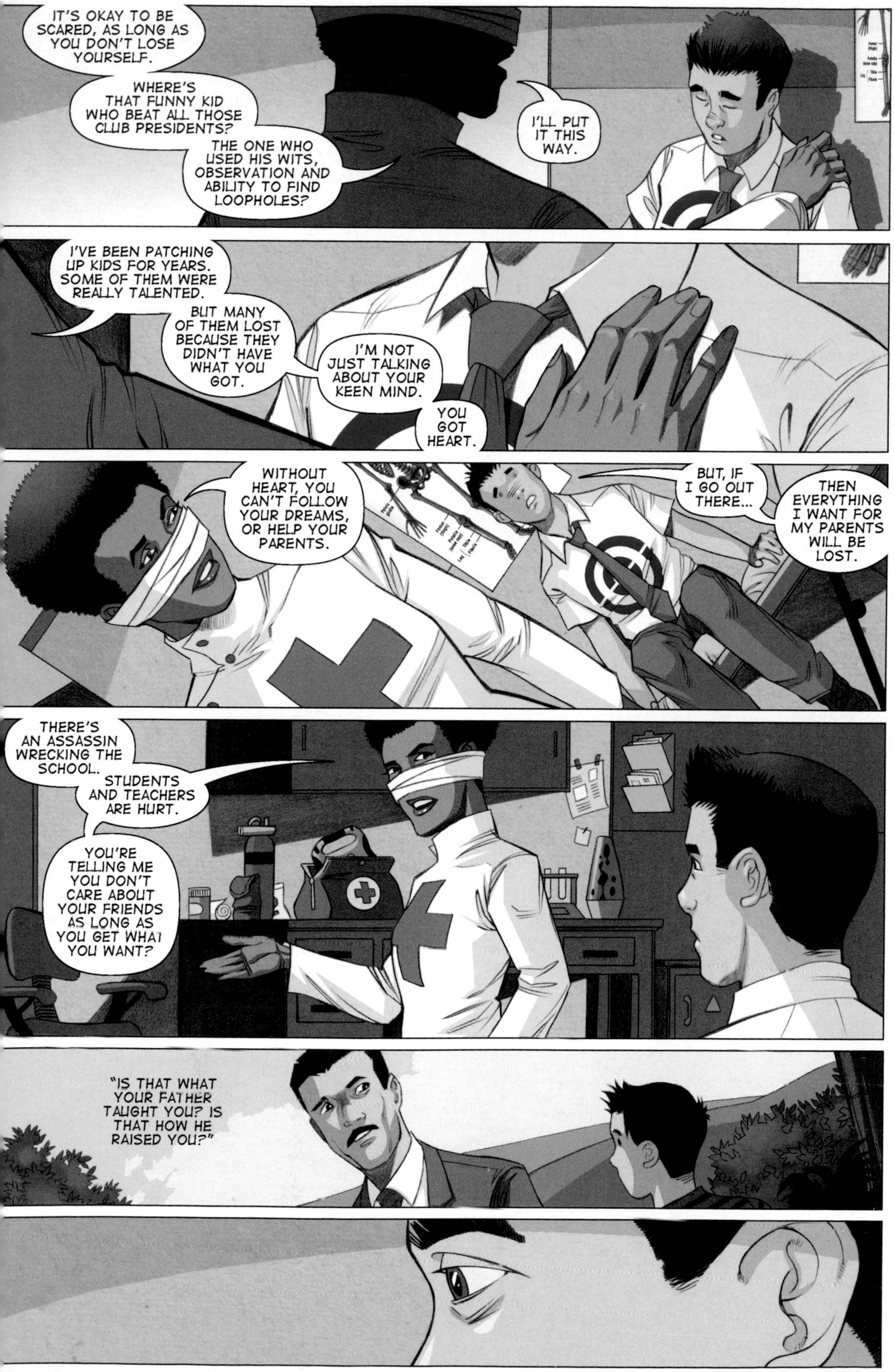
IT'S OKAY TO BE SCARED, AS LONG AS YOU DON'T LOSE YOURSELF.
WHERE'S THAT FUNNY KID WHO BEAT ALL THOSE CLUB PRESIDENTS?
THE ONE WHO USED HIS WITS, OBSERVATION AND ABILITY TO FIND LOOPHOLES?
I'LL PUT IT THIS WAY.
I'VE BEEN PATCHING UP KIDS FOR YEARS. SOME OF THEM WERE REALLY TALENTED.
BUT MANY OF THEM LOST BECAUSE THEY DIDN'T HAVE WHAT YOU GOT.
I'M NOT JUST TALKING ABOUT YOUR KEEN MIND.
YOU GOT HEART.
WITHOUT HEART, YOU CAN'T FOLLOW YOUR DREAMS, OR HELP YOUR PARENTS.
BUT, IF I GO OUT THERE...
THEN EVERYTHING I WANT FOR MY PARENTS WILL BE LOST.
THERE'S AN ASSASSIN WRECKING THE SCHOOL.
STUDENTS AND TEACHERS ARE HURT.
YOU'RE TELLING ME YOU DON'T CARE ABOUT YOUR FRIENDS AS LONG AS YOU GET WHAT YOU WANT?
"IS THAT WHAT YOUR FATHER TAUGHT YOU? IS THAT HOW HE RAISED YOU?"

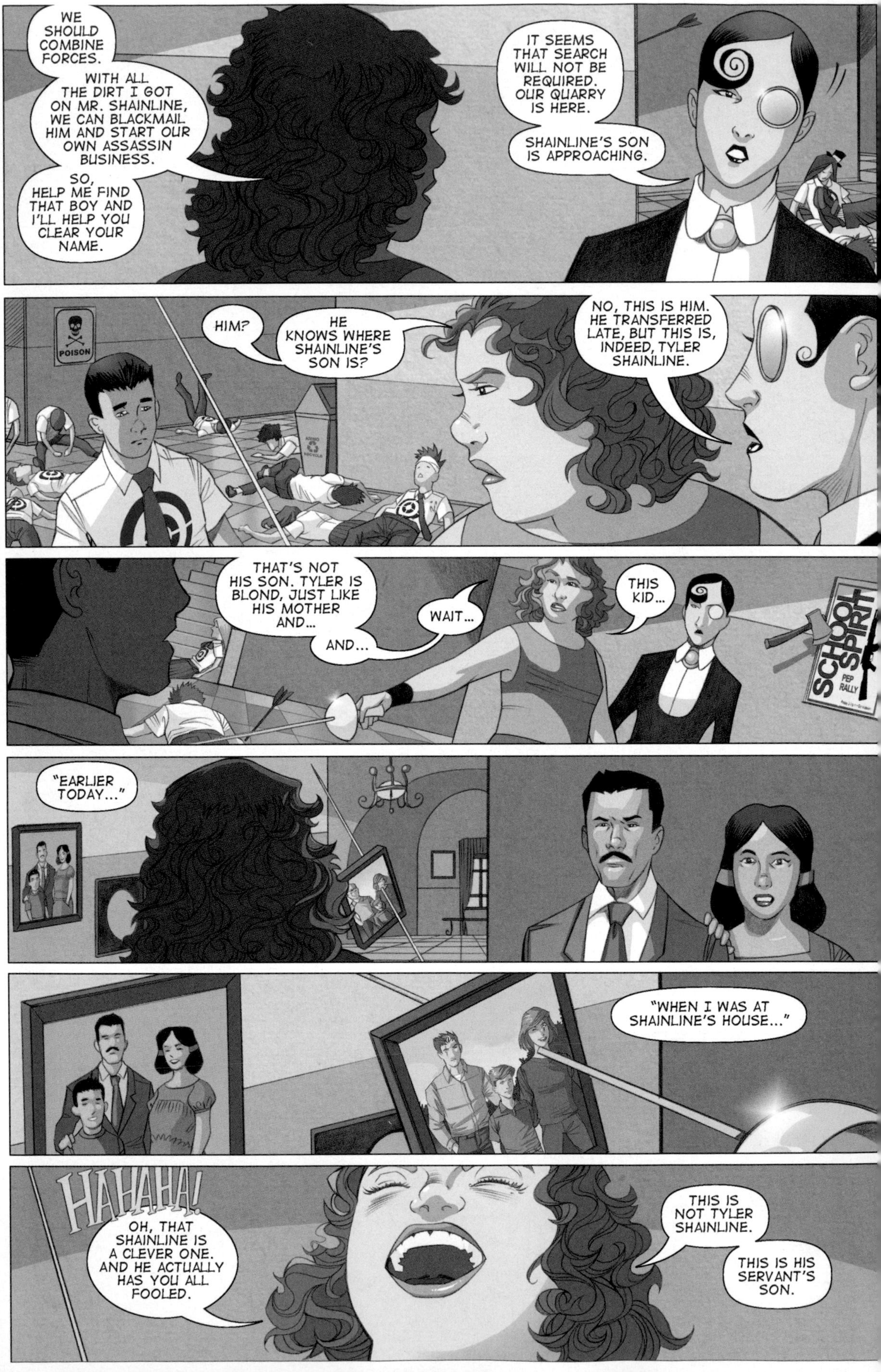

WE SHOULD COMBINE FORCES.
WITH ALL THE DIRT I GOT ON MR. SHAINLINE, WE CAN BLACKMAIL HIM AND START OUR OWN ASSASSIN BUSINESS.
SO, HELP ME FIND THAT BOY AND I'LL HELP YOU CLEAR YOUR NAME.
IT SEEMS THAT SEARCH WILL NOT BE REQUIRED. OUR QUARRY IS HERE.
SHAINLINE'S SON IS APPROACHING.
POISON
HIM?
HE KNOWS WHERE SHAINLINE'S SON IS?
NO, THIS IS HIM. HE TRANSFERRED LATE, BUT THIS IS, INDEED, TYLER SHAINLINE.
THAT'S NOT HIS SON. TYLER IS BLOND, JUST LIKE HIS MOTHER AND...
AND...
WAIT...
THIS KID...
SCHOOL SPIRIT
PEP RALLY
"EARLIER TODAY..."
"WHEN I WAS AT SHAINLINE'S HOUSE..."
HAHAHA!
OH, THAT SHAINLINE IS A CLEVER ONE. AND HE ACTUALLY HAS YOU ALL FOOLED.
THIS IS NOT TYLER SHAINLINE.
THIS IS HIS SERVANT'S SON.

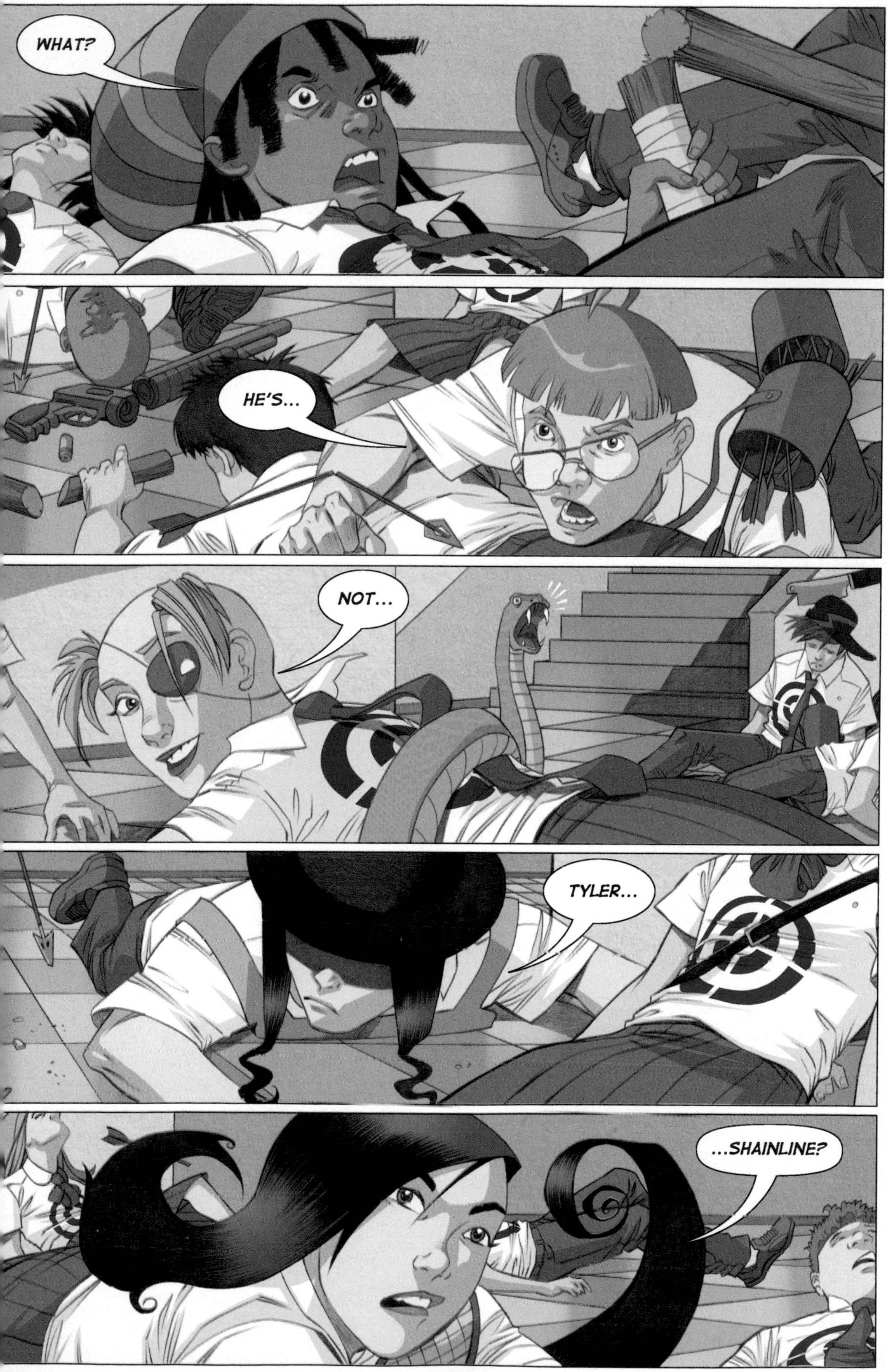
WHAT?
HE'S...
NOT...
TYLER...
...SHAINLINE?

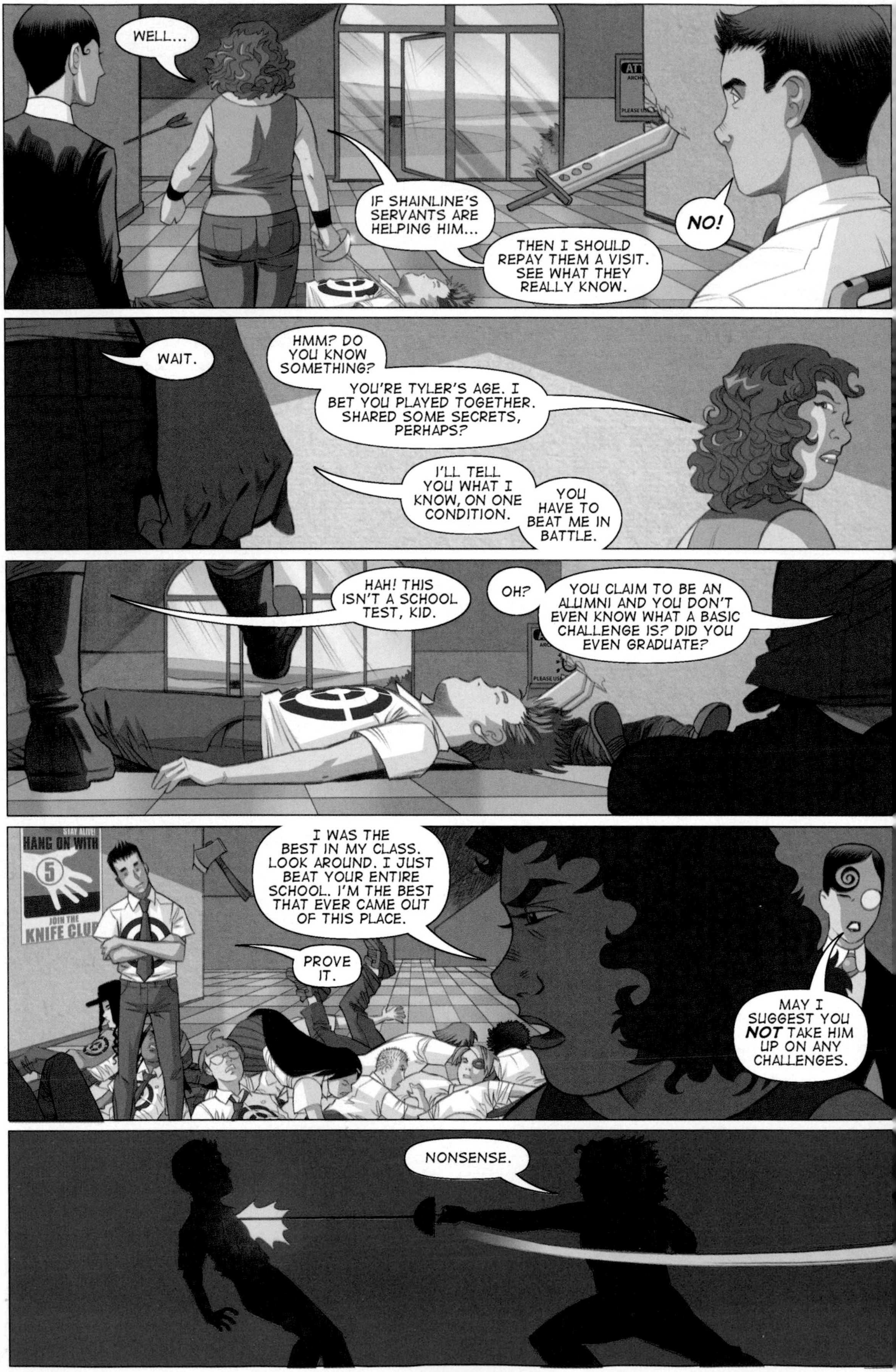
WELL...
IF SHAINLINE'S SERVANTS ARE HELPING HIM...
THEN I SHOULD REPAY THEM A VISIT. SEE WHAT THEY REALLY KNOW.
NO!
WAIT.
HMM? DO YOU KNOW SOMETHING?
YOU'RE TYLER'S AGE. I BET YOU PLAYED TOGETHER. SHARED SOME SECRETS, PERHAPS?
I'LL TELL YOU WHAT I KNOW, ON ONE CONDITION.
YOU HAVE TO BEAT ME IN BATTLE.
HAH! THIS ISN'T A SCHOOL TEST, KID.
OH?
YOU CLAIM TO BE AN ALUMNI AND YOU DON'T EVEN KNOW WHAT A BASIC CHALLENGE IS? DID YOU EVEN GRADUATE?
STAY ALIVE!
HANG ON WITH
5
JOIN THE
KNIFE CLUB
I WAS THE BEST IN MY CLASS. LOOK AROUND. I JUST BEAT YOUR ENTIRE SCHOOL. I'M THE BEST THAT EVER CAME OUT OF THIS PLACE.
PROVE IT.
MAY I SUGGEST YOU NOT TAKE HIM UP ON ANY CHALLENGES.
NONSENSE.

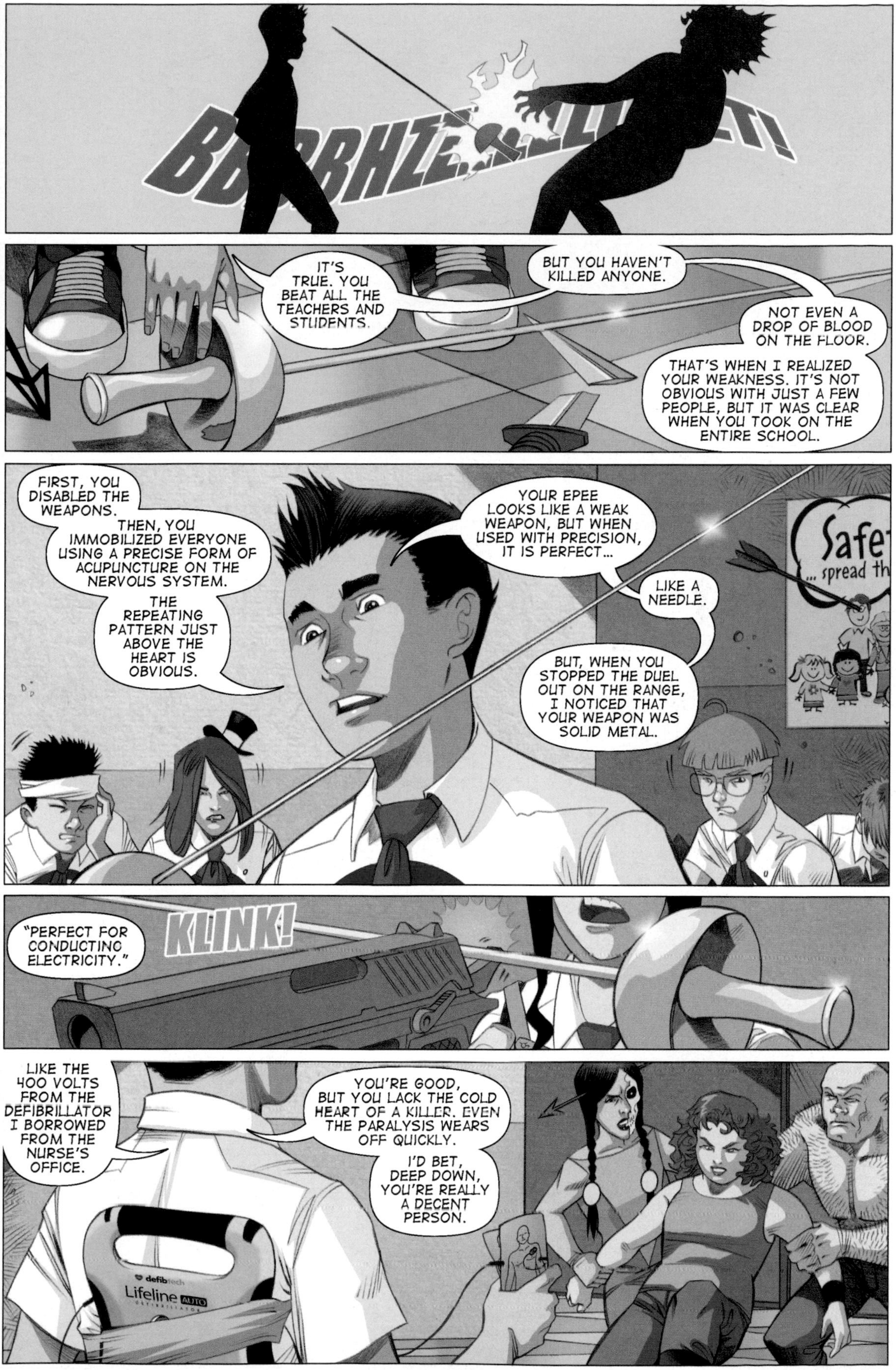
BBBRHZZ...ZZT!
IT'S TRUE. YOU BEAT ALL THE TEACHERS AND STUDENTS.
BUT YOU HAVEN'T KILLED ANYONE.
NOT EVEN A DROP OF BLOOD ON THE FLOOR.
THAT'S WHEN I REALIZED YOUR WEAKNESS. IT'S NOT OBVIOUS WITH JUST A FEW PEOPLE, BUT IT WAS CLEAR WHEN YOU TOOK ON THE ENTIRE SCHOOL.
FIRST, YOU DISABLED THE WEAPONS.
THEN, YOU IMMOBILIZED EVERYONE USING A PRECISE FORM OF ACUPUNCTURE ON THE NERVOUS SYSTEM.
THE REPEATING PATTERN JUST ABOVE THE HEART IS OBVIOUS.
YOUR EPEE LOOKS LIKE A WEAK WEAPON, BUT WHEN USED WITH PRECISION, IT IS PERFECT...
LIKE A NEEDLE.
BUT, WHEN YOU STOPPED THE DUEL OUT ON THE RANGE, I NOTICED THAT YOUR WEAPON WAS SOLID METAL.
"PERFECT FOR CONDUCTING ELECTRICITY."
KLINK!
LIKE THE 400 VOLTS FROM THE DEFIBRILLATOR I BORROWED FROM THE NURSE'S OFFICE.
YOU'RE GOOD, BUT YOU LACK THE COLD HEART OF A KILLER. EVEN THE PARALYSIS WEARS OFF QUICKLY.
I'D BET, DEEP DOWN, YOU'RE REALLY A DECENT PERSON.
defibtech
Lifeline AUTO

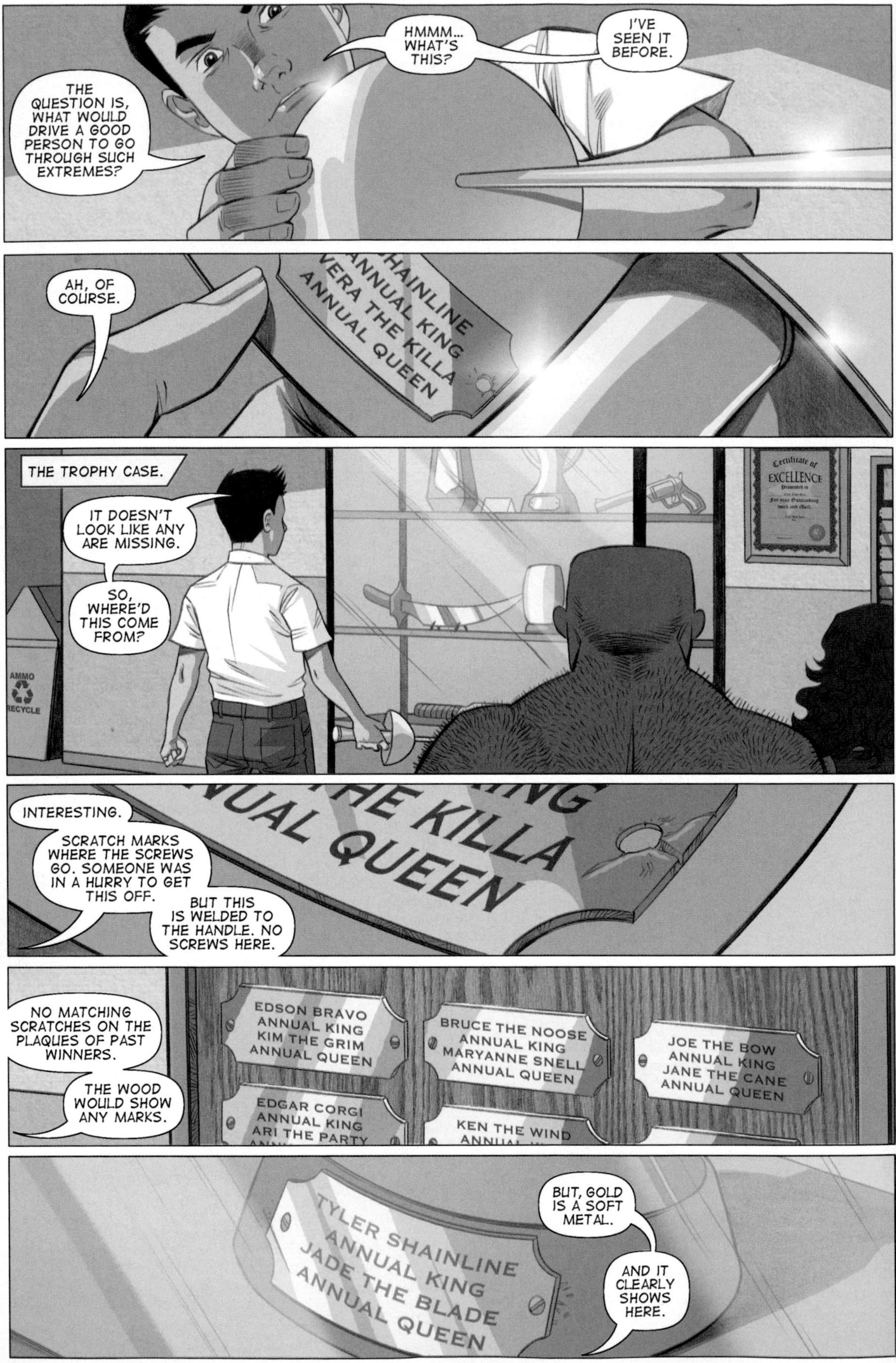
THE QUESTION IS, WHAT WOULD DRIVE A GOOD PERSON TO GO THROUGH SUCH EXTREMES?
HMMM... WHAT'S THIS?
I'VE SEEN IT BEFORE.
AH, OF COURSE.
SHAINLINE ANNUAL KING VERA THE KILLA ANNUAL QUEEN
THE TROPHY CASE.
IT DOESN'T LOOK LIKE ANY ARE MISSING.
SO, WHERE'D THIS COME FROM?
Certificate of EXCELLENCE
AMMO RECYCLE
INTERESTING.
SCRATCH MARKS WHERE THE SCREWS GO. SOMEONE WAS IN A HURRY TO GET THIS OFF.
BUT THIS IS WELDED TO THE HANDLE. NO SCREWS HERE.
THE KILLA QUEEN
NO MATCHING SCRATCHES ON THE PLAQUES OF PAST WINNERS.
THE WOOD WOULD SHOW ANY MARKS.
EDSON BRAVO ANNUAL KING KIM THE GRIM ANNUAL QUEEN
BRUCE THE NOOSE ANNUAL KING MARYANNE SNELL ANNUAL QUEEN
JOE THE BOW ANNUAL KING JANE THE CANE ANNUAL QUEEN
EDGAR CORGI ANNUAL KING ARI THE PARTY
KEN THE WIND
TYLER SHAINLINE ANNUAL KING JADE THE BLADE ANNUAL QUEEN
BUT, GOLD IS A SOFT METAL.
AND IT CLEARLY SHOWS HERE.

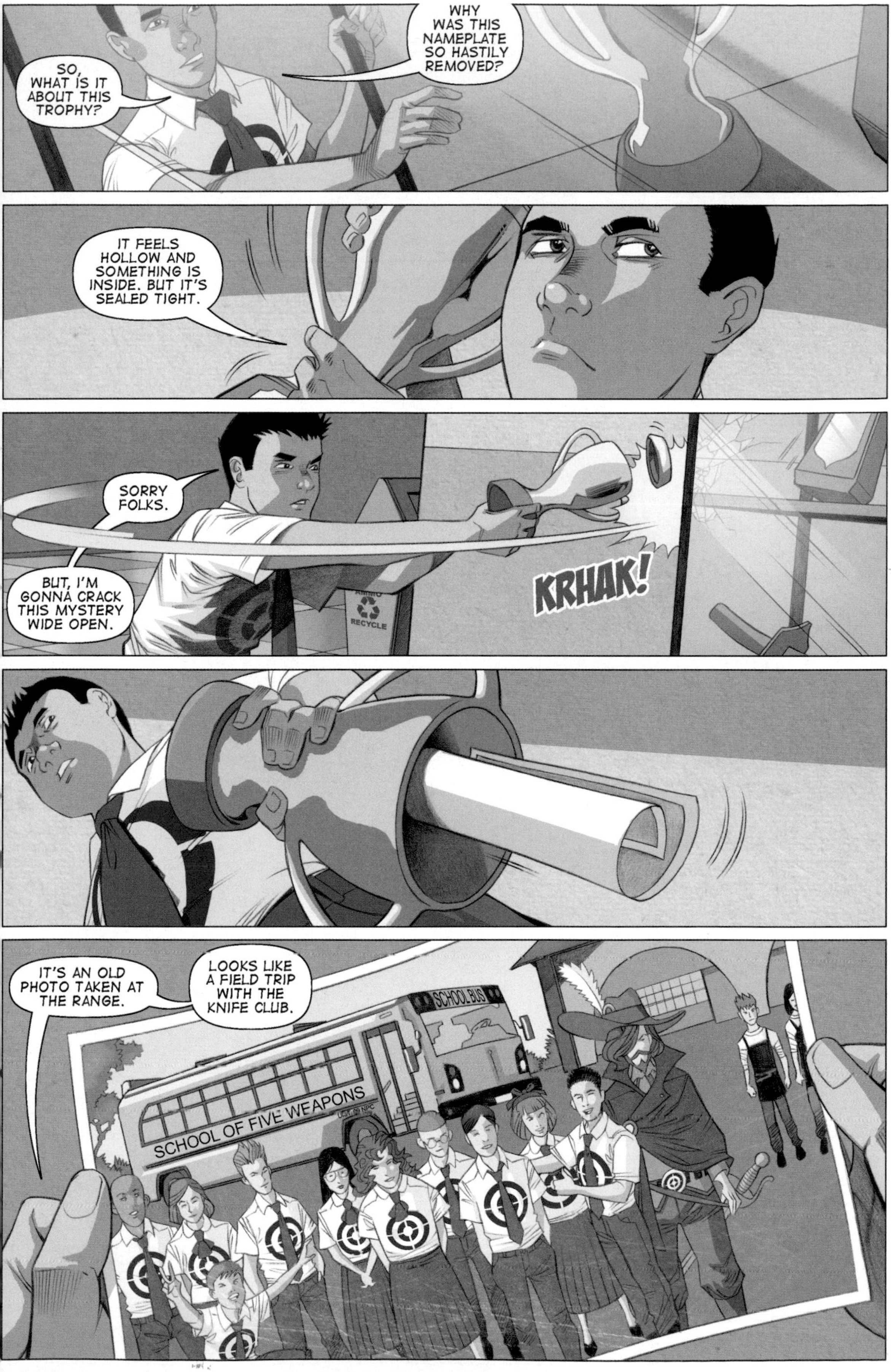

SO, WHAT IS IT ABOUT THIS TROPHY?
WHY WAS THIS NAMEPLATE SO HASTILY REMOVED?
IT FEELS HOLLOW AND SOMETHING IS INSIDE. BUT IT'S SEALED TIGHT.
SORRY FOLKS.
BUT, I'M GONNA CRACK THIS MYSTERY WIDE OPEN.
RECYCLE
KRHAK!
IT'S AN OLD PHOTO TAKEN AT THE RANGE.
LOOKS LIKE A FIELD TRIP WITH THE KNIFE CLUB.
SCHOOL BUS
SCHOOL OF FIVE WEAPONS

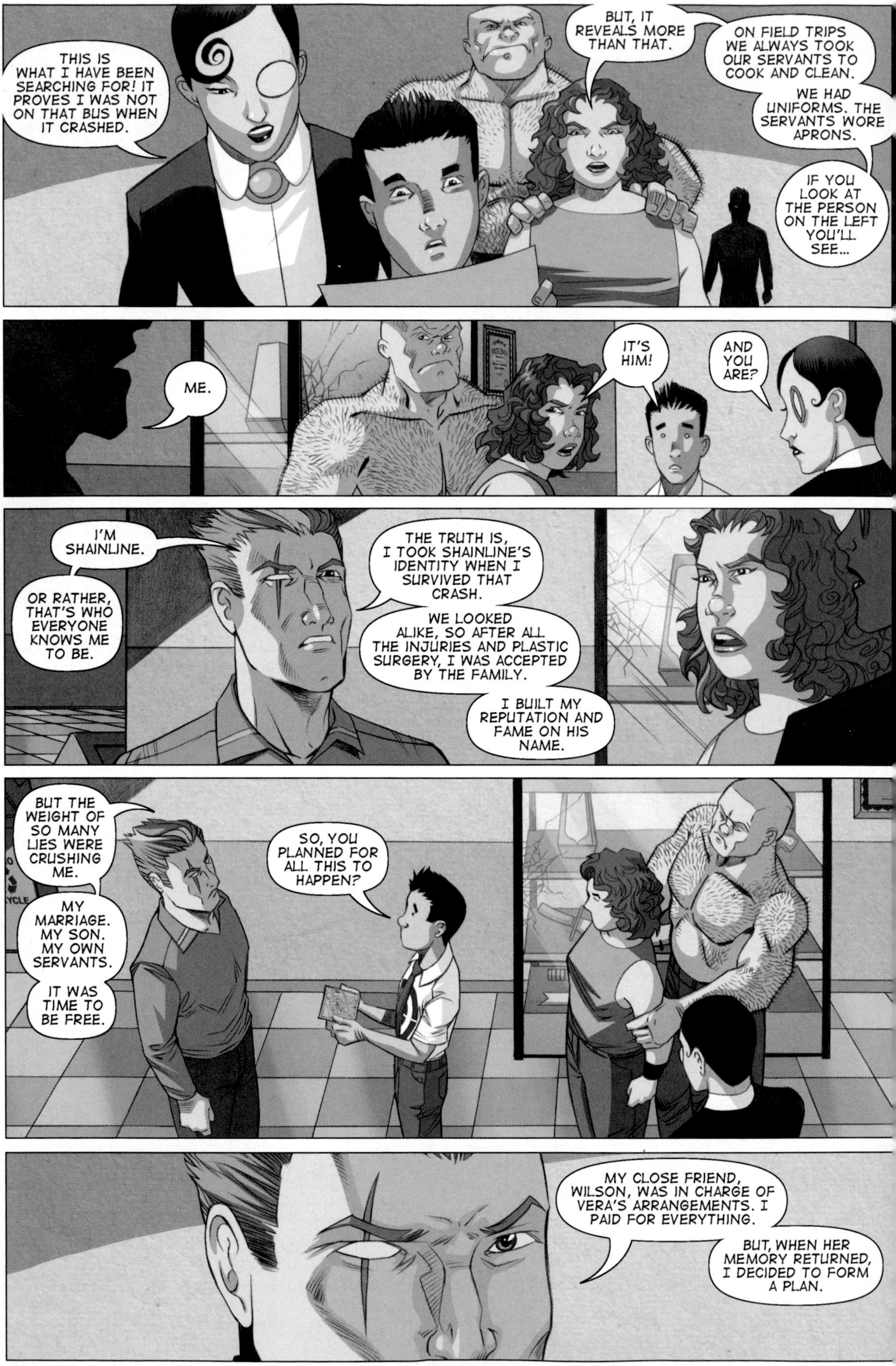
THIS IS WHAT I HAVE BEEN SEARCHING FOR! IT PROVES I WAS NOT ON THAT BUS WHEN IT CRASHED.
BUT, IT REVEALS MORE THAN THAT.
ON FIELD TRIPS WE ALWAYS TOOK OUR SERVANTS TO COOK AND CLEAN.
WE HAD UNIFORMS. THE SERVANTS WORE APRONS.
IF YOU LOOK AT THE PERSON ON THE LEFT YOU'LL SEE...
ME.
IT'S HIM!
AND YOU ARE?
I'M SHAINLINE.
OR RATHER, THAT'S WHO EVERYONE KNOWS ME TO BE.
THE TRUTH IS, I TOOK SHAINLINE'S IDENTITY WHEN I SURVIVED THAT CRASH.
WE LOOKED ALIKE, SO AFTER ALL THE INJURIES AND PLASTIC SURGERY, I WAS ACCEPTED BY THE FAMILY.
I BUILT MY REPUTATION AND FAME ON HIS NAME.
BUT THE WEIGHT OF SO MANY LIES WERE CRUSHING ME.
MY MARRIAGE. MY SON. MY OWN SERVANTS.
IT WAS TIME TO BE FREE.
SO, YOU PLANNED FOR ALL THIS TO HAPPEN?
MY CLOSE FRIEND, WILSON, WAS IN CHARGE OF VERA'S ARRANGEMENTS. I PAID FOR EVERYTHING.
BUT, WHEN HER MEMORY RETURNED, I DECIDED TO FORM A PLAN.

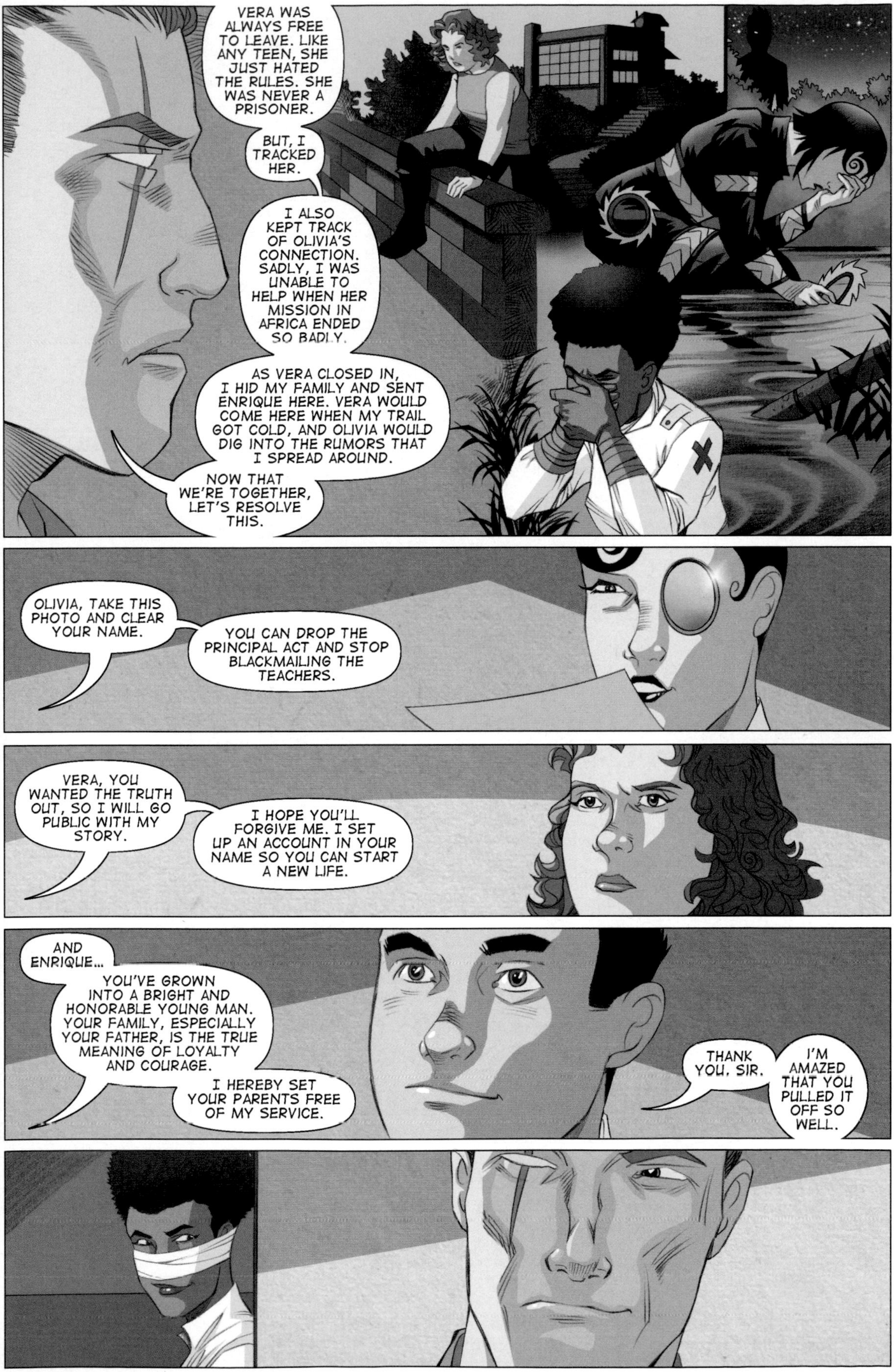
VERA WAS ALWAYS FREE TO LEAVE. LIKE ANY TEEN, SHE JUST HATED THE RULES. SHE WAS NEVER A PRISONER.
BUT, I TRACKED HER.
I ALSO KEPT TRACK OF OLIVIA'S CONNECTION. SADLY, I WAS UNABLE TO HELP WHEN HER MISSION IN AFRICA ENDED SO BADLY.
AS VERA CLOSED IN, I HID MY FAMILY AND SENT ENRIQUE HERE. VERA WOULD COME HERE WHEN MY TRAIL GOT COLD, AND OLIVIA WOULD DIG INTO THE RUMORS THAT I SPREAD AROUND.
NOW THAT WE'RE TOGETHER, LET'S RESOLVE THIS.
OLIVIA, TAKE THIS PHOTO AND CLEAR YOUR NAME.
YOU CAN DROP THE PRINCIPAL ACT AND STOP BLACKMAILING THE TEACHERS.
VERA, YOU WANTED THE TRUTH OUT, SO I WILL GO PUBLIC WITH MY STORY.
I HOPE YOU'LL FORGIVE ME. I SET UP AN ACCOUNT IN YOUR NAME SO YOU CAN START A NEW LIFE.
AND ENRIQUE...
YOU'VE GROWN INTO A BRIGHT AND HONORABLE YOUNG MAN. YOUR FAMILY, ESPECIALLY YOUR FATHER, IS THE TRUE MEANING OF LOYALTY AND COURAGE.
I HEREBY SET YOUR PARENTS FREE OF MY SERVICE.
THANK YOU, SIR.
I'M AMAZED THAT YOU PULLED IT OFF SO WELL.

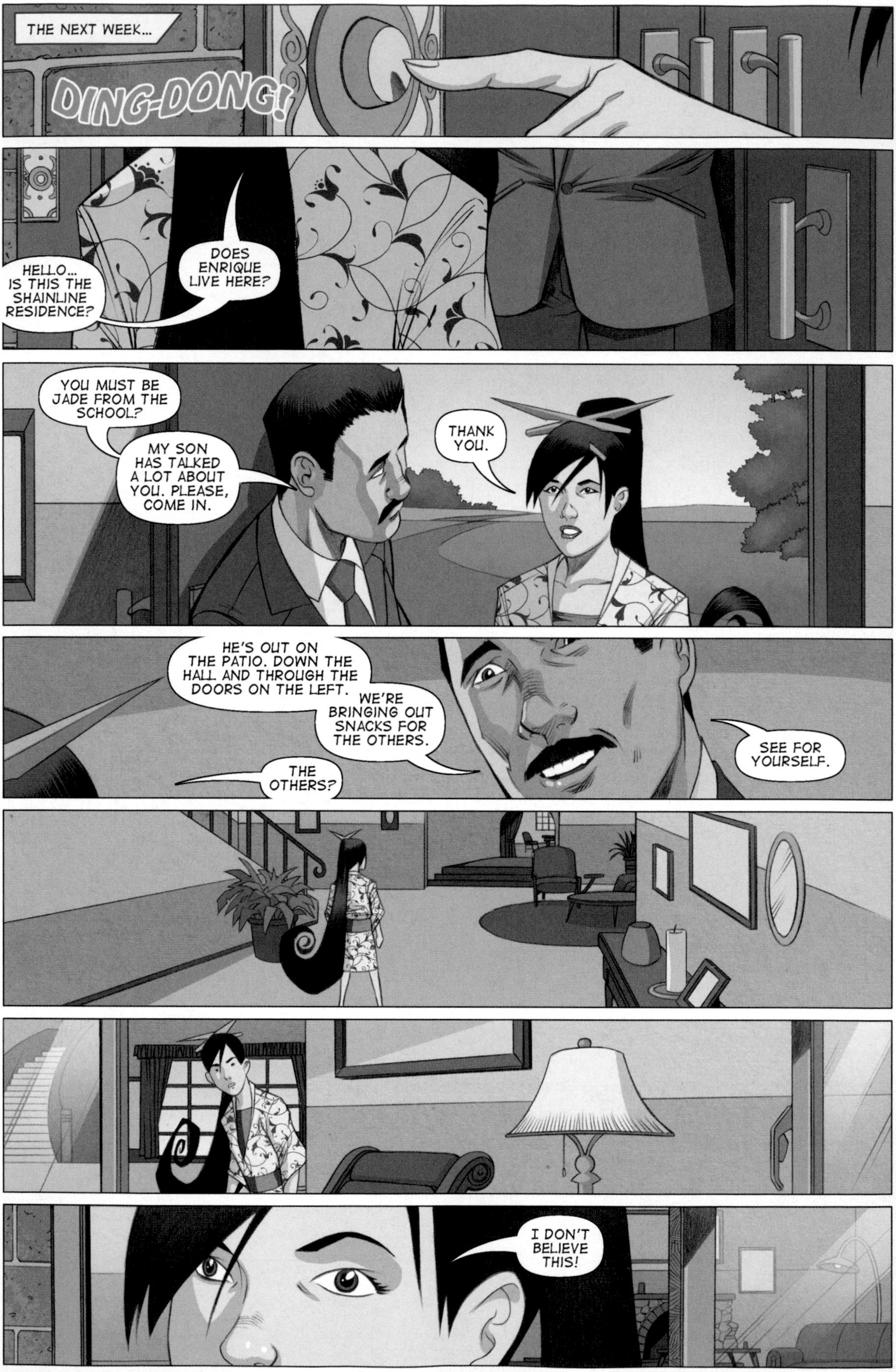
THE NEXT WEEK...
DING-DONG!
HELLO... IS THIS THE SHAINLINE RESIDENCE?
DOES ENRIQUE LIVE HERE?
YOU MUST BE JADE FROM THE SCHOOL?
MY SON HAS TALKED A LOT ABOUT YOU. PLEASE, COME IN.
THANK YOU.
HE'S OUT ON THE PATIO. DOWN THE HALL AND THROUGH THE DOORS ON THE LEFT.
WE'RE BRINGING OUT SNACKS FOR THE OTHERS.
THE OTHERS?
SEE FOR YOURSELF.
I DON'T BELIEVE THIS!

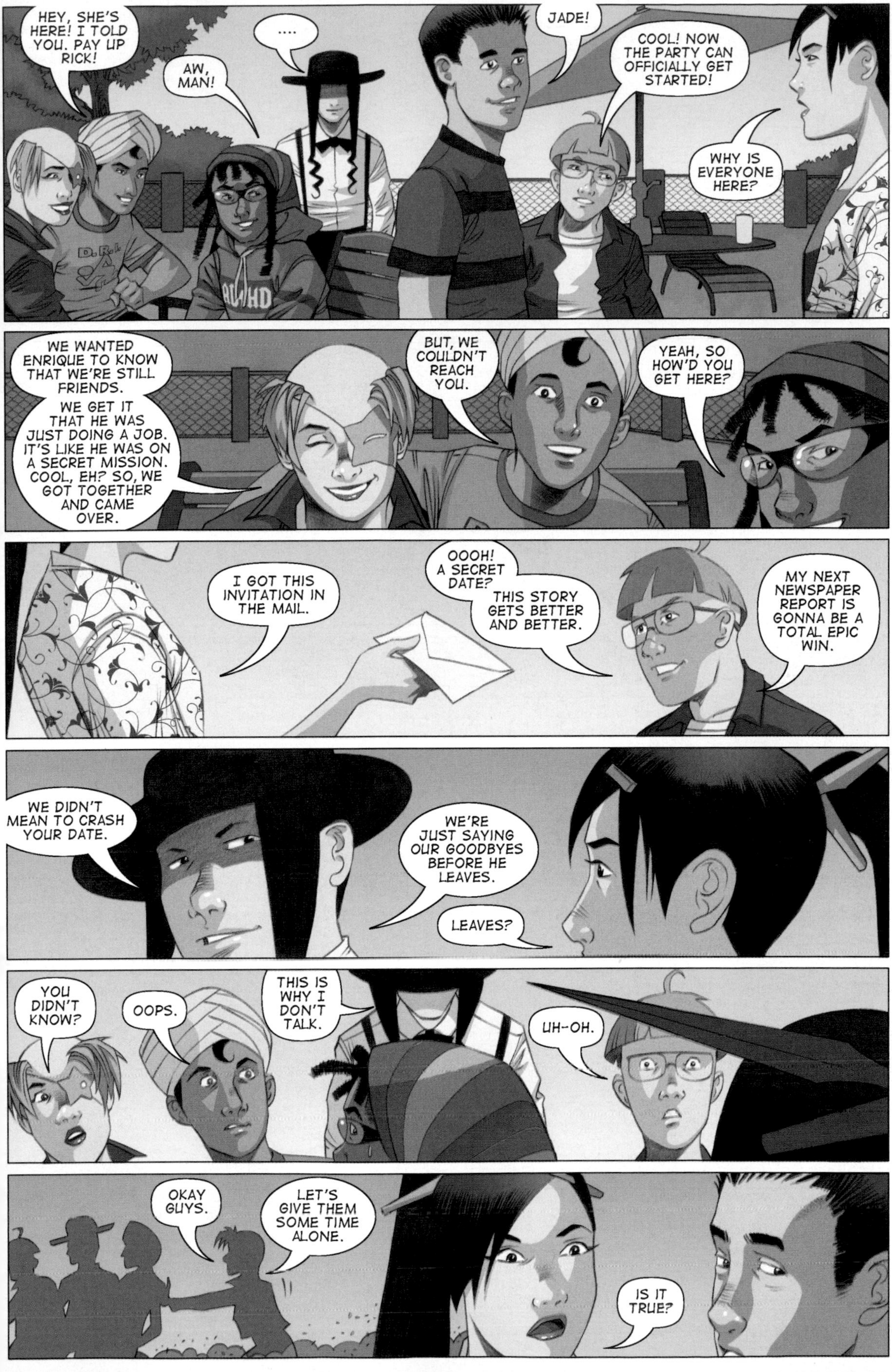
HEY, SHE'S HERE! I TOLD YOU. PAY UP RICK!
AW, MAN!
....
JADE!
COOL! NOW THE PARTY CAN OFFICIALLY GET STARTED!
WHY IS EVERYONE HERE?
WE WANTED ENRIQUE TO KNOW THAT WE'RE STILL FRIENDS.
WE GET IT THAT HE WAS JUST DOING A JOB. IT'S LIKE HE WAS ON A SECRET MISSION. COOL, EH? SO, WE GOT TOGETHER AND CAME OVER.
BUT, WE COULDN'T REACH YOU.
YEAH, SO HOW'D YOU GET HERE?
I GOT THIS INVITATION IN THE MAIL.
OOOH! A SECRET DATE?
THIS STORY GETS BETTER AND BETTER.
MY NEXT NEWSPAPER REPORT IS GONNA BE A TOTAL EPIC WIN.
WE DIDN'T MEAN TO CRASH YOUR DATE.
WE'RE JUST SAYING OUR GOODBYES BEFORE HE LEAVES.
LEAVES?
YOU DIDN'T KNOW?
OOPS.
THIS IS WHY I DON'T TALK.
UH-OH.
OKAY GUYS.
LET'S GIVE THEM SOME TIME ALONE.
IS IT TRUE?

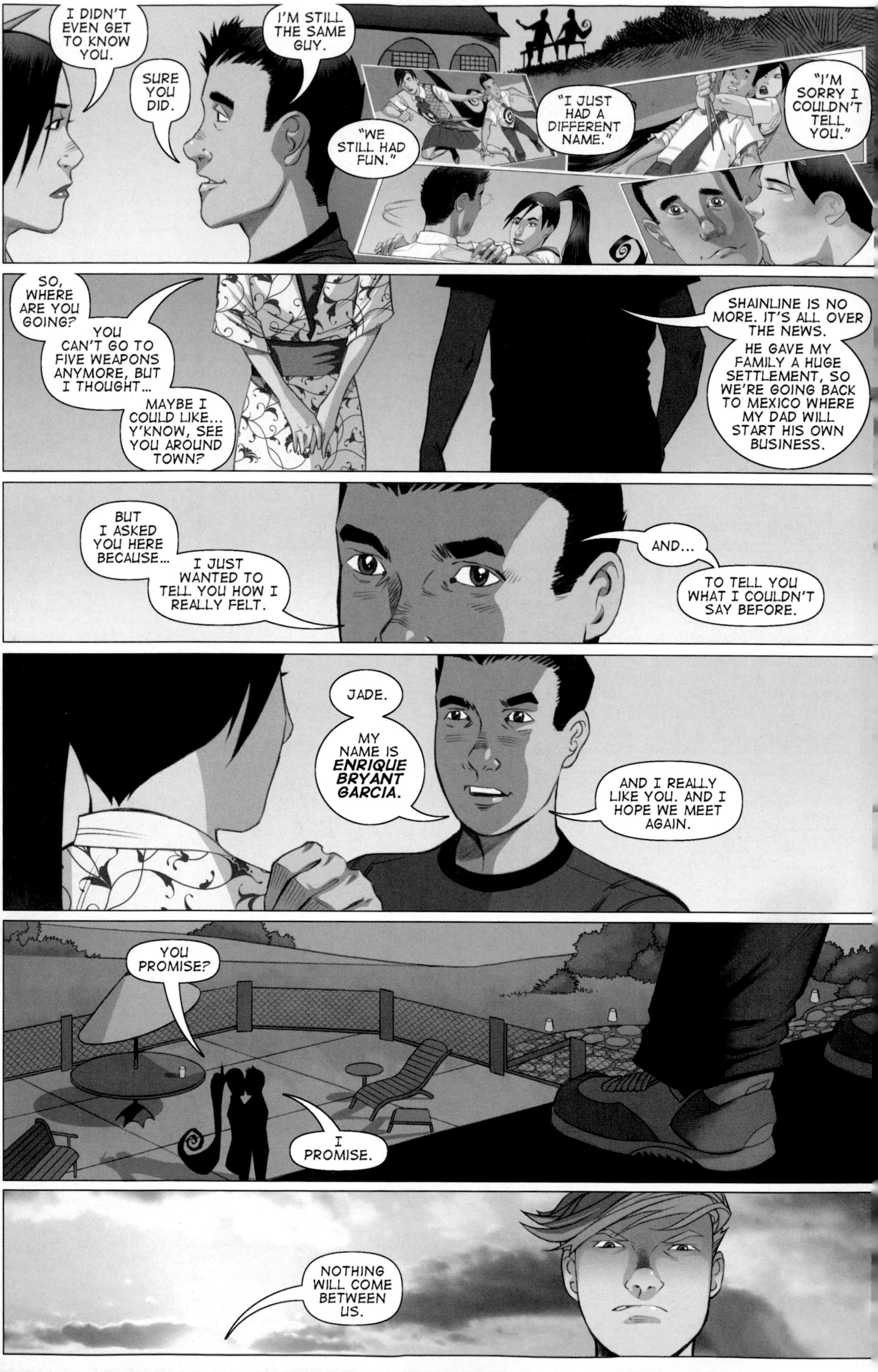
I DIDN'T EVEN GET TO KNOW YOU.
SURE YOU DID.
I'M STILL THE SAME GUY.
"WE STILL HAD FUN."
"I JUST HAD A DIFFERENT NAME."
"I'M SORRY I COULDN'T TELL YOU."
SO, WHERE ARE YOU GOING?
YOU CAN'T GO TO FIVE WEAPONS ANYMORE, BUT I THOUGHT...
MAYBE I COULD LIKE... Y'KNOW, SEE YOU AROUND TOWN?
SHAINLINE IS NO MORE. IT'S ALL OVER THE NEWS.
HE GAVE MY FAMILY A HUGE SETTLEMENT, SO WE'RE GOING BACK TO MEXICO WHERE MY DAD WILL START HIS OWN BUSINESS.
BUT I ASKED YOU HERE BECAUSE...
I JUST WANTED TO TELL YOU HOW I REALLY FELT.
AND...
TO TELL YOU WHAT I COULDN'T SAY BEFORE.
JADE.
MY NAME IS ENRIQUE BRYANT GARCIA.
AND I REALLY LIKE YOU. AND I HOPE WE MEET AGAIN.
YOU PROMISE?
I PROMISE.
NOTHING WILL COME BETWEEN US.

EXTRAS

Introductory story originally appeared in
BOMB QUEEN VOL. 7: ATOMIC BOMB

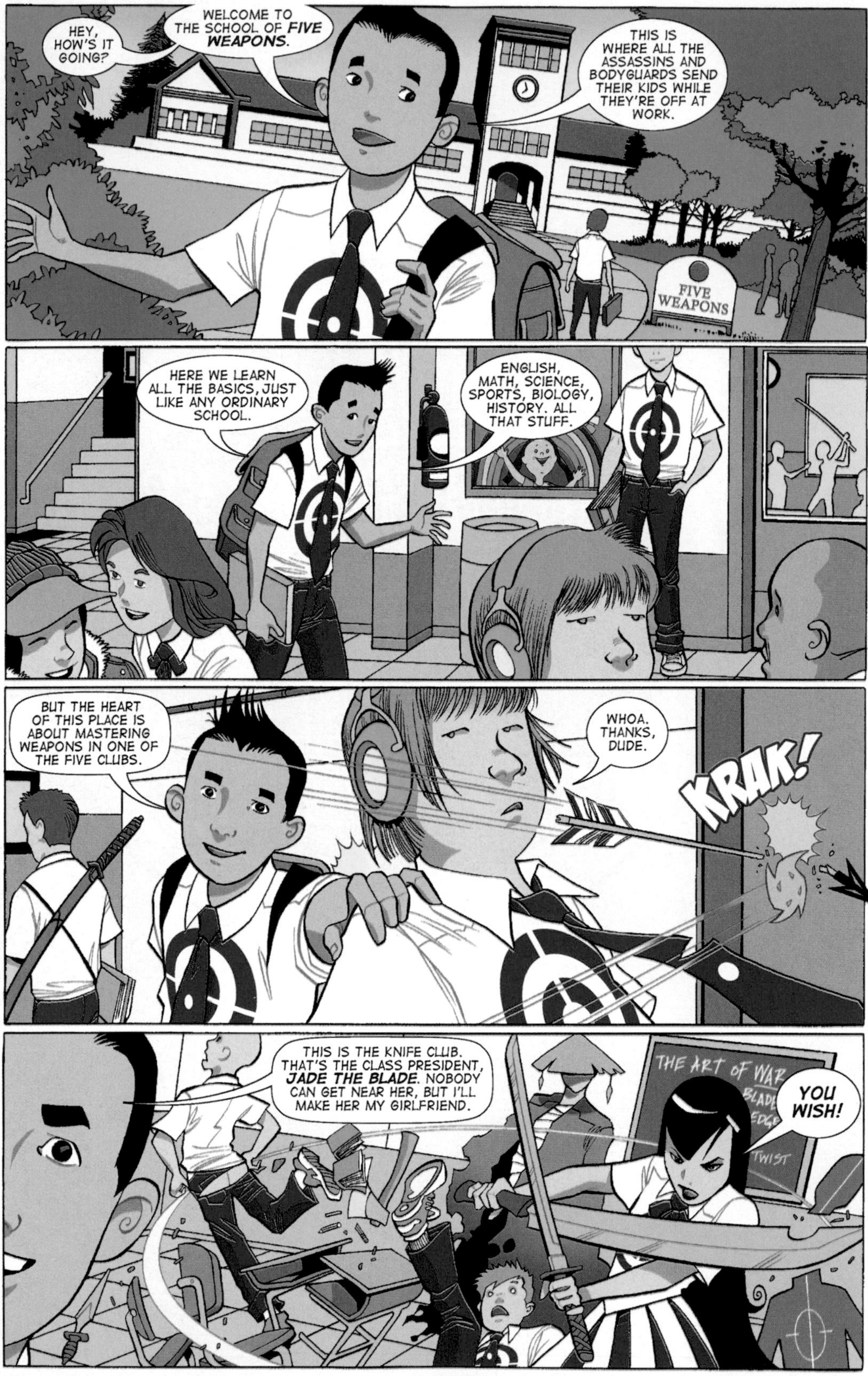
HEY, HOW'S IT GOING?
WELCOME TO THE SCHOOL OF FIVE WEAPONS.
THIS IS WHERE ALL THE ASSASSINS AND BODYGUARDS SEND THEIR KIDS WHILE THEY'RE OFF AT WORK.
FIVE WEAPONS
HERE WE LEARN ALL THE BASICS, JUST LIKE ANY ORDINARY SCHOOL.
ENGLISH, MATH, SCIENCE, SPORTS, BIOLOGY, HISTORY. ALL THAT STUFF.
BUT THE HEART OF THIS PLACE IS ABOUT MASTERING WEAPONS IN ONE OF THE FIVE CLUBS.
WHOA. THANKS, DUDE.
KRAK!
THIS IS THE KNIFE CLUB. THAT'S THE CLASS PRESIDENT, JADE THE BLADE. NOBODY CAN GET NEAR HER, BUT I'LL MAKE HER MY GIRLFRIEND.
THE ART OF WAR
YOU WISH!
TWIST

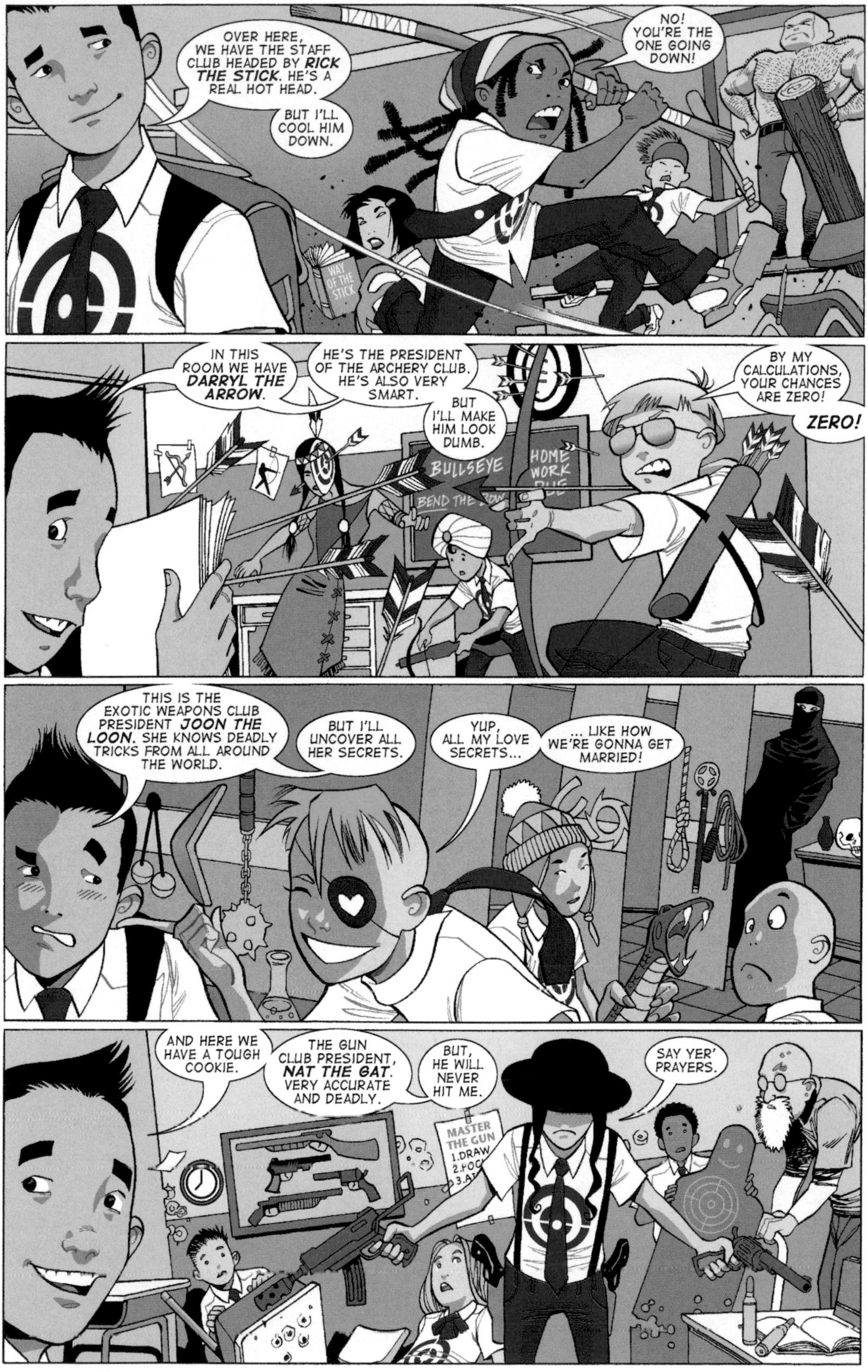

OVER HERE, WE HAVE THE STAFF CLUB HEADED BY RICK THE STICK. HE'S A REAL HOT HEAD.
BUT I'LL COOL HIM DOWN.
NO! YOU'RE THE ONE GOING DOWN!
WAY OF THE STICK
IN THIS ROOM WE HAVE DARRYL THE ARROW.
HE'S THE PRESIDENT OF THE ARCHERY CLUB. HE'S ALSO VERY SMART.
BUT I'LL MAKE HIM LOOK DUMB.
BY MY CALCULATIONS, YOUR CHANCES ARE ZERO!
ZERO!
BULLSEYE
HOME WORK
THIS IS THE EXOTIC WEAPONS CLUB PRESIDENT JOON THE LOON. SHE KNOWS DEADLY TRICKS FROM ALL AROUND THE WORLD.
BUT I'LL UNCOVER ALL HER SECRETS.
YUP, ALL MY LOVE SECRETS...
... LIKE HOW WE'RE GONNA GET MARRIED!
AND HERE WE HAVE A TOUGH COOKIE.
THE GUN CLUB PRESIDENT, NAT THE GAT. VERY ACCURATE AND DEADLY.
BUT, HE WILL NEVER HIT ME.
SAY YER' PRAYERS.
MASTER THE GUN
1.DRAW

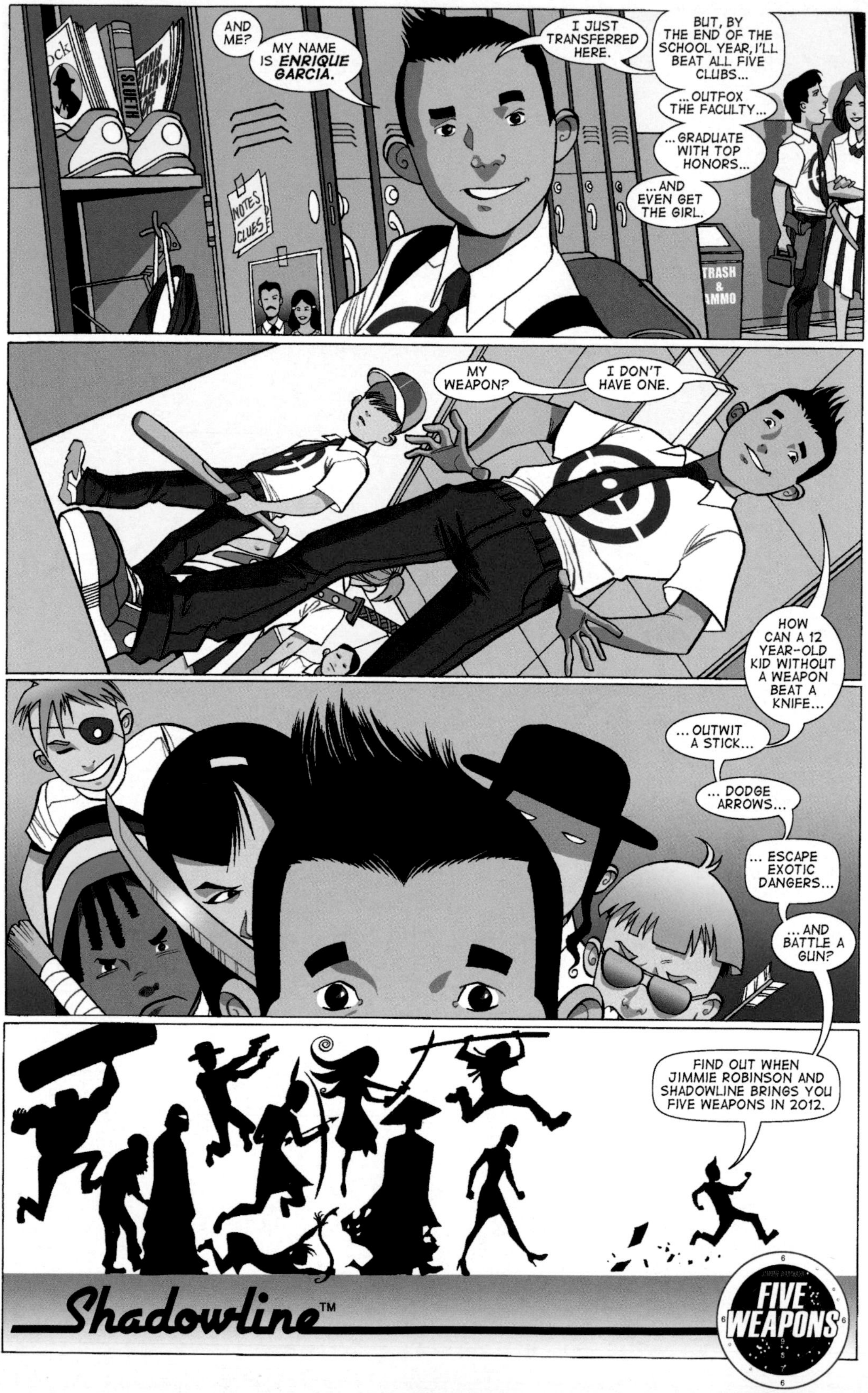
AND ME?
MY NAME IS ENRIQUE GARCIA.
I JUST TRANSFERRED HERE.
BUT, BY THE END OF THE SCHOOL YEAR, I'LL BEAT ALL FIVE CLUBS...
...OUTFOX THE FACULTY...
...GRADUATE WITH TOP HONORS...
...AND EVEN GET THE GIRL.
SLEUTH
NOTES
CLUES
TRASH & AMMO
MY WEAPON?
I DON'T HAVE ONE.
HOW CAN A 12 YEAR-OLD KID WITHOUT A WEAPON BEAT A KNIFE...
...OUTWIT A STICK...
...DODGE ARROWS...
...ESCAPE EXOTIC DANGERS...
...AND BATTLE A GUN?
FIND OUT WHEN JIMMIE ROBINSON AND SHADOWLINE BRINGS YOU FIVE WEAPONS IN 2012.
Shadowline™
FIVE WEAPONS

The following teasers announce the new series
and introduce the main characters.

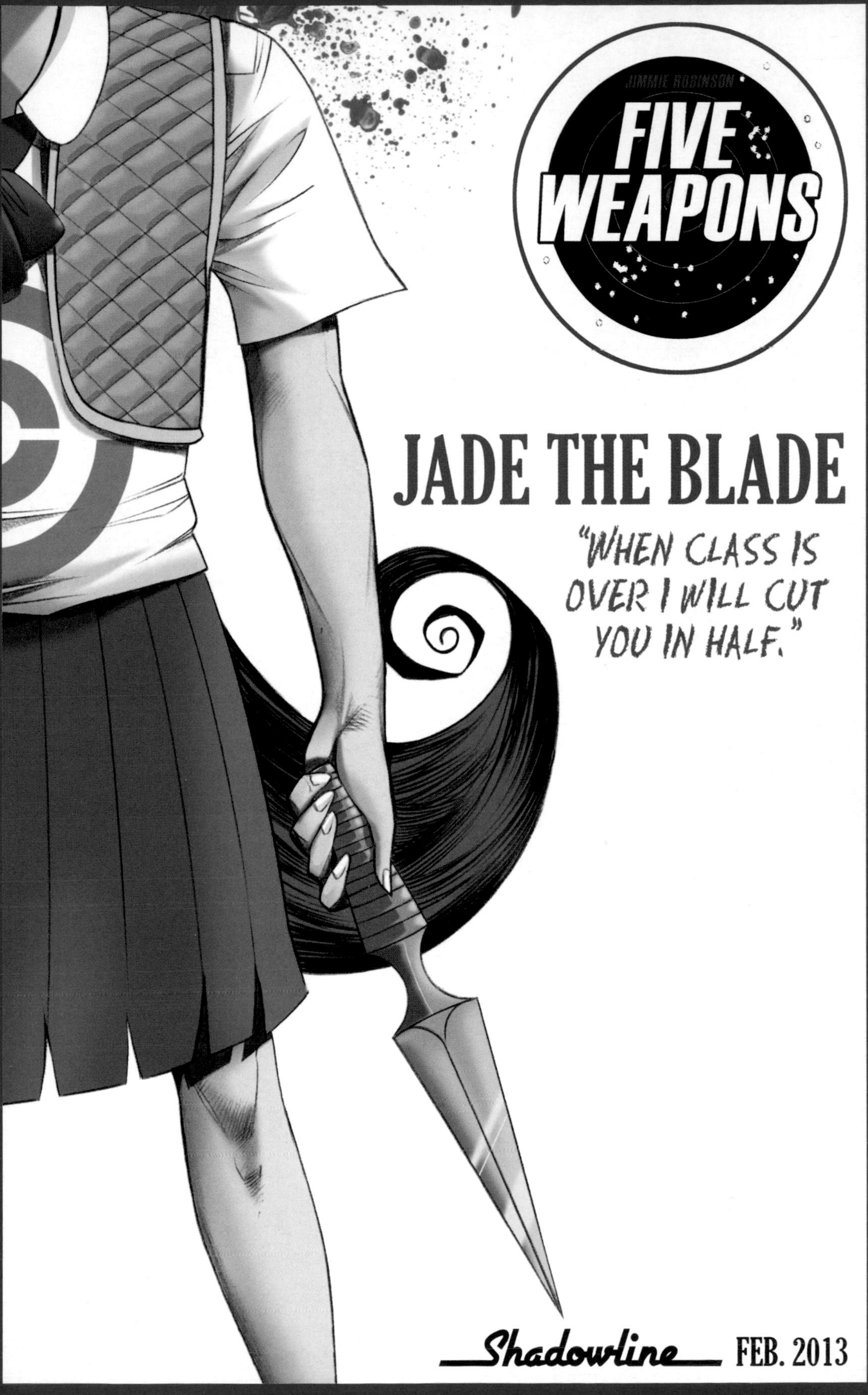
JIMMIE ROBINSON
FIVE WEAPONS
JADE THE BLADE
"WHEN CLASS IS OVER I WILL CUT YOU IN HALF."
Shadowline FEB. 2013

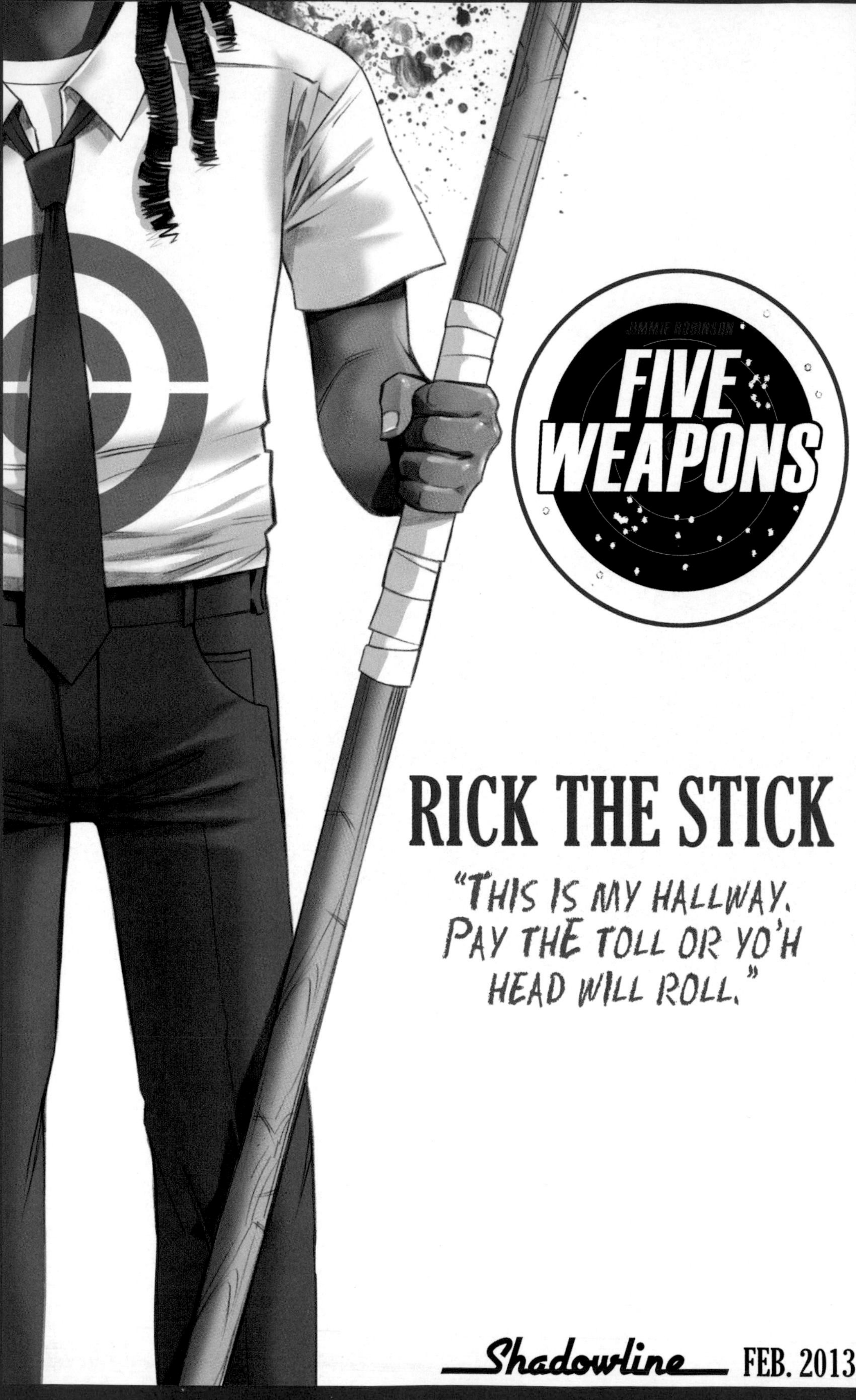

JIMMIE ROBINSON
FIVE WEAPONS
RICK THE STICK
"THIS IS MY HALLWAY. PAY THE TOLL OR YO'H HEAD WILL ROLL."
Shadowline
FEB. 2013

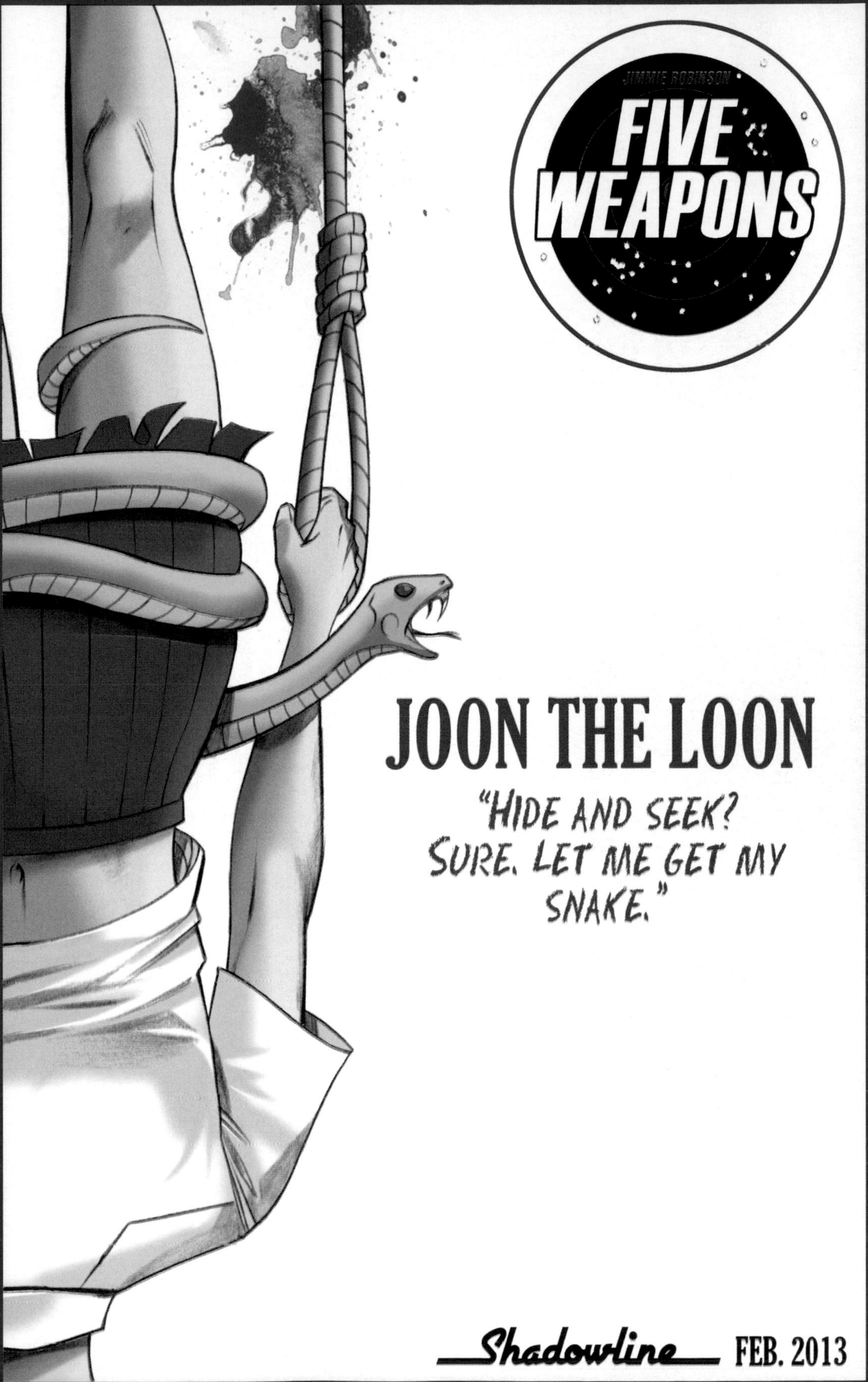
JIMMIE ROBINSON
FIVE WEAPONS
JOON THE LOON
"HIDE AND SEEK? SURE. LET ME GET MY SNAKE."
Shadowline FEB. 2013

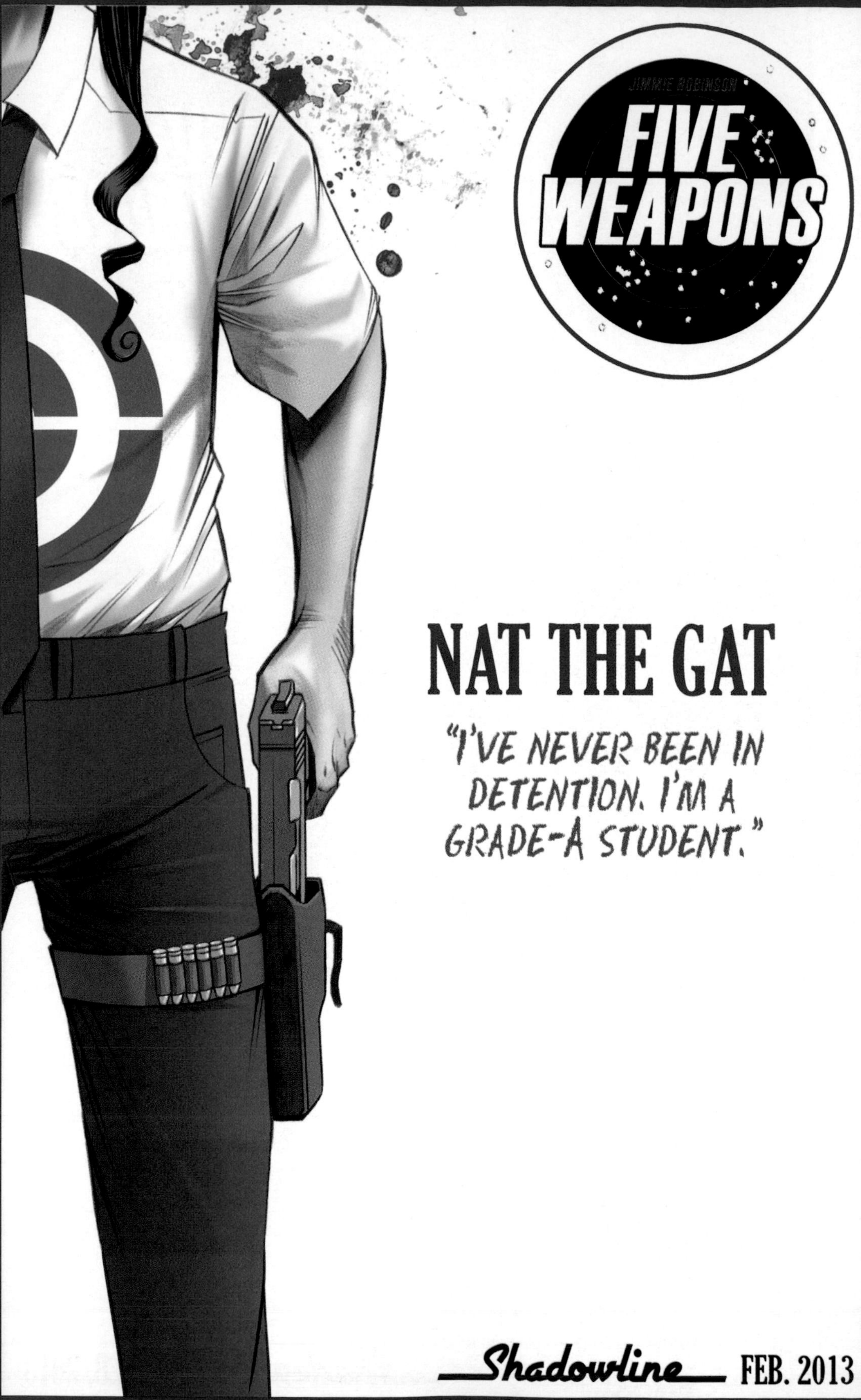
JIMMIE ROBINSON
FIVE WEAPONS
NAT THE GAT
"I'VE NEVER BEEN IN DETENTION. I'M A GRADE-A STUDENT."
Shadowline FEB. 2013

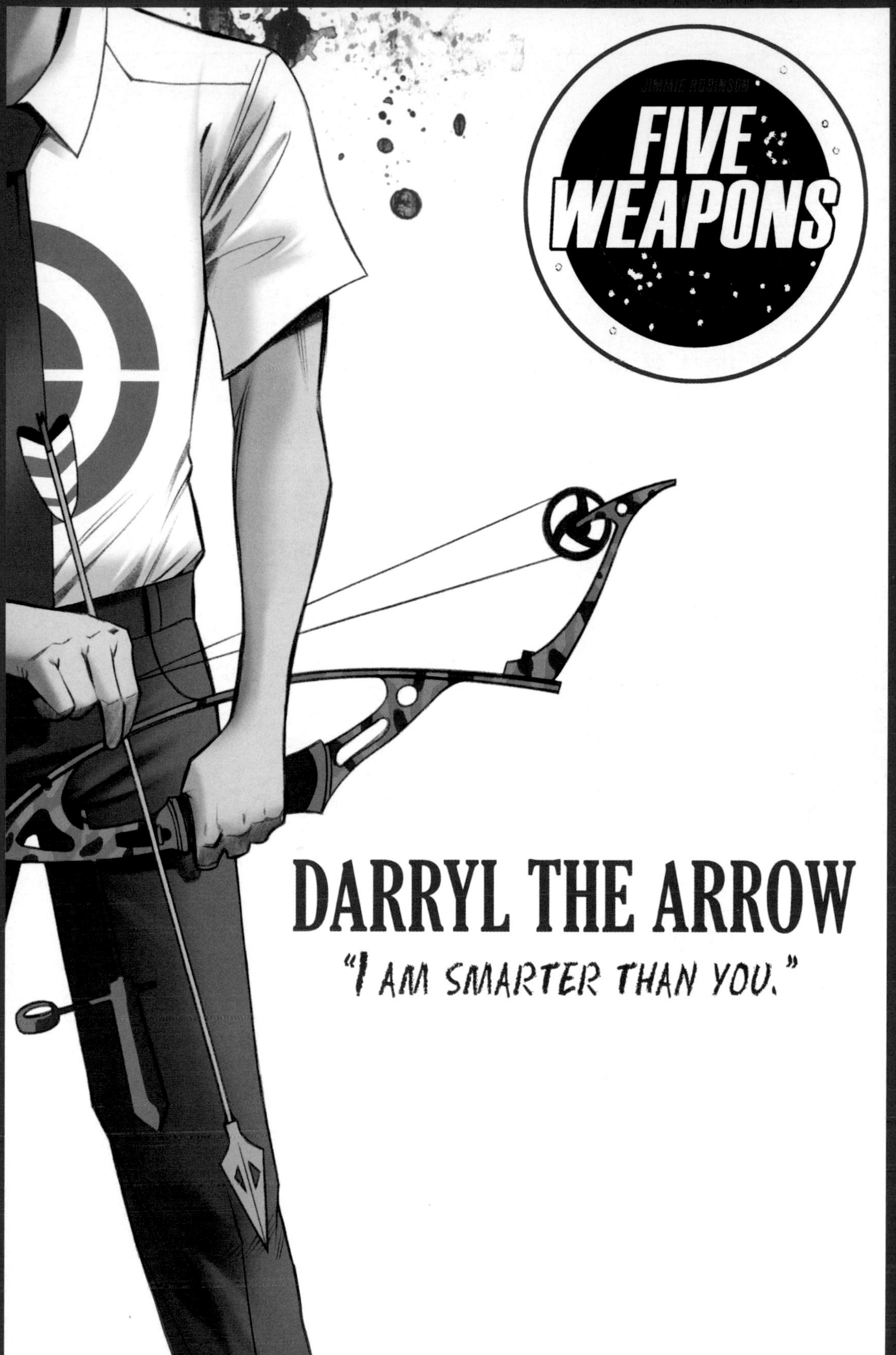
JIMMIE ROBINSON
FIVE WEAPONS
DARRYL THE ARROW
"I AM SMARTER THAN YOU."
Shadowline FEB. 2013

Promotional piece originally appeared in
BOMB QUEEN Vol. 7: ATOMIC BOMB

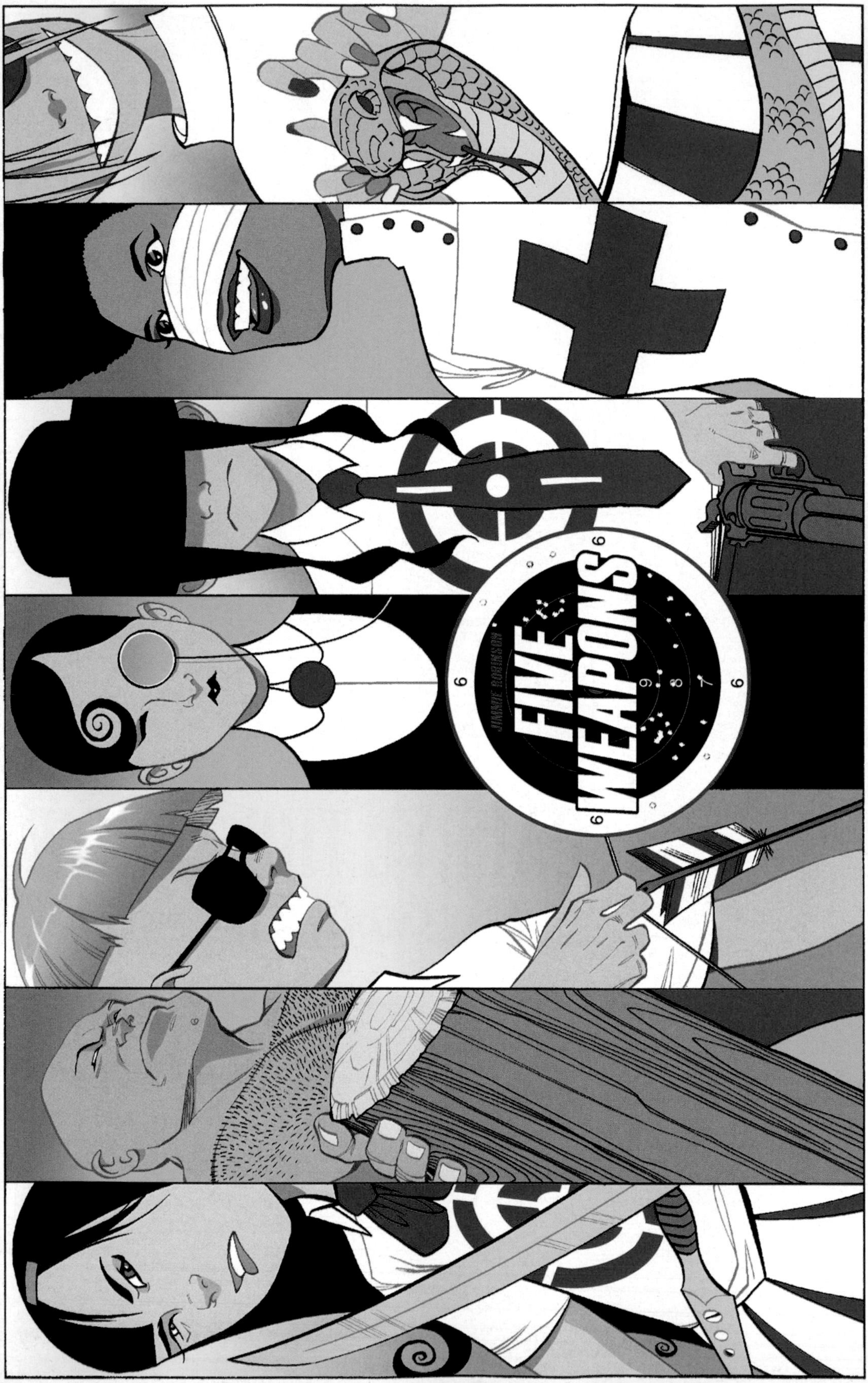
JIMMIE ROBINSON
FIVE WEAPONS

Unused cover for FIVE WEAPONS #1
second printing

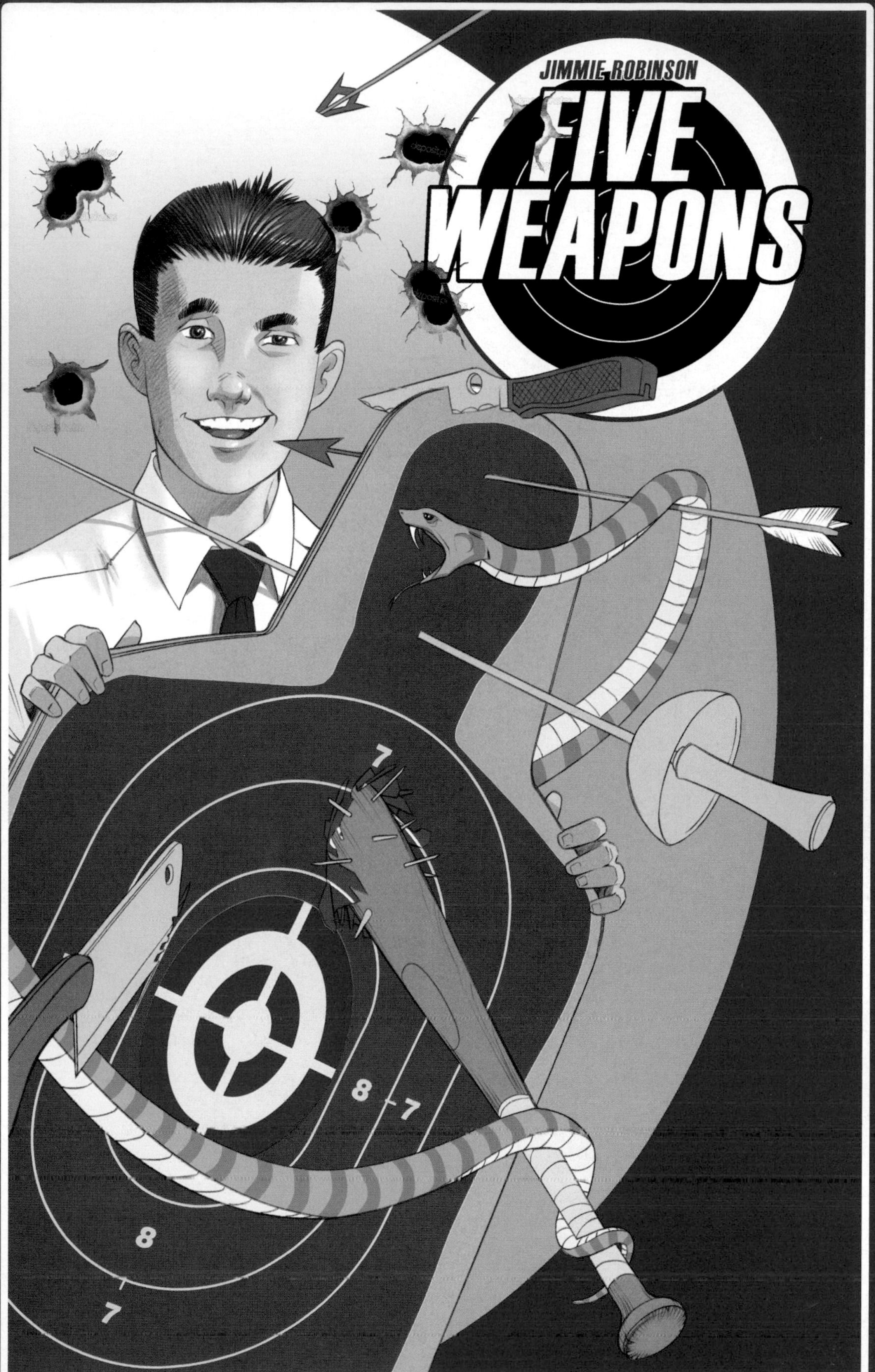
JIMMIE ROBINSON
FIVE
WEAPONS
7
8
7
8
7

JIMMIE'S SKETCHBOOK

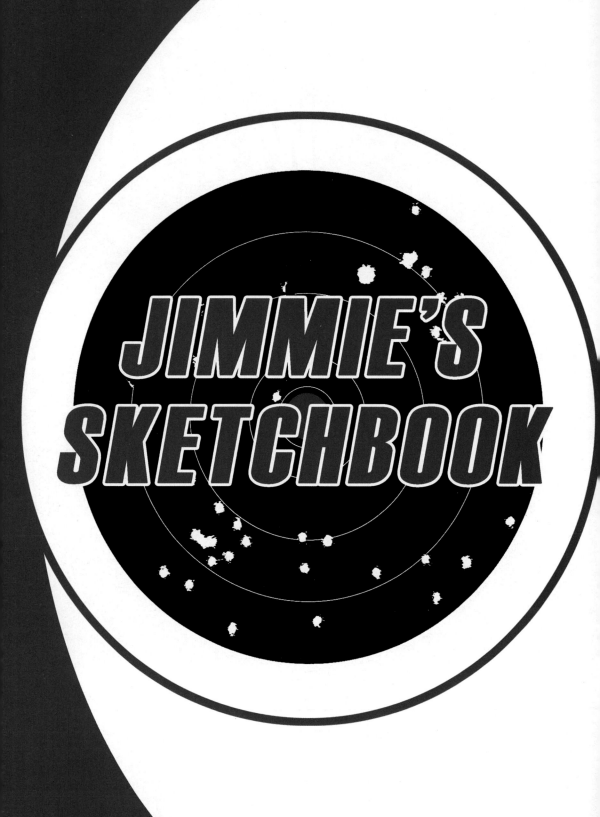

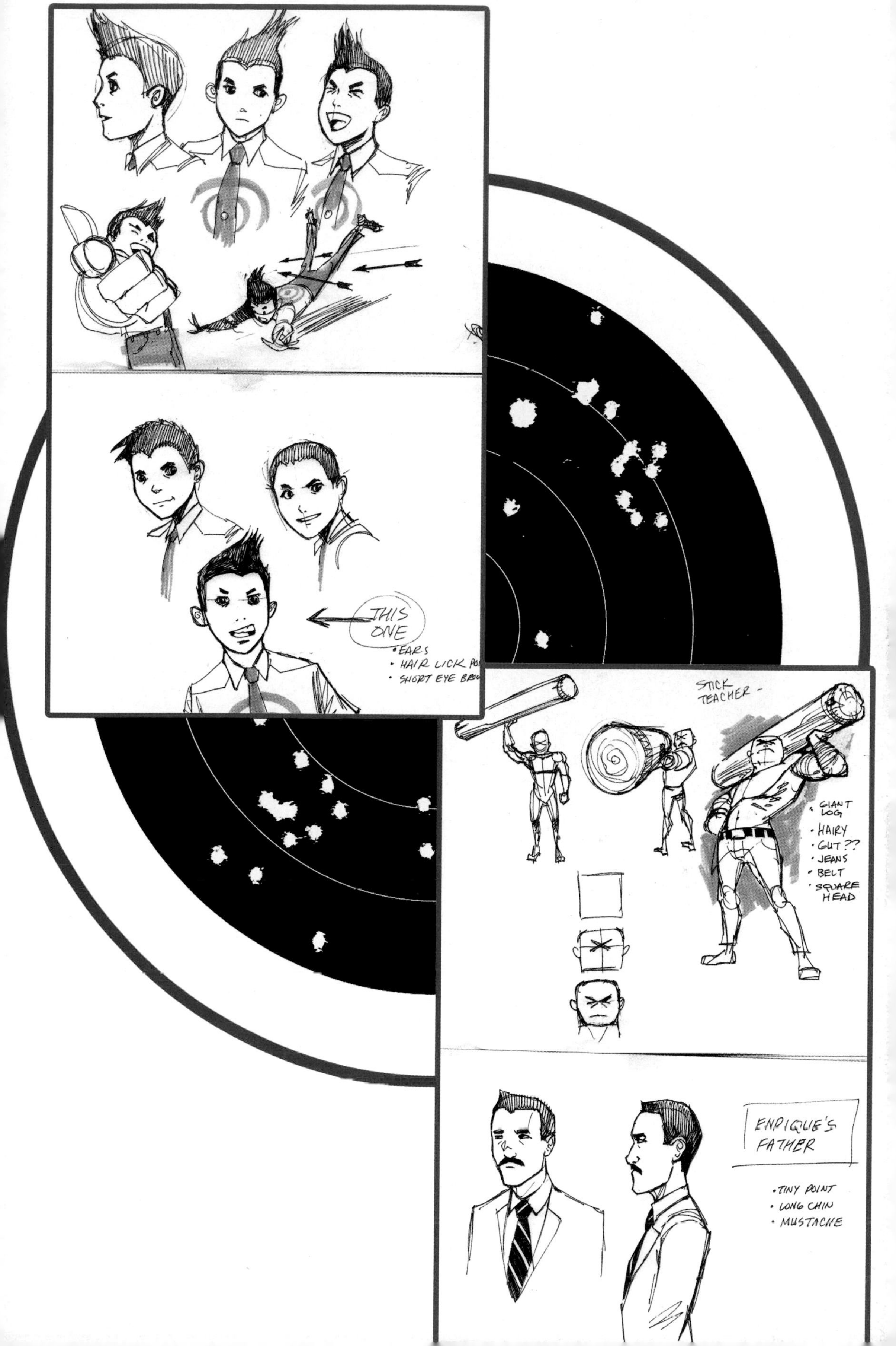
THIS ONE
• EARS
• HAIR LICK
• SHORT EYE
STICK TEACHER -
• GIANT LOG
• HAIRY
• GUT??
• JEANS
• BELT
• SQUARE HEAD
ENRIQUE'S FATHER
• TINY POINT
• LONG CHIN
• MUSTACHE

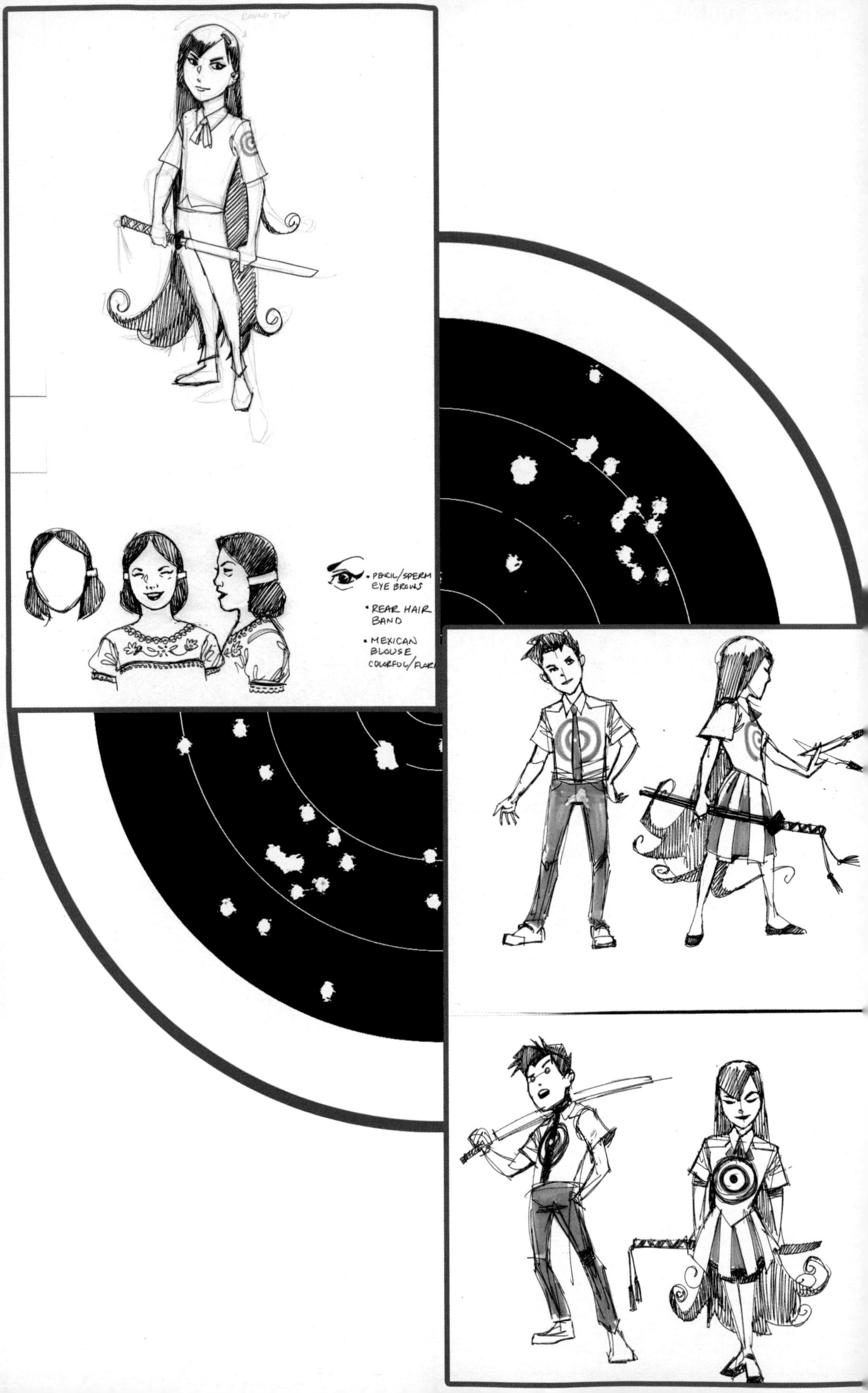

• PENCIL/SPERM EYE BROWS
• REAR HAIR BAND
• MEXICAN BLOUSE COLORFUL/FLOR

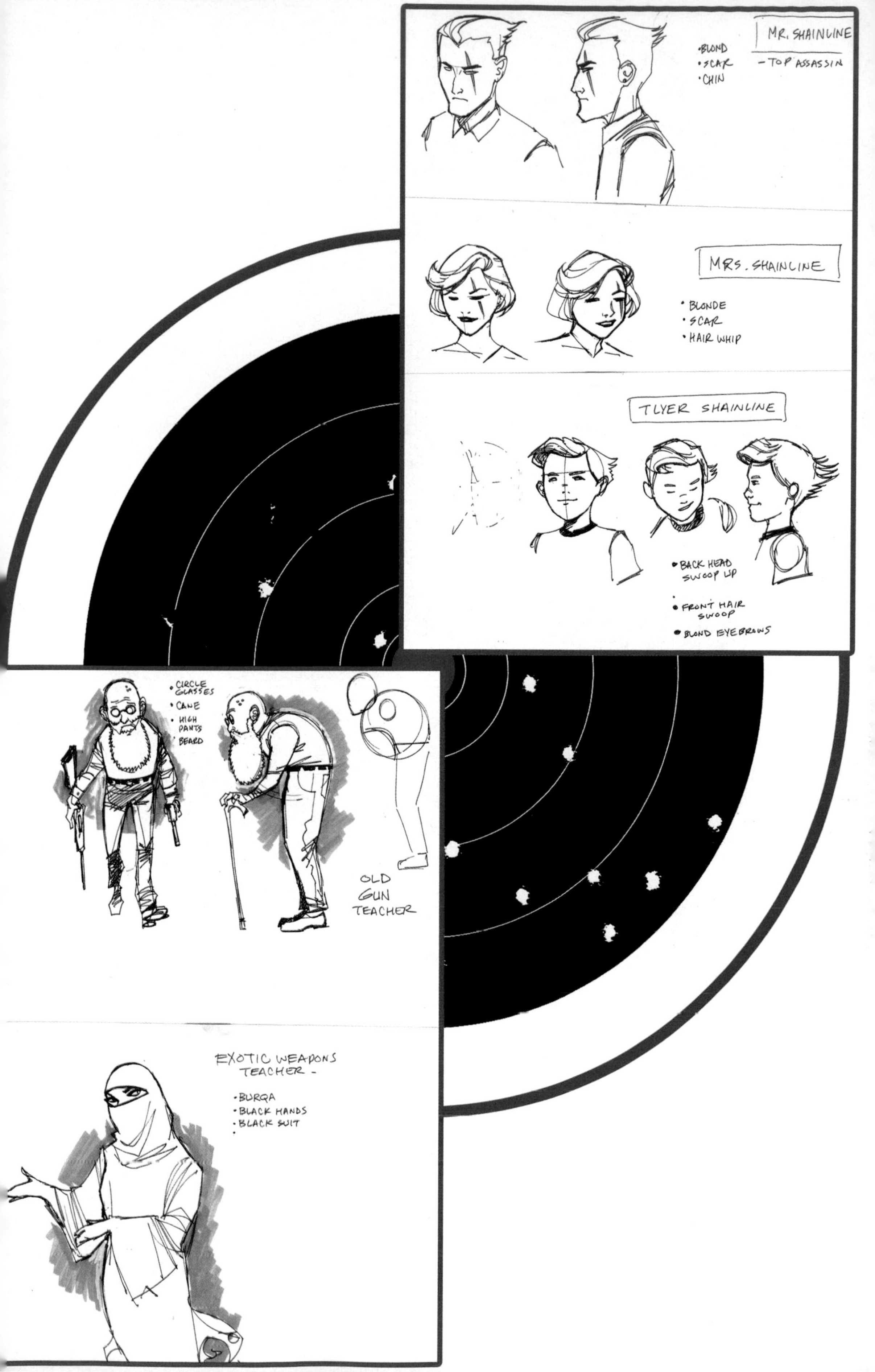

MR. SHAINLINE
- TOP ASSASSIN
•BLOND
•SCAR
•CHIN
MRS. SHAINLINE
• BLONDE
• SCAR
• HAIR WHIP
TLYER SHAINLINE
• BACK HEAD SWOOP UP
• FRONT HAIR SWOOP
• BLOND EYEBROWS
• CIRCLE GLASSES
• CANE
• HIGH PANTS
• BEARD
OLD GUN TEACHER
EXOTIC WEAPONS TEACHER -
• BURQA
• BLACK HANDS
• BLACK SUIT

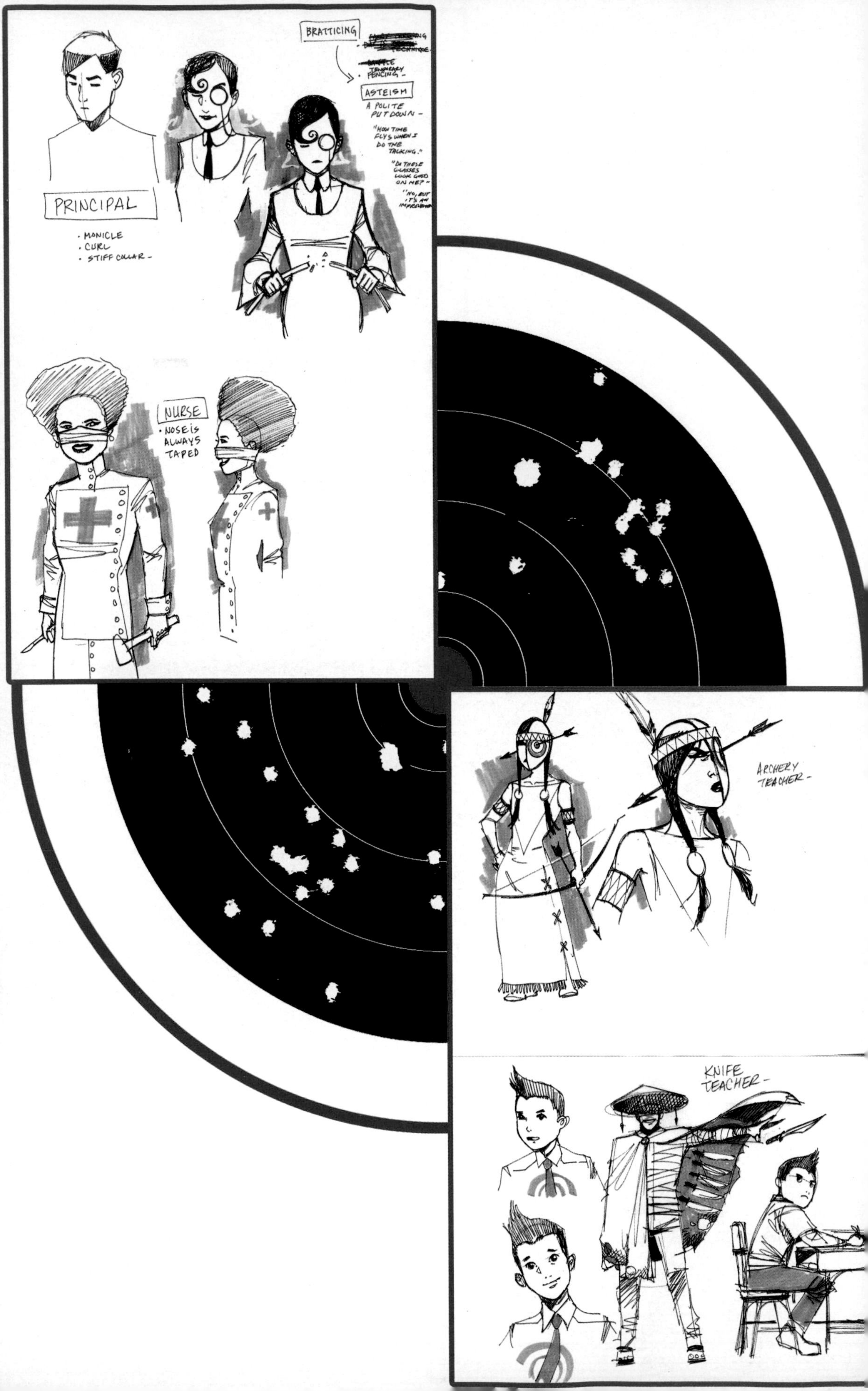
PRINCIPAL
· MONICLE
· CURL
· STIFF COLLAR -
BRATTICING
TEMPORARY
· FENCING -
ASTEISM
A POLITE PUT DOWN -
"HOW TIME FLYS WHEN I DO THE TALKING."
"DO THESE GLASSES LOOK GOOD ON ME?"
"NO, BUT IT'S AN
NURSE
· NOSE IS ALWAYS TAPED
ARCHERY TEACHER -
KNIFE TEACHER -

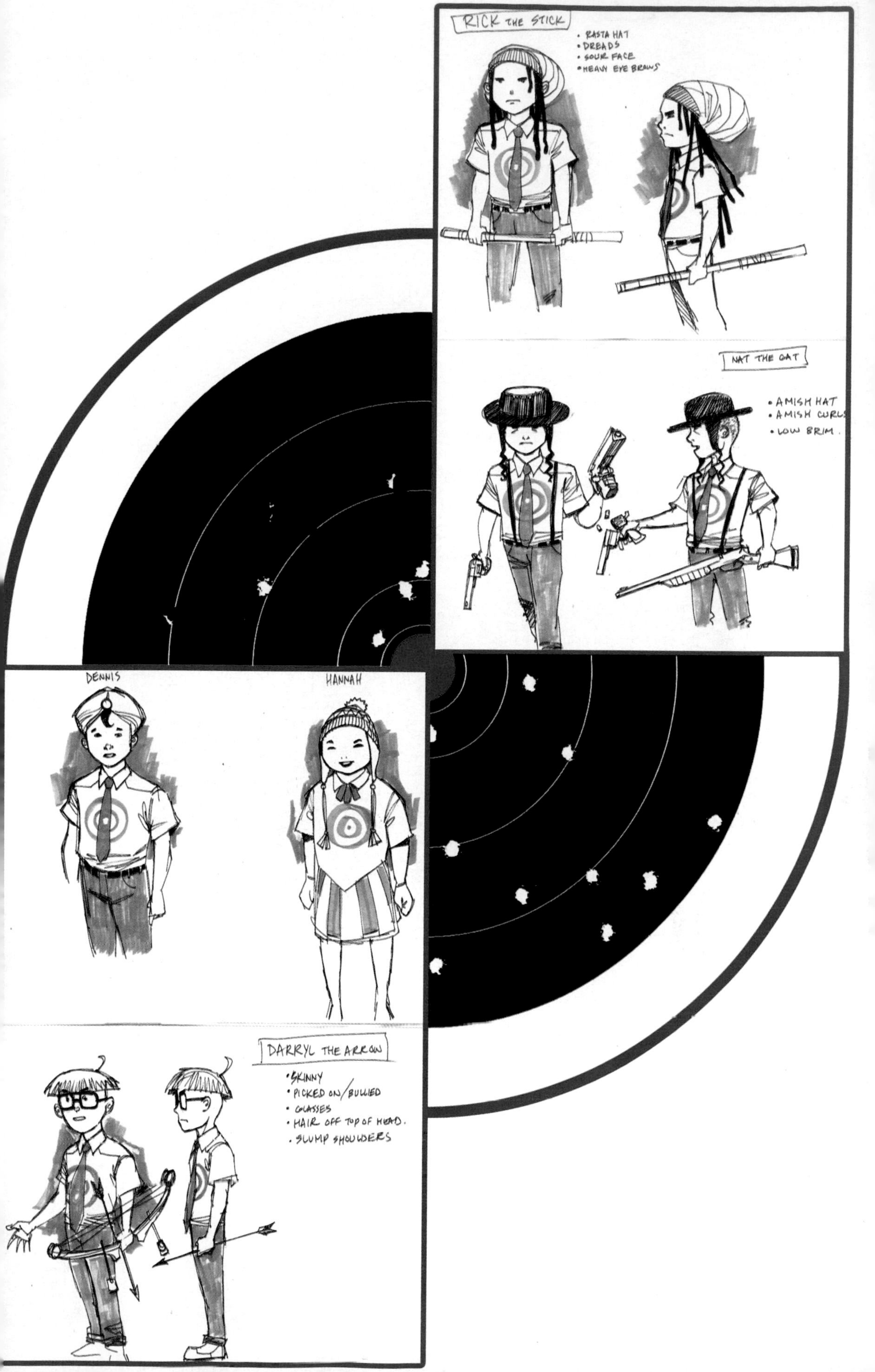
RICK THE STICK
• RASTA HAT
• DREADS
• SOUR FACE
• HEAVY EYE BROWS
NAT THE GAT
• AMISH HAT
• AMISH CURLS
• LOW BRIM.
DENNIS
HANNAH
DARRYL THE ARROW
• SKINNY
• PICKED ON/BULLIED
• GLASSES
• HAIR OFF TOP OF HEAD.
• SLUMP SHOULDERS

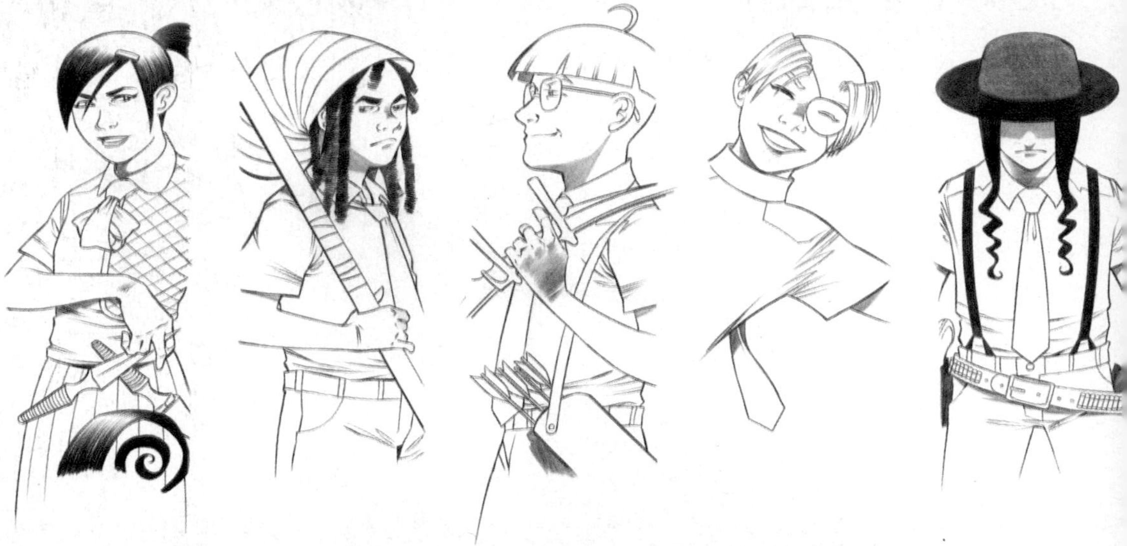

BOOKMARKS

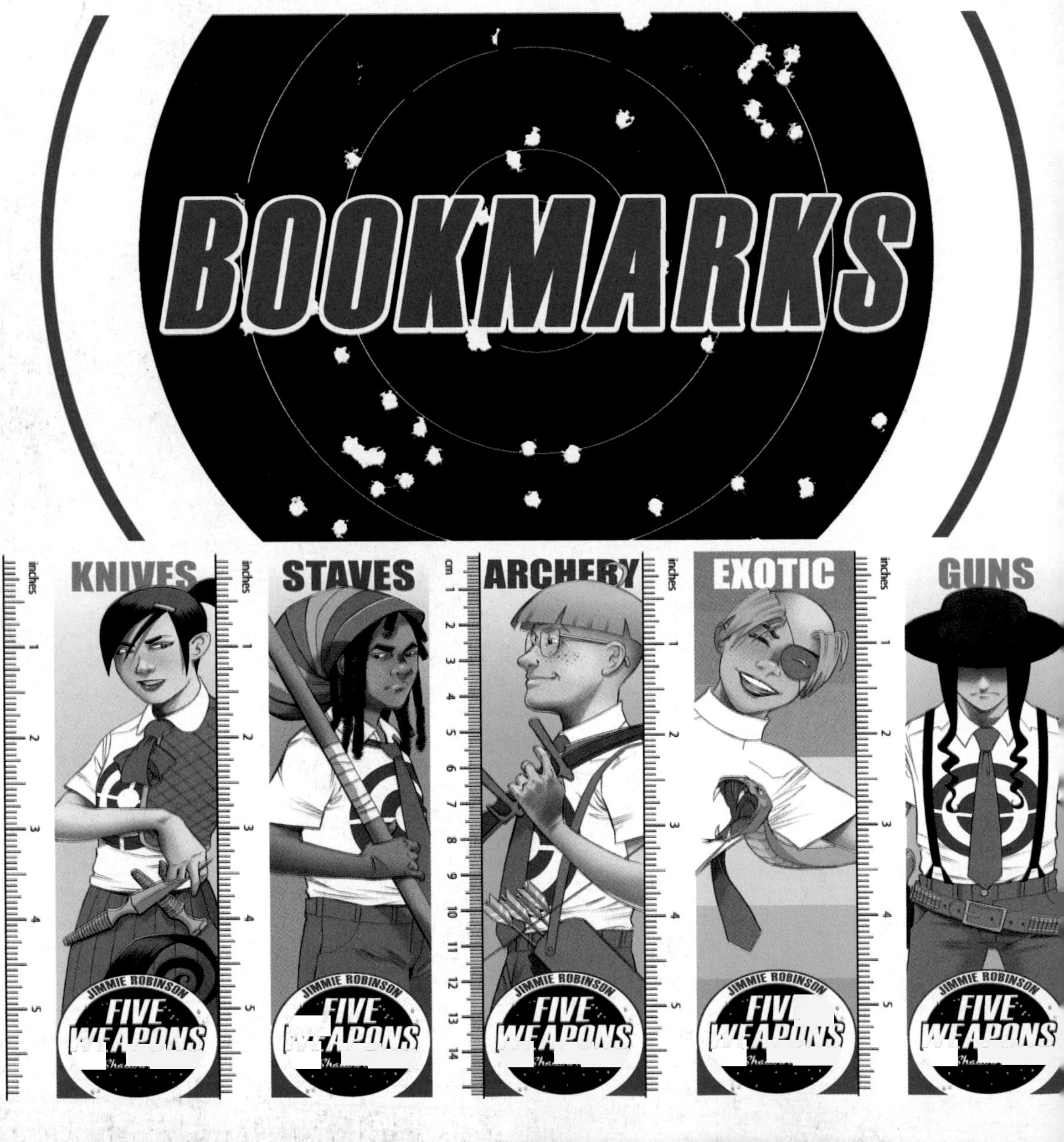
KNIVES
JIMMIE ROBINSON
FIVE WEAPONS
STAVES
JIMMIE ROBINSON
FIVE WEAPONS
ARCHERY
JIMMIE ROBINSON
FIVE WEAPONS
EXOTIC
JIMMIE ROBINSON
FIVE WEAPONS
GUNS
JIMMIE ROBINSON
FIVE WEAPONS

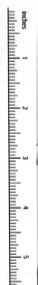

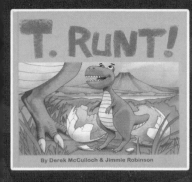

A Book For Every Reader...

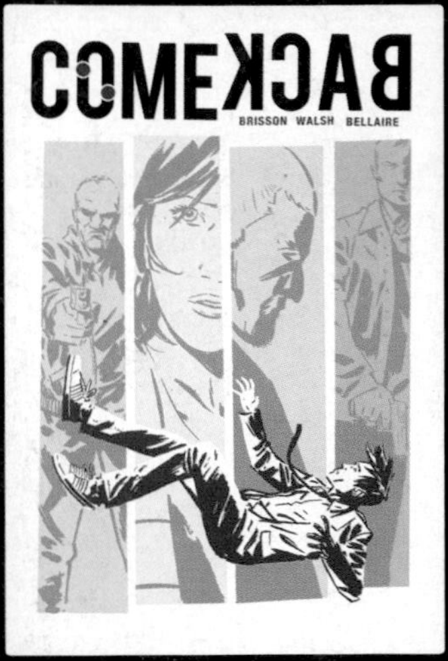
COMEBACK
BRISSON WALSH BELLAIRE

BRISSON/WALSH

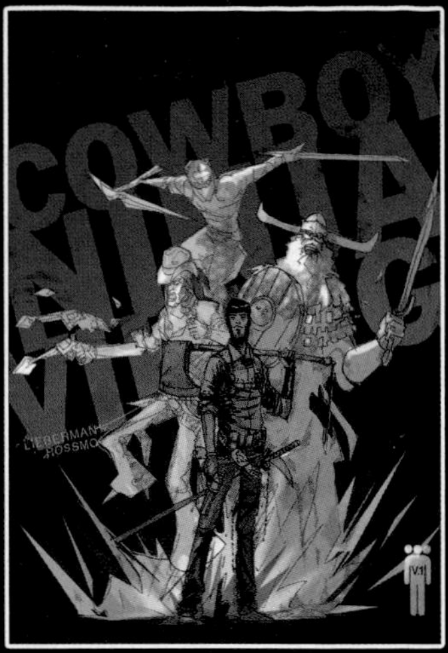
COWBOY NINJA VIKING
LIEBERMAN ROSSMO

LIEBERMAN/ROSSMO

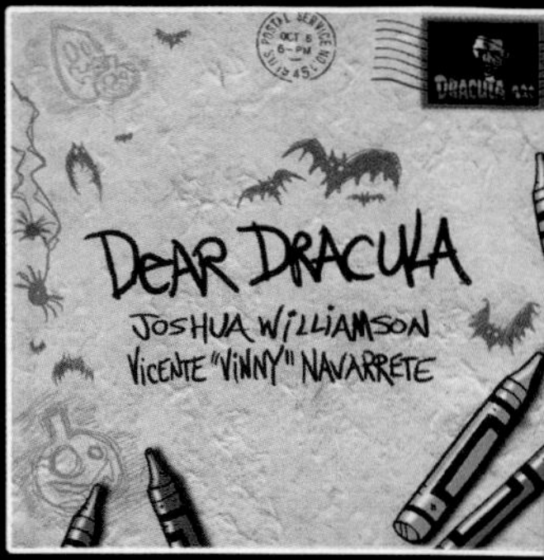
DEAR DRACULA
JOSHUA WILLIAMSON
VICENTE "VINNY" NAVARRETE

WILLIAMSON/NAVARETTE

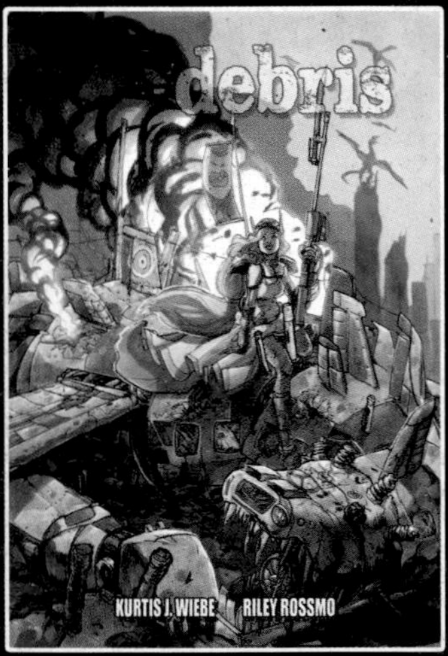
debris
KURTIS J. WIEBE RILEY ROSSMO

WIEBE/ROSSMO

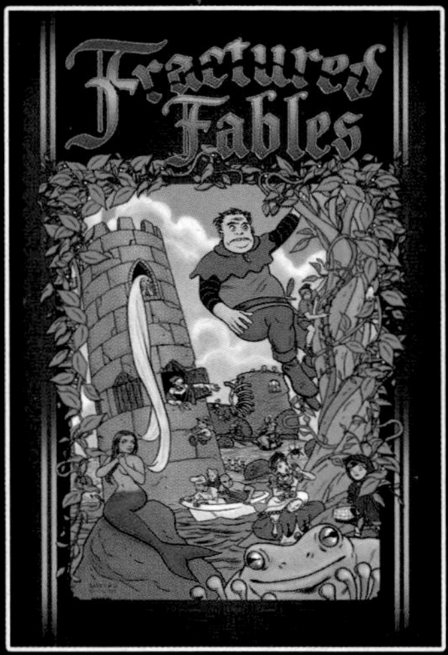
Fractured Fables

VARIOUS ARTISTS

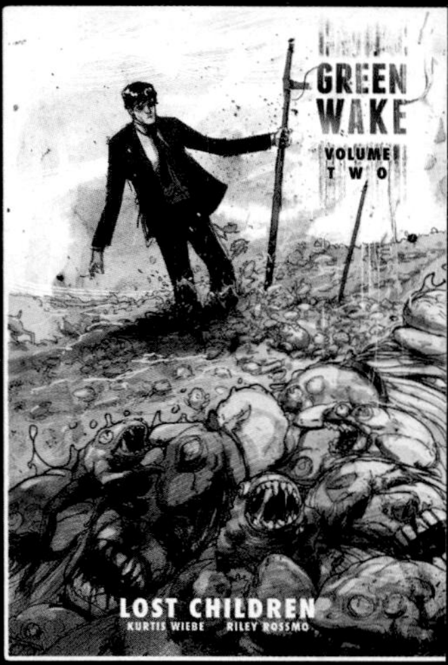
GREEN WAKE
VOLUME TWO
LOST CHILDREN
KURTIS WIEBE RILEY ROSSMO

WIEBE/ROSSMO

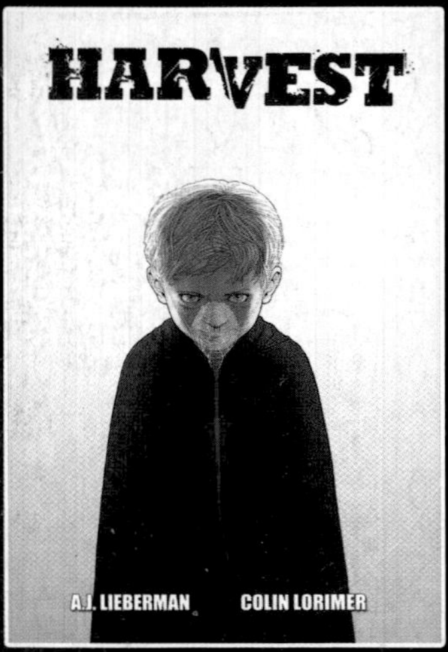
HARVEST
A.J. LIEBERMAN COLIN LORIMER

LIEBERMAN/LORIMER

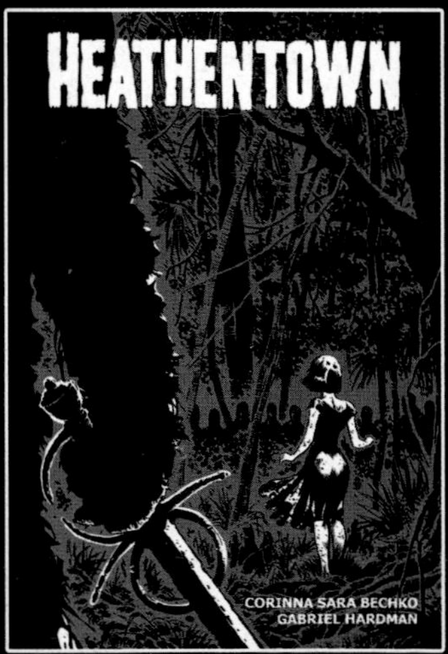
HEATHENTOWN
CORINNA SARA BECHKO
GABRIEL HARDMAN

BECHKO/HARDMAN

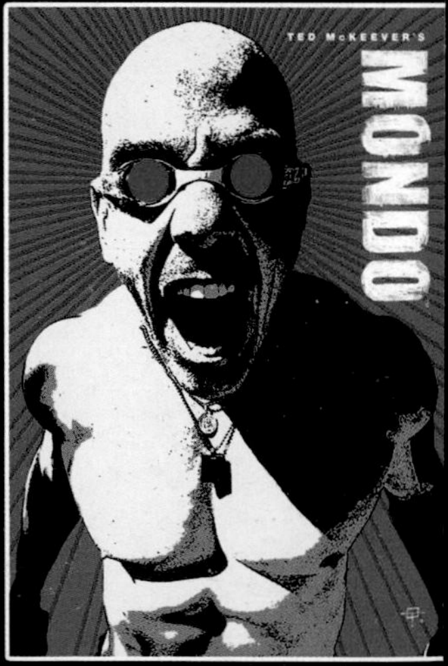
TED McKEEVER'S
MONDO

TED McKEEVER